Editec
David Pa

Forewo
the Archbish

FRESH
FROM
THE
WORD

**DAILY BIBLE STUDIES
FROM AROUND THE WORLD**

READ · REFLECT · GROW

IBRA

spck

First published in Great Britain in 2024

SPCK
The Record Hall
16–16a Baldwin's Gardens
EC1N 7RJ
www.spck.org.uk

International Bible Reading Association
5–6 Imperial Court
12 Sovereign Road
Birmingham B30 3FH
www.ibraglobal.org

British Library Cataloguing-in-Publication Data
A catalogue record for this book is available from the British Library

ISBN 978–0–281–09052–5
eBook ISBN 978–0–281–09053–2
ISSN 2050–6791

10 9 8 7 6 5 4 3 2 1

Typeset by Fakenham Prepress Solutions, Fakenham, Norfolk NR21 8NL
First printed in Great Britain by Clays, Bungay, Suffolk, NR35 1ED
eBook by Fakenham Prepress Solutions, Fakenham, Norfolk NR21 8NL

Produced on paper from sustainable sources

Fresh from The Word aims to build understanding and respect for different Christian perspectives through the provision of a range of biblical interpretations. Views expressed by contributors should not, therefore, be taken to reflect the views or policies of the Editor or the International Bible Reading Association.

The International Bible Reading Association's scheme of readings is listed monthly on the IBRA website at www.ibraglobal.org and the full scheme for the year may be downloaded in English, Spanish and French.

Contents

Foreword

If you're searching for meaning in life, or if you want to explore Christianity further, daily Bible reading is a fine way to grow your understanding and your faith. Engaging with scripture is a crucial part of the most exciting journey any of us will ever embark on! Whatever stage we're at, every so often it's good to remind ourselves of truths we know, but may have lost sight of, and I'm glad to touch on some aspects as I welcome you to *Fresh from The Word*.

Archbishop of York
Photo: Duncan Lomax, Ravage Productions

The word 'new' appears many times in the Bible. The story of Jesus and the first Christians is called the New Testament. The apostle Paul says that when we become Christians we are new creations. The Psalms tell us to 'sing a new song to the Lord'. Right at the end of the Bible, in the book of Revelation, God says: 'See, I am making all things new!' New life, new hope, new beginnings: the Christian faith is new every morning, and that's a wonderful reason to read the scriptures each day.

The Bible begins with the story of God creating the world and declaring it good. It tells us of God's love and purposes for the world. But then, in the Old Testament, we learn how creation got spoiled. God chose a people whose job it was to show the world the way – but they also got it wrong. And so, in the New Testament, we hear how God sends Jesus to reveal to us what life with God was truly intended to be.

The central event of the Christian story is the death and resurrection of Jesus. Born as a first-century Palestinian Jewish man, he shares our life on earth so that we can share God's life in heaven. As Romans 6:5 says 'if we have been united with him in a death like his, we will certainly be united with him in a resurrection like his' (NIV).

The word 'gospel' means good news, and the good news is that nothing bad – sin or death or evil – will ever have the last word. It means that whenever things feel desperate or whenever we feel lost, there is hope. God is with us in Jesus and he continues to help us through the power of the Holy Spirit.

The word 'disciple' means a follower or a learner – it is what the first friends of Jesus were called. We are Jesus' disciples today if we follow him and try to live like him. He gave us a new commandment to love one another – and by that he meant all humanity in its amazing variety. One of the most famous passages in the Bible reveals that what we do isn't really worth much if we don't have love. This is so important. We could read the Bible every day, say our prayers, go to church every Sunday and appear to be the best Christian ever, but if we don't love God, love our neighbour, and love ourselves, then it won't make much difference.

So let us seek to be encouragers to one another as we journey on together. My prayer is that as you read the scriptures each day, God will give you faith, hope and love for whatever the coming year brings.

Stephen Cottrell, Archbishop of York

How to use *Fresh from The Word*

How do you approach the idea of regular Bible reading? It may help to see daily Bible reading as spiritual exploration. Here is a suggestion of a pattern to follow that may help you develop the discipline but free up your mind and heart to respond.

- Before you read, take a few moments – the time it takes to say the Lord's Prayer – to imagine God looking at you with love. Feel yourself enfolded in that gaze. Come to scripture with your feet firmly planted.
- Read the passage slowly before you turn to the notes. Be curious. The Bible was written over a period of nearly 1,000 years, over 2,000 years ago. There is always something to learn. Read and reread.
- If you have access to a study Bible, pay attention to any echoes of the passage you are reading in other parts of the biblical book. A word might be used in different ways by different biblical authors. Where in the story of the book are you reading? What will happen next?
- 'Read' yourself as you read the story. Be attentive to your reactions – even trivial ones. What is drawing you into the story? What is repelling you? Observe yourself 'sidelong' as you read as if you were watching a wild animal in the forest; be still, observant and expectant.
- What in scripture or in the notes is drawing you forward in hope? What is closing you down? Notice where the Spirit of Life is present, and where negative spirits are, too. Follow where life is leading. God always leads into life, even if the way feels risky.
- Lift up the world and aspects of your life to God. What would you like to share with God? What is God seeking to share with you?
- Thank God for being present and offer your energy in the day ahead, or in the day coming after a night's rest.
- Finally, the † symbol is an invitation to pray a prayer that has been written for the day's reading. You are invited to say these words aloud or in silence with thousands of other readers around the world who will be reading these notes on the same day in dozens of languages.

Acknowledgements and abbreviations

The use of the letters a or b in a text reference, such as Luke 9:37−43a, indicates that the day's text starts or finishes midway through a verse, usually at a break such as the end of a sentence. Not all Bible versions will indicate such divisions.

We are grateful to the copyright holders for permission to use scriptural quotations taken from the following Bible versions, identified in the text by the version initials as below:

ESV   The Holy Bible, English Standard Version. ESV® Text Edition: 2016. Copyright © 2001 by Crossway Bibles, a publishing ministry of Good News Publishers. All rights reserved.

GNT   Good News Translation® (Today's English Version, Second Edition) © 1992 American Bible Society. All rights reserved.

KJV   The King James Version.

NIV   The Holy Bible, NEW INTERNATIONAL VERSION®, NIV®. Copyright © 1973, 1978, 1984, 2011 by Biblica, Inc.® Used by permission. All rights reserved worldwide.

NIVUK   The Holy Bible, New International Version (Anglicized edition). Copyright © 1979, 1984, 2011 by Biblica. Used by permission of Hodder & Stoughton Ltd, an Hachette UK company. All rights reserved. 'NIV' is a registered trademark of Biblica. UK trademark number 1448790.

NKJV   New King James Version. Copyright © 1982 by Thomas Nelson, Inc. Used by permission. All rights reserved.

NRSV   New Revised Standard Version of the Bible, copyright © 1989 by the Division of Christian Education of the National Council of the Churches of Christ in the USA. Used by permission. All rights reserved.

NRSVA   New Revised Standard Version of the Bible, Anglicised Edition, copyright © 1989, 1995 by the Division of Christian Education of the National Council of the Churches of Christ in the USA. Used by permission. All rights reserved.

Introduction from the Editor

From time to time, we gather things from around our home that are broken or no longer useful and take them to our local refuse collection point. It's a fascinating experience – everyone has rubbish in their lives and everyone needs to get rid of it, so here, in one place, we meet people from every background. The rich bringing their rubbish in their expensive new car, the not so well off in their old vehicle that looks like it might be part of the rubbish! Men, women, young, old, teachers, nurses, plumbers, scientists, unemployed, retired … every ethnicity, every gender, every political position, the fit, the healthy, the sick … I love watching this diversity unloading their rubbish, furtively checking to see what others have brought, some embarrassed, others joyfully throwing away that which was in the way, all leaving lighter than when they came.

It's a beautiful picture of the cross – here we all come, with our hopes, our prayers, our sin and brokenness. Here we come, materially rich or materially poor, here we meet those whom we would never otherwise meet – people across the religious, ethnic or political divides, people from different backgrounds living in very different locations. Coming together because of Jesus and because of all that the cross represents. A place of humility, a place of sacrifice, a place where we can leave that which is in the way, that which is holding us back, that which is heaping shame. A place where we can shed and leave our tears, a place where we can be made free.

And it reminds me of *Fresh from The Word*! A book compiled from writers who reflect that diversity – where else can you meet a refugee, a bishop, a trauma survivor, a Doctor of Theology, a recovering addict, the chronically ill, a Prime Minister and a group of displaced schoolgirls? Women, men, older, younger, married, single, teachers, poets, parents, healthy, sick … from around the globe geographically and around the Church theologically, coming together in this book to share their experience of the same God with you – a worldwide community of readers from different denominations, from different nations, from different backgrounds. All of us 'meeting' each day to read the same passage, for the most part unknown to each other, yet united as we reflect on the same words, drawing closer to the same God. Thank you for being part of this extraordinary community. May the God who reached down to raise us all meet with you as together we read his word.

Promises and resolutions

1 Bad promises

Notes by the **Revd Dr Peter Langerman**

Peter is a pastor in a Presbyterian church in Durbanville, Cape Town. From 2018 to 2021 he was Moderator of the General Assembly of the UPCSA. He is married to Sally, and they have four daughters, two sons-in-law and one grandchild. Peter is passionate about the dynamic rule and reign of God. He believes that God invites all to be part of God's transformative mission through love, and that the most potent and powerful agent for the transformation of local communities is the local church living out faithfulness to God. Peter has used the NIVUK for these notes.

1 January
Plans, prayers and promises

Read 1 Samuel 14:24–30

How much better it would have been if the men had eaten today some of the plunder they took from their enemies.

(verse 30)

As we move swiftly into another new year, think back and reflect on whether you have ever made a resolution, a promise or a commitment you regretted. A moment when you decided to say 'yes' to someone and sometime later regretted that, but felt you could not do anything about it. The interesting thing about such moments is that we usually could do something about it, but we don't want to, for fear of letting somebody else down or looking bad.

In this account, Saul had made a poor decision that his army should not eat until the enemy was fully defeated. Jonathan didn't hear the prohibition and ate. When challenged about his disobedience to his father's command, his response was, 'The king made a poor decision, and we should rectify it rather than slavishly obey it.'

A new year allows us a window of opportunity to reflect on the year that is past and start anew. As you begin the year, maybe you need to make a new start, or end something that has been hanging over you for a while. It takes courage, but this is the moment to do it.

† God who holds the past, the future and the present in your loving hands, help me to make wise decisions in the year ahead.

1

2 January
Numbered, weighed and divided

Read Daniel 5:13–30

This is the inscription that was written: MENE, MENE, TEKEL, PARSIN. *Here is what these words mean:* Mene: *God has numbered the days of your reign and brought it to an end.* Tekel: *You have been weighed on the scales and found wanting.* Peres: *Your kingdom is divided and given to the Medes and Persians.*

(verses 25–28)

In every time in history and every generation there have been people who have not been frightened to stand up for what is right in the face of persecution and unpopularity. Martin Luther, Florence Nightingale, Susan B Anthony, Dietrich Bonhoeffer, Mother Teresa and Dr Martin Luther King Jr, to mention just a few, were people who stood up for what was right, rather than popular, and in some cases paid for it with their lives.

By so doing they were standing in the tradition of a long line of faithful men and women who have done just this: chosen to do what God and righteousness require, despite the dangers of doing so, rather than that which is popular and safe.

Daniel was just such a person. Taken from Judah during the Babylonian exile, he became a trusted leader in Babylon itself. In a context of political intrigue, where prominent people often paid for their fall from political favour with their lives, Daniel prospered. Despite at least two attempts to kill him, we see him here, once again speaking truth to power without any thought as to his own safety.

You might be in a similar situation at some point in this year, faced with the option to play it safe or to take the harder route of doing what is right even if it may have consequences. Ask for the courage to do the right thing when the time comes no matter the consequences for yourself.

† Mighty God, grant me the courage to make the difficult decisions to do what is right rather than popular in the course of this year.

For further thought

Is there something you need to do that might have negative consequences, but which is necessary, in the light of what is going on around you?

3 January
Promoted, demoted and forgotten

Read Genesis 40
*But when all goes well with you, remember me and show me kindness;
mention me to Pharaoh and get me out of this prison ... The chief
cupbearer, however, did not remember Joseph; he forgot him.*

(verses 14, 23)

There is the well-known story of the queen who disguised herself
and went about the kingdom dressed as a peasant. As she did
so, many people treated her harshly as befitting her station as a
peasant. Only one man treated her kindly and cared for her. When
she returned to the palace, she called in the man who had treated
her with kindness and compassion and – to the surprise of the
entire court – gave him a place of prominence in her kingdom
because of the way he had treated her.

We love to hear such stories. On the other hand, have you ever
done something good for someone else and hoped to gain some
benefit from it, only to be disappointed? Unfortunately, these
stories are far more common than the former.

Joseph had good news for Pharaoh's cup bearer and bad news
for Pharaoh's baker. His only request was that the cup bearer
would remember him to Pharaoh when the good came to him.
Unfortunately, the cup bearer didn't remember Joseph, but God
did. What we must always remember is that in God's economy, for
those of us who live under the rule and reign of God, no kindness
is ever hidden; it is always noted by God and every kindness will
be rewarded by God.

So, do good, be kind, be hospitable, be gracious, be forgiving
and be generous. Maybe you will be rewarded in the here and
now, but be assured that whether that happens or not, each action
is seen, noted and will be rewarded by God.

† Loving God, help me to reflect your kindness and generosity in my life every day
whether that be rewarded or not.

For further thought
What can you do to serve, or show kindness to, someone with no
prospect of reward, trusting that your reward will come from God?

3

4 January
Choices and consequences

Read Judges 11:29–40

And Jephthah made a vow to the Lord: 'If you give the Ammonites into my hands, whatever comes out of the door of my house to meet me when I return in triumph from the Ammonites will be the Lord's, and I will sacrifice it as a burnt offering.'

(verses 30–31)

In November of 2023, I was returning to my home from a trip to Johannesburg. The victorious Springbok rugby team were then on their nationwide tour and were in the plane immediately following mine. When I came into the arrivals hall at the airport, there were hundreds of people to welcome them. As I came through the doors, since I was wearing a Springbok rugby shirt myself, a huge cheer went up, assuming that I was one of the support staff and that the team would be soon following me through the doors. The sense of disappointment when the crowd realised that I wasn't anybody important and that they would have to wait a little longer for the main attraction was palpable. When a person or a team returns home, usually there is something of an enthusiastic welcome from friends or supporters.

In the biblical world of bad decisions and poor choices, Jephthah stands head and shoulders above most others. In a prospective battle against the Ammonites, Jephthah made a vow that if God granted him victory, he would offer in sacrifice to God the first creature that he encountered on his return home. What he failed to consider was that the first creature he encountered might be his own daughter.

Sometimes we make rash promises or hasty resolutions that have unintended consequences. How do we guard against these? One way is to seek God's guidance in the making of the promise or the resolution in the first place. Is that thing we are promising or that resolution we are making in line with what God wants for and from us, or is it something we have just decided to do? If we have failed to consult God in the first place, we can't really blame God for the consequences that follow from our rash choices.

† Holy God, help me to not make hasty decisions and rash promises without reflecting on the possible consequences in the year that lies ahead.

For further thought

What can you do to prevent making regrettable choices that have far-reaching consequences in the year that lies ahead?

Promises and resolutions

2 Good promises

Notes by **Maya Lamberte Ineza**

Maya is a Burundian woman, raised in Lusaka, Zambia, and has spent some time in Rwanda. She is a wife, a mother, a Bible teacher, a worship leader and educator. Maya lived as a refugee for eighteen years before returning to Burundi in her early twenties, following God's call to go back to her home country. There she met and got married to Fabrice Nzeyimana, a Bible teacher and musician. Together they are raising two beautiful daughters. Maya has used the NIVUK for these notes.

5 January
Facing regret

Read Ruth 1:6–18

When Naomi heard in Moab that the LORD had come to the aid of his people by providing food for them, she and her daughters-in-law prepared to return home from there. With her two daughters-in-law she left the place where she had been living and set out on the road that would take them back to the land of Judah.

(verses 6–7)

Some years back, I walked away from the Lord and walked down a path that led me far from his purposes. After making the decision to repent, I remember asking God to give me a fresh start. By his grace, he enabled me to move to a new country soon after.

A new year can carry so much promise, but sometimes, a lot of regret.

Naomi and her husband had moved to Moab in search of a better life for them and their families, due to the famine in Israel. Unfortunately, Naomi lost her husband and both sons while in Moab. She even changed her name to Mara (meaning 'bitter') because it reflected how she felt about her life. Yet in these two verses, we see the one thing that changed the trajectory of the rest of her life.

Naomi heard that God had blessed Israel and she made the decision to return. This couldn't have been an easy decision. Not only did she not have anything to show for all those years, but she was actually worse off. No matter how bad she felt about her life, it could only change if she took a step to go back.

† God's love and his mercies are new every morning. Take time to bring your regrets to him today. It's never too late to start afresh.

6 January
Making promises

Read 1 Samuel 20:12–17

Then Jonathan said to David, 'I swear by the Lord, the God of Israel, that I will surely sound out my father by this time the day after tomorrow! If he is favourably disposed toward you, will I not send you word and let you know?'

(verse 12)

Jonathan and David had a special friendship. Saul, Jonathan's father, was jealous of David, and looked for ways to kill him. Jonathan loved his dear friend David and wanted to help save his life. He made a promise to his friend, one that could save David's life.

David placed his life in the hands of Jonathan, who could have betrayed him. He trusted that his dear friend had his best interests at heart and he waited to hear back from him. Jonathan kept his promise and their friendship was strengthened.

We live every day because we have promises. We go to work because we have the promise that we will be paid. We get married because of the promises we make to each other. Promises produce faith because we have the hope of the promise.

Hebrews 11:1 reminds us that faith is the assurance or confidence in what we hope for. This means we have things we are hoping will happen, and faith is the assurance that these things will happen. But where does that assurance come from? It comes from the promises we have been given.

Promises are only as reliable as the person who makes them. A faithful person is someone who is reliable and can be counted on to keep their promises. We trust in God today because he has kept his promises.

† Father, help me to keep my word and fulfil my promises to others. I want to reflect your character in being faithful through the power of your Spirit, as you sanctify me daily.

For further thought

What happens if we break promises? It can lead to hurt and disappointment, and the loss of credibility. Credibility is like credit that can lead to greater opportunity and the loss of it can cost you future opportunities.

Promises and resolutions – 2 Good promises

7 January
Keeping promises

Read 2 Samuel 9

'Don't be afraid,' David said to him, 'for I will surely show you kindness for the sake of your father Jonathan. I will restore to you all the land that belonged to your grandfather Saul, and you will always eat at my table.'

(verse 7)

My country has been plagued with generations of conflict because of so much hate and hurt. During each generation, the people in power take the opportunity to avenge the wrongs done to them, which keeps us in the cycle of continuous pain and suffering. In David's time, it was morally acceptable to punish family members for the sins of their fathers, which is why Jonathan asked David not to kill him. David's choice to open his heart and home brought this conflict to an end and ensured that future generations did not continue the cycle.

David had a special heart. One would wonder, where did he find the grace to forgive? Reading through the book of Psalms gives us an insight into David's strategy. In Psalm 55, we see how David prays. He asks God to defend him from his enemies, and he chooses to trust in the Lord. David surrendered his pain and disappointment to the Lord, allowing God to completely heal him. In the end, he honours Saul's family by restoring their wealth and by welcoming Saul's grandson to his table.

Mephibosheth's response shows how he was not expecting this kind of kindness from David because he thought of himself as undeserving. Yet David did not see him as the grandson of Saul, but as a human being deserving of love. Jesus teaches us in Matthew 5 that those who show mercy to others will also be shown mercy. What a beautiful illustration of the power of forgiveness and restoration.

† Lord, help me to show love and kindness instead of resentment, for your glory. Amen.

For further thought

What strategies do you have for preventing bitterness growing? What are the steps to forgiveness that we find in Matthew 18?

8 January
Wisdom for the assignment

Read 1 Kings 5:1–12

When Hiram heard Solomon's message, he was greatly pleased and said, 'Praise be to the LORD today, for he has given David a wise son to rule over this great nation.'

(verse 7)

The King of Tyre wanted to maintain a good diplomatic relationship with Israel, so he sent envoys to Solomon. God gave Solomon wisdom to identify the potential of this friendship, and that it was the key to him accomplishing his mission of building the Temple. Hiram the King of Tyre responded favourably and the two nations served each other, leading to mutual benefit.

Solomon was blessed with wisdom to not only know what to do, but how to do it and with whom. Every assignment we have needs all those three aspects: the what, the how and the who. Many people will come our way, but it takes divine wisdom to understand who God will use to help us fulfil our assignment. A divine assignment requires divine relationships. How I pray that God would open our eyes to recognise those people!

We are not meant to walk alone. Some of us struggle to allow people to meet our needs because we don't want to feel indebted to them. Or, if you are like me, being vulnerable is a very hard thing. But even Solomon with all his wealth needed people and he wasn't afraid to express his needs to them. Without him expressing his needs, Hiram would not have known how to meet them. Paul reminds us in 1 Corinthians 12 that we are like a body, and each part needs the others to survive. We were not created to be self-sufficient. We were created to depend on God and on others. That is the true meaning of being human.

† Thank you, Lord, that you have placed people in my life, so that we can serve each other.

For further thought
How can you serve those you are called to walk with this year?

9 January
Godly values

> **Read Daniel 1:8–16**
>
> *But Daniel resolved not to defile himself with the royal food and wine, and he asked the chief official for permission not to defile himself this way.*
>
> (verse 8)

Daniel was part of the people of Judah who were exiled to serve the kingdom of Babylon. Daniel and his friends were selected to be prepared to serve the king, but there was a big problem. Being devout followers of Yahweh, some of the expectations would require them to dishonour their God. In these particular verses, they faced issues with the food they were supposed to eat, and in future they would be challenged to bow down to idols. The meals served at the king's table, though considered to be the best, contained food that was considered unclean based on the laws of Moses.

Following God has never been easy at any point in history. Jesus compared it to a narrow road, because it is not the most popular route. Like Daniel, we need to 'resolve' to not compromise. As believers, our values are determined by scripture and God's standard for us. Values are principles that we live by and they should be non-negotiable. Through the wisdom of the Holy Spirit, God can help us navigate the different temptations that life brings us.

As we start this new year, may we resolve to hold on to our godly values, and may God give us wisdom to do so in a manner that honours others.

† Dear God, help me to stay committed to walking in your paths this year, no matter the cost. Help me to carry my cross and follow you. In Jesus' name. Amen.

For further thought

How can we encourage others who are finding the way challenging or the costs of following high?

10 January
Mercy outweighs judgement

Read Genesis 9:8–17

I establish my covenant with you: never again will all life be destroyed by the waters of a flood; never again will there be a flood to destroy the earth.

(verse 11)

Today's scripture focuses on the Noahic covenant. There are a number of covenants that are very significant to the narrative of scripture, and this one is one of them. God promises to not destroy humanity through a global flood again and gives a sign, the rainbow, as a reminder. This story is significant because it reveals God as the judge but also his heart of mercy. Both of those themes are made clear in this story, reminding us that he wants all of us to be saved, and 'Will not the Judge of all the earth do right?' (Genesis 18:25b).

He chooses to save, not because of Noah's righteousness, but because of his own love and mercy. We are today beneficiaries of that great promise. The writer of the book of Lamentations writes so beautifully 'Because of the LORD's great love we are not consumed, for his compassions never fail. They are new every morning; great is your faithfulness' (Lamentations 3:22–23). What a merciful God we have.

As we start this new year, let us embrace God's mercy towards us. Sometimes we know we are forgiven, but we find it hard to embrace God's mercy. When God forgives us, he does not remind us of our wrong. There is no sin that is too great for his mercy.

† Lord, thank you for your great mercy. Help me never to forget it and deepen my love as I meditate on it. Amen.

For further thought
Repent of any sin that the Spirit is convicting you of in this moment. Take time to thank God for your forgiveness and his mercy.

11 January
Keeping promises

Read 2 Corinthians 1:16–20

Was I fickle when I intended to do this? Or do I make my plans in a worldly manner so that in the same breath I say both 'Yes, yes' and 'No, no'?

(verses 17–18)

Paul had promised to visit the church in Corinth, but it seems he did not make it this time. He explained to them that he wasn't trying to intentionally deceive them, and that he understood the value of his word to them. He reminded them that believers are supposed to make sure their 'yes' means yes and their 'no' means no, and we must live up to God's standard for faithfulness when it comes to our words and our promises.

Recently, I made a promise to go and minister in music in another country with my pastor who lives in another continent. Two weeks before the event, I got a new job which did not permit me to take leave for those days. I did not want to seem uncommitted to my new job, so I tried to find a way to fly instead of taking the six-hour drive (meaning I could still keep my promise). But after failing to raise the funds for the ticket, I realised I had to break the promise that I had made, against my wish. It wasn't easy and it really hurt my pastor, and I asked for her forgiveness. Rightly, she told me how disappointed she was and how I had let her down.

Paul knew the importance of promises in relationships, he understood the natural disappointment and sense of being let down. He knew it was important for these to be expressed without being defensive. In that way, relationship can be restored and credibility rebuilt.

† Pray for wisdom only to make promises you can keep and for the humility and honesty to respond well when we hurt others if we are unable to fulfil them.

For further thought

Are there people who feel let down by you because of broken promises? Ask for grace and wisdom to offer apology without excuse.

Readings from Colossians (1)

Notes by **John Proctor**

John is a minister of the United Reformed Church. Now retired, he has served in a Glasgow parish, a Cambridge college and the United Reform Church's central office in London. John has written commentaries on Matthew's Gospel (BRF, revised edition 2022) and the Corinthian letters (WJK, 2015), also several Grove booklets on New Testament themes. John is married to Elaine and they live near Cambridge. John has used the NRSVA for these notes.

12 January
Firm and fruitful

Read Colossians 1:1–8

...we have heard of your faith in Christ Jesus and of the love that you have for all the saints ... the gospel that has come to you ... has been bearing fruit among yourselves from the day you heard it and truly comprehended the grace of God.

(verses 4–6)

Colossae was in the territory we now call western Turkey. Ephesus, on the coast, was the main city; Paul may possibly have written from there. Colossae was less important and well inland. Although Paul had spent time preaching in Ephesus (Acts 19), he had never visited Colossae, except perhaps in passing. The Colossian church was started by a friend of his, one Epaphras, and Paul knew few if any of its people. So, the opening of this letter seeks to bond with the recipients. Paul has heard good things about them and wants to assure them of his friendship and support. After that positive beginning, he will work around gradually to some specific pieces of teaching, advice and warning.

The Colossian Christians have 'truly comprehended the grace of God'. Good news gives people a grip on grace. It assures us that God is good, that we are loved and that Christ is with us and in us. This gospel is also 'bearing fruit among' them. The message of Jesus gives people confidence and enables us to love more joyfully and generously. The gospel reaches into our lives, to teach us grace, and then reaches outwards, in fruitful living and serving.

† Lord Jesus Christ, may your good news flourish within me and flow out constantly from me, in deeds and words of faith, hope and love.

13 January
A people changed

Read Colossians 1:9–14

...we have not ceased praying for you and asking that you may be filled with the knowledge of God's will ... He has rescued us from the power of darkness and transferred us into the kingdom of his beloved Son, in whom we have redemption, the forgiveness of sins.

(verses 9, 13–14)

Yesterday's theme was thanksgiving – for the positive impact the Christian message had made in Colossae. Today we hear Paul praying for the readers as they go forward with Christ. He longs that they will be sure and steady in their discipleship, faithful under pressure and joyful in spirit.

Paul wants his friends to be 'filled with the knowledge of God's will' (verse 9). Further on in the letter we shall see that other religious options were available in Colossae. Some people in the area appear to have been offering a spiritual top-up. They knew their way, they said, around the mazes of the spiritual world. For them Christ was not the focus; they wanted a more fulfilling religious experience (they would have said), with more mystery and intrigue about it. Paul will warn his friends not to stray into these winding paths. For the moment he speaks positively of the fullness that the Colossian Christians have already been given.

For a Christian is a person changed. We have a new loyalty: 'transferred ... into the kingdom' (verse 13) of Jesus Christ. We have a new light: rescued 'from the power of darkness' (verse 13) to learn 'the knowledge of God's will' (verse 9). And we have a new love: the word 'redemption' (verse 14) suggests a ransom, a costly action that enables and offers freedom and hope. 'Forgiveness of sins' (verse 14) comes to us through the loving gift of the cross of Christ. All of which leads into a grand statement of faith and praise, a so-called Christ-hymn, which we shall read tomorrow.

† Lord Jesus Christ, please help me to live today as a person under your rule, guided by your will, pardoned by your love. Amen.

For further thought

Have you ever faced arid times, when you did not feel 'filled with knowledge of God's will'? How would you advise a friend who was going through such a spell?

14 January
Heart of all creation, head of a new creation

Read Colossians 1:15–20

He is the image of the invisible God ... all things have been created through him and for him ... he is the beginning, the firstborn from the dead ... and through him God was pleased to reconcile to himself all things ... making peace through the blood of his cross.

(verses 15–16, 18, 20)

Was this a hymn? Maybe. The early Christians did sing (3:16, for example), but we know little about how they set words to music. Yet this passage is certainly lyrical and uplifting. The words stretch the mind and stir the heart. Whether spoken or sung, they draw us into worship. The focus is Jesus – all that he has done, and all that he means for the world. As we follow the verses through, two main threads emerge.

The first is Jesus in creation (verses 15–17). As in the opening of John's Gospel, Jesus is the hub and heart of God's creation. He was there at the beginning, working with his Father to give the universe shape and substance. Something rather similar to this is said in the Old Testament, about God's wisdom (Proverbs 8:22–31). Colossians helps us see that 'all spiritual wisdom' (verse 9) is found personally and permanently in Jesus Christ.

The second thread is Jesus in new creation (verses 18–20). As Risen Lord, he is the prototype of a new humanity, the leader of all whom he brings from death to life. His crucifixion was a mighty act of peace-making, drawing people together, offering promise and renewal to a tired and turbulent world – blood for blessing, pain for pardon, humiliation for hope.

If some in Colossae were tempted to look elsewhere for religious fulfilment, these lines shift the focus clearly and firmly back onto Jesus. In him is all the goodness of God, all the power of suffering love, all the fullness of an empty tomb.

† Lord Jesus Christ, as I travel through the years with you, please help me to understand ever more fully the scope of your power and the depth of your peace.

For further thought

Are there hymns that help you to direct your thoughts clearly and firmly to Jesus? Do they resonate at all with these lines in Colossians?

15 January
Renewing power and staying power

Read Colossians 1:21–23

And you ... he has now reconciled in his fleshly body through death,
so as to present you holy and blameless and irreproachable before him
– provided that you continue securely established and steadfast in the
faith, without shifting from the hope promised by the gospel ... I, Paul,
became a servant of this gospel.

(verses 21–23)

This short section of the letter has three linked purposes. One of these is the personal bonding with which the letter started. Paul is still outlining the rich network of Christian contact and belonging that connects him with the church at Colossae. The good news about Jesus has brought them hope, and this echoes in Paul's life. For his chief task, the centre of his thoughts and the main claim on his energies is the gospel – treasuring it, telling it and supporting the people who trust it.

Secondly, these verses connect yesterday's poetic words about Jesus as peace-maker to the personal experience of the Colossians. They have been reconciled through Jesus' death. Once living distantly and differently from God's ways, they have been given a new status, a new relationship with God and a new lifestyle. His dying has changed their living, powerfully and profoundly.

Finally, there is a hint of warning and challenge. It matters that these Christians 'continue' in the faith. The words 'securely established' (verse 23) speak of a building set on solid foundations. To be 'steadfast' (verse 23) implies stability and good support, to prevent wavering or wobbling. Not 'shifting' (verse 23) means not being dislodged or displaced. Together these words speak of solidity, steadiness and staying power. Paul will say more before long about things in Colossae that threaten to disturb or distract his readers, and he will offer some firm and cautionary advice. For the moment he reminds them gently but plainly that Christian living needs to involve commitment and consistency.

† Remember any Christians you know for whom life is troubling or testing at the moment. Pray for them to know the peace and new perspective that Jesus can give.

For further thought

What, do you find, gives people security and steadiness in their Christian living? And what experiences or influences tend to unsettle or undermine faith?

16 January
Struggle and glory

Read Colossians 1:24–29

...in my flesh I am completing what is lacking in Christ's afflictions for the sake of his body, that is, the church ... God chose to make known how great among the Gentiles are the riches of the glory of this mystery, which is Christ in you, the hope of glory.

(verses 24, 27)

In yesterday's reading Paul called himself a 'servant of the gospel' (verse 23). Today he is servant of the Church (verse 25). Commitment to the good news of Christ involves commitment to the people who believe it. They are the 'body' of Christ (verses 18, 24), a fellowship where Jesus is personally known, a people who represent his presence in the world.

Paul speaks of his own era as a key moment in history. There has been a 'mystery' (verses 26, 27) in the purpose of God, a purpose long hidden and now coming into the open. God is giving the world a glimpse of glory. This 'mystery' has two important aspects. One is breadth: it is for the nations, the gentiles, as well as for God's ancient people Israel. The life of Israel's God is reaching across the world. The second aspect is depth: 'Christ in you'. The gospel speaks of an organic bond between the Church and its Lord. He lives among us and within us. We embody his life, and this life stretches forward, from time into eternity, beyond death into resurrection – 'Christ in you, the hope of glory' (verse 27).

In the meantime, Christian service may be costly. Paul tells of 'toil and struggle' (verse 29). As Jesus suffered, he calls his people into a tough and testing way of life. Those who represent the gospel (as, in our different ways, all Christians do) may well find that the sufferings of Christ overflow into our own living (verse 24). If this happens to us, we shall find that the strength of Christ is present too (verse 29).

† Do you know (or know of) any Christians who are 'sharing in Christ's afflictions' because of their faith? Pray for them, and for courage and hope today.

For further thought

Do you often think of the Church as 'the body of Christ'? In what ways does this idea make sense to you?

17 January
Love's struggle

Read Colossians 2:1–7

...I am struggling for you, and for those in Laodicea, and for all who have not seen me face to face ... As you therefore have received Christ Jesus the Lord, continue to live your lives in him, rooted and built up in him and established in the faith.

(verses 1, 6–7)

Several of the ideas in yesterday's reading recur in these verses. Paul spoke of 'toil and struggle' (1:29), and now he says, 'I am struggling for you' (2:1). He makes an effort to support not only churches he has founded, but also Christians whom he knows only at a distance. By telling the Colossians this, he assures them that his guidance and teaching arise from serious and loving commitment. He invests work, not just words, in their well-being.

Many of Paul's hopes for this church we have heard before: unity and love (verse 2; as in 1:4); understanding and knowledge (verse 2; as in 1:9); steadiness and stability (verses 5 and 7; as in 1:11). Indeed, the repeated stress on sureness and solidity – 'firmness' (verse 5), 'rooted and built up in him and established' (verse 7) – recalls the challenge of 1:23. Paul fears that the Colossians may forget the basis of their faith and topple sideways, and now we start to see what he has in mind.

Persuasive speech, 'plausible arguments' (verse 4), were in the air. Some people thought they could offer the Colossian Christians a more advanced and fulfilling spiritual life. But Paul has already taken trouble to underline the priority and power of Jesus. There is no need to look elsewhere, is his main advice: 'live your lives in [Christ]' (verse 6).

As an aside, notice that Paul also mentions the nearby town of Laodicea (verse 1). The Colossians were in active contact with Christians there (4:15–16). But Paul tells us little about the church in Laodicea. There is more in Revelation (3:14–22), which may be a few decades later.

† Do you have any responsibilities towards Christians you have never met – praying, giving, practical help of some kind? Pray for them, amid anything that might undermine or weaken their faith today.

For further thought

Has anyone you never met invested effort in supporting your well-being and Christian growth? Have you ever had a chance to thank them? Could you?

18 January
God made you alive

Read Colossians 2:8–15

See to it that no one takes you captive through philosophy and empty deceit, according to human tradition, according to the elemental spirits of the universe, and not according to Christ ... God made you alive together with him, when he forgave us all our trespasses ...

(verses 8, 13)

The religious ideas being put before these Christians are sometimes referred to as 'the Colossian heresy'. But this 'heresy' is difficult to define or describe exactly. Indeed, as Paul writes from afar, he may not know all the detail himself. However, his mention of 'circumcision' (verses 11, 13) suggests a Jewish aspect to the matter. And his opening words here, that they shouldn't be taken captive (verse 8), imply that Christian freedom is at stake, which was also his concern in Galatians (5:1, 13). Even so, the issues behind these two letters do not seem identical.

'Philosophy and empty deceit' (verse 8) suggest that clever speech was part of the problem in Colossae. 'Human tradition' (verse 8) – the way we've always done it, ideas with pedigree, doing justice to our heritage – we can almost hear the 'plausible arguments' (verse 4) rolling out. 'Elemental spirits' (verse 8) are the components that make up the world – the words might imply physical matter, or astrological forces, or even vague and shadowy powers such as 'fate'. Someone may have wanted the Colossian Christians to align their lives more fully with 'the way the world worked'.

In response, Paul speaks of what Christ has already given us. He has planted new life in us; we are resurrection people; baptism displays this, visibly and powerfully (verse 12). We are pardoned; our sins are forgiven, erased, set aside and nailed to the cross (verses 13–14). And we need not fear. Our Lord is 'head of every ruler and authority' (verse 10). He has conquered the powers that cast shadows and superstition on the earth. Their reign is over (verse 15).

† Forgiven, erased, set aside, nailed to the cross: pray for someone who needs to know that God has really taken away their guilt and their sins.

For further thought

Have you been baptised? What does it mean to you? Thank God for this gift and for its power and promise.

Readings from Colossians (2)

Notes by **Bruce Jenneker**

Bruce Jenneker is a retired Anglican priest living alternately in Cape Town and in Johannesburg with his grandsons. During thirty-five years of ministry, worship, liturgy and Christian formation were his passion and primary occupation. He is 'completely retired', taking no vocational or professional commitments, although he has done some teaching recently. He remains engaged in personal academic study, provides short daily prayers with an image and a hymn for a Sick List, and similar evening prayers for Sundays and Feast Days. Bruce has used the NRSVA for these readings.

19 January
A new self: free from the past

Read Colossians 2:16–23

If with Christ you died to the elemental spirits of the universe, why do you live as if you still belonged to the world? Why do you submit to regulations, 'Do not handle, Do not taste, Do not touch'?

(verses 20–21)

Paul spent two years planting and nurturing the church in Ephesus. Whether he or some of his disciples planted the church in Colossae one hundred miles away, we will never know. Clearly the apostle had great affection for this fledgling community.

The Colossians were in trouble – dissension was rife among them: the seduction of Gnosticism, new philosophies and self-imposed scrupulosity were pulling them apart.

He writes to remind the Colossians of the divine mystery to which they have been called, in which they have been made new, and in which they are living. They are alive in Christ, the very image of the invisible God, in whom they are chosen, redeemed and called to a new life according to the image of their Creator.

Written as a pastoral response to a community at risk of breaking apart, losing its way, it is a careful and measured encouragement for the Colossians not to lose sight of who they are and what the love of God in Christ has made them. It is a passionate appeal for them to reclaim their high calling as those established in Christ.

Addressed to a community at risk, it speaks to us as well.

† Present Christ, keep the flame of faith burning within me, that no matter what tempts, tests and tantalises me, my gaze remains fixed on you.

20 January

A new self: free for the future

Read Colossians 3:1–4

So if you have been raised with Christ, seek the things that are above, where Christ is. Set your minds on things that are above, not on things that are on earth, for you have died, and your life is hidden with Christ in God.

(verses 1–2)

Life tumbles all around us, falling upon us in a thousand distractions. Here an urgent call insists on our attention. Here a looming crisis needs the intervention only we can make. Here a pressing financial situation will become calamitous without our speedy response. Here a relationship is teetering on a brink and we must nurture, save and restore it. We are juggling balls flying all around us. We must keep our eyes on each one, or disaster will be inevitable.

The distractions are unavoidable. The crises come unbidden. The calamities loom. And yet it is not about them. It is about our focus: where the heart of our attention is, what the source of our confidence is.

We need to know who we are, what we are made to be. That is the foundation on which we stand, the launching pad from which we dare to reach out and engage those distractions, crises, calamities. Often – perhaps even all the time – they are not of our own making or even our own choosing (although it is true that sometimes they are). We have little control over them. But we are who we are in Christ and that makes all the difference.

Who we are is given to us, a free gift of grace. We are victors with Christ over darkness, over all that threatens us, over the chains of evil and the cords of death. This wondrous gift cannot eliminate the distractions, the crises, the calamities. But it does something far more wonderful – it robs them of their power to unseat, derail and overcome us.

† Christ of gentle power, take and mould me, fill me with your life, that I may live, always and forever secure in the gift of your grace.

For further thought

Attempt to start and continue from today first focusing on the power of your new life in Christ, and then dealing with life's challenges.

21 January
Reborn: beyond slavery and freedom

Read Colossians 3:5–11

[You] have clothed yourselves with the new self, which is being renewed in knowledge according to the image of its creator. In that renewal there is no longer Greek and Jew, circumcised and uncircumcised, barbarian, Scythian, slave and free; but Christ is all and in all!

(verses 10–11)

The wonder of our new life in Christ is that nothing of the uniqueness we are made to be in the image of our Creator is lost in our rebirth and renewal. Rather, and by grace, our hallowed uniqueness is liberated, unshackled, released. What was imprisoned in prejudice and partiality is liberated. What was enslaved in captivity and oppression is unshackled. What was chained in conventional assumptions and conformist codes is released.

In our new life in Christ, in the image of our Creator, we are what we are created to be, at last, forever and notwithstanding all the evidence to the contrary. No longer confined to definitions that undermine, exploit and despoil God's image in us. No longer Greek or Jew, circumcised or uncircumcised, barbarian, Scythian, slave or free; but now Christ is all and in all.

While slavery, human trafficking, racism, sexism, abuse and war still rage all around us, we know that every shackling captivity is being eroded by the love and grace of the Creator whose image we are, and whose image is being revealed more and more in all creation. Our identity is a vocation to be the will of our Creator redeeming and liberating the whole creation.

This renewed, restored identity is not the end of our rebirth. Our renewal is continuing and lasting, for moment by moment we are being renewed according to the image of our Creator. Day by day we are becoming more and more like the Creator who made us, and whose fingerprints are all over us.

† Unshackling Christ, break every chain that fetters me. Free me from my selfish securities and petty condescension. Then use me to let freedom ring all around me.

For further thought

Attempt to start and continue from today to identify the captivities you choose and those you support and find ways to break free of them.

22 January
Living in Christ: God's chosen ones

Read Colossians 3:12–17

And let the peace of Christ rule in your hearts, to which indeed you were called in the one body. And be thankful. Let the word of Christ dwell in you richly; teach and admonish one another in all wisdom.

(verses 15–16)

Sometimes the smallest words have the most profound meanings. The little word 'let', which appears twice in today's extract, brings multiple layers into our meditation. It is an invitation and an offer. It is a request. It is an imperative.

In the midst of the upheaval and turmoil in the life of the Colossian church, its members are invited to receive the peace of Christ into their hearts as its pattern and rule. The 'shalom' of God is offered to them: that blessed peace in which creation is restored to its original wholeness through the saving and sacrificial love of Jesus Christ for a fallen universe and broken humanity. This wholeness is on offer, a free gift with no strings attached, and it is not simply offered as a take-it-or-leave-it option – it is an invitation from one heart to another.

The Colossians are buffeted by many competing distractions, each one seducing them away from the faith which at first they held so devotedly. This 'let' is a request, an entreaty, a tenderly made appeal. It comes as a quiet word in the midst of noise. It is as soft as the voice of a trusted friend taking you by your hand and leading you from chaos to calm.

And yet it is an imperative, a bold and urgent summons, lifting your head above the water, catching you as you fall, to protect and save you.

This saving peace is a penetrating word, the living Word of Jesus Christ, spoken in deep care and steadfast love.

Listen! It is addressed to you.

† Eloquent Christ, make your appeal, speak your word and soothe my troubled breast to bring calm where tumult rages and peace for brokenness.

For further thought

Attempt to start and continue from today to surrender to this 'let'. Allow the invitation to lay hold of you. Let go and let God.

23 January
Turning the world upside-down

Read Colossians 3:18 – 4:1

Whatever your task, put yourselves into it, as done for the Lord and not for your masters, since you know that from the Lord you will receive the inheritance as your reward; you serve the Lord Christ.

(verses 23–24)

At its heart, the gospel of Christ is countercultural. It invites us to go against the stream. It overturns cherished assumptions. It undercuts established privilege. It turns the world upside-down.

This is not what we want most from Christ and Christ's gospel, most of the time, if we are honest with ourselves. We want assurance that 'things as they are' is not just fine but is acceptable, admirable and worthy. We desire the affirmation that we, just as we are, and life, just as we live it, are faultless and irreproachable.

Then, in our complacency, we are assaulted by the ringing 'but' of the gospel. 'But' Christ is penetrating darkness and bringing light. 'But' Christ is 'casting down the mighty and lifting up the lowly' (Luke 1:52). 'But' Christ is establishing a new order that judges the old and establishes the peace that is the wholeness of all creation, and which surpasses all understanding.

This passage has for centuries been paraded as a warrant for patriarchy, and for slavery and the hierarchy that locks humanity into superiors and inferiors, the powerful and the voiceless. This is a gross misreading of the text, for in truth it demands of husbands and wives, parents and children, masters and slaves, a radical re-ordering of their relationships, exchanging patterns of privilege and power for a new paradigm of mutual respect and reciprocal dignity.

In this new way of living and relating, we are summoned to engage everyone and everything – each encounter and each task – as one more movement in our ongoing, mindful pilgrimage with God.

† God with us, stay close by and alert us to your presence in all around us, in all that we encounter, and in all that we do.

For further thought

Attempt to start and continue from today to discover the fingerprints of God in every aspect of who you are and what you do.

24 January

Seasoned with salt: prayerfully and graciously

Read Colossians 4:2–6

Devote yourselves to prayer, keeping alert in it with thanksgiving. Conduct yourselves wisely towards outsiders, making the most of the time. Let your speech always be gracious, seasoned with salt, so that you may know how you ought to answer everyone.

(verses 2, 5–6)

Our life in Christ, as God's chosen ones with our lives hidden with Christ in God, demands the discipline of prayer and requires the practice of thanksgiving.

First, we are called to risk entering the presence of God, to dare to enter the Holy of Holies, there to dwell with God in divine communion, listening, hearing and speaking. In a blissful way, this intimacy is nothing less than becoming a partner in the fullness of the divine conversation among the blessed and holy Trinity – loving Creator, living Word, life-giving Spirit. In prayer we are caught up in the joy and peace of this divine spiral of love.

Along with a vocation to a life of prayer, we are summoned to an all-embracing gratitude. In every moment we are to recognise the grace of God that comes to meet, uplift, redeem and save us – and give thanks: to stand in awe before God's handiwork, all things, great and small, and tremble with gratitude.

In both these identifying callings, we are invited to remove ourselves from the central place we have fashioned for ourselves in our little universes. Not only must we step out of our petty little worlds and take our place in the big wide universe, but there we become responders rather than pseudo-agents. The initiative is God's and remains with God, who invites us into the divine communion. So too with the vocation to gratitude. We are given gifts, we receive them, we give thanks. In our proper place.

† Generous God, keep inviting us into the intimacy of prayer with you, that the ears of our hearts will delight when you speak, and the eyes of our faith will thrill each time you give.

For further thought

Attempt to start and continue from today to enter into the divine spiral of prayer and to delight in the loving conversation of the Trinity.

25 January
A new community of shared faith and love

Read Colossians 4:7–18

Give my greetings to the brothers and sisters in Laodicea, and to Nympha and the church in her house. And when this letter has been read among you, have it read also in the church of the Laodiceans; and see that you also read the letter from Laodicea.

(verses 15–16)

God's chosen ones are real people, with real names and unique identities, living in real communities. Tychicus, Onesimus, Mark, Barnabas, Aristarchus, Justus, Epaphras, Luke, Demas, Nympha and Archippus are all mentioned by name – twelve people including Paul. These names are known and the people they name are participating members of the community they all share. The localities in which the church is at work are mentioned too – Laodicea, Hierapolis and the church in Nympha's house. All identifiable and real.

The community of God's chosen ones is a real, living, concrete community, living every day in out-in-the-world real places.

Christianity is founded on the incarnation, born of God's choice of humanity as a dwelling place for the fullness of God. Humanity matters to God: God loves humankind, the work of God's hands. The material world matters to God: God loves the creation of God's hands.

Christianity is rooted in the specificity of our identities, anchored in our time and places. It is there that we must encounter ourselves, encounter our world, encounter God. And it is there too that we must encounter our fellow pilgrims on the pilgrimage to our full potential as God's chosen ones, holy and beloved, clothed with compassion, kindness, humility, meekness and patience.

It is from them that we will receive compassion when we need it. It is to them that we will offer kindness when their spirits are broken. Together we will inject humility, meekness and patience into a world desperately in need of these qualities.

† Summoning God, you call us into community and make us one body, members of one another; empower us to be what we are.

For further thought

Attempt to start and continue from today to recognise the uniqueness of your fellow pilgrims and celebrate the community.

Sheep and shepherds

Notes by **Bola Iduoze**

Bola is an author, conference speaker and mentor. She began her career as an accountant over thirty years ago and began her entrepreneurial journey as a home business coach in 2000. Bola is also a co-pastor at Gateway Chapel, a multi-cultural church in Kent, UK, founded in 2003. She has a passion to encourage, equip and empower people to live their best life ever. Bola is married to Eddie, and they are blessed with two children, Asher and Bethel. Bola has used the NIV for these readings.

26 January
The power of the loved sheep

Read 2 Samuel 12:1–6

But the poor man had nothing except one little ewe lamb he had bought. He raised it, and it grew up with him and his children.

(verse 3)

Sheep are still a big part of life in the suburban parts of Nigeria in Africa. The condition of the sheep – as well as the number – acts as an indicator of how powerful a person the owner is. While many might think nothing of sheep, I come from a culture where wealth and leadership are still measured by land and cattle ownership.

In this scripture, the man does have authority, visibility as well as prosperity, which he used for personal gains. As against taking one of his own sheep to entertain his guest, he went for the only sheep owned by his poor neighbour. This neighbour has invested a lot of time, money and care for his sheep and the Bible makes this very clear.

Though the story is mainly about Nathan reflecting David's sin back to him, there are a couple of other lessons to be learnt from it. One is that we are never too little or insignificant to God and he can raise someone to fight or speak for us in places of authority, just like Nathan did in this story. Another is that God cares for his sheep and will judge all injustice towards his loved sheep, whom you and I are.

† Father, help me to value your sheep and treat all around me as you would. Help me to be kind and fair in my dealings with all around me.

27 January
The offering presented to the Lord

Read Leviticus 8:18–29

It was a burnt offering, a pleasing aroma, a food offering presented to the Lord, as the Lord commanded Moses.

(verse 21b)

God had a programme in place in the Old Testament that the people needed to adhere to, and he expected Moses who received the instruction to inform the people on how to prepare for their offering to the Lord. The offering God called for requires preparation to present the burnt offering without blemish to the Lord. The fragrance that comes from these burnt animals in sacrifice must be pleasing to the Lord.

We, in the New Testament, are told that Jesus offered himself as a perfect fragrant offering to the Lord (Ephesians 5:2) and we are to present our bodies as a living sacrifice, holy and acceptable to God, which is our spiritual and reasonable worship (Romans 12:1).

We tend to think that God is no longer interested in burnt offerings and the blood of bulls and goats. While that is correct because Jesus has paid the price, God is still interested in lives that are lived in a way that is pleasing to him. Every burnt (sacrificial) offering releases an aroma. It could be a fragrance that will attract or one which will repel. Let us always ensure we please God.

How do we present ourselves as a living sacrifice that pleases our God? By living by his statutes and following his will wholeheartedly. As we do that, God will be pleased with the sacrifice we offer: our lives.

† Lord, please give me the grace to offer you my life as you require and let my life please you always. In Jesus' name. Amen.

For further thought
God can be pleased with our lives and sacrifices if we live as he desires. He has shown us how to live to please him. Let us therefore follow his will in living for him.

28 January
Time to water the sheep

Read Genesis 29:1–10

'Look,' he said, 'the sun is still high; it is not time for the flocks to be gathered. Water the sheep and take them back to pasture.'

(verse 7)

The welfare of the sheep is essential to any shepherd. There is a routine for watering and feeding the sheep and that should be known to every shepherd. The hirelings in this story are waiting around for the right time to water and feed the sheep. If the sun is too high, it will not be safe for the flock to be gathered.

Sheep are helpless and need their keepers to watch over and care for them. A true shepherd should not expose the flock to the elements; but make all provision to feed, water and gather them at the appropriate times.

God is truly our good shepherd and will continually watch over us to provide for us. We as his sheep can trust in him daily.

Also, as under-shepherds, we must realise that God's people matter to him just like the sheep matter to the shepherd. We must continually give attention to and take care of God's flock; we must be aware of the expectations of the one who has committed the work of caring for the sheep into our hands.

Let us be mindful to take care of the sheep at the appropriate times and seasons. Jacob knew there is a time for the sheep to be fed and watered before they get taken back to pasture; and he reminded the shepherds of this.

† Thank you, Lord, for being the good shepherd who knows all our needs and who cares for us. Help us to equally be compassionate and caring of your flock within our pasture. In Jesus' name.

For further thought

God knows and cares for his children and we can trust him to meet our need according to his will.

29 January
Caring for the sheep

Read 1 Samuel 25:2–8

Now I hear that it is sheep-shearing time. When your shepherds were with us, we did not mistreat them … Therefore be favourable towards my men.

(verses 7–8)

Sheep shearing time is a regular occurrence in the cycle of a sheep farmer. The greater the number of sheep, the more time the farmers must give to this exercise. Though sheep shearing helps the sheep feel lighter and better, it is also a time of vulnerability for the sheep and an extremely busy time for the shearers.

David and his men helped with the protection of the shepherd during this sheep shearing period and he expected a level of hospitality for his people. He did not get the reward he was expecting and was going to fight Nabal for his decision, but for Abigail's intervention. Though he never got into battle, he was still rewarded for the help he provided.

God cares for the sheep and rewards anyone who equally cares for his sheep. He told us to be careful to know the state of our sheep and if we do that well, the sheep will provide clothing and wealth (Proverbs 27:23–26).

God's sheep are his children – be interested in God's children, care for them, and he will reward you abundantly. There is reward in caring for God's children.

† Lord, I acknowledge the fact that you care for your sheep. Please grant me grace to care for your sheep just the way you as a good shepherd do. In Jesus' name. Amen.

For further thought

God cares for his sheep and every time we align our actions with his, we please him. As we care for God's sheep, he rewards us.

30 January
Transferable skills

Read Psalm 78:70–72

He chose David his servant and took him from the sheep pens ... And David shepherded them with integrity of heart; with skilful hand he led them.

(verses 70, 72)

David was a well-known shepherd whom God used in leading and caring for Israel because of his heart and skills. His actions while he was a shepherd did not go unnoticed by God and those were also the qualities God wanted when looking for a leader for his people.

God still chooses people to serve and care for his flock and, as in David's case, our skills and character are not independent qualities. God uses all you have gone through and learnt in different areas of your life for his purpose. We all have transferable skills that do not go to waste because we are in different spaces of life. Your knowledge and training in your career path can be used by God in ministry and service.

No experience or skill is lost. My husband and I found ourselves in a cow farm in Cyprus a few years ago. As farm hands, we got a lot of skills taking care of the cattle – feeding, caring for, ensuring the safety of as well as protecting these cattle from hurting themselves. We learnt so much from the cow farm and this knowledge subsequently helped us when we became pastors of God's people. Shepherding would have been a different experience if not for this opportunity we had taking care of the flock.

God will use our skills and experience for his own glory if we co-operate with him.

† Lord, thank you for all the things I have gone through and experienced. Please help me trust you to use my skills and experiences to build the lives in your kingdom. In Jesus' name.

For further thought
God will use who you are and what you have learnt for his own glory if you allow him, so do not discount your history.

31 January
God will give you rest

Read Micah 2:12–16

I will bring them together like sheep in a pen, like a flock in its pasture; the place will throng with people.

(verse 12b)

God gave a prophetic word about how he was going to gather his people Israel together and bring them back to the land he promised them. God likened this action to that of how a shepherd gathers his flock in their pasture and brings them into the pen. This is indicative of the great love of the Father for his children and the extent he will go to to give us peace and rest based on his promise to us.

When Eddie my husband and I were working in Cyprus, our cow farm was next to a sheep farm. The shepherd has a daily task and that was to take the sheep out to graze and no matter how scattered or far they've gone; it is the job of the shepherd to ensure he brings back all the flock to the pen.

The sheep being back in their pen represents rest for them. It is the responsibility of the shepherd to ensure all his sheep are gathered and taken into their pasture daily.

Just as the shepherd knows his sheep and ensures their safety, God has made provision for his people to be gathered and led back to their safe land. He also knows us, cares for each one of us and is keen to ensure we lie down in safety and enjoy rest.

God will bring you and me together like a flock in its own pen. Let us trust him to lead us and direct us to a preprepared place of rest for us.

† Father, grant me the grace to trust you as a good shepherd. May I follow your leading into the pasture you have prepared for me in Jesus' name.

For further thought
God gathered the scattered people of Israel into their own pastures. As a good shepherd, he is still keen to gather his flock into their own pastures.

1 February
A shepherd knows their sheep

Read John 10:14–16

I have other sheep that are not of this sheep pen. I must bring them also. They too will listen to my voice, and there shall be one flock and one shepherd.

(verse 16)

The sheep and its shepherd have a unique relationship. The sheep being a defenceless animal depends mainly on its shepherd and the shepherd is committed to care for and keep his sheep safe.

The main way a sheep follows its shepherd is by recognition of its shepherd's voice. Each shepherd has a different voice or mechanism for calling their sheep and the sheep recognises its shepherd's voice. The sheep does not just follow any shepherd's voice but the recognised voice of its shepherd.

Just like the sheep knows the shepherd, the shepherd also knows his sheep. He calls them individually and knows if one of them is missing. The shepherd expects the sheep to listen to his voice. Be it the original sheep in his flock or the additional (newer) sheep that are added to the flock.

We are known, cared for, protected and gathered by the shepherd who knows us and expects us to get to know him and his voice.

Jesus said of the other sheep he will be adding to the flock that they too must hear his voice and come. The recognition of the shepherd's voice is essential to the gathering of a flock into a prepared pen. And voice recognition is a function of relationship.

So, let's make every effort to relate closely with our Father so we can recognise his voice always. In that is our safety and the assurance of our provision.

† Father, I thank you that you have called me as your own. I pray that I will continually recognise and respond to your call. In Jesus' name.

For further thought

Jesus knows his sheep and his sheep know his voice. Every sheep that knows and responds to the voice of the shepherd will enjoy the provisions of the shepherd.

The Gospel of Luke (1)

1 The ministry begins

Notes by **Audrey Jose**

Audrey and her husband serve with Radstock Ministries and divide their time between Canada and Albania where they mentor Albanian missionaries serving across the Balkans. An author and Bible teacher, Audrey speaks internationally and has a passion for people to have a transforming relationship with Jesus. Her book, *Guard Your Heart* (WhiteFire, 2010), challenges believers toward that kind of transforming relationship with Jesus. Audrey has used the NIVUK for these notes.

2 February
Preparing the way

Read Luke 3:1–22

The people were waiting expectantly and were all wondering in their hearts if John might possibly be the Messiah. John answered them all, 'I baptise you with water. But one who is more powerful than I will come … He will baptise you with the Holy Spirit and fire.'

(verses 15–16)

'The people were waiting expectantly'. The long-predicted Messiah was never far from the Jewish people's minds (Isaiah 9:6). They waited eagerly, excitedly – maybe even anxiously – in anticipation of the one who would change everything!

From childhood, John heard his father tell the astounding story of his conception, birth and unique purpose (Luke 1:11–17). John's perspective on life was rooted in Isaiah: 'A voice of one calling in the wilderness: "Prepare the way for the LORD"' (40:3–5). That voice was his, and the time to speak out had come.

A magnetic speaker of influence, John was compelling yet humble. When asked if he was the Messiah, he'd say, 'No, I'm not. But I'm pointing you to him, to the one greater than I, to the one whose sandals I am not even worthy to untie. Listen to me! Repent, because he is coming!'

Are we, as God's people, waiting expectantly – trusting that he has good reasons for saying 'Wait'? Rather than get anxious, let's do as John did: wait in expectation of God keeping his promises and living out our calling from God with humility, pointing everyone to Jesus.

† Lord, may repentance be part of my daily worship, and may I continually point others to you.

3 February
The temptation of Jesus

Read Luke 4:1–13

Jesus, full of the Holy Spirit, left the Jordan and was led by the Spirit into the wilderness, where for forty days he was tempted by the devil ... When the devil had finished all this tempting, he left him until an opportune time.

(verses 1–2, 13)

Jesus identified with sinners in baptism (Luke 3:21–22) and then in temptation. Baptism is a public testimony to our faith, and Satan doesn't like it when we take such steps to deepen our relationship with God. So, he goes into attack mode, as he did here with Jesus. During his forty days in the desert, Satan tempted Jesus to:

1. Make bread out of a stone – the temptation here is to take care of his own needs, rather than allowing God to meet these needs in his own way and timing.

2. Worship Satan in return for all the kingdoms of the world. This temptation is for Jesus to 'save the world' in a far less humiliating and painful way than dying on the cross. The focus is on what or who you 'worship' in order to achieve a goal.

3. Jump from the top of a building and rely on angels to break his fall. The temptation is to control or manipulate God. If he jumped, putting himself in unnecessary danger, it would force God to protect him.

Looking at Jesus' temptations again, it suddenly became personal. I often resort to taking care of my own needs rather than allowing God to meet them, and I have sometimes been tempted to say, 'God, if you do this then I'll do that.'

The spiritual battle is intense, it's relentless. Satan is desperate for us to fail. Yet, let's not forget the five most important words here: 'Full of the Holy Spirit'. You have all you need, in Jesus Christ, to stand firm (Daniel 11:32b).

† Father, give me the courage to look these temptations in the face, to see them for what they are, and a knowledge of your word to stand firm in the face of them.

For further thought

How have I experienced any of these same temptations? Do I believe Jesus can understand and cares about what I'm going through during these times?

4 February
Jesus is rejected

Read Luke 4:14–30

'Isn't this Joseph's son?' they asked. They got up, drove him out of the town, and took him to the brow of the hill on which the town was built, in order to throw him off the cliff.

(verses 22b, 29)

Immediately after his forty-day ordeal in the desert, Jesus went home to Nazareth – a 'safe place' where people knew and loved him. A place where his childhood friends lived, where his mom's friends were. Everyone was amazed at the changes they saw in him.

In the synagogue on the Sabbath, Jesus opened the scroll and read two verses from Isaiah's messianic prophecy beginning with the words, 'The Spirit of the Lord is on me' (see Isaiah 61:1–2).

He stopped, closed the scroll and sat down. He looked around at his family, friends, the town elders, the synagogue leaders – everyone was staring at him. 'Today this scripture is fulfilled in your hearing,' he said. There was an unspoken something in the air. How would they respond? At first, they were amazed at his words. But ... wasn't this Joseph's son?

Jesus continued explaining the truth: Elijah was not sent to the widows in Israel during the famine; he was sent to a gentile widow in Sidon. Elisha was not sent to cleanse the skin diseases of anyone in Israel; he was sent to a gentile leper in Syria.

His words sparked outrage! Who does he think he is? He's claiming to be the Messiah! He's saying God's blessings and mercy are for gentiles, not just for Israel! This is blasphemy!

The whole town moved swiftly from approval to offence then fury and finally to attempted murder. 'But he walked right through the crowd and went on his way' – heartbroken at their rejection, yet with unassailable power and authority: the Son of God.

† Lord, how do I respond to you? Do I just want you as a carpenter, to fix things? Or do I want all of you? I pray you would guard me from any way I might reject you.

For further thought

When faced with something Jesus teaches that we don't like, how do we respond? Do we reject it? Or do we embrace it and act on it?

5 February
Holy One of God

Read Luke 4:31–44

The people were amazed … and said to each other, 'What words these are! With authority and power he gives orders to impure spirits and they come out!' …[they] brought to Jesus all who had various kinds of illness, and laying his hands on each one, he healed them.

(verses 32, 36, 40)

In Nazareth the people were amazed at Jesus' teaching. In Capernaum people were amazed at his authority. If they had truly understood who Jesus was, they wouldn't have been amazed. Part of the Messiah's mission was to bring freedom for prisoners, to set the oppressed free (Luke 4:17–21).

While Jesus was in the synagogue teaching, a man possessed by an impure spirit approached him. The demon within the man cried out to Jesus as loud as it could, 'Go away! …Jesus of Nazareth! …I know who you are – the Holy One of God!' This man was in desperate need of being set free from the prison of demon possession. Jesus demonstrated his messianic calling by going on the spiritual offensive against the demonic and evil.

What the demon had said was true, but there was no way Jesus wanted the testimony of a demon. He wanted people to see his Messiahship for themselves; to see 'the Holy One of God' revealed in their midst. With immediate and piercing authority, Jesus commanded the evil spirit to 'Be quiet!' and 'Come out!' And it did! Evil cannot stand in the face of Jesus.

Like the demon-possessed man, we cannot free ourselves from what plagues our spirit or from whatever Satan is holding over us. Only Jesus has the power to do that. And even as he did not draw from his own strength and resources, neither should we. In human form, Jesus drew from consistent, private communion with God his Father. And so can we.

† Thank you, Lord Jesus, that you love me so much. Thank you for your power to transform my life. Thank you that you are the Holy One of God!

For further thought

Jesus has authority over illness and evil, as well as our own selves. Where are you submitting to Christ's authority in your life? Where are you resisting?

6 February
Calling of the first disciples

February

The Gospel of Luke (1) – 1 The ministry begins

Read Luke 5:1–26

Then Jesus said to Simon, 'Don't be afraid; from now on you will fish for people.' So they pulled their boats up on shore, left everything and followed him. Everyone was amazed and gave praise to God. They were filled with awe and said, 'We have seen remarkable things today.'

(verses 10b–11, 26)

When Jesus finished his teaching, he turned to Simon and said, 'Put out into deep water, and let down the net for a catch.' A seasoned fisherman, Simon had spent the whole night fishing, but had caught nothing! Nevertheless, Simon said, 'But because you say so, I will let down the net.' The catch of fish was so overwhelming he cried out to his fishing partners James and John to come and help.

Astonished at what had happened Simon fell at Jesus' knees and cried, 'Go away from me, Lord' – he was a sinful man, in the presence of holiness. But Jesus didn't go away. He had big plans for this 'sinful man' and his friends – to bring them into a right relationship with God and give them a new purpose.

'Don't be afraid,' Jesus said. 'Follow me' (Matthew 4:19). 'From now on you will fish for people.' If someone said to you, 'Come on! Follow me! Don't be afraid!' would you do it? My hesitation would be, 'Why are they telling me not to be afraid? What's the danger?' Yet this was exactly what Jesus said to these men! Their response? 'They left everything and followed him.' They could do this because not only had they heard his teaching, not only had they seen him do miracles, but they had just had a personal, first-hand encounter with him, and they trusted him.

Jesus' invitation was, and still is, open to everyone. While Jesus specifically called the twelve disciples, they weren't any more special or spiritual than the many others who followed him just as devotedly and closely. They heard him, they trusted him and they too stepped out into the unknown. And they all saw remarkable things!

† Lord Jesus, I'm asking you to give me the strength, both physically and emotionally, to follow you wherever you lead me with joy and anticipation as to what we will do together!

For further thought

This passage is about an invitation from Jesus. What is his invitation to you? What 'remarkable things' does he want to share with you?

37

7 February
Lord of the Sabbath

Read Luke 5:27 – 6:11

One Sabbath Jesus was going through the cornfields, and his disciples began to pick some ears of corn ... Some of the Pharisees asked, 'Why are you doing what is unlawful on the Sabbath?' Then Jesus said to them, 'The Son of Man is Lord of the Sabbath.'

(6:1–2, 5)

The practice of observing the Sabbath originated in the biblical commandment, 'Remember the Sabbath day by keeping it holy' – just as God, himself, rested on the seventh day after creation (Exodus 20:8–11; Genesis 2:2–3). He knows the importance of rest.

According to the Jewish traditions that grew up around the Sabbath day commandment, picking an ear of corn from a stalk was considered work – it was reaping. Working grain in one's hands to separate the wheat from the chaff was work – it was threshing.

The Pharisees and teachers of the law were looking for a reason to accuse Jesus, so they watched him closely to see if he would do any healing on the Sabbath. When they saw his disciples 'working' on this sacred day, they accused him of committing a serious breach of religious tradition.

Jesus never disdained the Old Testament scriptures. He respected them and quoted them. In response to the Pharisees' accusations, Jesus' actions and words were in effect saying that they had added to and encumbered the old so much that it was almost unrecognisable. He, Jesus, as Lord of the Sabbath, came in person, to set everyone back on the right track.

God's Sabbath principle is for us to set apart a portion of our time, free from the demands of work, and allow that time to focus on God in a way different from what the working week allows. A time to enjoy his blessings in a distinctive way.

There's freedom in Christ: freedom to obey the intent of God's commandments, freedom to be nourished, freedom to be healed.

† Lord God, my heart's desire is to have time with you, free from outside pressures, to focus solely on you and to enjoy your presence. Thank you for desiring this time as well.

For further thought

How can you find time in your weekly rhythm of life to prioritise a Sabbath time with God?

8 February
The disciples' journey begins

Read Luke 6:12–36

When morning came, he called his disciples to him and chose twelve of them, whom he also designated apostles. He went down with them and stood on a level place. A large crowd of his disciples was there and a great number of people from all over Judea ...

(verses 13, 17)

The disciples Jesus chose to be apostles were a diverse group. There were brothers (James and John; Peter and Andrew); business associates (Peter, James and John fished together); political opponents (Levi the Roman-collaborating tax collector, Simon the Roman-hating zealot); and even one who wouldn't remain committed (Judas Iscariot). This diversity was indicative of all Jesus' disciples.

While Jesus specifically singled out twelve, many of the men and women in the large crowd of disciples on the side of the hill that day followed him for all or part of his ministry (Mark 15:40–41; Acts 1:21–23). He saw in them a great faith and trust; yet he also knew some would exhibit selfishness and an astounding lack of comprehension.

What did Jesus think was important to teach his followers? Looking directly at all of the disciples in the crowd, he said: You are blessed! You are part of God's kingdom! You will be satisfied! You will laugh! You will be rejected; you will be rewarded! Love those who don't love you back; be merciful because God is merciful.

Discipleship begins at the feet of Jesus – daily choosing to spend time with him, to learn from him, and to follow his teachings with the goal of becoming more and more like him. Jesus said, 'If you hold to my teaching, you are really my disciples' (John 8:31).

And so, too, does your own journey of discipleship begin ... at the feet of Jesus, spending time with him, serving him, knowing he will give you the power to fulfil whatever you have been sent to do.

† Thank you, Jesus, that I can know that I am one of your true disciples as I abide in you. Thank you that you are steadfast truth, which frees me to become more like you.

For further thought

Which of the teachings in Luke 6:20–36 is Jesus focusing on with you at this point in your discipleship?

The Gospel of Luke (1)

2 Receiving the word

Notes by **Jessica Hewitt**

Jessica Hewitt is a mother of two with a wealth of personal experience navigating mental health difficulties and addiction issues. She is currently studying early childhood development, with a focus on the gentle parenting of children with ADHD and autism. Her own diagnoses have shaped her faith and motherhood journeys greatly, and she enjoys finding new ways in which to express spirituality with her children. She has a strong personal community within her local church that her whole family enjoys being a part of. Jessica has used the NIVUK for these readings.

9 February
Do as I do, not as I say!

Read Luke 6:37–49

Why do you call me, 'Lord, Lord,' and do not do what I say?

(verse 46)

We strive as Christians to be earthly representatives of God, and to embody Christ in our everyday lives. To show grace, forgiveness and compassion to our neighbours so that they may be encouraged to show those qualities to others. These things are also true, and key, to being an effective parent. It's so easy to get wrapped up in which lessons you should be teaching your children that we often forget how to teach them these lessons. Sometimes, we never knew how to in the first place. Children learn best from modelled behaviour; and they are watching us more often than we realise! How many times did you hear, 'Do as I say, not as I do!' when you were younger, and how unfair did that feel? Before we even know the word, we understand hypocrisy. When your actions line up with your words, children copy you confidently.

Living your life authentically by the values that matter most to you is also the best way to live a fulfilling life, full of integrity and free from hypocrisy. One of the most effective teachers in history was Jesus. People followed him everywhere because he lived the life he was preaching, and people could see it was good. He was, and is, the ultimate gentle parent!

† Dear Lord, I want my life to be a reflection of your values and teachings. Please help me embody your goodness honestly and wholly.

10 February
Say the word

Read Luke 7:1–17

That is why I did not even consider myself worthy to come to you. But say the word, and my servant will be healed.

(verse 7)

My oldest comes to me for comfort when she has nightmares because, as we know from yesterday, modelling values and truth works – I've demonstrated to her that I am capable of making things right. We talk about darkness and defeat any monsters that may be lurking there so she can sleep peacefully. To her, I have authority over darkness.

Likewise, the centurion had heard of Jesus' authority over sickness. He sent messengers to Jesus to ask for his healing, and before they even reached his house asked that Jesus just 'say the word'. The centurion understood what it was like to have faith in those he had authority over, knowing that they would follow his commands, and he knew Jesus had the same authority over sickness. What an incredible show of faith! Jesus demonstrated time and time again that he had power to heal, yet what always impressed me was the faith demonstrated by those in need of healing. They did not doubt that it would happen, Jesus just healed. He was renowned for his powers even in the face of death – as demonstrated by his interaction with the widow's son. I find it fascinating how Jesus spoke directly to the dead, commanding them to live. His word was the power through which death was defeated, as his words hold the power through which we may live.

† Is there anything in your life that needs to be put into words, or spoken out loud, so it may heal? Say these words to God so that he may shine a light on the darkness and defeat it.

For further thought

Are there people you know whose faith led to healing? What similarities to the centurion's story can you find?

11 February
John the Baptist's faith and doubt

Read Luke 7:18–35

When the men came to Jesus, they said, 'John the Baptist sent us to you to ask, "Are you the one who is to come, or should we expect someone else?"'

(verse 20)

I had many doubts when my first was born. I had so much to learn and often felt like I was drowning in choices, never making the right ones. Over time, I realised the key to raising my children was patience and faith. Patience to wait for the right time to teach and faith that the right time will arrive! I listen to my gut on when to hold my tongue and when to teach. But it can be hard to trust our instincts when we are bombarded with information from the media, well-meaning friends, family, professionals and even strangers. Of course, it's good to take on board others' genuine life experience, but sometimes it drowns out your own voice and the knowledge of what is right in your unique situation. We all experience doubt – it's a natural part of growth and learning, and a reasonable response to hardships and trials.

John was in a difficult predicament when he asked if Jesus truly was the Messiah. He was in prison for fearlessly speaking what he knew was the truth, yet here he was speaking from uncertainty and doubt. I love that, rather than berating him, Jesus praises his unwavering commitment to God, even in the face of doubt. He is a testament to the faithfulness that God seeks in his followers. Like John, we are asked to trust in God and to have patience and faith in his perfect timing even while being honest about our doubts! In that way, we can authentically and faithfully live out our purpose, preparing the way for Christ in the lives of others by teaching his word and practising his wisdom.

† May we be filled with gratitude and hope because we can have faith that God's plan will unfold with perfect timing. He will fulfil his promises, leading us on a journey of transformation and redemption.

For further thought

This passage highlights John the Baptist's humanity. Do you notice how his doubt doesn't invalidate his relationship with God?

12 February
Anointed by a sinful woman

> **Read Luke 7:36–50**
> *As she stood behind him at his feet weeping, she began to wet his feet with her tears. Then she wiped them with her hair, kissed them and poured perfume on them.*
>
> (verse 38)

When I was an alcoholic, I often wandered the streets aimlessly in the early hours. I remember acutely how sunrise in particular was a time of great emptiness for me. I had endured another night and had yet another full day to survive ahead of me. The contrast between a bright, clear new day, full of potential, and me – dulled, tainted and squandering any potential I once had.

One of these occasions happened to be a Sunday morning and I had meandered through town in a mire of my own struggles, avoiding the looks of other early risers out of embarrassment and shame. I knew they could see me, but they could not understand me. As I stumbled through town, I was drawn to the familiarity of my local church. After sitting on the steps for some time, I was ushered in by those I had once been among as part of the church community, who knew me and my mother. They showed me great kindness, love, forgiveness and compassion. They offered me food, shelter and a place to rest a while. I was a wretch on the steps, but I was humble, asking for mercy – and it was granted. I often think back to that day and I don't remember the faces of those who helped me, but I know whose face they reflected – as far as I am concerned, it was at the feet of Jesus that I fell and his face that offered forgiveness. That day was the brightest day I had seen in a very long time, and I am still reaping the harvest of love that was shown to me.

† Thank you, Lord, for always showing us love and forgiveness especially when we are at our most vulnerable. May your boundless mercy for our authentic selves help us to be humble and thankful every day.

For further thought

Can you remember a mercy shown to you when you were in need? Consider how even the smallest act of kindness can be life-changing.

13 February
Sower's parable

Read Luke 8:1–21

Therefore consider carefully how you listen. Whoever has will be given more; whoever does not have, even what they think they have will be taken from them.

(verse 18)

Being diagnosed with autism as an adult has been a difficult revelation to me. It uncovered truths about my life that I couldn't see, because I didn't have the language or the understanding to see what was happening. I've since had to relearn how to communicate effectively. It turns out I wasn't expressing myself to my full potential and I was suffering because of it. In my childhood, I had to hide the fact that I might not understand the same as others and that I would miss cues that were obvious to the rest. Learning how to ask for help has been revelatory to me, but it would be useless if I also hadn't practised actively listening. I now understand that if I am to grow as a person, I must be honest about gaps in my knowledge, which often includes the humility to admit I didn't understand in the first place.

What's interesting here is that Jesus' disciples had to ask him what he meant with this parable. Not only did they humble themselves in front of a multitude of people in order to reap the benefits of the lesson, but the lesson itself was one of receptiveness and transformation. Jesus explained that he was not laying things out plainly for everyone to understand, as a metaphor for the parable itself. Jesus' caution to 'consider carefully how you listen' underscores the importance of intentional listening. This principle highlights that receptive hearts actively engage with God's word, seeking to understand its deeper meanings and allowing it to take root and bear fruit.

† Lord, please help us to be humble enough to ask for help when we don't understand your messages and be listening closely enough to hear your response.

For further thought

Asking for help can be more important than offering it in many ways. Explore how asking for help can make you feel and how Jesus can help you do it more often.

14 February
The cost of spiritual transformation

Read Luke 8:22–39

...and the people went out to see what had happened. When they came to Jesus, they found the man from whom the demons had gone out, sitting at Jesus' feet, dressed and in his right mind; and they were afraid.

(verse 35)

I, like many other recovering addicts, have seen first-hand the cost of transformation. The journey to sobriety demands real, fundamental change in all aspects of your life. You have to work from the ground up, understanding that the roots of your current life have decayed along the way and require some difficult gardening. The end result, of course, is a life free from the darkness of addiction. A result you willingly sacrifice for; but the cost is real.

The cost of Jesus' transformative powers is demonstrated clearly during the encounter with the possessed man. The financial cost of the pigs that were sacrificed so that the man may be exorcised is first. It seems unfair that a stranger's property and livelihood be offered without consent, but this shows how little value God places on commodities, as should we, particularly when losing such things saves someone's soul. Secondly, the social cost of this terrifying spectacle – yes, Jesus performed a miracle, but it was so unsettling that the people of the town asked him to leave! Jesus willingly paid this price so that one man could live freely.

It may feel like the cost of our own spiritual transformation is too great, sometimes. The act of devoting your life to God wholeheartedly can certainly come with loss and grief, but it is a fair price for the life in return.

† Dear God, I am ready and willing to pay the price to follow you, as Jesus paid the ultimate price on the cross. I'm ready to accept your transformative love into my life anew.

For further thought

Is there any consequence of being a Christian that has seemed too much for you in the past? How did you overcome that?

15 February
The power of human connection

Read Luke 8:40–56

She came up behind him and touched the edge of his cloak, and immediately her bleeding stopped. 'Who touched me?' Jesus asked.

(verses 44–45)

My husband and I made a pact a long time ago to always reconnect via touch whenever we were greeting. We also agreed to put aside our egos during disagreements and touch hands, or a leg, even whilst continuing to argue. It helps us to remember that we are a team battling a problem together and not each other, to regain some intimacy and closeness whilst our words may create distance. My daughter has high sensory needs and regularly pauses what she is doing to come and 'touch base' with me throughout the day, anywhere and around anyone. Often it is as simple as her leaning into me for a second or resting her head on my shoulder. A very close family friend was bereaved recently, and at the first opportunity my mother went to visit to bestow a 'very long, very big hug', as she explained to my eldest. We know, understand and crave physical connection. It's instinctive – as instinctive as saying 'Bless you!' after a sneeze or yawning when another person yawns.

Humans at their core are a collective, social, community-driven species. I think these passages can be drawn to a simple, relatable conclusion – people need to touch one another to heal, and healing cannot be done alone. The bleeding woman instinctively knew that her illness would be healed if she just touched Jesus, and Jesus took the dead girl 'by the hand' when he commanded her to get up. To me, these verses are compelling, profound examples of the truth of Jesus and his human nature. His physical touch reveals his tangible presence amidst the heavenly framework of his miracles.

† God, thank you for sending Jesus to us to connect to us as humans, and not just the divine. Your understanding of us and all of our needs proves your enduring love for us wholly.

For further thought

Notice how often you use touch and non-verbal communication throughout the day. How has someone helped you through their physical touch?

Living with the Romans

1 At the time of Jesus

Notes by **Orion Johnson**

Orion lives in Warwickshire, UK, and has worked in publishing and marketing. When a young undergraduate, her studies in Classics presented the view of ancient Greek and Roman worlds from their own historians. While writing about this week's theme, she was interested to note how biblical accounts from that era provide a different angle and the story of those ruled over rather than ruling. Orion has used the NIV for these notes.

16 February

The powers that be

Read Luke 2:1–7

In those days Caesar Augustus issued a decree that a census should be taken of the entire Roman world.

(verse 1)

At the time of Christ's birth, his family's homeland had been occupied, governed and taxed by Rome for over sixty years.

Any large empire needs strong record-keeping, especially when extracting taxes – and the Roman empire was a spectacular model of bureaucracy. That and its powerful armed forces were attributes that allowed Rome to spread its reach so effectively.

Today's passage opens with icons of power and pomp: Caesar Augustus, the vast Roman empire, the governor of Syria. Suddenly the focus zooms in on two humble subjects: Mary and Joseph, simply doing what thousands of others are as they register on the census. Mary is pregnant and, away from home, gives birth in makeshift circumstances.

The imperial masters are aliens, with no interest in Jewish scripture, yet it is by Roman command that prophecies surrounding the Messiah are fulfilled: a child born in Bethlehem, with an animal's feeding trough for his cradle.

Rome's earthly might controls the ancient world around the Mediterranean and beyond, but God's power is greater. As if to prove it, God uses what the Romans think is their show of power in order to provide the signs that Jesus is the longed-for Messiah.

† Almighty Father, I praise you as the true commander of all things, working your plan through our lives whether grand or ordinary.

17 February
The extra mile

Read Matthew 5:38–42

If anyone forces you to go one mile, go with them two miles.

(verse 41)

Many commentators associate Jesus' statement about walking the extra mile with a rule that Roman soldiers could command any local to carry their army pack for them for one mile, but not further. Such a rule or law is not explicitly mentioned and does not appear to have contemporary evidence but is considered a likely practice by Roman soldiers in an occupied land. It would explain the choice of words, 'forces you', and why the walk is included in a list with two cases of abusive behaviour (violence and taking of possessions). Both the strike of a cheek and the taking of your shirt could be suffered from a brutal occupying force; the demand of a shirt perhaps alluding to excessive taxation by Rome?

It is a potential context for the comment, particularly for an audience then living under Roman rule. Alternatively, the 'extra mile' could be more general: simply providing over and above what was asked by someone who needs us to be alongside them for companionship and support.

Either interpretation connects to the common phrase (used in English at least) of 'going the extra mile', which originates from Jesus' words in verse 41. At work or with friends or strangers, 'going the extra mile' is commended as showing your dedication to the task or to helping others, and even cited as a key to success in business.

Christ's instructions might appear crazy at first – contradicting our usual eye-for-an-eye sense of justice – but they offer the opportunity to witness to others how wonderful and true his teachings are by willingly serving another's need beyond their expectation and our basic obligation.

† When you will it, Lord, grant me the grace and strength to turn the other cheek, offer my 'cloak', and walk the extra mile in your name.

For further thought
Can you think of a time when someone went 'the extra mile' with you or for you? Perhaps thank them for that and thank God for them.

The outsider understands

Read Matthew 8:5–13

…many will come from the east and the west, and will take their places at the feast with Abraham, Isaac and Jacob in the kingdom of heaven.

(verse 11)

The Roman rulers recruited soldiers from local, gentile areas for the lower ranks of their army of occupation, many coming from Caesarea or Samaria. But higher ranks were more likely to be Roman citizens and so this figure of authority is probably Roman or at least a representative of Rome. From Jesus' words we can tell the centurion is a gentile, and from his own words we know he is a commander.

Yesterday, we considered the harsh, overbearing idea of a Roman soldier forcing a local subject to carry their army pack for a mile. Today, we are presented with a man who, both as an army commander and as a Roman, holds greater power and bears some responsibility for enforcing Roman rule. Yet this centurion has compassion – he wants his servant to be healed and is going out of his way ('the extra mile'?) to secure it. He is also perceptive and articulate, showing respect to Jesus, whom most soldiers would consider beneath them.

At that moment in history, Rome is the oppressor with an alien culture, worshippers of a multitude of gods. Once Christ's early followers start spreading the word of the gospel, the breadth of the Roman empire – built to enrich emperors and a privileged population – will become a fruitful mission field, eventually assisting the spread of the Christian faith. The centurion is a promising forerunner of that future, and Jesus assures him and us that the kingdom of heaven offers a feast for everyone.

Like the centurion, we can ask of Jesus what we need.

† Thank you that I am invited to the feast with Abraham, Isaac and Jacob in the kingdom of heaven.

For further thought
Hold each day to that hope of feasting in the kingdom of heaven.

19 February

Tax or no tax?

Read Mark 12:13–17

Give back to Caesar what is Caesar's and to God what is God's.

(verse 17)

I may be the only one, but I occasionally feel sorry for politicians when a journalist pushes them on a question which is clearly asked simply to trip them up or commit them to an answer against their meaning or intent. Only occasionally, of course. Public figures should expect scrutiny. But if they are criticised for not giving a simple yes-or-no answer, when the answer is far from simple or not relevant to the debate the interview becomes nothing more than a game: 'Ha, caught you out!'

As was proven in plots leading to the crucifixion, opponents of Jesus were prepared to report him to the Romans as a means of silencing and even killing him. So we know that their intention in asking the tax question was simply to get Jesus into trouble – either with the Romans or with his fellow countrymen. But the question was irrelevant to Christ's message.

Throughout history, monarchs, emperors or presidents have stamped their claim on our money with their portrait, showing they are in command of the treasury. The Roman emperor's image was on the coin Jesus held, asserting Caesar's earthly power and the dues he demanded from his subjects. Christ's mission and God's will lie beyond the human obsession with money.

What is God's image stamped upon? Genesis 1 tells us that we are made 'in his image'. Money was important to Caesar. God has a different priority, and we are important to him.

Whoever we honour with fleeting tributes such as money and power, the Bible directs us to honour God in his world and with our lives.

† Focus my heart on the things that matter to you, Lord.

For further thought

What are the 'things of Caesar' in your situation? How do you reconcile your obligations to worldly authorities and those in the kingdom of God?

20 February
The outsider believes

Read Mark 15:37–39
Surely this man was the Son of God!

(verse 39b)

The reputation of Roman centurions has been rather boosted in our readings this week.

Roman soldiers had just put Jesus to death in the cruellest fashion, as a warning to the suppressed Jewish population not to stir up any trouble. Although not invented by them (but thought to have been adopted from earlier use by other civilisations), crucifixion has historically become a symbol of Roman authority: a brutal and humiliating method of execution.

This centurion must have witnessed dozens of victims dying, whether with a cry, scream, whimper or final sigh. He stands in front of Jesus, whose death affects him so much that he suddenly declares Jesus to be the Son of God. Golgotha was outside Jerusalem's city wall so although Mark includes a detail of the Temple curtain being torn in two, the centurion's reaction is not in response to that spectacle (which would have been away from his view inside the city) – it is in response to how Jesus dies.

There are already Jewish followers of Jesus who believe in him as the Son of God, but the very first to acknowledge faith as a result of his death is a Roman, and one with command over the executions. That is indeed a remarkable response, quite in contrast to the cynical one from soldiers in earlier verses: those who taunt Jesus and joke about his fate.

I wonder whether the centurion given the gruesome task of overseeing crucifixions was somehow *privileged* to witness the death which gave him this epiphany, catching a glimpse of Christ's divinity? He knew in his heart that this man's death was different from the many others he must have seen.

† Jesus – let me see your divinity and be aware of your power.

For further thought

Can you remember when you first recognised Christ as the Son of God? If you don't feel that way, what would be the 'signs' for you?

21 February
Keeping the Romans at bay

Read John 11:45–53

...it is better for you that one man die for the people than that the whole nation perish.

(verse 50)

The Romans were generally content to allow Jewish people to worship their one God and the priests to run their temples and to oversee religious practices, as long as it did not upset or challenge the political balance of power held by Rome – unlike some other areas of their empire where Roman culture and religion were more widely adopted.

Here, the priests and Pharisees are terrified of losing their 'place' and nation to the Romans. That was understandable perhaps, but unfortunately for Jesus they think that his growing popularity and belief in him will bring about the Roman destruction of what is currently their own domain.

Caiaphas identifies Jesus as a political saviour, whose martyrdom would secure the survival of Jewish nationhood. His prophecy echoes that of Isaiah's: that Christ would be a sacrificial lamb led to the slaughter. And Caiaphas is determined to bring that sacrifice about.

The political situation made the priests defensive against the Romans, and yet they used the Romans to secure the death. Hypocritical but clever, I suppose: their unwelcome governors are the ones with the authority and facilities to arrange execution, and if there is any backlash from fellow countrymen then they can blame the Romans.

Unfortunately, through the centuries since then, some Christians have themselves acted in a similar way in the name of protecting the Church: sacrificing 'heretics' or other victims in order to keep their own hierarchy in place. At times, in order to preserve their own domain, Christians have allied themselves to organisations or practices that contradict the gospel messages of love and peace.

† Lord and Master, keep my focus on your will and guidance, even when that seems to conflict with my own advantage.

For further thought

The priests and Pharisees decided what they wanted Jesus to be. What do I want Jesus to be?

22 February
Jerusalem trampled

Read Luke 21:20–24

When you see Jerusalem being surrounded by armies, you will know that its desolation is near.

(verse 20)

When the Roman army lays Jerusalem under siege in AD 70, breaking through its walls, burning the city and destroying the Temple, people with the memory of Jesus' words would have thought they were indeed witnessing his prophecy. Luke probably wrote this Gospel around AD 85–90, and it must have been in his mind when recording this reported warning from Jesus, whose words indeed seem a very accurate forecast of the destruction of Jerusalem at the hands of the gentile Romans crushing a Jewish revolt.

After AD 70, there would be two further Jewish–Roman conflicts. This region has known many dozens of attacks during its history. As I write, I know that tears and blood will be shed this very day from bitter fighting in the area; and probably more by the time you are reading this.

'Wars and rumours of wars' (Matthew 24:6) seem never far from our daily news or even personal experience.

The world moved on after AD 70, and many Jews or early followers of Christ not killed or enslaved were dispersed far and wide, away from their Jerusalem home but continuing their lives and faith. In earlier verses, Jesus points out that we will encounter terrors but cannot know whether each sign truly heralds the end of the world as we know it. He also promises to give us 'words and wisdom' (Luke 21:15) as we face the worst of times.

† Through war and conflict, grant me the 'words and wisdom' you promise.

For further thought

Read verses 8–9 and 15 of this chapter and consider the reassurance of God's support and presence, despite the circumstances we may be enduring.

Living with the Romans

2 In the early Church

Notes by **Christopher Lamb**

Christopher is a retired Anglican priest living in Warwickshire with his wife Tina. He looks back on an immensely formative time as a CMS mission partner in Pakistan which led to many years of ministry specialising in relations between the world faith communities of the UK, particularly with Muslims. He works at reading the Old and New Testaments and the Qur'an in their original languages. He is a regular prison visitor and enjoys bread-making and the local science study group. Christopher has used the NRSVA for these notes.

23 February

Cornelius ... was a devout man who feared God

Read Acts 10:1–24

Cornelius, a centurion of the Italian Cohort ... was a devout man who feared God with all his household; he gave alms generously to the people and prayed constantly to God ... he had a vision in which he clearly saw an angel of God coming in and saying to him, 'Cornelius.'

(verses 1–3)

This is the beginning of a great turning point in the Christian story, when the gospel begins to be announced to those outside the Jewish community and gentiles are gathered into the infant Church. If Theophilus is a real individual (Luke 1:3; Acts 1:1), Luke is writing for just such a person and he is himself the one non-Jewish writer of the New Testament. He might have been content with the brief reference to gentiles being drawn into the church at Antioch (Acts 11:20) but his canvas is the great Roman empire, from Jerusalem to Rome. He tells the story carefully and in considerable detail. Cornelius is a significant figure, his military unit specified, and his base noted as the key town of Caesarea. As a centurion he was in charge of several hundred men, reminding us of the centurion whom we met last week, who said to Jesus, 'I am a man under authority, with soldiers under me.' Yet like some other Roman officers whom we meet in the Gospels, Cornelius is unexpectedly deeply attracted to the Jewish faith, and a man of great personal devotion.

† Lord, how much you have done in secret to prepare people to receive your gospel! How careful, how wise you are with your human agents.

God has no favourites

Read Acts 10:25–48

Then Peter began to speak to them: 'I truly understand that God shows no partiality, but in every nation anyone who fears him and does what is right is acceptable to him.'

(verses 34–35)

Peter had protested 'I have never eaten anything that is unclean', yet he has accepted gentile hospitality, with the risks that implied for faithfulness to Jewish law. Now, in a pivotal moment, he realises the true breadth of God's care for humanity. It is not that Jews thought gentiles like Cornelius were beyond God's concern. The very Temple in Jerusalem included the Court of the Gentiles. But the Temple authorities had permitted its misuse, and this roused Jesus' anger when he quoted Isaiah 56:7 to declare it a house of prayer for all peoples (Mark 11:17). God's concern for the gentile world made a huge impression on Peter on the rooftop in Joppa. Now he comes face to face with a devout Roman officer to whom the Spirit has directed him. Baptism demonstrating his inclusion must be next.

The significance of this story for our own day is massive. At a time of resurgent nationalism in many countries, and talk of 'white supremacy' and other forms of ethnic and religious superiority, the message of God's impartiality is hugely liberating. Waves of migration due to conflict and climate change are driving defensive policies and hostility to any identified as strangers. Yet the first letter of Peter specifically addresses its Christian readers as aliens and exiles, using a word (*paroikoi*) which paradoxically is the origin of our 'parish' and 'parochial' (1 Peter 2:11). So we are spiritually 'aliens' in a world of warring tribes, yet bearing a commission to make that world's Lord known as loving and accepting of everyone who aims at what is good.

† Lord, show me if there is any trace of racial or cultural superiority in my own attitudes and assumptions.

For further thought

Find out about the story of your own local church. Who was it built for, and by whom?

25 February
'Sneak us out by the back door? Oh no!'

Read Acts 16:19–39

Paul replied, 'They have beaten us in public, uncondemned, men who are Roman citizens, and have thrown us into prison; and now are they going to discharge us in secret? Certainly not! Let them come and take us out themselves' ... So [the magistrates] came and apologized to them.

(verses 37, 39a)

We may be surprised at how familiar the first Christians were with courtrooms and prisons. The early chapters of Acts record two arrests and appearances of the apostles before the supreme Jewish council, the stoning of Stephen, the arrest and imprisonment of believers by Saul, the judicial murder of James and the arrest of Peter. Christians who remembered the warnings of Jesus would not have been surprised: 'they will hand you over to synagogues and prisons, and you will be brought before kings and governors because of my name' (Luke 21:12). Now Saul/Paul himself is imprisoned in Europe, detained by the magistrates of Philippi for disrupting the business of fortune tellers. Jewish law forbade divination and Paul and Silas were accused as Jews of promoting un-Roman customs.

The result of the earthquake and the conversion of the jailer and his family is that Paul and Silas are free to go, but Paul doesn't want an unobtrusive exit after the way they have been treated. Luke's claim to his reader Theophilus is that the Christian movement is led by honourable people and no threat to Rome. Centuries before any idea of universal human rights Paul has to rely on his Roman citizenship, which many did not share or had to buy at a high cost (Acts 22:28). But his real concern is equally relevant today: that justice should be seen to be done and the innocent publicly exonerated. Too many victims of injustice are made to feel guilty by powerful authority figures, whether abusive husbands or judicial officers, but Christians are not called to be doormats!

† Pray for all in the criminal justice system, and especially for those imprisoned with little hope of release and the prospect of dying in prison.

For further thought

'I was in prison and you visited me' (Matthew 25:36). There are many kinds of prison – poverty, addiction, chronic illness. Do you visit Christ there?

26 February
'I am appealing to the emperor's tribunal'

Read Acts 25:1–12

Festus ... asked Paul, 'Do you wish to go up to Jerusalem and be tried there before me on these charges?' Paul said, 'I am appealing to the emperor's tribunal; this is where I should be tried. I have done no wrong to the Jews, as you very well know.'

(verses 9–10)

Luke's intent, throughout the Acts of the Apostles, is to show that Christians are constantly accused of breaking Jewish law and creating social unrest and even riots, but in each case they are found to be innocent. Jews hostile to the new faith in Jesus, as Paul once was, try to persuade the Roman authorities of their guilt and even plan to assassinate Paul. The Romans are generally indifferent to specifically Jewish issues but cannot ignore public disorder. They consistently act sympathetically to Paul the Roman citizen, but can be subject to Jewish pressure. All this repeats the behaviour of Jewish and Roman authorities in the trial and crucifixion of Jesus, even echoing Jesus' appearances before the Sanhedrin, Pilate and Herod as Paul is brought before the Jewish council, the Roman governor and a Jewish king. Paul knew that he could not expect justice from a trial in Jerusalem, so the alternative was to appeal to Rome itself, which was his right as a Roman citizen. Festus the governor, no doubt glad to be rid of the responsibility, agreed.

Christianity took root in the exceptional stability of the *Pax Romana*, the relative peace of the empire, which Paul and the early Christians constantly relied upon to travel safely and spread the message of Jesus. Today Christians in many countries would be glad to have that visa-free travel and a judicial system at least as fair as that of Rome. They may also lack Paul's protected status as a citizen, but at least can share his trust in God's guiding hand whatever the forces against them.

† Pray for Christians living under discriminatory laws and social prejudice against them, especially those unjustly accused of blasphemy.

For further thought

Consider supporting one of the organisations dedicated to exposing violations of human rights or helping those who have suffered from them.

27 February
Another governor out of his depth

Read Acts 25:13 – 26:1

I found that he had done nothing deserving death; and when he appealed to his Imperial Majesty, I decided to send him. But I have nothing definite to write to our sovereign about him … it seems to me unreasonable to send a prisoner without indicating the charges against him.

(verses 25–27)

The experience of Paul continues to echo that of Jesus at his trial when Governor Festus judges that, as Pilate had concluded, he had 'done nothing deserving death'. But unlike Pilate, Festus is effectively protecting Paul from his Jewish accusers, at Paul's own request. His speech to Agrippa (Acts 26) shows how firmly Paul held to his Jewish identity and claimed faith in Jesus as its real fulfilment. Yet he preferred to be tried by Roman justice on the charge of public disorder rather than by the Jewish council on alleged violations of the Temple and the Mosaic law. Festus clearly felt out of his depth in knowing how to deal with Paul, and called upon the Jewish king Agrippa II and his sister Bernice for advice as both were significant voices in the Jewish world. They agreed with Festus about Paul's innocence (26:32).

Despite his eventual martyrdom at the hands of the Emperor Nero, Paul's trust in Rome rather than Jerusalem was justified. He was able to live in Rome with a significant degree of freedom. Christians and other religious believers have often had to seek redress for wrongdoing from the secular power, even against their own religious institutions. The latter can be too prone to protect their own standing at all costs. Across the world there has been a tsunami of cases of sexual and physical abuse by priests and church leaders against the young and vulnerable, and again and again allegations have been met with denial and obfuscation. Yet an institution's reputation is finally damaged more by cover-up than by transparency.

† Pray that all in authority 'may truly and impartially minister justice, to the punishment of wickedness and vice, and to the maintenance of thy true religion and virtue' (*Book of Common Prayer* 1662).

For further thought

Note that it is only after many safeguarding scandals that church leaders are urged to report every allegation to independent bodies and the police.

28 February
Fear God. Honour the emperor.

Read 1 Peter 2:13–17

For the Lord's sake accept the authority of every human institution, whether of the emperor as supreme, or of governors, as sent by him to punish those who do wrong and to praise those who do right … Fear God. Honour the emperor.

(verses 13, 17)

The first letter of Peter is written to Christians of non-Jewish, gentile origin, but the author addresses them with precious Old Testament terms of honour given to the Israelites in Exodus 19:6, 'You are a chosen race, a royal priesthood, a holy nation, God's own people' (1 Peter 2:9). He even refers to them as living among the gentiles (2:12), with the implication that they are not themselves *goyim*, people outside the law and the covenants of Israel. They have been called out of darkness into his marvellous light. Yet they are also exiles of the Dispersion (1:1), the 'diaspora' or scattering of God's people around the eastern Mediterranean and beyond, another term used initially about and by Jews. They are aliens and exiles (2:11), as we noted on 24 February subject to misunderstanding and suspicion.

Minorities everywhere live in apprehension of being stereotyped by the majority after any negative behaviour of their members. It is not surprising that leaders like Peter should counsel obedience to the authorities – 'the powers that be', as Paul called them (Romans 13:1, KJV). As a minority Christians could not afford to be seen as a threat to the order of the Roman empire, so Peter calls for what today may seem an unduly submissive attitude to authority. Democracy and human rights as understood now were unthinkable in a world of universal slavery and enforced social privilege. Social reformers fighting racial discrimination, harsh employment practices or restrictive gender roles have always had to face accusations from the authorities that they were endangering social order, although their intention was justice and peace.

† Pray for those who have the heavy burden of national leadership and make decisions affecting millions of people, that they may be challenged with courtesy, grace and freedom within the law.

For further thought

Who are your heroes among social and political reformers, and what do you admire about them?

1 March

Whoever resists authority resists what God has appointed

Read Romans 13:1–7

There is no authority except from God, and those authorities that exist have been instituted by God ... Pay to all what is due to them – taxes to whom taxes are due, revenue to whom revenue is due, respect to whom respect is due, honour to whom honour is due.

(verses 1b, 7)

In his letter to the Romans, Paul writes to Christians at the heart of the Roman empire and declares his faith in Christ in detail, in advance of the visit he hopes to make to Rome itself. His series of greetings in chapter 16 indicates how many of them he already knew, for Christian leaders made full use of the relative ease of travel in the empire. Like Peter (see yesterday's passage), he was concerned for the reputation of the Church, especially in the empire's capital city, where some years earlier the Emperor Claudius had ordered the expulsion of Jews because of disturbances *impulsore Chresto* – a phrase which may refer to arguments between Jews and Christians in Rome. Paul had worked closely with Aquila and Priscilla, Jewish Christians who had had to leave Rome because of Claudius' edict (Acts 18:2).

Like all effective governments the Roman empire had its eyes and ears close to the ground with a network of spies and informers. The edict of Claudius suggests that a weighty letter like Paul's would have been of particular interest to those in power. This may explain what can sound to modern ears like an unqualified endorsement of the imperial state. Paul, like Jesus (John 19:11), did indeed support the Jewish view that governance is part of the divine order and meant for human good. But he makes no suggestion that public officials should be obeyed under all circumstances. Criticism of official decisions is not the same as rejecting authority. Those with the privilege of living in a democracy should call governments to account.

† Pray for those living in countries where government is ineffective, corrupt or actively persecuting those who stand for the truth. Pray for integrity in public life and for honest and compassionate legal systems.

For further thought

Revelation 17 represents Rome (called Babylon) as a prostitute drunk with the blood of God's people. Was Paul mistaken in Romans 13 or would he have agreed?

Living with the Romans

3 Pilate and his soldiers

Notes by **Terry Lester**

Terry has served as an Anglican priest in the Diocese of Cape Town for over four decades and is currently serving in Constantia. His first wife, Colleen, died over eight years ago and he has since married Nicolette. Together they share five children. He loves being a parish priest and has a passion for community building, especially considering the legacy that apartheid has left. This he does through encouraging storytelling, working for justice and strengthening interfaith ties. Terry has used the NRSV for these notes.

2 March
Jesus, the way, the truth and the life!

Read John 18:28–40

Pilate asked [Jesus], 'What is truth?'

(verse 38)

The final hours of Jesus' earthly life are told with profound effect by St John and, in the first part of the week, cover the person and actions of Pontius Pilate and how love and light shine through these darkest hours of Jesus. We can use the 'See, Judge, Act' process of reading the Bible for these readings – starting with simple reflection and moving to 'forcefully good' action as we journey from Ash Wednesday and into Lent.

In the mid-1980s being arrested, charged, arraigned and driven off to prison for defying apartheid's unjust laws was common. Once I found myself in court facing a magistrate who was also a parishioner where I served as curate! The magistrate was livid and sent us straight to the holding cells to await the remand to prison. Our appearance placed him in an invidious position. But he stood by his truth, the law, and I stood by mine: protesting the continued incarceration of Nelson Mandela who was jailed for opposing racial discrimination. We had each chosen our path to walk guided by our truth.

Choose a path, for Pilate's question results in mere talk which maintains the status quo. Where no one chooses, nothing changes.

† Lord, may I speak when necessary and act when needed. Amen.

3 March

Truth is eternal

Read John 19:1–16a

Jesus answered [Pilate], 'You would have no power over me unless it had been given you from above; therefore, the one who handed me over to you is guilty of a greater sin.'

(verse 11)

Our South African story has taught us that power is fleeting but truth is eternal! History shows that despotic leaders are slow to learn this. Instead, they flaunt their power instilling fear and deflect from their excesses and brutality with 'whataboutisms' and obfuscation. But they are constantly at work exerting their influence and targeting those who dare to speak. They use humiliation and brutalisation of those they deem a threat while making it clear that it is in their power to have you live or have you die! This is common practice – it was then, and it is still far too prevalent in many parts of our world today.

The powerful can often regard the very existence of those who oppose them as an affront. It was true of Herod and John the Baptist, and it was true of the one to whom John pointed. Jesus was and is indeed a 'stumbling block'.

Yet choices matter, even here. Pilate is hemmed in by Rome, by the Jewish authorities, by the baying crowd, by the dreams of his wife and perhaps by his own conscience. Judas, by contrast, has witnessed the full love of God in Christ and chooses betrayal.

Choices may be difficult, but the comfort for the faithful is this: that the true light which came into the world not only exposes but also overcomes darkness! Jesus, as victim, identifies with all victims and declares them innocent.

† Thank you for the insults you endured and the wounds you bore. Help us to heal and restore our trust. Amen.

For further thought

Look up current Amnesty International reports and add some names and situations to your prayer list.

4 March
People are complex

Read John 19:16b–25

Pilate answered [the chief priests], 'What I have written I have written.'

(verse 22)

My country's story is often told through the binary lens of right and wrong, of victim and villain. In its telling there are those who are perpetually consigned to eternal shame with others elevated to perpetual rightness! But people are complex, hence mere simplistic binary representations and caricaturing does most an injustice!

Some years ago, a former president of my country announced at the opening of parliament – and most unexpectedly – the release from prison of Nelson Mandela, together with all political prisoners. He went further and announced the immediate unbanning of political organisations! His party had introduced racial segregation yet now he was consigning those policies to the dustbin of history! Unthinkable! Yet, in doing so he set our country on a totally different path. Many are still not on it! Our racial silos and binary thinking had to recalibrate to the new, and away from our racially simplistic mantras. The seismic event caught most unawares but created a whole new reality. The previous path had been shut for good, while the new path promised a profound new learning and engagement, trust, faith and hope.

Pilate, for all his previous shortcomings and uncertainties, in this moment was certain of *one* thing: a new reality had come into being, not just for Jews, but for all nations who stop to read as they pass by: the King of the Jews!

† Forgive me for settling for simplistic descriptions of complex situations and for not giving more credence to the human spirit to surprise. Amen.

For further thought

Identify situations which need new paths to be opened in what appear, on the face of it, to be dead ends. Think about how you can help to bring these about.

Walking with Jesus: Christian life

1 Our example

Notes by **Terry Lester**

You can read Terry's biography on 2 March.

5 March
Scriptures bear witness to Jesus Christ

Read John 5:36–39

And the Father who sent me has himself testified on my behalf.

(verse 37)

What do you identify as? More and more the question is being asked about both one's genetic make-up and the pool from which we are drawn. These days too, it refers to where you place yourself on the gender spectrum. Who one identifies as is quite a thing! I loved watching a programme called *Who Do You Think You Are?* in which celebrities share their beliefs and thoughts on who they think they are. Then, when their genetic code is deciphered and explained, it is either confirmed or they are shocked to learn who they truly are! One such celebrity thought himself to be of slave ancestry; he was Black, came from the Caribbean, and, based on this, concluded that his forebears were brought from Africa as slaves. He was proud of his ancestry, it had shaped his mindset and thinking. When the 'reveal' happened, though, he was found to also have Caucasian ancestry, meaning that he also had 'slave owner', which shocked him.

Jesus is speaking about identity! He is trying to encourage the Pharisees to be less harsh in their judgement of law breakers and to find kindness and compassion for the man healed on the Sabbath who for years couldn't access the pool for healing. Jesus tells them that his identity is wrapped up in the identity of the Father, to which John had earlier testified. God offers life to all, as a gift, the true identity of all, and through Jesus that life and identity can be accessed and realised for every moment of every day.

† Thank you for the rivers that have flowed into nourishing my existence. Free me of all prejudice. Amen.

For further thought

Research your family tree and celebrate the richness contained in it.

6 March
Peter heals crippled beggar in name of Jesus Christ of Nazareth

Read Acts 3:1–10
Peter looked intently at him, as did John, and said, 'Look at us.' And he fixed his attention on them expecting to receive something from them.

(verses 4–5)

It fascinates and impresses me when I see athletes with severe mobility constraints competing at a high level. The design of the equipment, so closely matching their unique needs, combined with the courage and determination to develop their natural talent despite the additional hurdles, is inspiring.

I have a physiotherapist friend who does work on the African continent modelling fit-for-purpose wheelchairs to ensure the greatest benefit to the patient. Small adjustments can give rarely used muscles the best chance to develop so enhancing the person's mobility, enabling them to grow in independence and confidence. The world is full of such people: those like Peter, who look intently at the person and using all their expertise and know-how, work with the individual to create what is the best fit for each unique situation.

As for this man, it can lead to a total change in outlook and possibility with access to schooling, sports, dancing, work – in fact, any activity which once seemed an impossible dream becomes doable! Shame and pain can be dispelled and confidence restored.

Notice that Peter wasn't afraid to tell the man what he couldn't do, nor did Peter meet what the man first thought of as his needs. Instead, prayerfully, Peter offers what he has – Jesus reveals what the perfect fit was for this unique individual. Sometimes we can be afraid of helping because we don't have the specific thing we think the person needs – or indeed, what they feel they need. Let's prayerfully put ourselves at their service in the name of Jesus.

† Make me jump for joy for all that I have and all that I am. Amen.

For further thought
Find where you can help with those who have mobility constraints and need a hand up, whatever that might mean for them.

Temptation of Jesus in the desert

Read Matthew 4:1–11

Then Jesus was led up by the Spirit into the wilderness to be tempted by the devil.

(verse 1)

In the mid-1980s I joined a course at St George's College, Jerusalem, called 'The Bible in its Setting'. We travelled the length and breadth of Israel, visiting all the known sites including a few days (and nights) in the Negev desert. The terrain is harsh, and the sun is relentless during the day and at night cool, with a breeze which blows off the sea. On those desert nights I loved nothing better than to sit outside and take in the beauty of the night sky and its vastness as it reminded me of home – but we were warned that leopards roamed there and that nights were their hunting time! In the daytime, snakes loved the hot sun but were so well blended with the shrubbery that one had to be extra vigilant then too.

Deserts and wildernesses feature widely in the scriptures. The desert serves as a prelude to Eden in Genesis, where no plant grew and there was no water to water the earth (Genesis 2:5) yet, with the barest of ingredients, God's journey with humanity began! Then, after Eden, the breakdown of the relationship between God and humanity also affected the created order causing enmity, schism and a scorched earth – a new wilderness.

No wonder then that the wilderness is where Jesus chooses to confront the enemy. Sin has turned paradise into desert and Jesus has come to begin the process of bringing life out of dead places. Perhaps we are surprised when we follow the leading of God to find ourselves in a desert place. Perhaps we question whether we heard right. Yet so often the Spirit leads us through times of refinement, desert places, before launching us into ministry.

† Help me to find and commit to working towards building up and restoration with the people and places where I am active. Amen.

For further thought

Find a local project which involves restoration and rebuilding of the environment, or care of something old like furniture, a house or a vehicle, and commit to giving some of your time.

God will not let you be tempted more than you can bear

Read 1 Corinthians 10:12–13

So, if you think you are standing, watch out that you do not fall.

(verse 12)

Benjamin Franklin is credited with saying that nothing is certain except death and taxes. I wonder if we could add the certainty that people tend towards disagreeing!

As a church leader I have often needed to hold diverse individuals together in a group. Our history of racial suspicion and mistrust results in intransigence even when such positions are not rationally justifiable. Emotions are triggered and people dig in, leaving little or no room for moving forward. The protagonists assert their rightness with such conviction and certainty as to threaten any possibility of building closeness. Often the original reason for being together gets completely lost as the heat is ratcheted up to greater levels of conflict and chaos.

The Christian church at Corinth must have been the envy of many. There was the manifestation of various spiritual gifts, they were materially well off, they were diverse socially and economically and reflected a healthy ethnic and gender mix. They had so much in their favour, yet they couldn't function as one community when love and unity are the core calling for the church as St Paul describes in his analogy of the body. Many in Corinth stood so firm on their convictions that it became a hindrance to the unity and blessing that awaited them and those they served.

Certainties are not of themselves fatal, yet stubbornness can make us wrong even if we are right and can rob us of a deeper experience of the oneness of God.

† Thank you for the blessing of difference and diversity. Help me to value and treasure it. Amen.

For further thought

Join a group which has a spread of people with diverse backgrounds, views, faith and cultures who are tackling a common need or problem in the community.

Walking with Jesus: Christian life

2 Following the way

Notes by **Louise Jones**

Louise Jones lives and works in Winson Green, Birmingham, in an embedded, community-based organisation (Newbigin Community Trust) which aims to create a sense of family, purpose and social cohesion in a community that is often overlooked. Louise has recently finished an MA in Theology (Social Justice and Humanitarian Development) and has a passion for empowering, resourcing and loving those who have slipped through the cracks of our systems, to help people see their immense value and worth in Jesus. Louise has used the NIV for these notes.

9 March
Introducing the upside-down kingdom

Read Matthew 5:1–12

His disciples came to him, and he began to teach them. He said: 'Blessed are the poor in spirit, for theirs is the kingdom of heaven. Blessed are those who mourn, for they will be comforted. Blessed are the meek, for they will inherit the earth.'

(verses 1b–5)

The Beatitudes are so well known and recited that it can be easy to gloss over their significance. The fact that Jesus begins his famous Sermon on the Mount by elevating the 'poor' and 'meek' rather than the religious leaders or those considered by society as worthy is astounding. This radical passage works in direct contrast to the world where those who have wealth or celebrity or hold power are most celebrated.

In this, Jesus is giving us a not-so-subtle insight into God's upside-down kingdom – he loves everyone, longs for the best for everyone, but those with the least, those who are most vulnerable, those without choice are closest to God's heart. It was this passage that ultimately led me to move to Winson Green as I followed Jesus into a community often overlooked, but filled with beauty and joy.

Of course, following Jesus doesn't always mean moving physically, but the command to 'go' does require a change of location: we need to be in a different place in our hearts and minds. Perhaps this passage can help us reassess what is truly of value.

† Lord, teach us about your upside-down kingdom as we follow you to unexpected places, people and conversations.

10 March
Putting the upside-down kingdom into practice

> **Read Matthew 25:31–46**
>
> *'Lord, when did we see you hungry and feed you, or thirsty and give you something to drink?' … The King will reply, 'Truly I tell you, whatever you did for one of the least of these brothers and sisters of mine, you did for me.'*
>
> (verses 37, 40)

In every personality test I have taken, the results show that I am the personality type that loves ticking things off lists in order to feel productive. This passage appeals to that side of me – there are concrete things that I can do to put this upside-down kingdom into action!

The risk that I've found, though, is that everything becomes a task – things that started out motivated by love become ministries or projects – and we busy ourselves, ticking them off our list when they're done … But people aren't projects. Loving people can never be accomplished treating them as tasks to be completed! Loving people is more than just doing things for them; it's all about relationship.

I have a colleague – let's call her Samantha – who goes above and beyond just completing tasks for the people who come to our drop-in centre. She truly has compassion for everyone she meets which means that she notices when someone is lonely and needs an hour of her time just to chat. She makes sure her day is interruptible and sacrifices her time to make sure that the 'least of these brothers and sisters' feel seen and loved when they spend time with her.

I'm reminded and challenged by the story of Jesus and the woman who was bleeding. Jairus, the 'important' leader of the synagogue has an urgent task for Jesus – to heal his daughter. Yet Jesus gives the time this woman needs, not just to heal her physically, but to restore her dignity by knowing that she has been heard.

† Thank you, God, that you give us so much of your time and love. Would you help us to also be interruptible and know how to extend help to those in need today?

For further thought

Why not set yourself the challenge of giving someone five extra minutes of your time today to really get to know them better?

11 March
Studying Jesus' character

Read John 14:1–7

Jesus answered, 'I am the way and the truth and the life. No one comes to the Father except through me. If you really know me, you will know my Father as well. From now on, you do know him and have seen him.'

(verses 6–7)

Jesus teaches us in this passage that if we want to know what God is like, if we want to learn about God's character and his heart, then we need only to look at Jesus. 'If you really know me' Jesus says, then you know God as well. This is always something I find comforting as the idea of getting to know an omnipresent, omniscient God can feel overwhelming. But getting to know Jesus is something that feels doable. As we learn about Jesus' character in the New Testament, we begin to build a picture of a person who faces the same troubles we do, but who always treats those around him with divine kindness, love, justice and humour. We see someone who constantly chooses to serve, to put others first and ultimately to lay down his life for us.

This, Jesus says, is both the way to know God – and the *only* way to God himself. So, how do we live that 'way'? How do we become like Jesus?

I remember being taught as a child that who we spend time with shapes us. And looking back I can see this – I grew up in a middle-class town and absorbed that worldview without noticing. When I moved to work and live alongside those from very different socio-economic backgrounds, I found myself changing the sort of clothes I wore, the way I spoke and even my sense of humour. This is no bad thing in itself, but it highlights that the only way to be like 'the way' is to spend a lot of time with Jesus.

† Jesus, would you teach us something new about your character today as we continue to follow your way?

For further thought

Take a moment to think about the people you are spending the majority of your time with and how this could be influencing your character.

12 March
Upside-down kingdom in action

Read Acts 9:1–9

'Saul, Saul, why do you persecute me?' 'Who are you, Lord?' Saul asked. 'I am Jesus, whom you are persecuting,' he replied. 'Now get up and go into the city, and you will be told what you must do.' The men travelling with Saul stood there speechless.

(verses 4–7)

It's all too easy to look around impoverished communities, or individuals who seem antagonistic to our way of life, and presume that they can offer nothing to God, that they are of little value. Yet Jesus always looks beyond the outward prosperity of a community or the challenging behaviour of the individual – he sees the heart, the intrinsic worth, and calls it out.

In this passage we see how this upside-down kingdom of God works out as Jesus interacts with Saul, a man actively persecuting Christians. No one or no situation is ever too far gone for God to redeem and work through, and this is a message I find deeply inspiring! Jesus sees beyond Saul's actions, and where we might have seen a violent opponent, Jesus sees a zeal that he can redirect and leadership abilities that he can use. Above all, he sees a man that he deeply loves.

All too often we see situations or communities and focus on what they lack and simply throw our resources at them in an attempt to fix the problems. But this doesn't empower people to become agents for change themselves. The upside-down kingdom way is to invest in people, looking at their gifts, looking at the value people have. It's what Jesus does in this passage with Saul.

What a difference this makes, when people know that they are being heard, seen for who they are. When people can see how they can contribute, when they are valued and loved. In the passage, what the enemy meant for evil, God was able to turn into something good. A beautiful example of the upside-down kingdom in action.

† Would you help us to look at situations and individuals with your asset-based eyes, God, and help us to see the gifts and potential in the people and communities we are working in?

For further thought

Where in your life has God taken something that you considered bad and turned it into something beautiful?

13 March
Demonstrating another way

Read John 9:1–12

As he went along, he saw a man blind from birth. His disciples asked him, 'Rabbi, who sinned, this man or his parents, that he was born blind?' 'Neither this man nor his parents sinned,' said Jesus ... 'we must do the works of him who sent me.'

(verses 1–4)

Our actions speak louder than words. And Jesus' actions in the form of miracles were certainly very loud. However, in this passage Jesus' miracle seems to serve two purposes. It appears that he is doing more than just healing a sick man, as he engages in a theological discussion about the relationship (or lack of one) between sickness and sin. This miracle seems to be a way for Jesus to undo the 'bad theology' they had acquired from teachings at the time around physical disability and sin. In this interaction Jesus liberates the man by healing him so he can see – but he also liberates the people watching as he liberates them from their misunderstanding of God's character and helps them to see the truth.

Following the way and Jesus' teachings means questioning our preconceived beliefs. Whether we have grown up in Christian contexts or come to faith later in life we all have beliefs that we attribute to God but are actually the result of bad teaching or simply things we have absorbed from the world around us. Jesus teaches us that it is healthy to question what we have been taught and I think it is so important that we find safe people to question things we have accepted as truth. In fact, following Jesus will always involve questions and doubts as we are confronted by things that don't make sense. Jesus shows us in this passage that following the way involves being open and ready to learn new things about who God is.

† God, would you help us to be open to a fresh perspective and new revelations on who you are? May we not be afraid of learning new things about your character.

For further thought

When was the last time you let someone challenge your beliefs and you truly listened to what they had to say?

14 March
Becoming a light in the world

Read Matthew 5:14–16

You are the light of the world. A town built on a hill cannot be hidden. Neither do people light a lamp and put it under a bowl. Instead they put it on its stand, and it gives light to everyone in the house.

(verses 14–15)

This verse is often used to teach that we should not be ashamed of our faith and to encourage evangelism. Recently I've been reflecting on this. When I was a student, I remember the pastor encouraging us to pray about someone we wanted to bring along to church. As I did this, a close friend – let's call her Bella – came to my mind. However, as I thought about messaging her, I felt God say not to invite her to church! At first, I was convinced it was me being ashamed or scared to ask her, but God gave me a picture of Bella on a train and said, 'She's doing this journey at her pace, just enjoy being her friend.'

Fast-forward six years, Bella has become more like a sister than a friend to me, and we've had deep chats about life and our beliefs about the world. Her beliefs have changed some of my views and mine have influenced hers. Bella now has a relationship with God, and I truly believe this is because instead of seeing her as someone I needed to convert, I valued her as a human being who had things to offer me in our friendship. Bella has said that it was more the way I was choosing to live out my faith practically than any of the theological chats we had that challenged her views.

A lamp lights up a room simply by being. And my journey with Bella has taught me that evangelism should be about living differently and loving people as humans rather than projects.

† Lord, would you help us to have the patience to form genuine friendships with those we want to know you, and would those friendships shape and guide us too?

For further thought

Why don't you take some time today to pray for your closest friends and see what God has to say about them?

15 March
No condemnation

Read John 3:17–21

For God did not send his Son into the world to condemn the world, but to save the world through him. Whoever believes in him is not condemned, but whoever does not believe stands condemned already because they have not believed in the name of God's one and only Son.

(verses 17–18)

This week we have looked at various ways we can follow Jesus in the way by seeing how he lived his life so radically differently from how the world tells us to. But what happens when we get it wrong, when we mishear, when we choose a different path, when the call to live radically seems just too hard? Is that the end of the journey for us? Will Jesus disown us, discard us?

In this verse we learn that God isn't out there looking for us to fail, waiting to pounce on our mistakes, ready to condemn. His purpose is to save – and that makes all the difference. It means we can step out in faith, confident that this is what God approves of – this is 'the way'.

When we choose to journey with Jesus, he acknowledges that we are going to make mistakes, we will never perfectly follow 'the way'. But we are not condemned for that. In the same way a parent loves their child despite the mistakes they make, God's opinion of us, his love for us, doesn't waver when we journey with him.

Too often, people live under the weight of condemnation – from teachers, parents, friends, partners, colleagues, bosses, pastors … If God, the ultimate judge, chooses not to condemn us when we make mistakes in our journey with Jesus, then let's not fall into the trap of judging others in their journey.

† Thank you, God, that there is nothing we can do to separate ourselves from your love. May we know that love even deeper as we continue to live out our lives with you.

For further thought

Take a moment to reflect on the things you are consciously or subconsciously condemning yourself for and ask God what he thinks about those things.

Walking with Jesus: Christian life

3 Walking through the world with Jesus

Notes by **Dafne Plou**

Dafne is a retired social communicator, a women's rights activist who participates in the women's movement in her country. She is a member of the Methodist Church in Argentina. In her local church, in Buenos Aires' suburbs, she works in the area of 'Community building and fellowship in liturgy'. In 2023 she was invited to lead the weekly Bible studies focused mainly on Acts and St Paul's epistles. Dafne has a big family and loves spending time with her ten grandchildren. Dafne has used the NIVUK for these readings.

16 March
Joy in discipleship

Read John 15:8–11

I have told you this so that my joy may be in you and that your joy may be complete.

(verse 11)

In the calmness of the small church, I can listen to them coming down the street. A talkative group of middle-aged women and men, some church members, all of them neighbours, in a hurry to get to the weekly Bible study on time. Coffee is ready – and cookies too. A nice way to start our 'Coffee with Jesus' gatherings just before we open the scriptures and start to analyse the text and reflect on it.

Participants have been looking for different sources in books, websites, YouTube videos and online publications during the week to share findings in the Bible study. Their thoughtful contributions and insights remind me that Jesus encouraged his followers' commitment by creating a space of freedom, a new kind of fellowship, in which their questions, doubts, uncertainties or lack of confidence were not barriers to being accepted and included in love and understanding.

'Meeting you all here makes me feel good, happy,' said one of the newcomers one evening. 'I find what we talk about and discuss so challenging and reassuring at the same time.'

Glad and sincere hearts (Acts 2:46) is what we need so as to grow and bear much fruit as Jesus' faithful disciples.

† Help us, Jesus, to keep your words alive and understand that you call us to remain in your love, in deep joy, in all circumstances and ways of life. Amen.

17 March
Main command

Read John 15:12–18

This is my command: love each other.

(verse 17)

It was Advent Sunday in 1511. Eight members of the Dominican Order of Preachers prepared the sermon to be pronounced in front of Viceroy Diego Columbus and his court in the New World conquered by the Spanish in 1492. These friars were horrified and shocked by the cruelty of slave owners and traders who were oppressing the once diligent and peaceful native peoples. Friar Antonio de Montesinos was chosen to deliver the message: 'What are your arguments to enslave these people in such a horrible way? Are they not human beings? Don't they have souls? Are you not obliged to love them as you love yourselves?' he challenged them. Slave traders wanted to expel the friars back to Spain, but King Ferdinand listened to their plea and in 1513 new rules were passed to stop injustice and abuse in the conquered land.

Centuries have passed and we still face similar situations in many of our countries. Migrants, inhabitants of shanty towns, those with darker skin or poor education are discriminated against, bullied, exploited, paid less, diminished in their opportunities, looked down on as if they don't have souls or rights. Should we not love them as we love ourselves?

Jesus calls us to be part of his movement of love and solidarity with all people. Caring for each other also means caring for a world fit to live in. We are challenged to 'pursue righteousness, faith, love and peace' (2 Timothy 2:22) to enlighten Jesus' command and redemptive actions.

† Come to us, Jesus, and inspire us at these difficult times to open our hearts, minds and doors to those who need our understanding, respect and love. Amen.

For further thought

Are there any migrant groups or organisations in your neighbourhood or near your church? Get in touch with them, ready to share and learn!

Churchgoers or Christians?

Read Galatians 5:16–26

Those who belong to Christ Jesus have crucified the flesh with its passions and desires.

(verse 24)

A popular preacher in youth ministries affirmed in an interview that although churches had grown quite a bit in the country, there were many churchgoers but few Christians. He argued that quite a few churches have been preaching an 'aspirin message', soothing, easy-going, that very seldom questions people's personal behaviour, spiritual conflicts or their commitment to others. Many feel at ease attending sugar-coated services in pleasant environments. Don't we call to repentance in our services any more? Is it that our preaching of the gospel is not challenging us to a radical change in our lives and compromises? Is it that questioning our way of living, our individualism and selfishness, our materialistic consumerism, our lack of engagement with our neighbours' needs and refused rights would keep us away from church?

When Jesus started his ministry, he announced his demands openly: 'The kingdom of God has come near. Repent and believe the good news!' (Mark 1:15). His call is to a new start, to become part of an active new community. We are challenged to discover the hidden treasure, the precious pearl and give away everything we have to follow Jesus, recreating our lives and putting into practice the kingdom's rules.

Are we ready to break ties with our passions and desires and conduct ourselves 'in a manner worthy of the gospel of Christ' (Philippians 1:27)? Jesus' disciples were no saints. They were women and men like us, with their virtues and imperfections. Still, they understood that repenting and starting a new life were essential to being part of a movement that announced God's redeeming love.

† Jesus, help us to shake off our false comfort and reassurances and guide us to follow your call to solidarity and engagement with all who need your good news. Amen.

For further thought

What passions and desires should we overcome? Let's think about it with sincere recognition of our faults and prayers for forgiveness.

19 March
Building up in faith

Read Ephesians 4:1–16

So Christ himself gave the apostles, the prophets, the evangelists, the pastors and teachers, to equip his people for works of service, so that the body of Christ may be built up.

(verses 11–12)

The church building had been closed for four years. It wasn't only because of the global pandemic. That city area had changed a lot long ago. The once old bohemian neighbourhood with its artists, painters and artisans had turned into a gloomy place. The buildings were taken over by street gangs and criminal rings exploiting prostitutes and small peddlers. Few dared to walk around after sunset. The area seemed to have been erased from any city initiative. Did the same happen to this church? Had it been removed from church projects and mission objectives? Would it ever re-open its doors?

A small pastoral team accepted the challenge. Gates were unlocked, tea and refreshments were served in the once empty hall and, little by little, neighbours and passers-by started to come in, shyly at first and with renewed interest after a while, when they realised that a serene and understanding environment invited them to share their concerns, needs, fears, questions and doubts with women and men of faith equipped for these 'works of service'. As attendance at the different activities grew, more volunteers from different congregations in the city decided to take up the call and dedicate their time and expertise to this new Christian group that kept growing in the margins.

We know well in our hearts and minds that if a church closes its doors to the surrounding world and circumstances, it is also closing its doors to the gospel. Jesus' call pushes us to be his witnesses even in situations we find dingy and obscure. His Spirit always encourages us.

† Help us to understand, Jesus, that we are called to share your gospel and abundant love in all places, even those we would like to avoid. Amen.

For further thought

Are there any Christian ministries in difficult areas in your town or city? What would be the best way to help or contribute?

20 March
Examining ourselves

Read Ephesians 4:17–32

You were taught, with regard to your former way of life, to put off your old self, which is being corrupted by its deceitful desires; to be made new in the attitude of your minds.

(verses 22–23)

Paul had a hard time preaching to new Christians that they were called to abandon their old selfish ways of living and breathe new life in their relations to others. When watching *Thursday's Widows*, a series based on an Argentine best-seller on Netflix, I felt it showed clearly that our so-called Christian Western society has not abandoned its 'old self' nor its 'deceitful desires'. Self-interest and lack of generosity are pictured to be the rule, even in family and intimate relations, and people are more valued for their physical beauty, their possessions and social status than for who they really are.

How do we 'put on the new self' (verse 24) and reject these seductive rules? Our societies can't go on disregarding other people's needs and hopes. We need to transform attitudes in our minds and hearts. We must consider in the first place that God listens to the cry of the poor, the victims, the suffering, the dispossessed and that we are called to put our gifts, talents and abilities in his hands to serve others. We should do this in community, together with other faithful and activists, with open and generous hands.

Believing in Jesus and being faithful to his gospel entails the unfailing appeal to love God and our neighbours. We show our love to God by adoring and trusting him with deep engagement – and our love for others by walking in solidarity with them, seeking for justice, inclusion, genuine opportunities and an enjoyable future for all. Let's break with 'former ways of life' and put into practice these essential mandates!

† Inspire us, Jesus, to share with others your gospel's call to do away with our old selves and be guided by generosity and commitment to those in need. Amen.

For further thought

Ready to look inside your 'current self'? Take your time to examine and be ready to put aside and overcome 'old ways' still hiding there ...

21 March
Difficult prayers

Read Philippians 1:3–20

In all my prayers for all of you, I always pray with joy because of your partnership in the gospel from the first day until now.

(verses 4–5)

Watching the queue of Russian young couples and mothers with their newborn babies at the register office makes me feel sad. They want their children to have another nationality. They have made the effort to travel to Argentina to deliver their babies here, so that they may have a citizenship that will help them to avoid discrimination in the future. Some will stay, some others will leave soon. Will they ever get to know Argentina at all? It's hard to 'pray with joy'.

Today an official press release read on the radio tells us that dozens of Jewish Argentinians have requested the government bring them back from Israel, where a bloody war currently escalates at high speed. The Jewish community is quite big in my country and their members carry out all sorts of professions, industries and trade. We even have 'Jewish gauchos', from the old migrant colonies in the rural inland, where they settled in the late nineteenth century. They now see destruction in their land and suffer the death of their dear ones. It's hard in war to pray with joy.

Paul was imprisoned and in chains but in spite of these hard circumstances, he prayed with joy because he felt confident that the Christian community he had nourished was a firm witness of the gospel and shared God's Spirit and grace with him. As Christians, many of us have learned that personal piety cannot be divorced from community engagement and that our hope for a new order of justice and peace must be an inclusive hope, in which there is a place for joyful prayers.

† Be with us, Jesus, in our distress! May your Spirit fill us with everlasting hope, so that we may stand fearlessly by those who need you. In your grace. Amen.

For further thought

Are there any war refugees in your community? What are their needs? Listen to them and give them a hand.

22 March
Love and belonging

Read John 21:15–19

Simon son of John, do you love me?

(verse 16)

Coffee time after the weekly service has become a key component of our church life. Some days these noisy and pleasant gatherings last longer than the service itself! Is this all right? What's going on? The pastor and lay leadership wondered at first, but it was clear after some weeks that this new, unofficial get together was opening the door to a new sense of belonging, to a different way of sharing the gospel and its blessings between members and newcomers, old and young, women and men.

In his book, *Life Together,* Dietrich Bonhoeffer says that the Word of Jesus Christ brings 'redemption, righteousness, innocence, and blessedness' and that God has put this Word into our mouths so that we may pass it on to others (*Life Together: The Classic Exploration of Christian Community* trans. John W Doberstein, HarperOne, 1954, p. 22). God has wanted us to seek and find his living Word in the testimony of our brothers and sisters, in their Christian experience told by themselves. As Christians we need other Christians to tell us how Jesus has cleared the path that leads to God. During coffee time people talk about almost everything and as conversations get deeper and more personal, Jesus' mandate to Peter becomes real: 'Feed my lambs', 'Take care of my sheep', and do it lovingly.

Believers should know that where there is love, there is a future. Jesus' call to love him and our neighbours and serve them in community opens the way to put all our sensibilities and potential at his service.

† Humbly, we want to put our capacities and abilities in your hands, Jesus, so that we may contribute to strengthening our communities of faith with joy and understanding. Amen.

For further thought

Read Psalm 133. What does it tell you about the community of believers? Is there any other psalm that relates to it?

Walking with Jesus: Christian life

4 Opposition

Notes by **Alesana Fosi Pala'amo**

Alesana is Head of Department for Practical Theology at Malua Theological College in Samoa. An ordained minister of the Congregational Christian Church Samoa, his research interests include social ministries, Pacific research methodologies, theology and pastoral counselling. Alesana's PhD research through Massey University New Zealand explored pastoral counselling practices of Samoans. Alesana and his wife Lemau co-founded a pastoral counselling agency called Soul Talk Samoa Trust. Alesana has used the NRSVA for these notes.

23 March
A love–hate relationship

Read John 15:18–25

If you belonged to the world, the world would love you as its own. Because you do not belong to the world, but I have chosen you out of the world – therefore the world hates you.

(verse 19)

Raising children has allowed us to observe the behaviours of two of our sons who are one year apart in age. When younger they would share toys, food and drink, and generally enjoyed each other's company. Yet moods would change where they would argue, push and shove one another to get what the other wanted. Their older brother would often mediate to settle such brotherly disputes. Our younger sons displayed a love–hate relationship, where brotherly love was always there, mixed with emotions of hate when competing for the same desires.

Walking with Jesus has its challenges where love is opposed by hate, such as a love–hate relationship. Belonging to the world shows a love that values worldly matters. Yet walking with Jesus means that one has been set apart from the world and become a brother or sister of Christ. This draws hate from all things worldly by having a Christ-like mind in one's thoughts and in actions. This week looks at what opposition to walking with Jesus looks like, with key messages of how to overcome and persevere through opposing forces in our daily and private individual walk with Jesus, one step at a time.

† Lord God, help me in walking with you to not stumble, but to move forward one step at a time, sharing your love onto others. Amen.

24 March
Disbelieving your own

Read Matthew 13:54–58

And they took offence at him. But Jesus said to them, 'Prophets are not without honour except in their own country and in their own house.' And he did not do many deeds of power there, because of their unbelief.

(verse 57)

The constitution of the Congregational Christian Church Samoa (CCCS) states that one cannot become a *faifeau* (minister) in the village where you were born and raised. Respecting one's elders and upholding relational space *(vā)* as a sacred place between people are important values for all Samoans. If a *faifeau* ministered within their home village, any of their decisions that contradicted the wishes of their elders might be considered as disrespectful and a breach of the *vā* between them. This article of the constitution connects with today's Bible account, protecting relationships in our context.

Jesus taught the crowds about the kingdom of God using parables, followed by his explicit explanations. These teachings often drew disbelief in his hearers and especially when he returned to his birthplace Nazareth. They knew him to be the son of a carpenter, yet here he was contradicting the traditional teachings of the respected rabbis.

Our daily walk with Jesus is such that those closest to us may display disbelief in the changes they see in us, having known us from birth. Just as Jesus was more than the carpenter they knew, so Christ can change us to become more than they knew of us as we leave our past and rejoice in our new-found life and love of Christ. It would be wonderful if instead of holding onto the knowledge of our historical selves, those closest to us believed in what God is capable of and rejoiced with us. Yet we should not be surprised when our new life and our new beliefs meet with resistance or hostility from some of those closest to us.

† Lord, forgive me if I display disbelief in my own family members in their walk with Jesus. Help me in my walk with Jesus to lead a righteous life worthy of your glory. Amen.

For further thought
Nothing is impossible to God; let us rejoice in our new-found life and love of Christ, rather than holding onto our old selves.

25 March
Expect to be hated

Read Matthew 10:5–23

...and you will be hated by all because of my name. But the one who endures to the end will be saved.

(verse 22)

Most journeys (*malaga* or *folauga* in Samoan) begin from a specific starting point and travel towards an intended destination. The setting of the journey – whether on land, across oceans or through the sky – is important to determine how best to prepare for it. The selected twelve from today's reading were given clear instructions of the purpose of this specific journey – to proclaim the good news that the kingdom of heaven was near. They were also instructed on the destination of their journey – to the lost people of Israel, identified as those who had turned their backs to God. Instructions for this journey also included where they should avoid: towns of the non-Israelites (gentiles) as well as the Samaritans. Future journeys would have different instructions, depending on the purpose and setting – some would include going to the very places they were told to avoid on this one. We must be careful not to make rules for all journeys out of the specific instructions given for this one.

Journeying with a purpose was not an easy task, as they discovered. Just like most journeys, challenges presented themselves – as they proclaimed the name of Christ, they encountered hatred and opposition. The hope that Jesus gave was that those who persevered in the journey through to its end would be saved.

One's walk with Jesus is not an easy journey, given the many worldly obstacles and challenges. Yet being faithful to God and seeing the journey out to its destination means that the struggles faced are all worth it – the purpose of that journey will be fulfilled, the kingdom of heaven will have drawn near and salvation will be ours.

† Our supreme and loving God, may you use me as a disciple of Christ to spread the gospel to others through my journey with you, amidst the challenges of the world in which we live. Amen.

For further thought
Allow yourself to be called by God as a disciple of Christ to journey and take the gospel to the world.

26 March
A bad apple spoils the bunch

Read 2 Timothy 3:10–17

...so that everyone who belongs to God may be proficient, equipped for every good work.

(verse 17)

Group dynamics are such that sometimes there is that one person who always talks negatively and looks at the bad side of things. Today's theme is a proverbial saying that means when there is one rotten or 'bad' apple in the bunch or basket, often the neighbouring, good apples also become bad. Considering perishables such as apples, it is understandable that when left to nature, eventually all the apples will decay and become rotten. Yet when this saying is applied to a group of people, is it possible then for all the 'non-negative' people in the group, who see the good things in life, to rub off their positivity and good will onto others in the group? In other words, how do we resist becoming 'spoiled' by the negative ones? How do we avoid absorbing their false view of the world, of people and of God? How, instead, do we influence them so that they too have the joy and peace that is promised?

Paul was approaching the end of his work, and today's narrative speaks to Timothy, his devoted follower in Christ, about this very issue. He warned him to beware of those who opposed his teachings and who displayed through their lifestyle that they were 'rotten apples'. The antidote is to stand steadfast, following Paul's example by living in faith and persevering through all types of sufferings.

For all those who belong to God are equipped for the good work ahead, to counter all the wickedness they face and, in so doing, some of those who were 'bad apples' see true goodness and repent.

† O God, help me to see the good in people and encourage them to worship and honour you in all that we do, for the glory of our Lord and Saviour Jesus Christ. Amen.

For further thought

Be the 'good apple' for others and let our love for Christ rub off onto others so they too can experience for themselves God's love.

Walking with Jesus: Christian life – 4 Opposition

March

27 March
Conflicting belief systems

Read Acts 19:23–41

Some of the crowd gave instructions to Alexander, whom the Jews had pushed forward. And Alexander motioned for silence and tried to make a defence before the people. But when they recognized that he was a Jew, for about two hours all of them shouted in unison, 'Great is Artemis of the Ephesians!'

(verses 33–34)

One of the challenges in our walk with Christ includes dealing with conflicting belief systems. The apostle Paul faced similar opposition when he revisited the ancient Greek city of Ephesus during his third missionary journey. The ancient city's location today lies on the western shores of modern-day Turkey. The temple in Ephesus and the statue of its deity were the pride of locals in its worship of the ancient Greek goddess Artemis, otherwise known as Diana to the Romans. Artemis was often represented as a statue with a crescent on her head, a bow in her hand and dressed as a hunter. The Ephesians' worship of hand-made idols conflicted with Paul's teachings about God, that he taught for three months in the synagogues before being rejected, then almost two years in a public domain. The increasing number of Jewish and gentile converts Paul encouraged over to Christ led to the riot in Ephesus when the idol-making and shrine-building trades were gradually declining.

The world in which we live today continues to have several belief systems, some religious, others secular. Often, their voice seems loud and vehemently opposed to us, just as must have been the case at the riot in Ephesus. Just as with Paul though, our response is not to shout louder but to live our lives reflecting the love of Christ, who for our sake became flesh, taking the form of a servant, even to death on a cross.

† Lord God, encourage and equip me to stand strong in my faith as I daily walk with Christ amid the abundance of different and conflicting belief systems in the world we live in. Amen.

For further thought

Do we place our belief in worldly material things, or do we have faith in our gracious and loving God who provides for us always?

28 March
False witnesses

Read Acts 6:1–15

They set up false witnesses who said, 'This man never stops saying things against this holy place and the law; for we have heard him say that this Jesus of Nazareth will destroy this place and will change the customs that Moses handed on to us.'

(verses 13–14)

If we are to understand a witness to be a person who gives testimony about something in its verbal, written or implied form, how then does one distinguish between a false witness and a true witness? According to Jewish law, the answer was simple – if the testimonies of two or more witnesses agreed, then the issue was deemed to be settled (Deuteronomy 19:15). If, however, someone was shown to have provided false testimony, then they suffered the same penalty that would have been due to the accused had their testimony been true.

The witness of Stephen was not just his eloquent speech; it was the life of service to which he had been called. From today's reading, we see that he was a faithful servant to the cause of spreading the gospel of Christ at the beginning of the Christian Church. Stephen also was a capable preacher and debater when defending his faith. Yet where there are true witnesses to Christ, you will also find false witnesses who attempt to draw people away from God.

Stephen's life lined up with his words. The two agreed and therefore, under Jewish law, his testimony was true. Yet the people listened more to the false witnesses than to the truth that Stephen's life embodied. I wonder why. Perhaps the lies they heard conveniently connected with their own lifestyle, meaning that they didn't have to change anything. This is a danger that we all face – if we claim the name 'Christian' yet live a life that is not Christ-like, we are being a false witness. But when our lives and words agree, Jesus is made visible, just as Stephen proclaimed at the end: 'I see ... the Son of Man' (Acts 7:56).

† O Lord, I pray that you will bless me through faith and knowledge to separate all false witnesses who distract me from you in my daily walk with you in my life. Amen.

For further thought

True witnesses to God bring you closer in your relationship to our Lord. Be aware of testimonies from false witnesses that do the opposite.

29 March
Challenged by suffering

Read 1 Peter 4:12–19

Yet if any of you suffers as a Christian, do not consider it a disgrace, but glorify God because you bear this name. For the time has come for judgement to begin with the household of God; if it begins with us, what will be the end for those who do not obey the gospel of God?

(verses 16–17)

Admitted to hospital unexpectedly while recently on holiday in Sydney visiting our son and family may seem an experience that constitutes some degree of suffering. Yet considering the conditions observed of neighbouring patients in the ward, my illness appeared petty and minor in comparison. The care received at Prince of Wales Randwick, particularly its newly opened Emergency Department and the Community Assessment Unit 3 South, was nothing short of five stars to a visiting traveller from Samoa. Although holiday plans suddenly changed, the five-day hospital admission became a forced time to reflect on the year that was near its end and a time to stay put and rest, being in recovery mode from surgical procedures and illness.

When we ponder upon the suffering that Christ endured because of us, then all other suffering that we know – physical, emotional, mental, spiritual – does not compare. Jesus was tortured and whipped, then nailed to a cross and died, although he was innocent. Jesus was wrongfully accused by his own people and was crucified on behalf of all sinners as part of God's plan. The good news is that Jesus was resurrected from the dead to eternal life, because God's love has no limits. In our daily walk with Christ, we need to share the suffering of Christ for all sinners. We must also share that we have been cleansed of our sins and earned entry into eternal life through faith in Christ as our Saviour. What good news that glorifies God, to be shared with others, as we bear the name of Christ in walking with our Lord.

† Christ my Saviour, thank you for making me a new person through your sacrifice on the cross. May I share and glorify you always as I walk with you each day. Amen.

For further thought

Are we challenged by suffering? How does the knowledge that in this we are sharing the sufferings of Christ impact our situation?

Walking with Jesus: Christian life

5 The One who goes with us

Notes by **The Honourable Fiamē Naomi Mata'afa and Lemau Pala'amo**

Fiamē and Lemau met when they both attended the Malua Bible School and formed a friendship based on their shared faith in God. Fiamē Naomi Mata'afa is a deacon of the Congregational Church of Samoa in the village of Lotofaga. She has been an MP since 1985 and became Prime Minister of Samoa in July 2021. Lemau Pala'amo is a lecturer's wife at Malua Theological College. She is a mother of three boys. She is co-founder of Soul Talk Samoa Trust. Fiamē and Lemau have used the NRSV for these notes.

30 March
Seeking wisdom (Fiamē)

Read Ephesians 1:15–23

I pray that the God of our Lord Jesus Christ, the Father of glory, may give you a spirit of wisdom and revelation as you come to know him.

(verse 17)

The story of Solomon's wisdom in dealing with the two mothers claiming the same child is well known. For me, the main value of that story is the revelation of the true nature of love – that of sacrifice, the one mother that would rather give up her claim than risk the child's death. Such is the love of God, when he chose to sacrifice his only Son for our salvation.

As a leader at multiple levels I am often faced with having to make decisions on competing interests and to resolve disputes. I am therefore constantly bringing these matters to the Lord in prayer, seeking the wisdom and revelations referred to in our scripture of today.

We pray to God for many things, but I have found that praying for his clarity in situations of dispute and angst has been a special pathway in my walk with him. In truth, coming to resolutions in such matters are mere by-products of a greater revelation, that of the nature of God.

Growing in the understanding of God brings me such peace of mind and spirit but most importantly it has given me a confidence of spirit to walk forward with a stronger faith.

† Lord God, we pray for wisdom and a fresh revelation of your love. Amen.

31 March
Building a strong and solid foundation (Lemau)

Read Ephesians 2:14–22

In him the whole structure is joined together and grows into a holy temple in the Lord.

(verse 21)

This verse reminds me of a Sunday here in Samoa. Every village in Samoa has a church building, some villages have more than one church building, which is built to be strong and unbreakable. Every Sunday morning without a doubt, you see people dressed in white, holding their Bible bags and walking into a big white church. One by one they walk into church getting ready to sing, reflect on the Bible reading, listen to the sermon and pray to God.

This verse teaches me that the Church is compared to something solid and enduring, just like a building structure. It is a place where people can come together to experience God's presence and to worship him. The Church is not stagnant; it is growing and it is constantly moving. Working together to build the Church and support one another, encourage one another and love one another. In Ephesians 2:21, Paul writes a beautiful comparison for the Church, as the body of Christ. We are all individual believers, but we are also part of something much bigger. We are united in Christ, and together we form a holy temple, a dwelling place for the Spirit of God. Paul is actually referring not to the physical sense of the building structure but the community of believers that is united in Christ. Let us be thankful for the gift of the Church. Let us commit to living holy lives that are pleasing to God. And let us walk together to build up the body of Christ.

† Lord, thank you for the gift of the Church. Help us to continue to live, serve, help and grow your Church. Help us to know your will every day. In Jesus' name we pray. Amen.

For further thought

God is not restricted to worship only in a church building. God is everywhere.

1 April
God's love (Fiamē)

Read 1 John 4:7–21

The commandment we have from him is this: those who love God must love their brothers and sisters also.

(verse 21)

The message of our chosen scripture is very clear: that if we do not love our brother, we cannot truly then love God. This is very challenging for me as I would imagine is the case for many other people. Many disputes and differences happen between people. The deepest hurt, real or imagined, is often inflicted within the closest circle of family.

Samoan society is structured around large extended families. The heads of these families are chieftains and the succession to these titles has traditionally been settled through family consensus but in more recent times, by court arbitration. My accession to the title Fiamē was by arbitration. There were twenty-one parties in the arbitration with thirteen candidates.

As a new leader, the first order of business was to restore family unity. It was important in that process to reassure all members of the family that despite our differences aired during the arbitration process, I was their leader, not just for those who had supported my candidature. Mending the relationships took time in which we performed our respective roles and functions, bringing to the fore the value of family for all of us. It was not just talking and communicating but also the collective activities, be they smaller or larger, regular or intermittent.

Building our relationship with God as our Father, the Alpha and the Omega in our lives, is the blueprint to building loving relationships with our brethren.

† Lord, we pray that you shower us with your love and for your continued guidance in our lives to nurture and share the love. Amen.

For further thought

What are the challenges that still face us in loving our brothers and sisters?

Walking with Jesus: Christian life – 5 The One who goes with us

2 April
Jesus is our Saviour (Lemau)

Read John 1:10–18

And the Word became flesh and lived among us, and we have seen his glory, the glory as of a father's only son, full of grace and truth.

(verse 14)

Being a counsellor and helping those in need takes a lot of energy and time. The impacts and complexity of people's problems have helped me understand God's love in a deeper way. People feel overwhelmed by problems that they are facing and I am constantly reminiscing on how Jesus came to earth to experience suffering and to give hope to us all. When the struggles of people are real, their minds seem to be cloudy and not focused. People who are going through problems tend to also forget that it is important to forgive others as well as themselves.

Reminiscing once again on Jesus, Jesus came to earth to forgive our sins and to show us how to love others. This thought gives comfort, strength, courage and hope to continue the path that God has given us. John 1:14 has helped me to fulfil my duties as a mother, as a Reverend's wife, as a counsellor and as a member of the congregation. To see myself as God sees me. This verse gives me the courage to face fears and challenges, knowing that Jesus is always with us and he will help us through anything. Jesus inspires us to love and serve others. He gives us hope for the future. Jesus came to earth to serve others, and we want to follow his example. Jesus also came to earth to teach us about God, to forgive our sins and to give us eternal life. God's love and grace for us is never ending and through his Son, Jesus Christ our Saviour, we are saved.

† Lord, help us to have courage, strength, comfort and hope in all that we do. Help those who are lost and are in need for you to guide them. Amen.

For further thought

What verse helps you continue your journey in life?

3 April
The armour of God (Fiamē)

Read Ephesians 6:10–17

Take the helmet of salvation, and the sword of the Spirit, which is the word of God.

(verse 17)

There are many Samoan proverbs that speak to the importance of words, words to carry messages, words to record significant events and spoken words of commitment and commemoration. One such proverb speaks of words that teach and nourish: 'the young of birds are fed on fruits and berries but the human child is fed on word and stories.' Such is the word of God as shared in these pages of *Fresh from The Word*. It is our daily bread, sustaining our spirit and joining our minds and hearts as a world community of believers.

Throughout the ages, the sword is a symbol of corporeal authority and physical might and in Samoan mythology Nafanua, the Samoan war goddess, had four named war clubs:

1. Ta Fesilafa'i: Facing the enemy. Used at the onset of the war.

2. Faauliulitō: Purposeful resolve. Used by allies holding the flank to protect the centre.

3. Ulumasao: To free. Used to end the war.

4. Faamategatama: Weapon of death. It was never used as it would have laid waste to both allies and enemies.

Victorious in battle, Nafanua brought unity to the country taking possession of the four paramount titles reconstituting the traditional chiefly system that continues in Samoa today.

In God's kingdom, the sword (the word) is part of God's armour that both protects and enables us to fight the good fight to bring the word of salvation to the world.

† Lord, with your armour we pray that you are always our protector, giving us the strength to spread your word in our daily routines. Amen.

For further thought

What parts of the armour of God give you courage and strength?

Walking with Jesus: Christian life – 5 The One who goes with us

4 April

All good things come to those who wait (Lemau)

Often you see people lining up at the bank to be attended by a bank teller or lining up at the grocery store to be served by the cashier. Then you see those who don't have patience push their way closer to the front of the line and cause frustrations to those who were first. I have experienced the latter and wonder: would it have made any difference if they did not push in front of the line? There have been times when I have prayed for certain things to happen and God has not answered my prayer immediately. But even in those times, I have been able to hold on to hope because I know that God is faithful and that it is all in his time and his way for us.

Waiting for good things to happen takes a lot of patience. Waiting is an opportunity to develop a strong trust in God and remember that there is hope, as God knows what is best for us and it is all his timing of when and where things will happen. This verse is a reminder that hope is a gift from God. It is a gift that helps us to persevere through difficult times and to look forward to the future with confidence. If you are waiting for something in your life today, be encouraged to hold on to hope. Trust God that he knows what is best for you and trust him to provide for you in his timing and his way. Wait with patience and grow your faith in God.

† Dear Lord, help us to have patience and for us to know that it is your timing and not ours. Teach us to have hope and trust in you, through Jesus Christ. Amen.

For further thought

Let us all follow God's lead in becoming patient people in our everyday living.

5 April
In all things (Lemau)

Read Romans 8:28–39

And we know that in all things God works for the good of those who love him, who have been called according to his purpose.

(verse 28)

Moving countries is not easy and when we (my husband and I) moved to study at Malua Theological College it meant that we moved from Sydney, Australia, to Apia, Samoa. The organisation, logistics and list of what we needed to take took a while to compile. Not knowing which house we were going to stay in upon arrival, not knowing what furniture or kitchen appliances were needed at the time was difficult. Moving countries and going through a new journey in life was not easy and the sense of fear over whether it was the right decision we had made came with doubt and uncertainty. Feeling overwhelmed, feeling sad about moving away from family and especially facing the language barrier were not easy at the time.

When we arrived in Samoa, the feeling was a fresh breath of air and the sensation of starting our new journey together was somewhat exciting! Knowing that we were going to learn more about God and his ministry gave us a source of comfort and strength. Our strength was knowing that God is with us and that he would help us through these times. And he did. God gave us the strength to persevere.

When we love God, when we are called according to his purpose, God is always working things together for our good, even when we don't understand it.

† Lord, we thank you that you are sovereign, and we pray that we will continue to know you first through Jesus Christ our Saviour. Amen.

For further thought

Are you excited about what God has planned for your life in the future?

The Gospel of Luke (2)

1 The events of Holy Week

Notes by **Angharad Rhys Davies**

Angharad has served with YWAM in England, China, France, Romania, Argentina and South Africa. She lived in Cape Town for seven years, where she helped set up The Dignity Campaign (https://dignity.org.za). She has recently completed a book based on her personal experience of overcoming eating disorders and depression – the first of its kind in the Welsh language. Angharad has a BA in Welsh Literature and currently home educates her two lovely kids while studying for an MA. Angharad has used the NRSVUE for these notes.

6 April
Betrayal

Read Luke 22:1–6

So, he consented and began to look for an opportunity to betray him to them when no crowd was present.

(verse 6)

When I was at university, I dated a Christian man. I came to love and trust him and eventually, we became engaged. Then he had an affair with my friend. Ouch. I felt betrayed and publicly humiliated. Truth is, I would never have chosen to date the guy if I could have foreseen how it would turn out!

Yet in today's passage we see that Jesus deliberately includes in his close friendship group people who had the potential to betray him. He knew from the start that one of them would: 'One of you will betray me,' he said. It could have been Peter; he came close to it: 'Get behind me, Satan,' Jesus warned! In the end, as we read, it turned out to be Judas. But the amazing thing is that knowing all this, Jesus still befriended him, still shared himself with him. No sane person would do that! Unless they had an astronomical hope in a worthwhile outcome!

Wisely for me, I broke off the engagement. For our sake, despite the pain, Jesus followed through with the plan he and the Father and the Holy Spirit had agreed – that in the end, we might be his bride.

† Jesus, thank you for the emotional pain that you chose to endure, so that we can experience the comfort of a relationship with the Father.

7 April
Bread and wine

Read Luke 22:7–23

Then he took a loaf of bread, and when he had given thanks, he broke it and gave it to them, saying, 'This is my body, which is given for you. Do this in remembrance of me.'

(verse 19)

Simon (my husband) and I spent a few months living in a Muslim community called Bo-Kaap, in central Cape Town. Apparently, this was the stronghold and 'birthplace' of Islam in the Western Cape province of South Africa. We ran a church planting seminar and hosted experienced teachers; some had lived among the unreached and had worked with un-churched believers. During this six-month internship we attempted to deconstruct the culture of the Western Church and tried to be open to different expressions of Christianity.

One day, we sat at an Eastern food cafeteria in downtown Cape Town with our Muslim-background believer friends – a man from Morocco and a lady from a South African township, who had both been renounced by their families for converting from Islam to Christianity. Neither of these people could use their mother tongue to communicate with us and attending churches with unfamiliar traditions could be uncomfortable. We tried to speak what little of their language that we knew, and we made a safe space for them to communicate.

Our time of fellowship felt so special and we were humbled by the stories that they shared – their challenging upbringings, the pain of being ostracised because of their faith and their love for Jesus. We could not help but use our Peshwari naan and sweet chai tea to share the Lord's Supper with them. There we were, representing seven unique nations, gathering in unity to celebrate everything God had done for us all.

† Jesus, your kingdom knows no bounds. We don't want to be a stumbling block that hinders others from expressing thanksgiving to you. Expose our cultural biases and show us how you transcend all cultural differences.

For further thought

When we consider all that Jesus has done, how can we not put down our knives and forks and take time to remember him?

8 April
Friends through trials

Read Luke 22:24–30
You are those who have stood by me in my trials.

(verse 28)

Recently a friend went through a crisis and for six months I visited her to keep her company and look after her daughter so that she could rest. Knowing that she was actively adhering to New Age practices, we were surprised to be invited into her home for a meal; she wanted to chat about Christianity. We truly thought that she was curious about becoming a follower of Jesus. Sadly, as she recovered in strength, she stopped searching for truth and turned to others who reinforced the lies that had led to her breakdown. It was very painful to watch her separate herself from me, knowing where it would lead.

Jesus knows how I felt: having stood by the Twelve, he knows that they will all soon desert him. Yet still he says: 'You are those who have stood by me ...' Even though they would run away – back to fishing, back to the familiar, back to the comfortable lies – Jesus acknowledges the value of when they stood with him. Their future failure did not invalidate the previous good. God sees a bigger picture – a lesson I'm still learning!

Learning, because I've been blessed by people who have stood with me, despite times when I wanted to run away. Often, it's been the small gestures of standing with from the consistent people in my life that have been invaluable. In the ten years of my marriage, there have been multiple dark nights of the soul. There's nothing my husband can do to 'fix' me in those times. But his unrelenting presence has been an anchor.

† Open our eyes to see the people in our lives who just need to know that we are there for them, come what may, and to be more aware of those who support us.

For further thought
Maybe the people around us don't want anything from us, other than for us to not leave them alone in their suffering.

9 April
God never fails

Read Luke 22:31–38

Jesus said, 'I tell you, Peter, the cock will not crow this day until you have denied three times that you know me.'

(verse 34)

Integrity is a key value in the kingdom; hypocrisy was something that Jesus constantly pointed out. There's a simple reason: if our words don't match our actions, our words lack credibility, and our witness becomes invalid. Often, we speak words that describe where we would like to be in our journey, rather than where we are – just as Peter does here.

I used to make the mistake of flippantly promising something to my kids – usually to distract them from discomfort. But I wouldn't always follow through and I have had to become very intentional at restraining myself from uttering appeasing promises! And I'm learning to keep my word with them, even if the conditions aren't perfect and even if it seems trivial – such as playing cars for ten minutes with my four-year-old. I want them to be able to trust that I am an honest person.

Of course, sometimes the reason we fail to speak the truth is shame – as with Peter and the serving girl. It's easy to let fear or shame alter our words or impose silence. I had such an experience recently: I was with three other mums, and they began to discuss Christianity in a very negative way. I was deeply offended at their words because I felt that they were insulting my best friend. Yet, I was silent. At the time, I justified it to myself because I wasn't part of their discussion, but inside I was mortified at my incapacity to stand up for what I know to be true about Jesus.

† Jesus, forgive me the times that I have been ashamed to be called your friend, and forgive me the times that my silence has been a denial of my relationship with you.

For further thought

Who were the disciples who didn't run away? What was the difference? Could it be something to do with a deep integrity?

10 April
Turning points

Read Luke 22:39–46

Father, if you are willing, remove this cup from me, yet not my will but yours be done.

(verse 42)

Most of us will face times when everything in us longs to choose a different path; the current trajectory looks bleak, we can't see a bigger picture that would make it worthwhile, or perhaps it's just that the other path seems safer, more comfortable.

When my husband and I were newly-weds, we were living on an extremely tight financial budget – if the value of the pound went down in comparison with the South African rand, then things would get even tighter. But we were offered a position that seemed to be an answer to all our woes. Simon was offered a job as a minister, in his city of origin – the job came with a set annual salary and a house big enough for a family in close proximity to the church. It wasn't a 'bad' or 'sinful' option – it could have made perfect sense for Simon to take the job, with financial security, safer than his work in Cape Town, close to his parents and in his own culture. But the still small voice of the Lord persisted in whispering that this was not the calling he had for our lives. We were to continue working in the townships and prisons in Southern Africa. We wrestled with the decision but in the end, the prayer of our heart was, 'Your will be done, not ours.'

I'd love to say that as a reward for saying 'yes' all our concerns were proved baseless. But of course, that isn't how it works. It was as tough as we anticipated. Choosing God's way doesn't make that way easier!

We have no regrets.

† Give us the tenacity to make decisions that coincide with your plan for our lives and cultivate in us a resilience to accomplish all that you have for us to do.

For further thought

In the prayer, God the Son makes it clear to God the Father that the cross is not his will. Meditate on this – how agonising a decision it must have been, how much bigger it made Jesus' eventual decision to submit to the Father.

11 April

He is the way

> **Read Luke 22:47–53**
>
> *But Jesus said, 'No more of this!' And he touched his ear and healed him.*
>
> (verse 51)

Peter is up way past his normal bedtime. He's had a fair amount of wine to drink. He's a fisherman not a soldier. But he's told Jesus, 'I'll die before I let you be taken.' So, tired and tipsy, he pulls out his sword to begin the revolution, takes a wild swipe, misses and nicks someone's ear. If it weren't so tragic it might almost be darkly comic.

The truth is the chief priests, the officers, the Temple police were bullies; they exercised power illegally, in the dark away from the crowds who might oppose them. Bullies are usually cowards who tend to work in groups. My husband has worked with hardened criminals in a maximum-security prison in South Africa; when the men are with their gang, they're tough, but if my husband speaks to them individually, the tears roll and the trauma stories pour out.

'Put your sword away,' responds Jesus – and heals the man's ear. The solution to bullying is not to bully back, but to walk in God's way, whatever that might look like.

We can also feel bullied: by 'the system', by bosses, by the global economy, by the unnecessary expectations of Christian culture and much more. We could fight the 'bullies' head on, but that's likely to result in lots of people getting hurt (futile). We could surrender to the pressures and walk the easier path (compromise). Or we can remember God's plan and live accordingly (faith).

By faith we will walk the path less taken – facing obstacles and enduring threats; by faith we will keep our eyes on him and allow him to direct our steps.

† Lord, sometimes I feel like I can't breathe because I feel that everything is against me. Please help me to have a clear view of you and the narrow path that leads to life.

For further thought

Following God can mean that we have to be radically countercultural and frequently act in ways that others find unexpected.

The Gospel of Luke (2) – 1 The events of Holy Week

Take heart

Read Luke 22:54–62

And he went out and wept bitterly.

(verse 62)

At the time when Jesus would have needed as much support as possible, Peter turned his back on his rabbi. What a tragedy for Jesus and a gut-wrenching experience for Peter. It's easy for us to skip to the end of the story – to the BBQ on the beach and Peter's restoration – but skipping over painful bits, trying to short-cut the journey, means we miss out on opportunities to grow.

When I was about seventeen, I stopped sitting with the group of girls that I had been best friends with – I went to sit on the 'cool girl' table and began to hang out with a brand-new set of people. At the time, I was just attempting to survive my first ever serious heartache. But after I became a believer, I was filled with guilt and remorse for the awful way that I had turned my back on people I had been close to and went back and apologised to those whom I had hurt. I'd love to blot that out of my memory, or skip to an ending that included forgiveness and reconciliation. But actually, it's the stark memory of the cost of my actions that helps me determine not to be like that again. Skipping to the end, minimising the pain for myself and those I hurt, is a recipe for repeating the disastrous choices in the future.

Owning our choices, accounting for the cost of those choices, is the only true basis for relationship repair and restoration. Sometimes we just need to weep bitterly.

† Have mercy on us when we fail you. Extend grace to us when we do not advocate for you. Give us courage when we are weak. Let us not hide our light.

For further thought

When we fail, let us mourn our weakness and own our choices and their consequences. God uses our lament, our confession, to bring true repentance and growth and in that place he can comfort and embolden us.

The Gospel of Luke (2)

2 Holy Week continues

Notes by **Tim Yau**

Tim is an Anglican Ordained Pioneer Minister serving in the suburbs of Norwich, trying to reach new people, in new places, in new ways. He's one of the few Chinese heritage priests in the Church of England and wants to see more vocations from UK Minority Ethnic/Global Majority Heritage (non-white people of African, Asian, Latin American descent), believing: 'to be it, you have to see it'. He's frequently found enjoying sci-fi epics and still dreams of becoming a superhero. Tim has used the NIVUK for these notes.

13 April
Revolutionary resilience

Read Luke 22:63–65

The men who were guarding Jesus began mocking and beating him.

(verse 63)

During Passion Week, we enter a time of reflection, repentance and anticipation of the joy of Easter. However, we must first walk with Christ through the remembrance of his sufferings.

Today we encounter Jesus withstanding the worst of human behaviour: mockery, insults and brutality. Chained and bruised, he responds not with anger or vengeance but with inner strength and embodying a radical resistance.

In secular society, religion is often marginalised and faces ridicule and dismissal. Some Christians get defensive and lash out against the inequity, demanding their freedoms; others hide away and don't engage with the world. Jesus though shows us how to respond by exemplifying his teachings of forgiveness, love and endurance with revolutionary resilience. When we respond to negativity with grace and determination, we highlight the depth of our convictions and challenge misconceptions about religion.

Jesus' example invites us to be agents of change in a dismissive culture. By demonstrating the revolutionary resilience of our faith, we can challenge preconceived notions and inspire others to reconsider their perspectives. Jesus said: 'In this world you will have trouble. But take heart! I have overcome the world' (John 16:33).

Will you join Jesus in his holy revolution?

† Lord God, ignite in us the revolutionary resilience of Christ. In a society sceptical of faith, grant us courage to face trials with grace. Amen.

Council in crisis

Read Luke 22:66–71

'If you are the Messiah,' they said, 'tell us.'

(verse 67)

While Israel had some religious freedoms, the Jewish authorities faced an unwelcome challenge: preserving their freedoms and culture in the face of radical religious and political groups that threatened the *Pax Romana* (Roman peace and stability).

Jesus was disturbing this fragile peace. He was more than a religious reformer; he was a holy revolutionary. So, the conclave confronted him, but were not presented with a triumphant warrior king, but a poor itinerant miracle-working rabbi in chains. Jesus was not their kind of Messiah!

The Jewish authorities' anxiety over losing their grip on power mirrors the UK Church establishment's own fears about a declining role in a secular society. Church traditionalists are pitched against progressives, some advocating the status quo, others pioneering or planting new congregations. Some trying to be culturally relevant, others advocating religious distinctiveness. Ultimately, I imagine pragmatism will prevail. Whatever happens, I believe we'll see adaptation to the evolving spiritual landscape.

Jesus challenged received wisdom and expectations – his message of love, acts of compassion and proclamation of spiritual liberation remain a timeless source of inspiration, transcending the confines of what came before him. Maybe in the same way, when we are confronted with novel or controversial ideas and practices, we shouldn't jump to judgement but adopt the 'Gamaliel Principle' where the honoured Pharisee responded to the new followers of Jesus, declaring: 'Leave these men alone! Let them go! For if their purpose or activity is of human origin, it will fail. But if it is from God, you will not be able to stop these men; you will only find yourselves fighting against God' (Acts 5:38–39).

† Almighty God, lead us through the ever-changing currents of culture. Grant us the courage to honour our spiritual heritage while embracing innovation, knowing that your divine purpose can emerge in surprising and unforeseen ways. Amen.

For further thought

How will you listen to new perspectives when they challenge your traditions? What traditions will you adapt to meet the needs of a changing world?

15 April
Pilate perplexed

Read Luke 23:1–7

Then Pilate announced to the chief priests and the crowd, 'I find no basis for a charge against this man.'

(verse 4)

The Roman governor Pilate is confronted by irate Jewish leaders accusing Jesus of sedition and tax avoidance. So, Pilate probes the prisoner, but Jesus doesn't plead his innocence, or throw allegations back at his accusers, nor deny the legitimacy of Pilate to judge, but simply reflects the question back.

Whether Pilate is aggrieved, unconcerned or amused by Jesus' response we don't know. Nevertheless, the governor declares him guiltless and sends him to Herod Antipas, the ruler of Galilee, to be cross-examined.

In the face of relentless accusations, political pressure and the uproar of the crowds, Jesus remains the epitome of integrity, not vengeful or pleading but focused and assured. We too are called to emulate Jesus' stance, even when the prevailing winds of public opinion clash with the values and purposes of the kingdom of God.

Church, at its best, embodies Jesus' revolutionary holiness by being a community of grace. Therefore, we no longer need to protect ourselves because we belong to something bigger: the kingdom of God! With Christ as our example, we create sacred space for communal integrity, accountability and forgiveness. It's no longer about me, my rights, my wants and needs; instead, it's about 'us' and God.

Jesus' revolutionary holiness is the antidote to the culture of Western individualism. Together as church we relinquish self-interest and selfishness by demonstrating that true transformation occurs within a community that seeks the greater good of the kingdom of God. Knowing we're not on our own encourages us to be virtuous, and experiencing God's Spirit with us makes us holy like Jesus.

† Gracious God, empower us to embody Jesus' revolutionary holiness. Give us strength to forsake self-interest and pursue church communality, for your kingdom's greater good. May your Spirit guide us, making us holy like you. Amen.

For further thought

What can your church collectively prioritise for God's kingdom? What actions can you take to exhibit the revolutionary holiness of Jesus in your life?

16 April
Silence as sedition

Read Luke 23:8–12

[Herod] plied him with many questions, but Jesus gave him no answer.

(verse 9)

Wealth, status and might have always been the staples of political power. Palaces, thrones and armed guards are there to intimidate and cause people to adulate, cower or rebel. Yet in the meeting between Jesus and Herod, the embodiment of earthly privilege and authority, we encounter a profound act of revolutionary defiance: silence.

Herod Antipas ruled Galilee, Jesus' heartland, but still had to navigate the political dynamics of the time: maintaining Roman support, placating Jewish religious leaders, whilst striving to expand his territory. This unanticipated royal court hearing was Herod's chance to interrogate this celebrity miracle-maker and win some political kudos.

The seemingly vulnerable and defenceless Jesus stood before Herod's strength and splendour, whilst the gathered inquisition anticipated a spectacle. Would the Galilean holy man denounce Herod, plead for mercy or reveal his supernatural abilities?

Yet Jesus responded in unwavering silence. He refused to engage in the theatrics of power. His silence became a revolutionary act of defiance against Herod's intimidation tactics, a dignified response transcending Herod's tarnished sovereignty.

Jesus' refusal to perform miracles at Herod's request wasn't a sign of weakness but a display of strength. He didn't succumb to worldly pressures, recognising that genuine power and authority emanated from a higher source: God, his heavenly Father.

In that moment of silence, Jesus challenged the powers of this world. He affirmed that God's kingdom couldn't be manipulated or overpowered; it stood resolute in its own truth and purpose. Silence in the face of corrupt power can be a potent resistance, a non-verbal allegiance to the kingdom of God that defies without resorting to retaliation.

† Almighty God, teach us the revolutionary power of silence in the face of intimidation. May we find the strength to stand with dignity and refuse to bow to the false allure of worldly power. Amen.

For further thought

How has silence been used as a tool by social justice movements for resistance and dignity?

17 April
Perils of populism

Read Luke 23:13–25
But they kept shouting, 'Crucify him! Crucify him!'

(verse 21)

While the mob were baying for his blood, we can only imagine what was going through Jesus' mind and emotions as he processed his predicament: abandoned by his disciples, victimised by a corrupt legal system, the crowds turning against him, the injustice of Barabbas being released, the threat of imminent violence and execution; and all the time obeying his heavenly Father's will over his own personal well-being (see Luke 22:42).

The cries of 'Crucify him!' expose the perilous power of populism when intertwined with unfair legal processes. The crowd had succumbed to manipulation by religious leaders, abandoning justice for political gain. Mob rule often seeks hasty solutions and scapegoats individuals, sidestepping underlying issues.

The inequitable legal process was glaringly obvious as the Roman governor acknowledged Jesus' innocence but yielded to the mob's pressure anyway. Tasked with upholding the law, he agreed to the crowd's demands, endorsing and enabling the grave injustice suffered by Jesus. Today, in many Christian traditions, they regularly recite the Apostles' Creed, declaring that Jesus 'suffered under Pontius Pilate'.

The depth of Jesus' love, obedience to God's will and his unwavering commitment to rescuing humanity reminds us that even in the face of injustice, rejection and personal agony, faith and divine purpose can provide the strength to endure.

Therefore, we are challenged to champion justice, seek truth and withstand the enticement of populism. We are called to emulate Jesus, who endured injustice with grace and extended forgiveness, even amidst a flawed legal system and the chaos of mob rule. Through our actions, we too can create a fairer and more compassionate society.

† Heavenly God, in times of turmoil and injustice, help us find strength in faith and purpose, just as Jesus did. Guide us to champion justice, seek truth and stand against the allure of populism. Amen.

For further thought

How can you champion justice and seek truth in your own life and community? What is God asking you to be obedient to today?

Christ's crucifixion

Read Luke 23:26–49

...he breathed his last.

(verse 46)

Today, when walking the Via Dolorosa through the Old City of Jerusalem, nobody takes any notice – the people are used to pilgrims and tourists parading the traditional 'Sorrowful Way' through the bustling, narrow bazaars. How different must the commotion have been when they saw a Roman cross of execution being dragged through the city.

Crucifixion was primarily reserved for individuals who were considered serious threats to Roman authority or who had committed heinous crimes. The main objective of this public punishment was for it to serve as a deterrent and a means of maintaining Roman control and order.

Today, in some parts of the world, the death penalty is still enforced. Sadly, legal systems can be prone to error and exploitation. Incarcerated innocent people can end up being dismissed, forgotten and disposed of by tyrannical regimes: the powerless prisoners of the powerful!

In the tragedy and drama of these final moments of Jesus' life we could mistakenly see him as a powerless victim of a corrupt system, a political pawn stuck between the machinations of Roman rule, the Jewish crown and the Temple authorities. But something greater was going on, something so world-changing that even the sun seemed to stop shining and the curtain separating the Temple's Most Holy Place from the world was torn apart. Jesus willingly gave up his life, not as a victim but as a revolutionary victor.

† Lord Jesus, as we recognise the injustices in the world, we contemplate your transformative sacrifice. Through your crucifixion, you sparked a momentous shift. May we join your revolution to fight corruption with divine love. Amen.

For further thought

Jesus said: 'He has sent me to proclaim freedom for the prisoners ... to set the oppressed free' (Luke 4:18). How can you support oppressed imprisoned innocents?

19 April

Joseph and Jesus

Read Luke 23:50–56

Going to Pilate, [Joseph] asked for Jesus' body.

(verse 52)

Joseph of Arimathea had been waiting for the kingdom of God, and through Jesus I suspect that he saw something of God's love, light and life breaking out. Therefore, as a respected member of the Jewish council at Jesus' trial, he dissented. To stand with a pariah must have cost him his reputation, nevertheless he exhibited the power of personal conviction in the face of adversity.

Following the crucifixion, in a time when Jesus' followers were largely in hiding, Joseph took a bold step. He approached Pilate, the same authority that had condemned Jesus, and requested his dead body, labelled 'King of the Jews' (verse 38). Joseph's courage stands as a testament to the strength of his character and the depth of his compassion.

Joseph's willingness to provide for Jesus' funeral, to endure ridicule and suspicion from the Jewish elite and the Roman authorities, reflects the revolutionary aspect of his actions. Just as Jesus had faced derision and opposition for his teachings, Joseph, too, faced danger for his burgeoning faith.

Days of sorrow – from Gethsemane to a cross – had ended in the sad spectacle of failure as the hoped for Messiah was buried, and with him the dream of the kingdom of God. Joseph's actions urge us to reflect on our own responses to adversity and the power of personal conviction. They prompt us to consider how we show respect and compassion to those who have seemingly failed. Ultimately, we are reminded that even in challenging circumstances, faith and compassion can shine through, just as they did in Joseph's remarkable act of bravery and love.

† Lord Jesus Christ, as we have walked with you through your sorrows and sufferings, grant us strength and compassion in adversity to stand resolute in challenging times. May your holy revolution continue in us. Amen.

For further thought

How does Joseph's example inspire you to respond to adversity? How might the themes of Passion Week impact your faith and daily life moving forward?

The Gospel of Luke (2)

3 Resurrection

Notes by **Georgie Tennant**

Georgie lives with her husband and two teenage sons in England, UK, where she is a part-time teacher of English. She is the author of the devotional book, *The God Who Sees You* (2023). As someone who has experienced significant bereavement, she writes about grief, loss and hope on her blog www.somepoemsbygeorgie.blogspot.com, as well as volunteering for Care for the Family, a charity that supports families experiencing difficult times. Georgie has used the NIVUK for these notes.

20 April
He is risen!

Read Luke 24:1–8

He is not here; he has risen!

(verse 6)

When my sons were small, they would wake on Easter Sunday, expecting a chocolate egg hunt, a tradition for children in England. Their excited anticipation showed their trust in us that what they hoped for would materialise and that they wouldn't be left disappointed.

Even as they went to bed with no visible sign of the chocolate that would adorn the house and garden when they awoke, they always expected and were always rewarded. Do we wait with the same confident expectation when our lives feel dark, that God will break in?

In Luke 24, the dawn of Easter Sunday at last replaces the cloying darkness of Saturday. The women arrive to anoint Jesus' body. But they find a rolled-away stone and angels in gleaming clothes, announcing the words that would be spoken for centuries, in churches across the world on Easter morn: 'He is not here; he has risen!' (verse 6).

Easter Saturday's transient gloom gives way to Sunday's glorious news. The wait was over: everything Jesus had promised was true! In the same way, whatever darkness we face in our own lives, the light of Jesus' resurrection power can break in, bringing life and hope to every dark corner.

† Lord, let the light of your resurrection illuminate my darkness, that I might live in the hope that it brings. Amen.

21 April
Pondering and wondering

Read Luke 24:9–16

Jesus himself came up and walked along with them; but they were kept from recognising him.

(verses 15b–16)

A few years ago, my son, suffering with a high temperature, stumbled into our bedroom at 3 a.m. to announce there was a frog in the toilet. I put my hand to his head, concerned that his temperature had triggered hallucinations, but I let him guide me to the bathroom to check. Sure enough, there was a frog – in an upstairs toilet – swimming happily around. My confused husband was summoned to catch it in a jug and return it to the garden.

We disbelieved our son's experience until we saw it with our own eyes. Peter did the same with the women here. Their testimony counted for little in the culture they were in, but Peter found their words compelling enough to prompt him to go and check for himself. The strips of linen he found in place of a body left him pondering and wondering if the women's words could be true after all.

Then the scene shifts to two disciples, travelling wearily home to Emmaus from Jerusalem. They are talking and trying to process the traumatic and upsetting events of the weekend, when Jesus comes up and walks with them but, 'they are kept from recognising him' (verse 16).

Even those who experienced him in the flesh struggled to see the truth that Jesus was risen and walking among them. It is not uncommon for our doubts and fears to prevent us from experiencing Jesus' comforting presence, but we must cling fast to the truth that Jesus never stops walking right beside us, whatever we are going through.

† Lord, thank you for walking beside me. Help me to recognise your presence in my life and allow you to help me make sense of things that confuse me. Amen.

For further thought

What evidence can you bring to mind to reassure yourself that Jesus is alive and at work in your life, even amidst doubt and uncertainty?

22 April
Tell me all about it

Read Luke 24:17–24

One of them, named Cleopas, asked him, 'Are you the only one visiting Jerusalem who does not know the things that have happened there in these days?' 'What things?' he asked.

(verses 18–19)

The English language boasts many idioms. One of them is relevant to today – 'Have you been under a rock?' If you asked someone this question, you would be expressing your shock that they have no idea about a current event, even though everyone else in the world knows all about it. Other cultures have similar phrases: 'Have you come down from the mountains?' and 'Have you been living on Mars?' are just as evocative to describe someone who has apparently missed all the latest news.

Yesterday we read about the two disciples, trudging home, discussing all they'd seen. In today's reading, Jesus (yet unrecognised by them) asks them what they are talking about. Cleopas, one of the two, essentially asks Jesus if he has been under a rock (verse 18), astonished that anyone who had been in Jerusalem for the past few days wouldn't have heard the headline news.

Why does Jesus ask them this question at all? It certainly isn't because he doesn't know what has happened. When the disciples reply, their explanation encompasses who they had believed Jesus to be, the tragedy they had witnessed, the hopes that looked dashed and the glimmer of possibility that it might not be over after all. Jesus, already knowing all this, simply invites them to share their pain and sadness, their misunderstandings and disappointments with him as they walk.

Isn't this a bit like our relationship with Jesus? He is omniscient and omnipresent, yet longs for us to share our hearts with him anyway – including our pain and sadness as well as our hopes and triumphs.

† Lord, thank you for caring about everything on my heart today. Thank you that I can come as I am, raw and real, and pour out my hopes and my fears to you. Amen.

For further thought

If Jesus was physically sitting or walking next to you today, what would you want to share with him, directly from your heart? Go ahead!

A lightbulb moment

> **Read Luke 24:25–35**
>
> *Then their eyes were opened and they recognised him, and he disappeared from their sight. They asked each other, 'Were not our hearts burning within us while he talked with us on the road and opened the Scriptures to us?'*
>
> (verses 31–32)

Have you ever had a 'lightbulb moment'? When you grasp something that you hadn't seen before as if a light has suddenly shone on it? As a teacher, there is nothing better than seeing things 'click' for students – when those who have been struggling have a lightbulb moment. It was a memorable lesson for me when a student who had fled their homeland (speaking no English) spoke in class for the first time. It was thrilling to hear them answer a question in halting English – they had grasped a concept and found the confidence to articulate it.

Perhaps Jesus felt this way in today's scripture, when the disciples he had walked and talked with finally recognised him. After Cleopas' narration of events in yesterday's reading, it's Jesus' turn to speak. He puts their fears in context, reminding them of everything scripture said about himself. Even as they received his teaching, they didn't recognise him, but, later in the passage, we find out that they had felt something stirring as he shared his message (verse 32).

At last, taking Jesus as a guest into their home and breaking bread with him (had they been present at the Last Supper and experienced this before?), their lightbulb moment finally came. I think I would have wished that Jesus had stayed around for longer; I would have had so many questions! But his brief presence with the two disciples is enough to spur them on to walk the seven miles between Jerusalem and Emmaus for the second time that day. They had seen the risen Lord and they simply had to tell others the good news.

† Lord, thank you for lightbulb moments when things feel dark. Thank you for revealing things about yourself afresh to me at the moments I need them most. Amen.

For further thought

What do you think triggered the disciples' recognition of Jesus at last? What do you need him to reveal about himself to you today?

24 April
The bringer of peace

Read Luke 24:36–43

While they were still talking about this, Jesus himself stood among them and said to them, 'Peace be with you.'

(verse 36)

Have you ever waited for something, spiritual or otherwise, lurching wildly between hope that it will work out and terror that it won't? When I found myself expecting a baby again after a stillbirth, I experienced this on a daily basis, especially as my due date approached. All signs pointed to a good outcome – a strong, healthy baby. But the doubts and fears kept rising, until the moment he was delivered safely into my arms.

I wonder if this was how the disciples were feeling here. Today's scripture depicts Cleopas and his companion, returning to Jerusalem to share the incredible news that they have encountered the risen Jesus. Until now, the waiting eleven had only had the word of the women and the ponderings of Peter to feed what little hope remained. Perhaps, like me, they swung between hope and fear.

Into this atmosphere, Jesus steps. The disciples' fear and uncertainty illustrate that they haven't yet dared to believe he is truly alive, instead fearing that the apparition they see before them is a ghost. I love what the disciples do next: 'They gave him a piece of broiled fish' (verse 43). Surely this is their statement of faith that, at last, they believe Jesus is who he says he is. As they offer, Jesus responds, eating the fish in their presence – all the confirmation they need that they can finally dare to believe all they had been promised was true.

His presence and his peace are enough to replace our fears and doubts with fresh hope and faith for all our circumstances and concerns.

† Lord, thank you that your presence and your peace change everything. Please bring both into my heart and mind today, stilling my troubled thoughts and restless soul. Amen.

For further thought

What helps you to feel God's presence and peace? Listening to worship? Getting outdoors? Something else? Make a point of doing that today.

A promised gift

Read Luke 24:44–49

I am going to send you what my Father has promised; but stay in the city until you have been clothed with power from on high.

(verse 49)

Have you ever experienced the excruciating wait for the delivery of an eagerly anticipated parcel? In the days of modern technology, we might be able to track our package on a phone app or online. But sometimes an unwelcome email arrives, announcing a rescheduled delivery, causing disappointment and frustration.

When my book was published, I was so excited about seeing it in print for the first time. I tore open a parcel, expecting it to be copies of the book, but it turned out to be the padded envelopes I had ordered to send out the book by post to kind purchasers. My son even videoed the unfortunate error!

God's timing for the delivery of his gifts and promises is never amiss though, and he never packages up the wrong thing. In today's scripture, Jesus gives the disciples the gift of understanding, at last, how everything he explained to them about himself is being fulfilled. He appoints them as witnesses to explain to others what they now grasp for themselves.

But the biggest gift for the disciples is yet to arrive and they must stay in the city to await it. Jesus explains that the Father is going to send 'power from on high' – the Holy Spirit – to strengthen and enable the disciples to face the daunting days ahead and share the good news of the resurrection far and wide.

As he sent his Holy Spirit to the disciples, so too he sends it to us, for our strengthening and enabling. It is a gift he will never fail to deliver.

† Lord, thank you that every good and perfect gift comes from you, the perfect giver. Please send the gift of your Holy Spirit to strengthen and empower me today. Amen.

For further thought
Spend some time today naming the many gifts God has given you in your lifetime and thanking him for them.

26 April
Awakened to his glory

Read Luke 9:28–36

Peter and his companions were very sleepy, but when they became fully awake, they saw his glory and the two men standing with him.

(verse 32)

We finish this week by rewinding back to a significant event that took place just before the final period before Jesus' death and resurrection – the transfiguration. Many Bible scholars see this as a preview of Jesus' resurrection glory.

Until now, the disciples had seen Jesus' walking, talking, eating, sleeping humanity. Of course, they had seen miracles and heard his bold claims, but here on a mountainside they catch a glimpse of his supernatural glory. I wonder if that extraordinary moment, in the midst of the ordinariness of their everyday lives, sustained them and drove them on when things looked bleak.

In the Old Testament, it was common for people to set up stones as altars to ensure they and the generations to come didn't forget key events in their lives with God. It may be that Peter is thinking of the Jewish Festival of Booths here when he suggests building shelters, but it is more likely that he is seeking a way of marking this extraordinary encounter. But this altar was not to be on the mountainside, but in Peter's heart to sustain him through his later trials.

I know, personally, I can point to moments like these, where I can clearly remember a supernatural encounter that strengthened me and spurred me on, even in the toughest of times. It is for those moments that I metaphorically build an altar in my heart, to sustain me through the ordinary times and to remind myself that what God has done before, he can do again, many times over. Jesus, the risen Son of God, walks among us and makes his power available to us, always.

† Lord, help me to recall times of supernatural encounter, miracles and breakthrough to sustain me in the ordinary days. And pour out your resurrection power afresh on me today, I pray. Amen.

For further thought

Spend some time revisiting old 'altars' today, thanking God for past encounters and breakthroughs and reaffirming that you trust him with your future.

Trees

1 Trees for life

Notes by **Catherine Williams**

Catherine Williams is an Anglican priest who works as a freelance spiritual director, retreat conductor and writer. She writes biblical reflections for a variety of publications and is the lead voice on the Church of England's Daily Prayer App. Catherine lives on the Sandringham Estate in Norfolk, where her husband Paul is Domestic Chaplain to the Royal Household. Catherine enjoys reading, singing, theatre, cinema and poetry for leisure. She keeps chickens and is passionate about butterfly conservation. Catherine has used the NRSVA for these notes.

27 April
Trees

Read Genesis 2:8–10

Out of the ground the Lᴏʀᴅ God made to grow every tree that is pleasant to the sight and good for food, the tree of life also in the midst of the garden, and the tree of the knowledge of good and evil.

(verse 9)

Today we begin a two-week forage through scriptural passages relating to trees. Climate change and deep concern for our planet have led to the rediscovery of the significance of trees for well-being. Trees, rooted deeply in the ground, stretch their branches to the sky, symbolic of the connection between earth and heaven. Trees reside in one place communicating underground through networks of roots and symbiotic relationships with fungi, nurturing their own young while providing shelter for other plants, birds and animals. Trees absorb carbon dioxide and produce oxygen, lowering the air temperature and cleaning the atmosphere. Planting trees makes a big difference to our world.

In our passage today we read that trees, created by God on the third day, provide food and give pleasure. Joy comes from spending time with 'The Standing People', as Native Americans call them. In the middle of Eden, God placed the tree of life and the tree of the knowledge of good and evil. Both have a part to play in the faith journey of our forebears, both away from God and back into loving relationship. So, in this next fortnight, let's be open and curious to all that God wishes to teach us about trees.

† Lord God, thank you for your gift of trees. Open my eyes to all that they teach me of you. Encourage me to love and to respect your creation.

28 April
Rooted in living water

Read Psalm 1

Happy are those who do not follow the advice of the wicked ... but their delight is in the law of the Lord, and on his law they meditate day and night. They are like trees planted by streams of water, which yield their fruit in its season, and their leaves do not wither.

(verses 1–3)

In my childhood, my Auntie Iris lived in a small stone cottage in deepest rural Devon in the south-west of England. Her garden was vast and wild. It included a small wood through which ran a lively stream. My family spent many long summers having adventures in this wild outdoor space, so different from the busy, noisy town we lived in. For me, Psalm 1 always brings to mind happy memories of sitting amongst the trees on the bank of the stream on a hot summer's day dangling our feet in the cool water. Sometimes the sticklebacks would nibble our toes, and once we watched in silent awe as an otter played in the waters in front of us.

Psalm 1 opens the Psalter with the word 'happy'. This happiness is a state of ongoing contentment that comes from engaging deeply and continuously with the law of the Lord. The Law (Torah) is found in the first five books of the Hebrew Bible. For Christians, this Law becomes incarnate in Jesus: God with us. Deep engagement with God promises fruitfulness and well-being through all seasons and down the generations. Delighting in Jesus is like the psalm's image of trees that are rooted beside plentiful fresh water, or children who find adventure, liberation and wholeness in the natural world. As well-watered, healthy trees give many and varied blessings to the environment, so Christians firmly rooted in God, filled with the living water of Jesus and alive to the Spirit's guidance, are a blessing to all around. Are you delighting in Jesus? Have you found the happiness that the psalmist speaks of?

† Lord, root me deeply in your living water so that as your disciple and witness I may be happy, blessed and fruitful.

For further thought

Take a walk alongside a river or look at a picture of flowing water. How do you experience God in this place?

April

Trees – 1 Trees for life

An abundance of trees

Read Ezekiel 47:6b–12

On the banks, on both sides of the river, there will grow all kinds of trees for food. Their leaves will not wither nor their fruit fail, but they will bear fresh fruit every month because the water for them flows from the sanctuary. Their fruit will be for food, and their leaves for healing.

(verse 12)

In Ezekiel's vision, the water flowing from the Jerusalem Temple's sanctuary will be life-giving and abundant. Starting shallow, it will continually deepen until everything in its path is drenched and overwhelmed with life. Stagnant waters will become fresh and teem with life so that fishing will be a plentiful employment. It's not just any region that this water flows into, but the low-lying Arabah that leads to the Dead Sea, the lowest place on earth, in whose waters nothing can survive. All along the banks of this mighty living waterway will be trees, so abundant, diverse and healthy that there will be a constant supply of leaves for healing and fruit to eat. It will be a return to the Garden of Eden. Here is a vision of God renewing the land, bringing the dead back to life, just as in Ezekiel's earlier vision of the valley of dry bones (37:1–10).

This is no impossible dream. We see God acting to bring the dead to life in Lazarus (John 11) and then in Jesus himself, who is the first fruit of the resurrection – the new life in God which is open to all. Part of this new creation foreseen by Ezekiel celebrates the important role of trees in our world. Trees are essential for human life and flourishing. They remove pollution, improve air quality and generate life-sustaining oxygen. They are a source of food, medicine and shelter. Reforestation is one of the ways to combat climate change and renew our dying planet. Planting trees enables God's life-giving water to flow.

† Lord, help us to make Ezekiel's vision of a renewed earth a reality in our time. Show us ways to bring your living water to our needy world.

For further thought

Resolve to plant a tree or make a donation to a charity dedicated to reforestation.

30 April
Forest-bathing

Read Isaiah 41:17–20

*I will put in the wilderness the cedar, the acacia, the myrtle, and
the olive; I will set in the desert the cypress, the plane and the
pine together, so that all may see and know, all may consider and
understand, that the hand of the LORD has done this …*

(verses 19–20)

Forest-bathing has become a popular practice recently in the UK.
During the Covid-19 pandemic, many people reconnected with
the natural world through daily walks. Spending time in wooded
areas amongst a variety of trees, plants and animals is very good
for our well-being. It enables us to reconnect with our place in the
natural world and God's incredible creation. Recently relocated
to a rectory in the middle of a forest, I am both astonished and
delighted by the way a daily walk amongst trees has enhanced my
experience of God's loving presence and provision.

In today's passage, the writer of Isaiah assures the people of
Israel exiled in Babylon that God has not abandoned them. God
will answer their cries and bring life to their wilderness experiences.
The imagery is lively and refreshing. From pools of fresh clear
water and life-giving streams in the desert, an abundance of trees
will spring up. Not fruit trees for sustenance this time but trees
that will provide shelter, shade and protection on the long journey
home. It's a fortifying and much-needed promise given to a people
far from home, weary and in need.

Seven trees are mentioned in our passage. Seven is a holy
number, so these trees represent God's divine presence and
provision. Some of these trees are used in the Temple: cedar and
cypress for its construction and acacia wood for the Ark of the
Covenant containing the Ten Commandments. Notice too the
diversity of the trees – large and small, evergreen and deciduous.
God's loving presence and provision are abundant and diverse.

† Lord, as you promised to lead your people out of exile by secure and sheltered
paths, so provide for and protect your Church today and lead her to abundant and
fruitful living.

For further thought

If possible, take a walk in a wooded area. Be attentive to the trees
around you. How do they speak of God's presence and provision?

1 May
Leadership: the cedar and the cross

Read Ezekiel 31:3–9

Consider Assyria, a cedar of Lebanon, with fair branches and forest shade ... All the birds of the air made their nests in its boughs; under its branches all the animals of the field gave birth to their young; and in its shade, all great nations lived.

(verses 3a, 6)

The image of a great tree has long been used to describe a significant leader, a monarch or an empire. Ezekiel likens the mighty empire of Assyria to a cedar of Lebanon, the largest tree he had encountered. Today we might use the massive ancient sequoia or redwood in America and China as an example of power, longevity and strength.

Ezekiel's description is not just about Assyrian power. The tree is strong and beautiful because its roots go deeply into the waters below enabling it to grow tall with large boughs and long branches. These in turn provide shade and shelter to the birds that nest there and the animals that find there a safe place to birth and raise their young. Great nations too find it a place of protection and security. The tree is a benign and protecting presence enabling all to flourish. With significant position and great power comes serious and considerable responsibility for the well-being of others.

There is much to note here for those in positions of leadership, whether in the Church, the local community or the world. Leaders need to be deeply rooted in life-giving water – that which sustains and enables them to grow. For the Christian leader that living water is Jesus, who shapes and defines leadership by his willingness not only to provide and protect but also to serve and ultimately to sacrifice himself. It is not the mighty cedar tree that symbolises the leadership of Jesus but the humble cross, a broken tree that enables the salvation of the world.

† Lord Jesus, teach me your serving and sacrificial model of leadership. Help me to exercise any power I have wisely and well.

For further thought
What models of leadership can you see being exercised around you? What leadership lessons might we all learn from the cedar and the cross?

May

Trees – 1 Trees for life

The scent of water

> ## Read Job 14:7–9
>
> *For there is hope for a tree, if it is cut down, that it will sprout again, and that its shoots will not cease. Though its root grows old in the earth, and its stump dies in the ground, yet at the scent of water it will bud and put forth branches like a young plant.*
>
> (verses 7–9)

I recently visited the church of St Melangell in the Welsh Berwyn Mountains. Melangell – a seventh-century Irish princess – is the patron saint of hares, which she is said to protect. The beautiful church and shrine are set in an ancient grove of yew trees, some of which are 2,000 years old. The trees have huge circumferences and are hollow inside. When the centre of the tree decays it renews itself by sending out runners which plant new saplings so that each tree is in effect a colony of relatives – watered by a natural spring and nourished by fungi living inside the trunk and around the roots. Despite being ancient, the trees are strong and vigorous commanding considerable awe and respect. Living on a different timescale from us there is something mysterious and holy about them: they have seen and survived so much.

Job, besieged by all manner of disasters, is pondering the fragility of human existence. People's lives, it seems to him, are fleeting, frail and full of trouble. Job struggles to understand why God should care about people when their lives are short and death is the end. In contrast, he recognises that trees are hard-wired to hope. When a tree ages or is cut down it can renew itself. Just the scent of water will enable it to sprout and regenerate. With the hindsight of the life, death and resurrection of Jesus, Christians are hard-wired to hope too – like trees. We are assured that Christ's resurrection leads to the possibility of eternal life for all. This is our scent of water.

† Lord, thank you for your promise of eternal life made possible through Jesus. Help me to trust in this promise and live each moment with commitment and joy.

For further thought

What part does hope play in your life as a disciple of Jesus?

3 May
The tree of life

Read Revelation 22:1–5

On either side of the river is the tree of life with its twelve kinds of fruit, producing its fruit each month; and the leaves of the tree are for the healing of the nations.

(verse 2)

Ending this week, we have come full circle back to the tree of life. We began our exploration with the tree of life in the middle of the Garden of Eden. A few days ago we enjoyed Ezekiel's vision of the water of life flowing from the Temple producing an abundance of trees. Now in the book of Revelation, a final vision reveals these trees as the tree of life restored and multiplied. The tree of life grows on both sides of the river – perhaps it is now a colony, like the yew trees we explored yesterday. Here is a vision of paradise regained. The garden has become a city full of the life and light of God. All nations flock to the city of God, and the tree of life produces abundant monthly fruit and leaves that heal division and enmity.

Have you noticed before how the tree of life begins and ends the Bible? The tree of life – sometimes identified as the cosmic tree, world tree or sacred tree – is a potent and positive symbol for many faiths and cultures. With a variety of spiritual meanings that point to the harmony, balance and well-being of creation, and the linking of heaven and earth, it transcends time and is a symbol of longevity, wisdom and strength. For Christians, the tree of life analogy finds its deepest fruition in Jesus Christ. Not only does the cross represent the tree of life, it represents Christ himself. The one who feeds, heals, restores, protects and saves is for all of us the eternal tree of life.

† Lord Jesus, may the tree of life remind us of your presence in all things. Be for us one who feeds, heals, restores, protects and saves.

For further thought

Find or make a picture of the tree of life that resonates with you. Use it in a creative way to enhance your prayer life.

Trees

2 The trees of the field

Notes by **Catherine Williams**

You can read Catherine's biography on 27 April. Catherine has used the NRSVA for these notes.

4 May
Under the vines and fig trees

> **Read Micah 4:1–4**
>
> *...they shall beat their swords into ploughshares, and their spears into pruning-hooks; nation shall not lift up sword against nation, neither shall they learn war anymore; but they shall all sit under their own vines and under their own fig trees, and no one shall make them afraid.*
>
> (verses 3b–4)

Abundant throughout the Middle East, vines and figs have been symbolic in Middle Eastern, Greek and Roman cultures since ancient times, where they represent prosperity, well-being, joy, wisdom, knowledge and sensual love. Figs were a sacred food for the Egyptians, whilst the Romans connected grapes to Bacchus the God of wine.

Vines and fig trees are potent symbols in the Hebrew and Christian scriptures. Both came to symbolise the health of the house of Israel. Jesus used the analogy of the vine and the fig tree regularly in his teachings, as examples of community, growth and fruitfulness. In today's passage, Micah looks to a time when everyone will respond to the reign of God and live in peace and harmony with their neighbours. Weapons will be refashioned into tools to aid productivity and no one will need to learn how to fight. Everyone will have their own vine and fig tree to sit under in freedom, peace and safety. Where do you feel most relaxed, secure and peaceful? What constitutes your own vine and fig tree?

† Thank you, Lord, for Micah's vision of a future without war. Bring peace to the war-torn and hurting places of our world. May each person live in safety, free from fear and oppression.

For further thought

How is conflict handled in your church and community? What more can you do to encourage peace in your neighbourhood?

5 May
Grapes, thorns, figs and thistles

Read Matthew 7:16–20

You will know them by their fruits. Are grapes gathered from thorns, or figs from thistles? In the same way, every good tree bears good fruit, but the bad tree bears bad fruit. A good tree cannot bear bad fruit, nor can a bad tree bear good fruit.

(verses 16–18)

Continuing the analogy of vines and fig trees, today's passage, which comes at the end of the Sermon on the Mount, finds Jesus drawing on their fruit – grapes and figs – to warn his disciples about false prophets. How do we tell which people speak the truth of God and which are waiting to lead us astray? False prophets can be very plausible, seemingly trustworthy, reasonable and kind. Jesus encourages us to look at the fruit of a person's life not just listen to their words. A good tree will produce good fruit and a bad tree bad fruit. Put like that it sounds straightforward.

In the garden of our new rectory, there are several elderly fruit trees: apples, pears, plums and quince. It's too exposed where we live for vines or figs. All the trees have produced fruit this year: some healthy and delicious, some sadly diseased and rotten. It wasn't possible to tell from looking at each tree whether it would bear good fruit or not – we had to wait to see what was produced. The healthy trees we will continue to nurture and cultivate, the less good trees we will cut right back to encourage healthy growth. Sadly, the most diseased trees will have to go.

As a disciple of Jesus are your words and actions consistent with the new life that he brings? Are you producing attractive healthy fruit that shows you are well tended by the word of God? Do your words and behaviour lead people to Jesus, or turn them away?

† Lord Jesus, tend my life so that it bears good fruit and draws many to you.

For further thought

Take some time to identify the good fruit that God is growing in your life. How are you using this fruit to encourage others into the kingdom?

6 May
Nesting space

Read Matthew 13:31–32

The kingdom of heaven is like a mustard seed that someone took and sowed in his field; it is the smallest of all the seeds, but when it has grown it is the greatest of shrubs and becomes a tree, so that the birds of the air come and make nests in its branches.

(verses 31b–32)

Sometimes when we see the state of the world, and all the problems that are around us in our communities, we can feel very small and useless. We ask ourselves: 'What difference can I possibly make?' Jesus' parable of the mustard seed speaks to that scenario. The mustard seed is tiny – barely perceptible – yet it becomes the greatest of shrubs, says Jesus. Humble beginnings can lead to extraordinary conclusions. Faced with the mighty Roman empire, the infant Church must have felt minuscule – but look what happened. Two thousand years on, the Christian Church has spread throughout the world and continues to grow. From a handful of disciples has come a worldwide faith. So don't give up! You never know how the kingdom may ripple out and grow from your little faith, your desire to serve and your small acts inspired by the living God.

Jesus says the tiny mustard seed will become a shrub and then a tree in which the birds will find a safe space to nest and raise their young. Have you ever seen a mustard tree? I don't think such a thing exists! Mustard is definitely a shrub, not a tree. Perhaps Jesus is saying that with God all things are possible and the growth that God gives is beyond both our imagination and the limits of the natural world. So next time you are feeling small and insignificant remember that from tiny hidden things, God can do the impossible. Not only that: your words and works in God's name will enable others to grow and thrive too.

† Lord Jesus, when I think I have almost nothing to offer, remind me that God can bring remarkable growth from very little.

For further thought

Find a small venture or charity that is producing significant good for others. Thank God for this work and support it in some way.

All creation rejoices

Read Isaiah 55:12–13

For you shall go out in joy, and be led back in peace; the mountains and the hills before you shall burst into song, and all the trees of the field shall clap their hands.

(verse 12)

In our passage today from Isaiah, the prophet looks to a time when God's people will be freed from exile in Babylon and return home to Jerusalem. This homecoming will be a cause of great rejoicing – not just from the house of Israel but from the whole of creation. The people will be filled with joy and their return will be marked by peace. As they make their journey the landscape will sing, and the trees will clap. Weeds and thorny bushes that hinder the journey will be replaced by stately and gracious trees as the landscape is transformed in celebration of God's everlasting love and commitment. It's a beautiful poetic vision for a restored future guaranteed to give hope to weary souls far from home.

The writer has given the mountains and trees human characteristics. The landscape doesn't have a human voice and trees don't have hands. However, you only have to walk in a forest in stormy weather to know that trees can make a lot of noise when animated by the wind! It is a feature of our faith that the non-human creation has its own relationship with the living God. Nature praises its Creator and groans as it waits for God's redemption (Romans 8:22–23). Jesus curses the fig tree that doesn't bear fruit when the Messiah needs it (Matthew 21:18–19) and reminds us that even if we forget to worship, the rocks will cry out to God (Luke 19:40). As you worship the Lord in whatever way works best for you, imagine creation worshipping in its way alongside you.

† Thank you, Lord, that in your precious name, I am set free and brought home. Help me to see all creation rejoicing with me.

For further thought

Go for a walk outside or spend time looking out of a window. In what ways can you see creation praising God?

Jesus Christ the apple tree

Read Song of Solomon 2:1–5

As an apple tree among the trees of the wood, so is my beloved among young men. With great delight I sat in his shadow, and his fruit was sweet to my taste.

(verse 3)

The Song of Solomon in the Hebrew Bible is a beautiful dialogue between the lover and his beloved. Christians have long identified the lover as Jesus, and the beloved as his bride the Church, the body of Christ to which each of us belongs. In today's passage, which is filled with references to flowers, trees and fruit, the beloved likens her lover to an apple tree in whose shade she is delighted to sit. She tastes the delicious fruit and is sustained and refreshed. It's a beautiful and potent image of love, protection, nurture and fruitfulness.

When we see the apple tree in Song of Solomon as a metaphor for Jesus the imagery takes on new spiritual depth and richness. Jesus is the one who stands out above all others. He is the one in whose shadow we can rest secure. We are fed, sustained and refreshed by his body and blood in the Eucharist. His sacrificial love for us on the cross – the tree of life – ensures that we will make our home with him for eternity.

In eighteenth-century England, Richard Hutchins wrote a poem called 'Jesus Christ the Apple Tree' inspired by this passage. There are over 2,500 varieties of apple in England and it's thought the poem was written to Christianise ancient wassailing ceremonies which wished health and fertility to apple trees in orchards on Christmas Eve. Set to music, the poem has become a popular Christmas carol. It's a lovely example of how scripture is living and active, shining the light of Christ creatively in surprising places.

† Use these words from the poem in prayer: 'I'm weary with my former toil / Here I will sit and rest awhile / Under the shadow I will be / Of Jesus Christ the Apple Tree' ('Jesus Christ the Apple Tree', ascribed to the Revd Richard Hutchins, 1761).

For further thought

Find a copy of the poem 'Jesus Christ the Apple Tree' or listen to the carol. What is God saying to you through these words?

Grafted in

> **Read Romans 11:17–25**
>
> *But if some of the branches were broken off, and you, a wild olive shoot, were grafted in their place to share the rich root of the olive tree, do not vaunt yourselves over the branches. If you do vaunt yourselves, remember that it is not you that support the root, but the root that supports you.*
>
> (verses 17–18)

Olive trees grow abundantly throughout the Mediterranean and Middle East. Olives are strong and hardy trees which can live for thousands of years. Some are cultivated, some are wild. In this passage, Paul is writing to the early Church in Rome and shows how the gentile Christians have been grafted into the rootstock to become part of the same tree as those Christians with Jewish heritage. Grafting is a process by which one tree is encouraged to bond with another, growing together to produce a healthier specimen. It encourages both strength and fruitfulness as the energy from one tree is tied to the strength of another. It's a skilful process which takes time and expertise. Paul knows this and reminds the Roman Christians that they and others within the body of Christ are equal – one is not better than another. Both draw from the same source – Jesus Christ.

One of the most exciting features of Christian churches is the variety of believers they attract. People worship together who might never meet or interact in secular situations. This can have its ups and downs as we all learn to be disciples together within the body. Bringing together different ethnicities, genders and ages makes for a strong and diverse community with many gifts that enhance the body of Christ. Like the grafting process, growing such a community takes time and skill, and it doesn't always work. Reminding ourselves that all members are equal in the body of Christ and there is room for everyone helps to grow a vigorous, fruitful and resilient Christian community.

† Thank you, Lord Jesus, for your body, the Church. Help me to take my place with openness and grace.

For further thought

Think about the church or fellowship you attend. Who needs to be grafted in to make this community more diverse and fruitful?

10 May
Oaks of righteousness

Read Isaiah 61:1–3

They will be called oaks of righteousness, the planting of the LORD, to display his glory.

(verse 3b)

The iconic oak tree is solid, sturdy and hardy. Its deep system of roots draws over fifty gallons of water each day from the earth ensuring that it can withstand adverse weather, storms – even hurricanes. A mature oak can absorb a tonne of carbon dioxide every six years – enabling us all to breathe easier. Oaks are a symbol of utter reliability. Houses, roofs, panelling, flooring, furniture, ships and barrels made of oak are long-lasting and able to withstand considerable wear and tear. Some of our most famous trees in the UK are ancient oaks, dating back hundreds of years. Some even have names: 'Cathedral', 'Gog and Magog', 'Old Knobbly'. They are individuals – silently standing and witnessing all manner of events down the centuries. Our Celtic forebears saw these trees as mystical bearers of wisdom. Sentinels in the landscape, they live on a different timescale from humans and animals.

The prophet Isaiah recognises God's anointing Spirit, who brings good news, freedom, restoration and comfort. The promise is that those who have been dispossessed of the land will become oaks of righteousness. Sturdy trees planted by the Lord: solid, resilient and timeless. This is the passage read by Jesus in the synagogue in Nazareth and applied to himself (Luke 4:16–19). Jesus is the good news that brings salvation. Through him, we can move from being broken, grieving and captive, to standing tall and confident – drawing deeply on God's love and enabling those around us to live more fully. Faithful Christian communities rooted in Christ and full of the Holy Spirit are like mighty oaks, displaying God's glory.

† Lord, grant me a fresh anointing of your Spirit. Heal my brokenness and grief. Set me free to be an oak of righteousness, planted for your glory.

For further thought

Think back through the past fortnight. What have you heard God say through these reflections on trees? What is your response to God?

Readings in Joshua

1 Into the promised land

Notes by **Andy Heald**

Andy is a communications, marketing and fundraising consultant, and has led fruitful young adult, small group and family ministries. Lifelong pilgrims, now living in Scotland, in 2019 he, his wife and three daughters travelled through Europe in a motorhome exploring God's principles of faith, freedom and family and living differently from the world. Their ministry is to introduce a fatherless generation to their heavenly Father. Discover their adventures at www.adifferentway.org.uk. Andy has used the NIVUK for these notes.

11 May
Promises, promises

Read Joshua 1

...you and all these people, get ready to cross the River Jordan ... I will never leave you nor forsake you. Be strong and courageous, because you will lead these people to inherit the land I swore to their ancestors to give them.

(verses 2a, 5b–6)

God's pledge of the promised land to the Israelites was a landmark step in the restoration of their relationship with him, providing a base from which Israel could bless the nations. Exiled from Eden, all God's children became separated from their Father. Out of love, God initiated his covenant of restoration to Abraham (Genesis 12, 15 and 17) and, following the former generation's rebellion, Joshua picks up the mantle to lead God's people to their promised land.

Yet, this place is more than a place to belong; it is a foretaste of the new creation, where God will dwell with his people (Revelation 21:3). This is the promise that we share in, of our complete restoration as children of God. But for now, humanity lives in exile, banished from eternity and the fullness of God's presence by sin.

I wonder how Joshua felt when God commissioned him as leader? God knew that the way ahead would be scary, repeatedly telling Joshua to be strong and courageous, and promising his presence wherever he went. Embracing God's promise of eternal life can be scary, but we too have God with us – his Holy Spirit to guide and comfort us.

† Jesus, help us to be strong and courageous as we repent, believe and follow you, to receive your promise of life in your eternal kingdom.

12 May
Look before you leap

Read Joshua 2

I know that the LORD has given this land to you and that a great fear of you has fallen on us, so that all who live in this country are melting in fear because of you.

(verse 9)

Are you the kind of person who jumps straight into an activity or do you need to think about it first? I am definitely the latter, needing to consider the consequences, resources – even if it's worth doing at all! Therefore, I value the practice of sending spies ahead, to check out the dangers, obstacles, fruit and treasure of the land. I'm keen to peer over the fence before leaping over it.

Jericho was a walled, well-defended city: a hard target for the Israelites, standing in the way of them possessing their promised land. Joshua recognised the benefits of reconnaissance; after all, he had spied on this land a generation ago. But this story doesn't reveal anything about Jericho's defences. Instead, the spies learn from Rahab that the people of Jericho are terrified, knowing that God goes with the Israelites and he has given the land to them. In contrast, when Joshua spied on the promised land, he wasn't afraid. Because he knew that God was with the Israelites, and they would devour the giants.

On our journey of faith, we can come up against an obstacle like Jericho that seems insurmountable and frightening. Looking before leaping can help prepare us for the faith challenge ahead but trusting in God is the key to overcoming it. God invites – commands – us to live by faith, not by sight. Joshua's long-held belief that God was with them was affirmed by Rahab's testimony. When we believe God is with us, we can trust in him with all our heart and lean not on our own understanding, obediently following where he leads.

† Lord, as we move towards the promised land of eternal life and encounter impenetrable walls, help us to see by faith, beyond human vision, and obediently trust in you.

For further thought

Has God ever invited you to move into a 'promised land' in your life? Did you need to take steps in faith? Has God provided unexpected help, like he did through Rahab, when you've needed it?

13 May

When God is with you, expect to be amazed!

Read Joshua 3

This is how you will know that the living God is among you ... as the priests who carry the ark of the Lord – the Lord of all the earth – set foot in the Jordan, its waters flowing downstream will be cut off ...

(verses 10a, 13b)

Recently, my wife was offered a job in Scotland, 600 miles away. Eighteen months previously, we'd felt God telling us to move there but in that time had found nowhere to live. Despite this, she accepted the job, believing that if God wanted our family there, he would make a way. So we prayed. Just weeks before her start date, about to become homeless, a friend messaged – someone we didn't know was moving out of her home for a month to get us started. It was enough, so we stepped out in faith and moved.

Most of the Israelites would have only heard stories of God parting the Red Sea, yet they followed Joshua's command, as he followed God's. There might not have been an Egyptian army bearing down on them, but this time, the Israelites had to step into the water before it would stop flowing. What's more, God created a path through the river directly opposite their destination, Jericho, whose already fearful inhabitants may well have watched this miracle.

I think it's unlikely that many of us will see a sea or river part as they did, but God still requires us to follow him obediently, which can mean encountering war zones (metaphorical or real), barren places or immovable objects. Yet the Israelites' story is our history, from which we can draw strength and encouragement. When God asks us to move into hard places, we must trust that he will do the amazing things that are outside our control and understanding, and which reveal his presence with us.

† Father, help us follow you obediently into hard places, trusting you to make the way, when we perceive there is no way. Help us expect to see your amazing works when you go with us.

For further thought

Have you ever been told by God to move somewhere difficult or undertake a seemingly impossible task? Did he do amazing things? Was it also a witness to others of his power and glory?

The promise for a new generation

Read Joshua 4:1 – 5:1

He said to the Israelites, 'In the future when your descendants ask their parents, "What do these stones mean?" tell them, "Israel crossed the Jordan on dry ground." For the LORD your God dried up the Jordan before you until you had crossed over.'

(4:21–22, 23a)

After Joshua's death, another generation grew up that knew neither the Lord nor what he had done for Israel (Judges 2:8–10). Can you believe that? The generation that left the wilderness dwelt with God and knew he had parted the Red Sea, yet the generation that followed them had no idea that he had held back the Jordan's flow and crossed with them, to give them their promised land.

When we are gone, how will others know about the works of God in our lives? I grew up hearing who God was, but not about who God is; I didn't hear testimonies of what he does in people's lives today, so I felt him to be distant and irrelevant; I walked away from him. I made many bad life choices, yet he revealed himself to me (even though I did not seek him) and transformed my life. He freed me from addiction, restored me from the pain of abuse and, most importantly, saved me into eternal life.

As the writers of Psalms 78 and 145 did, I want my children to know who God is and what he's done for me. I hope they will place their faith in him. We move around too often to have 'stones' as a memory aid, so we regularly share stories about the mighty works he has done in each of our lives. Telling others about God is a command (Matthew 28:19–20) but it should be a desire and a delight, yet somehow we can easily forget. How do you remember God and what he's done for you?

† Jesus, thank you for the mighty works you have done in our lives, rescuing and restoring us. Help us never to forget your sacrifice and love. Inspire us to tell these stories to the coming generation.

For further thought

Jesus gave us the practice of communion to remember him and what he's done for us. Why not have a meal with friends and talk about what God has done for you in your life?

15 May
A sign of God's promise

Read Joshua 5:2–15

And after the whole nation had been circumcised, they remained where they were in camp until they were healed. Then the LORD said to Joshua, 'Today I have rolled away the reproach of Egypt from you.' So the place has been called Gilgal to this day.

(verses 8–9)

This is perhaps the most significant moment in the Israelites' approach to their inheritance, the land that God had repeatedly promised them. Circumcision was a sign of God's covenant, first given to Abram, that the land of Canaan would be an everlasting possession for him and his descendants and, more importantly, that God would be their God. This outward sign was to be an everlasting covenant, and every male was to be circumcised in the flesh – any who weren't were considered to have broken God's covenant. The sons raised in the wilderness who had not been circumcised following the disobedience of the generation of their forebears bore the shame of that disobedience and lack of trust in God. Until now.

God cleansed them. He wiped away the shame of their past, doing what they could not do – make themselves right in his sight by their own merit. He restored them to the covenant and their inheritance. On our journey of faith, we too need cleansing to enter the promised land of salvation. Only in the new covenant of Jesus' blood, where he is the sacrifice, are we cleansed when we are born again, of the Spirit. We, in Christ, are a new creation (2 Corinthians 5:17), no longer condemned for our sins, or those of our fathers!

Circumcision was the sign of the covenant for the Israelites – but what is our outward sign? Perhaps it is the new commandment Jesus gave, to love one another as he has loved us – then others will know that we are his followers (John 13:34–35) and that he is our God.

† Jesus, thank you that your death for our sins washes our guilt away so we can receive the promise of living in eternity with you. Help us to live in the Spirit, as new creations.

For further thought

How do you display the signs of God's promise in your life? Think and pray about the ways in which Jesus loves you, and ask him to help you show that same love to others.

16 May
Destroying strongholds

> **Read Joshua 6:1–14**
>
> *See, I have delivered Jericho into your hands ... When you hear them sound a long blast on the trumpets, make the whole army give a loud shout; then the wall of the city will collapse and the army will go up, everyone straight in.*
>
> (verses 2b, 5)

When I first believed that God existed and started going to church, my life was messy. I struggled with severe anxiety and (in part consequently) alcohol and drug dependencies, as well as other worldly issues. I was accepted by the family of God but there were some powerful strongholds of sin in my life that needed destroying, and brokenness that needed healing. Two years later, having learnt about Jesus, I made a commitment to follow him. The day after my water baptism, I was miraculously healed from my drug dependency and my addiction to cigarettes – I simply couldn't smoke anything any more! Praise God! Nothing I had tried previously had freed me of these chains – only God, in his power and grace, broke them for me.

Joshua had a powerful army, thousands of experienced soldiers, and yet God revealed his unimaginable power, commanding them not to attempt breaching the walls using their own strength. The defeat of Jericho required them to obediently trust in God, as we must on our journey towards eternity. Deciding to follow Jesus does not always remove the fractured areas of our lives. We may enter the 'promised land' as a new creation on this earth but there are still battles to fight, obstacles to overcome, strongholds of sinfulness and worldliness that need destroying, or brokenness that needs healing – things that we cannot do on our own. But we don't have to. We have the Holy Spirit of God dwelling within us. We need to be obedient to his leadership, humbly trusting his authority and power over our limited knowledge, strength and experience.

† King Jesus, search our hearts and know our thoughts, reveal in us any strongholds of sin and worldliness in us. Help us to be obedient to your command, and draw us closer to you.

For further thought

'Be still, and know that I am God.' 'The LORD Almighty is with us; the God of Jacob is our fortress.' Pray through Psalm 46 to acknowledge God's power over any strongholds in your life.

17 May
Wholly faithful promise-keeping

Read Joshua 6:15–27

But keep away from the devoted things, so that you will not bring about your own destruction by taking any of them. Otherwise, you will make the camp of Israel liable to destruction and bring trouble on it.

(verse 18)

'I promise to be good.' This phrase often follows an act of disobedience. I've said it, as have my children – yet, sadly, it's a promise we fail to keep. God's standard for goodness is complete obedience, a standard no one but Jesus can meet.

When God commissions Joshua, he instructs him to 'be careful to obey all the law my servant Moses gave you' (Joshua 1:7), advising him that then he will be prosperous and successful. We don't get to pick and choose the commands we want to obey; God's complete and perfect law sets out the standard for goodness – because God knows what's good for us. Whenever we disobediently choose our will over his, we sin, revealing our inability to be righteous. Not long after committing my life to Jesus, I faced hard times. To alleviate the pain, thinking I knew best, I turned not to God but to my trusted 'medicinal' dependencies ... and my life fell apart.

Our entry to the promised land of God's kingdom is only in part. We remain sinful, broken children, justified but not fully restored. Our sin reveals the need for salvation; our inability to be fully obedient to God's commands reveals our need for a saviour. With help, I did reach out to Jesus, and was mercifully rescued once again. Our individual life stories differ but we all fall short, yet our God is faithful, keeping his promises (Deuteronomy 7:9), even when we break ours. We must endure, believing in Christ as our Saviour until we worship him in the fullness of his promised kingdom, dwelling with him forever.

† Thank you, Lord Jesus, for dying on the cross to save us from our sins. Help us to place our faith in you each day and experience your kingdom now, and forever. Amen.

For further thought

Are there areas of your life where you know you have disobeyed God and need to confess and repent? Remember, he loves us and forgives all of our sins when we believe in him.

Readings in Joshua – 1 Into the promised land

Readings in Joshua

2 Living in the land

Notes by **David Painting**

David's passion is to see people encounter God more profoundly. A science graduate, David has held senior roles in industry and commerce alongside a pastoral ministry in Baptist churches in the UK. Having spent time in YWAM leading and teaching on Discipleship Training Schools in the UK and overseas, he currently divides his time between software development, co-leading a house church, teaching and writing. David enjoys being a grandfather and all things related to space. He is excited to be Editor of *Fresh from The Word*. David has used the NRSVUE version for these notes.

18 May
Representing God

Read Joshua 7:1–15

Proceed to sanctify the people and say, 'Sanctify yourselves for tomorrow, for thus says the LORD, the God of Israel: There are devoted things among you, O Israel; you will be unable to stand before your enemies until you take away the devoted things from among you.'

(verse 13)

Joshua, a former spy, sends out spies to Ai to assess what is needed to win in this first battle in the process of taking the land. But victory in the kingdom of God is not won by an assessment of relative strengths; it is never by might or power, but by the Spirit of God. You cannot build the kingdom of God unless you act as the King would.

And so, the people have been told not to plunder – the point is to inhabit the land in such a way as to be a witness to who God is. But Achan doesn't know God, doesn't love him or his ways, and in keeping the items for himself, he misrepresents God. This is the heart of the sin, misrepresenting who God is, to us and to others, coming as a usurper, a conqueror rather than as Jesus would – humbly, lovingly, laying aside his rights.

Now God cannot associate himself with their actions – he cannot, by giving them victory, imply that he endorses their view of him or their approach. And so, they are defeated, not because they had too few men in the battle, but because they had too little love for who God is.

† Help us to come humbly, laying aside our agenda in order to serve and to love.

19 May
The wages of sin

Read Joshua 7:16–26

So Joshua rose early in the morning and brought Israel near tribe by tribe, and the tribe of Judah was taken. He brought near the clans of Judah, and the clan of the Zerahites was taken, and he brought near the clan of the Zerahites by households, and Zabdi was taken.

(verses 16–17)

Have you ever been in a situation where disaster was impending, but you didn't move, convinced until too late that somehow it would avoid you? I remember standing on the beach in Romania where I was teaching. The evidence was that the tide was coming in, that the route back to higher ground was becoming narrower. Yet still I stayed, somehow convinced that the tide was going out and that these last few waves were an anomaly. Too late I became convinced of my error, resulting in me giving the next talk dripping wet …

I wonder if Achan was similar? Even when their tribe had been identified, even when their clan had been singled out, still Achan didn't come forward. Did he hope, even at that last point, that God didn't know or wouldn't expose his sin?

Acknowledging our sin does not lead to death; it leads to life! Genuine confession evokes God's mercy and forgiveness (1 John 1:8–9). It is our unwillingness to own our sin that ultimately leads to death – in our reading, people physically died as a result of their sin. In other situations we encounter, we also experience death as a result of our sin. Greed kills those who, as a result of it, do not have enough; deceit leads to the death of trust; unfaithfulness to the death of relationships. The wages of sin is death – that's the outworking, the consequence, the payment that sin earns.

Confessing our sin doesn't make us a bad person; it simply reveals what is true, allowing us to become a better person. Repentance is not something to be feared, but something to embrace. It's about changing our mind about ourselves, about others, about God.

† Father, thank you that we can come to you honestly and openly. Thank you that being real with you leads to life, not condemnation.

For further thought

Reflect on the truth that God loves you, that acknowledging your sin to him is not something to be feared.

20 May
A cunning plan

Read Joshua 9:3–21

But when the inhabitants of Gibeon heard what Joshua had done to Jericho and to Ai, they on their part acted with cunning: they went and prepared provisions and took worn-out sacks for their donkeys and wineskins, worn out and torn and mended, with worn-out, patched sandals on their feet and worn-out clothes, and all their provisions were dry and moldy. They went to Joshua in the camp at Gilgal and said to him and to the Israelites, 'We have come from a far country, so now make a treaty with us.'

(verses 3–6)

In the face of grave danger, sometimes our instincts lead us to fight, at other times to run away – the classic fight or flight responses. Psychologists have identified others as well – the victim might collapse, appearing as if they are already dead and therefore not a threat, or they may seek to appease their attacker – the so-called flop and fawn responses. We see two of these in the passage – most of the inhabitants of the land put their differences aside and join together to fight Israel, but the Gibeonites choose to appease, to fawn. Neither approach works in the long term – ultimately Israel will drive out the inhabitants and possess the land, while Gibeon will survive in the land but as servants of Israel for generations.

Opposing God's ways can never end well! We can kick against them as Saul did and end up spiritually blind: 'Saul, Saul, why do you persecute me? It's hard for you to kick against me' (Acts 9:4–5; 26:14, paraphrase). Or we can seek to suppress them as the Sanhedrin sought to do with the apostles, only to have Gamaliel point out: 'I advise you: Leave these men alone! Let them go! For if their purpose or activity is of human origin, it will fail. But if it is from God, you will not be able to stop these men; you will only find yourselves fighting against God' (Acts 5:38–39, NIV).

In the end, God's will is accomplished and we can either have the joy and blessing of co-working in seeing it done, or remain blind to the love of God and slaves to the world.

† Father, open our eyes to your love, to see your hand at work when others see only darkness.

For further thought

Are there areas of your life where you are fighting God's ways or where you are compromising with the world and being a slave to it?

21 May
Inheriting by faith

Read Joshua 13:1–14

Now Joshua was old and advanced in years, and the LORD said to him, 'You are old and advanced in years, and very much of the land still remains to be possessed.'

(verse 1)

Joshua is getting old and the job isn't done – not all the land has been possessed and not all the tribes have been allocated their part. I notice a couple of things – first, God doesn't chide Joshua, but nor does he ignore the problem. And secondly, he provides a way for Joshua to finish well without being unrealistic. In faith, the tribes are to be allocated their allotted portion of the land, believing that they will convert that faith into practical reality.

There are good principles for us here! As leaders we must never believe that the task is to be carried by us alone. We are called to lead and that implies that there are more people involved in this than just us! But so often we put leaders (and they put themselves) in the impossible situation of carrying the burden for the task. That pressure leads to burn-out, dishonesty, disappointment and a sense of failure.

By contrast, notice how God manages the situation: he doesn't blame or put pressure on Joshua. The reality is that the people haven't fully bought into the project and haven't fulfilled their part. So, God encourages buy-in by allocating land to tribes and devolving responsibility to them for the fulfilment of their part of the overall.

This is a key approach – it moves responsibility away from some intangible 'the nation will do it' or some unrealistic 'Joshua will do it' to the meaningful 'the tribe of which I am a member will do this bit'. It's a principle repeated in Nehemiah as he allocates responsibility for rebuilding parts of the wall to families – and one which Paul highlights when he speaks about the body and each part having a unique contribution.

† Thank you, Lord, that you place us in teams, that we are as a body to accomplish your calling, that it isn't down to us alone.

For further thought

Do we sometimes enjoy a feeling of importance that leads us to take on responsibilities that are not ours to carry alone?

22 May
Distance and relationship

Read Joshua 22:10–31

No! We did it from fear that in time to come your children might say to our children, 'What have you to do with the LORD, the God of Israel? For the LORD has made the Jordan a boundary between us and you, you Reubenites and Gadites; you have no portion in the LORD.' So your children might make our children cease to worship the LORD.

(verses 24–25)

Sometimes friends or family move away and the geographical distance risks putting a distance in the relationship. You no longer do things together in the way you used to, and the people who moved gain new friends, embrace a new culture, become different …

The same is happening in our reading today. Some of the tribes have been allocated land on the other side of the Jordan. There's a physical barrier between them and the rest of the nation and, already, the fears of where that might lead have unsettled both sides and suspicion has crept in. The Reubenites, Gadites and Manassites are worried that in future generations the larger group of ten tribes will presume that they have lost their faith, while the ten tribes see their building an altar as evidence that they already have! Fortunately, direct communication about these fears and presumptions leads to honest dialogue, and all is well.

There are some key principles for relationships and reconciliation here:

- A willingness to confront and an honesty about what is feared.
- A willingness to give up something in order to lower the barrier to unity.
- A focus on things in common rather than on present or future differences.

Maybe these are key to our relationships too. Let's be open and honest about our fears. Let's be willing to put aside narrow self-interest for the sake of the relationship, and let us focus on that which unites rather than on the things that separate.

† Lord God, you who are three yet perfectly one, help us to be whole like you and to live in unity with those who also love you.

For further thought

We sometimes shy away from confronting issues. How can we raise issues without becoming defensive or aggressive?

23 May

Covenant and consequences

Read Joshua 23

A long time afterward, when the LORD had given rest to Israel from all their enemies all around and Joshua was old and well advanced in years, Joshua summoned all Israel, their elders and heads, their judges and officers, and said to them, 'I am now old and well advanced in years, and you have seen all that the LORD your God has done to all these nations for your sake, for it is the LORD your God who has fought for you.'

(verses 1–3)

God will finish the job. Some things are multi-generational – the key is to understand what our part is in the big picture and to find satisfaction in doing that to the best of our ability, in relationship with the God who will see it to completion.

Handing on to the next generation is always challenging – 'What if they don't do it like we would have? We now have all these years of experience, they are still so young – they are bound to make mistakes, it will be a disaster, they risk undoing all the good work we spent years doing! Maybe we should just hang on another year, or two, or ten …'

How many organisations have we seen struggle with this 'founder syndrome' and how do we avoid perpetuating it?

The key for Joshua was to recognise who had accomplished that which had already been done. 'You have seen all that the LORD your God has done' (verse 3). That wasn't to minimise his part, it wasn't said out of false humility; it was simply to acknowledge God's pivotal role in the team effort! A role that he would continue to exercise with the new generation – and that would be the foundation of Joshua's confidence that, despite their inexperience and his absence, the plan would be fulfilled.

But he ends with a warning. If they forget this fundamental truth, if they think they can do it in their own strength, if they move away from the plan, from the God who loves them, then they will discover in the starkest of ways that he is the one who brings things to fulfilment.

† Lord, thank you that you call us to co-work with you in building the kingdom. Help us to gladly invite others to participate as well.

For further thought

How do we encourage a new generation to take over when we are gone?

A covenant renewed

Read Joshua 24:16–33

Then Joshua said to the people, 'You are witnesses against yourselves that you have chosen the Lord, to serve him.' And they said, 'We are witnesses.' He said, 'Then put away the foreign gods that are among you, and incline your hearts to the Lord, the God of Israel.'

(verses 22–23)

'I didn't know' is so often an excuse we hear (or to be honest, that we make!). 'I didn't know the speed limit was xxx', 'I didn't know my homework was due …', 'I didn't realise I needed to declare that income for tax purposes.'

Joshua is aware of this tendency to claim ignorance as an excuse, so he reminds them of their covenant with God and they seek to reassure him: 'Oh, yes, we remember that, don't you worry, we'll stick to it after you're gone.' It sounds a bit like the child promising not to eat the sweets after the parent leaves the room! The truth is that even as they recommit themselves to the covenant, they are already in breach of it, as Joshua points out by telling them: 'Then put away the foreign gods … incline your heart to the Lord' (verse 23).

How easily we become blind to the real condition of our hearts and minds – just like the people then, we make promises on a wave of emotion that we are not keeping even as we speak the words! For all their words and promises, they were not being open about the reality of the situation. And this, more than the sin itself, is the problem. If we are open about our condition, God can draw alongside and work with us to transform it. If we deny the condition, we remain forever in it. As Jesus said, 'If you were blind, you would not have sin. But now that you say, "We see", your sin remains' (John 9:41).

† Thank you for shining your light into our lives. Help us to respond honestly with what is true, rather than what we would like to be true!

For further thought

When God's light shines on a situation, the only basis for loving relationship is to respond with what is actually true. We need to trust that in so doing, God picks us up – the purpose of his light is not to shame, but to enable healing.

The Gospel of Luke (3)

1 Working for God's kingdom

Notes by **John Birch**

Based in South Wales, John is a Methodist local preacher, and writes prayers and Bible studies for his website faithandworship.com. From here, they find their way all over the world, with some prayers adapted for use within both choral and more contemporary worship settings. John has published several books of prayers and Bible study material, and in his spare time enjoys folk singing and, with his wife Margaret, exploring the countryside in a campervan called Lola. John has used the NIVUK for these notes.

25 May
On the job training

Read Luke 9:1–27

When Jesus had called the Twelve together, he gave them power and authority to drive out all demons and to cure diseases, and he sent them out to proclaim the kingdom of God and to heal the sick.

(verses 1–2)

Some years ago, contemplating where my education might lead me, I read a book which inspired me to consider the food industry, and I began what was aptly entitled a 'sandwich course'. The 'sandwich' involved several months' practical experience, seeing how theory was put into practice, working as part of a team, and making the transition into an actual job a little easier. That was the theory anyway!

When taking on any new job or task, practical experience can be as valuable as head knowledge. The disciples had already found inspiration through Jesus or via Simon Peter and others. They experienced miracles, listened to Jesus' teaching, and in their journey of faith understood it was about freely sharing God's love, rather than making a profit as others had done.

That is why Jesus insisted the disciples travelled light and relied on the good will of people as they moved from town to town. When they returned, we are told that they reported to Jesus everything they had done. Feedback was important, an important part of their training to become the people Jesus knew they could be, his apostles carrying on in the power of God the work he had begun.

† Loving God, may all those who feel your call on their lives find the help and support they need to become the people you know they can be.

26 May
We are on a journey

Read Luke 9:37–45

'Listen carefully to what I am about to tell you: The Son of Man is going to be delivered into the hands of men.' But they did not understand what this meant. It was hidden from them, so that they did not grasp it, and they were afraid to ask him about it.

(verses 44–45)

Some things in life I am reasonably knowledgeable about, but ask me how my mobile phone plays music through a Bluetooth speaker and I'll simply shrug my shoulders, because all I need to know is that it does. If my laptop stops working, I'll try to fix it, but I may have to take it to a repair shop. And that's OK, because I know my limits.

I can empathise with the disciples as they walked alongside Jesus, listening to his teaching, enjoying fellowship with him. They had experienced many miracles and returned enthusiastically from a successful time of mission training, proclaiming the kingdom of God, and healing the sick. But then comes one of those moments: when faced with a screaming boy thrown to the ground in convulsions and foaming at the mouth, they suddenly seem powerless, as his father makes clear to Jesus.

Perhaps the disciples thought they'd reached their limits. If so, they were wrong, because Jesus had made it plain when he sent them into the mission field that they had all the power they would ever need. Fortunately, the boy receives healing through Jesus, and the disciples discover that they are very much still on a journey.

We all have those moments where faith seems tested to the limit, and it's important to realise that God is still there, as Jesus was when the disciples struggled. We are all on a journey, and this incident did not stop Peter and the others becoming the confident Spirit-filled apostles Jesus knew they would become.

† Be with us in those times when faith is tested, and in our weakness may we discover the strength and confidence we need.

For further thought

When the daily journey of faith becomes a struggle, are there particular Bible passages that bring strength and reassurance, and would it help if you could write these down, to share with others?

The cost of discipleship

Read Luke 9:46–62

*As the time approached for him to be taken up to heaven, Jesus
resolutely set out for Jerusalem. And he sent messengers on ahead, who
went into a Samaritan village to get things ready for him; but the people
there did not welcome him, because he was heading for Jerusalem.*

(verses 51–53)

As a teenager, I found it difficult to talk about my faith with other
kids in school. I knew it would leave me open to ridicule and
isolation, as it had with another boy, so I kept quiet. Looking back,
I know I should have been braver, stood by him, but that wasn't
me back then. Jesus is remembered for reaching out to those on
the margins, the outcasts, lepers, tax collectors and Samaritans,
while finding himself rejected not only by the Jewish authorities
but even by those in his home town.

Jesus knows he is heading toward the cross. He takes a direct
route from Galilee to Jerusalem through Samaritan territory, a
people long hated by the Jews. However, Jesus is happy to hold
out the hand of friendship as he seeks overnight accommodation,
and even rejection in one village doesn't stop him finding a more
welcoming one. He will have nothing to do with his disciples'
demand for God's judgement on the one place and its people.

In their later ministry, the disciples would find both welcome
and rejection following their call to mission. Opposition can often
be the experience of those who have chosen to follow Jesus, as
well as so many others in this world, whether for reasons of race,
religion or gender. I am pleased to see so many of our churches are
now happy to hold out the hand of friendship and fellowship and
say that 'all are welcome here'.

† Thank you, Lord, for all who regularly offer the hand of friendship and welcome
to those entering our churches and chapels.

For further thought

Offering the hand of friendship is so important for those who are
on the margins. Should it be a bigger part of who we all are today?

May

The Gospel of Luke (3) – 1 Working for God's kingdom

28 May

Mission work

> **Read Luke 10:1–24**
>
> *After this the Lord appointed seventy-two others and sent them two by two ahead of him to every town and place where he was about to go. He told them, 'The harvest is plentiful, but the workers are few.'*
>
> (verses 1–2a)

When I read about Jesus training his followers to become his messengers to the world, what comes to mind is my own journey of faith. This really began with a friend inviting me to a youth fellowship in a local Anglican church, where I discovered a real enthusiasm to know more about Jesus and share this growing faith with other young people in the town. And this simple pattern of evangelism has its roots in Luke's message, as he explores how Jesus entrusted the task of spreading his message to a group of people very much like us.

Jesus starts by sending his closest disciples out, and as that goes well, so mission training expands, and in Luke's mind, Jesus is thinking global, with seventy-two being symbolically the number of nations in the known world. What impresses me is that this was not a high intensity, no-expense-spared mission, but as low-key as it could possibly be. Two people walking into a town, accepting the hand of friendship and hospitality if offered (moving on if not), getting to know the locals, sharing the good news about Jesus, and offering prayer for the sick.

And it worked, with the seventy-two returning with truly positive feedback. Jesus had established a pattern which would continue after his death and resurrection, as scattered believers met in houses, became involved in the local community, and invited their friends to join them – just as my friend invited me to join his fellowship group. And I pray that will continue!

† Bless all whose calling is to mission work, in their local community or further afield, and may the seeds they sow, being watered and fed by your Holy Spirit, produce an abundant harvest!

For further thought

Does your local church offer a safe and accessible space for everyone to feel welcome?

29 May
Ascension

Read Luke 24:50–53

When he had led them out to the vicinity of Bethany, he lifted up his hands and blessed them. While he was blessing them, he left them and was taken up into heaven. Then they worshipped him and returned to Jerusalem with great joy. And they stayed continually at the temple, praising God.

(verses 50–53)

In the church calendar, Ascension Day officially marks the end of the Easter season and falls ten days before Pentecost. We break the flow of this week's passages to read about Christ's Ascension, which is only recorded in the Gospel of Luke.

There is a familiar phrase, 'When one door closes, another opens', attributed to the scientist Alexander Graham Bell, and which I can relate to both in my working life and in the direction my faith has taken me. However, what I didn't realise was that Bell apparently went on to add, 'But we often look so long and so regretfully upon the closed door that we do not see the one which has opened for us.'

How easy it is to continue looking sadly at a closed door, seeing it as the end of something we thought would go on for ever while failing to see another door swinging open. Change is often feared instead of embraced, and of course not all change means loss or failure. The disciples had been dependent upon the visible flesh-and-blood presence of Jesus. That had ended within a few weeks of his resurrection, and a door had seemingly closed. They could have left Bethany distraught and broken-hearted, all their hopes shattered, but instead were full of joy because they could see the open door of new possibilities, where nothing could separate them from the love of God in Christ Jesus (Romans 8:38–39).

Don't focus on the door that closes. Watch out for the one that's about to open.

† For all who have followed God's call into new areas of ministry, may their faithfulness be a blessing to both them and those among whom they work.

For further thought

How well do you accommodate change, in both your working and spiritual life, and could you be more open to God leading you through a door to new opportunities?

30 May

The good neighbour

Read Luke 10:25–42

On one occasion an expert in the law stood up to test Jesus. 'Teacher,' he asked, 'what must I do to inherit eternal life?' 'What is written in the Law?' he replied. 'How do you read it?' He answered, '"Love the Lord your God with all your heart and with all your soul and with all your strength and with all your mind"; and, "Love your neighbour as yourself."'

(verses 25–27)

Who'd have thought it! There's sometimes a risk in being a good neighbour of the kind Jesus was highlighting! The traveller was taking a risk, walking alone in an area where assault and robbery were common, and paying the penalty. The priest and Levite play it safe, walking quickly by, and it's the man Jesus' listeners would expect to be the villain of the story who ignores the risks to help and support the victim.

Refugees often walk along dangerous roads to uncertain destinations. Victims of severe flooding, storms and earthquakes would struggle to survive without the help of good neighbours offering what they can via aid agencies, whose workers on the ground accept the risks of helping those who have lost so much – helping them find shelter, clean water and the medical care they need, rather like the Samaritan highlighted in Jesus' story.

Being a good neighbour is not, of course, just about giving money to charity. It's also about reacting to situations we come across in our daily lives, in and around our local neighbourhoods. It can mean the sacrifice of our time, skills and knowledge to help others. It doesn't always end well, as I discovered when scammed by someone apparently in need. But if we do nothing, if we always walk by like the priest and the Levite, then can we be sure that anyone else will stop and help? There may be risks, but loving God and being a good neighbour are at the core of our Christian life.

† May all those who spend their days being 'good neighbours' to those in need in their local communities be truly blessed.

For further thought

Could you, without over-burdening your work/life balance, become more involved in your local community, or indeed further afield, where your skills or resources might help others?

The Gospel of Luke (3) – 1 Working for God's kingdom

31 May
Lord, teach us to pray

Read Luke 11:1–13

One day Jesus was praying in a certain place. When he finished, one of his disciples said to him, 'Lord, teach us to pray, just as John taught his disciples.'

(verse 1)

It was custom for a rabbi to offer his disciples a prayer that would become a regular part of their spiritual life. Try putting yourself in the place of one of those disciples, still on a steep learning curve in their spiritual training, seeing Jesus in prayerful conversation with his heavenly Father and needing help with their own prayer life. Jesus offers the familiar framework of the 'Lord's Prayer', although I prefer 'Disciples' Prayer' which some suggest, as Jesus offers his disciples the building blocks of a prayer encompassing daily needs and a sense of togetherness as a community, dependent on God the Father for so much in their daily lives.

It is easy to repeat familiar words without really thinking how they speak to you at that moment. Having grown up in a churchgoing family, engraved somewhere inside my memory are the words of so many liturgies and hymns, even if I don't use them so regularly now. What I really appreciate are new ones that cause me to concentrate more on the words and their meaning. This disciples' prayer can be repeated as the version we are familiar with, but also form the basis of our whole prayer life. To love God and love our neighbour is at the heart of being a Christian, and this prayer encompasses that theme, embracing God's forgiveness, mercy, generosity and grace. This is the framework by which Jesus wants all his disciples to live their lives, proclaiming God's kingdom and love through both words and deeds.

† Dear Lord, may those well-loved words of Jesus be at the heart of our daily worship and reflected in our daily journey of faith.

For further thought

Read again, but slowly and with pauses, the familiar words of the Lord's Prayer, and let it speak to you anew.

May

The Gospel of Luke (3) – 1 Working for God's kingdom

The Gospel of Luke (3)

2 Prepare yourself

Notes by **Amari Yogendran**

Amari is a poet and creative writer in her early twenties. She loves words and loves to think and pick apart meanings. She's learning that by leaning into the hard things and finding words that get close to our experiences, we can show up fully to ourselves, others and God. She works as a photographer in North London. Amari has used the NIV for these notes.

1 June
Beholding and becoming light

Read Luke 11:14–36

Your eye is the lamp of your body. When your eyes are healthy, your whole body also is full of light. But when they are unhealthy, your body also is full of darkness. See to it, then, that the light within you is not darkness.

(verses 34–35)

I was flying home from a short trip to Italy. It was about 9 p.m. when the captain announced that we were approaching England – instinctively we all looked out of the window. I saw the clusters of lights from buildings that made up towns and cities, but outside these clusters was an intense darkness. In the UK, our constant access to electricity and screens means that we don't get to experience much total darkness like this.

In Jesus' pre-electricity age, people were reliant on oil lamps as their sole light source during darkness. Therefore, when Jesus compares our eyes to lamps, he is speaking of our total reliance on our eyes in leading us. Like a lantern held out in front of us, we lead with our eyes. So where is your gaze directed?

Jesus doesn't impose cast iron rules on us. He doesn't tell us that we can't enjoy our friends with a different faith from us or engage with secular TV, music and books. Instead, Jesus says, 'See to it, then, that the light within you is not darkness.' He asks us to see to it that we take ownership and discern what produces light and promotes health within us.

† Father, thank you that you have called us to be bright lamps. We ask that you make us bright, wake us up and keep nudging us to behold and become light.

2 June

Jesus cares about the inside of you

Read Luke 11:37–54

But now as for what is inside you – be generous to the poor, and everything will be clean for you.

(verse 41)

I work as a photographer. My role is to capture the appearance of things, to freeze real life and create something beautiful. But the outside can be deceiving. I love my job, but I wrestle on a daily basis with the ethics of contributing to our culture's obsession with the appearance of things.

The outside can be deceiving – it tells us very little of what is going on inside. Jesus saw this and was well acquainted with religious people who were doing things for the sake of appearances, yet lacked true substance and depth in their lives.

Instead of scrubbing up our external appearances, Jesus says 'be generous to the poor, and everything will be clean for [us]' (verse 41). Jesus wants purity from within. Jesus wants to bring our outsides and insides, our beliefs and our actions, what's done in public and private, into alignment.

Thankfully, we don't have to strive to instantly become people who hang out with the less fortunate. We don't have to, overnight, become people who live lives of integrity or lead lives that don't seek praise from others. Transforming the inside takes time – when we first get to know him some of these things may well come flowing out of us, but there are no shortcuts to holiness. It's only by Jesus that we are met, transformed and inspired by the radical vision of the upside-down kingdom – the kingdom that flips the pecking order of our societies.

Cleaning up our outside appearance will only get us so far. What a relief. If we'll let him, Jesus wants to purify our hearts instead.

† Jesus, thank you that you care about the inside of us more than the outside. Thank you that we are transformed by your presence, not by scrubbing ourselves or by striving for cleanliness.

For further thought

Jesus cleanses the inside of us, making us able to be more than who we appear to be on the surface and to do more with us than we could ever expect.

June

The Gospel of Luke (3) – 2 Prepare yourself

3 June
Being rich towards God

Read Luke 12:1–21

But God said to him, 'You fool! This very night your life will be demanded from you. Then who will get what you have prepared for yourself?' This is how it will be with whoever stores up things for themselves but is not rich toward God.

(verses 20–21)

My dad has a huge, ever-growing collection of CDs and records, which is remarkable in today's world of streaming and free music. I guess old habits die hard. It's safe to say that my mum isn't the happiest about it – so much so that she'll often use the phrase 'storing up grain in the barn' as a way of coercing my dad into trading them in. It hasn't yet worked.

The phrase in our passage 'rich toward God' is interesting to me because the word 'towards' has motion and direction. The grain in the barn was stored up and stagnant. However, God is asking that our richness has a direction, and that it should be directed towards God as a form of our worship.

You might not be wealthy with money like the rich man, but I think this passage calls us to think beyond material possessions. We can be rich in our character, rich in our giftings, rich in our relationships. The 'grain' we have might be our dreams, our energy, our time. Everything of value to us, directed towards God and those things that he values.

Like Moses with his staff, perhaps the Lord is prompting us to look at what's in our hand. Perhaps abundant grain or perhaps just enough for today. How can we be rich towards God with what we have?

What does it look like to go into today with a posture of abundance? As with the manna in the desert, a posture that says there will be more tomorrow even if I give today's abundance to God today.

† Thank you, God, that you are an extravagant God – we don't have to store your goodness up in barns of self-protection. Help us see what you have made us wealthy with today.

For further thought

Perhaps something of yours has been preserved in a jar for a while. A skill, an idea or your time. Perhaps God is wanting you to bring this into the light so that he can use it.

4 June

In your worry, observe the small things

Read Luke 12:22–48

Consider the ravens: They do not sow or reap, they have no storeroom or barn; yet God feeds them. And how much more valuable you are than birds! Who of you by worrying can add a single hour to your life?

(verses 24–25)

It's painful to worry but often it's hard not to worry. Sometimes worry can feel like something we can rationalise away; other times, worry feels like more of a bodily anxiety that can't be reasoned with.

Jesus knew that worry can have a strong grip on us and this is why he chooses to talk about it. He compares us to the ravens, the wildflowers, the grass, the birds. It's a list of seemingly very different groups. Some with consciousness, others without. According to research, what sets human beings apart from the other creatures on this list is our complex capacity for self-analysis, mental time travel, imagination, abstract reasoning, cultural establishment and morality.

Our relative complexity, however, does not mean that we have all the answers. What if the very reason why Jesus groups us with the grass and the birds is because we have something to learn from them? These creatures exist with a language, a way of life that is alien to us. They have an ease about them, living moment to moment, and bend with the winds. We can learn from such creatures, from the practice of slowing down and being present.

Admittedly, at times I've seen this passage as an oversimplification of my problems. Of course, the birds are not worried – they don't have meetings, deadlines or the ability to feel complex emotions like regret, hopelessness and disappointment! But Jesus loves to use the little things, the seemingly insignificant creatures, to teach us that we, like them, can live in his care.

† Thank you, God, for the gift of stillness. Thank you, Father, that you are working for our good and can be trusted with our worries.

For further thought

Unclench your jaw. Let your worries for the day surface. Hand them over to the Father, one by one. Ask the Father to help you trust that he will meet all of your needs.

June

The Gospel of Luke (3) – 2 Prepare yourself

5 June
Sometimes building looks like breaking

Read Luke 12:49 – 13:9

Do you think I came to bring peace on earth? No, I tell you, but division. From now on there will be five in one family divided against each other, three against two and two against three. They will be divided, father against son and son against father, mother against daughter and daughter against mother, mother-in-law against daughter-in-law and daughter-in-law against mother-in-law.

(12:51–53)

When Jesus was first born, the angels sang a message of peace on earth and goodwill to all mankind (Luke 2:14) – a wonderful, hopeful declaration. Yet in this passage, that same Jesus says something much less comfortable: that he didn't come to bring peace but division on earth.

The truth is that Jesus has always been a peace-bringer, that's his ministry, to restore wholeness, shalom, peace to that which has been broken. But he also knew this: that sometimes you have to dismantle before you can rebuild. Sometimes, at the beginning, building looks like breaking. Misplaced walls have to be torn down and the rubble removed. Unhealthy turns in relationships might need to be undone before true unity can be created; unhelpful worldviews need to be dismantled before new ones can be received.

Jesus has also always polarised, evoking strong reactions from those who beheld him – some immediately accepting him, and some rejecting him, and those in between, following in a crowd, sitting in a tree or on the fence. In this passage, Jesus is ushering in a new method of belief system that does not come by bloodline or familial association but by an individual heart response. Under this belief system, even one small family can all have different responses to the message of Jesus. This is why it is divisive.

Accepting Jesus requires our whole lives to shift, as we break generational patterns, deconstruct our worldviews and the shaky foundations of our lives for a different blueprint. Sometimes building looks like breaking, but it's a breaking of pieces to build something beautiful and eternal.

† Father, we ask for perspective and vision so that in the face of division and discomfort, we can see you building your kingdom among us.

For further thought

Doubt is another form of division that we can encounter in faith. In the light of this passage, how might doubt serve to build the kingdom?

6 June
Our imaginations and the kingdom of heaven

Read Luke 13:10–35

Then Jesus asked, 'What is the kingdom of God like? What shall I compare it to? It is like a mustard seed, which a man took and planted in his garden. It grew and became a tree, and the birds perched in its branches.'

(verses 18–19)

I'm tempted to imagine the kingdom of heaven as a place: heaven. This place exists in the sky and is characterised by angels and clouds. Perhaps I imagine this because it's easiest to get my head around, thanks to the paintings of heaven depicted by Renaissance artists. But the kingdom of heaven, as Jesus refers to it, is a bit more abstract than this. Results of a Google search define the kingdom of heaven as the spiritual realm and government that God reigns over as king. The kingdom of God is therefore more of an abstract concept.

In this passage, Jesus asks a rhetorical question, 'What is the kingdom of heaven like?' (verse 18).

I love the question. Jesus uses the word 'like' as if the real kingdom of heaven can't ever be fully encapsulated in language. It has to be spoken about in similes, in likeness. We can identify the earthly things that the kingdom of heaven is akin to but ultimately, this is not a question with a straight answer.

With friends, and with ourselves, sometimes we can rush to the answer. I grew up in quite an intellectual Christian culture where we learnt theological answers to questions that our friends might ask about our faith, in order that we might have an answer ready for them. But Jesus also knew the importance of the question itself and the process of figuring out what he meant.

I think it's interesting that the left side of our brain processes facts and logic, and the right side of our brain is for imagination, intuition and feelings. Jesus asks questions to provoke our intellectual engagement; he offers us similes to spark our imagination. He wants us to lean in with our whole selves.

† Father, thank you for choosing to speak in questions and metaphors. Speak to us today on the ways your kingdom is like a 'mustard seed' and like 'yeast' mixed through dough. Give us imagination to hear you.

For further thought

If you had to describe the presence of God in 'like' statements, what would you liken it to? Perhaps write down three statements. There's no right or wrong.

The Gospel of Luke (3) – 2 Prepare yourself

7 June
Needing to feel significant

Read Luke 14:1–24

But when you give a banquet, invite the poor, the crippled, the lame, the blind, and you will be blessed. Although they cannot repay you, you will be repaid at the resurrection of the righteous.

(verses 13–14)

I've got a friend who has very similar values, goals and ambitions to me. Our similarities are the basis of our friendship. However, sometimes I can find myself wanting to compete with her. I feel an itch to appear impressive when I'm around her, to tell her how well I'm doing and the interesting thing I did that I know will get her approval and elevate me in her estimations.

Jesus is speaking to 'elevators' like me when he tells the Pharisees that not only should they not assume the best seats at the dinner table, but also they should dine with the poor instead of their distinguished guests and relatives. Ouch. Jesus is calling out the hypocrisy of the Pharisees who are deeply religious in their adherence to customs and yet have normalised a culture of elevating themselves above others.

Jesus says that when we elevate ourselves, we choose to receive our reward now, an earthly reward. Maybe some approval, a 'win' in that moment or an ego stroke. But if you humble yourself, you will receive a heavenly reward later. It's a choice, sometimes a split-second choice, to restrain from the need to feel big, powerful and in control.

As quite a competitive person, I often think that if I'm not competing or trying to be the best, then I lose. But the invitation is to remember who we are in Christ. We have been given purpose, authority and a unique path for our lives from the only one who can give it to us. If we are in him, we cannot lose.

† Jesus, thank you that you chose humility at every step. From your humble birth to laying down your life. Holy Spirit, please give us the courage to be humble like Jesus.

For further thought

Elevating myself robs me of fellowship and enjoyment of friendship. What might elevating yourself be robbing you of?

June

The Gospel of Luke (3) – 2 Prepare yourself

Prayer in the New Testament letters

Notes by **Paul Nicholson SJ**

Paul is a Roman Catholic priest belonging to the Society of Jesus, a religious order popularly known as the Jesuits. He works in London as Socius (assistant) to the Jesuit Provincial. He edited *The Way*, a Christian spirituality journal, from 2007 to 2022, and is author of *An Advent Pilgrimage* (2013) and *Pathways to God* (2017). Since ordination in 1988, he has worked principally in ministries of spirituality and of social justice, and was novice master between 2008 and 2014. Paul has used the NRSVA for these notes.

8 June
The Holy Spirit, prompter of prayer

Read Acts 2:1–18

And suddenly from heaven there came a sound like the rush of a violent wind, and it filled the entire house where they were sitting. Divided tongues, as of fire, appeared among them, and a tongue rested on each of them. All of them were filled with the Holy Spirit.

(verses 2–4a)

This week we'll consider the variety of ways in which prayer is presented in the New Testament letters. Today's reading gives the foundation for this. The coming of the Holy Spirit, at Pentecost, enables those gathered in the upper room to pray in the way that they do, and, prompted by their prayer, to go and speak of the risen Lord fearlessly to people from across the world.

Those of us who write for *Fresh from The Word* are invited to carry on that same mission. We're expected to be people of prayer ourselves, whose prayer leads us to share the scriptures with others. What we write is translated into many languages, languages we do not speak, and is sent out across the globe to people we never meet. The same Holy Spirit who stirred the hearts of the apostles continues to stir all involved with this publication, writers and readers alike.

So, your own prayer, too, has its foundation in what happened on the day of Pentecost. The Holy Spirit works in you, today, to fulfil the words Peter spoke to that crowd in Jerusalem. God enables you to bear witness to him, by your words and your life.

† Come, Holy Spirit, fill the hearts of your faithful, and kindle in them the fire of your love.

Approaching the light, aware of the darkness

Read 1 John 1:5–10

This is the message we have heard from him and proclaim to you, that God is light and in him there is no darkness at all. If we say that we have fellowship with him while we are walking in darkness, we lie and do not do what is true.

(verses 5–6)

Over the centuries, some of those the Church has come to recognise as closest to God have thought of themselves as the greatest sinners. Why is this? Is it some sort of false humility? You might be reminded of Uriah Heep, in the novel *David Copperfield* by Charles Dickens. He continually presents himself as a very humble person, but only to draw attention to his supposed piety.

Today's reading, though, offers another way to approach this question. 'God is light, and in him there is no darkness at all.' Inevitably, then, the closer I come to the light, the more I become aware of whatever darkness there is in me. And it is those who are closest to the light which is God who are thereby most aware of their own shadow side.

This awareness can lead me down two different paths. One cuts me off from God. Here, the more I am convinced of my own sinfulness, the surer I become that God wants nothing to do with me or will judge me harshly. The other path takes me in precisely the opposite direction. The more conscious I become of darkness within me, the more certain I am of my own need of God. Paradoxically, it is awareness of my sin that binds me to God most strongly, the God who is loving and infinitely forgiving.

Which path will I go down? It is prayer that will ensure that I am kept close to God, even when, indeed perhaps especially when, I feel I have nothing to offer God in return for his love.

† Lord, when I am most aware of the darkness within me, let that awareness bind me ever more closely to you, confident in your forgiving love.

For further thought

Try to remember a time when you felt far from God but can now see that God was in fact very close to you there.

10 June
See God at work and give thanks

Read Ephesians 5:15–20

Be careful then how you live, not as unwise people but as wise, making the most of the time … giving thanks to God the Father at all times and for everything in the name of our Lord Jesus Christ.

(verses 15–16, 20)

Ignatius of Loyola, founder of the Jesuits, the religious order to which I belong, was a great teacher of prayer. One of the prayer-forms that he most encouraged is called the examen. It can be thought of as a response to Paul's exhortation to the people of Ephesus to 'be careful then how you live'. Ignatius invited people to pause briefly, once or twice a day, and consider how God had been working with them over the last few hours, and how they had been responding to God's work.

His basic assumption is that this should be a positive experience. First, because God will always have been there, supporting and strengthening even in the most difficult of circumstances, whether recognised or not. Secondly, because my own response can always bring me closer to God. If I have been working well with God in the time leading up to this prayer, I will be encouraged by that. If I have been ignoring God, or even turning away from him, this prayer gives me a chance to redirect my efforts.

In this way the examen prayer leads naturally into that 'giving thanks to God the Father at all times' that Paul also hopes will be the way in which the Ephesians respond. Recognising things for which we can be genuinely thankful in all circumstances may take a bit of practice. But there is almost always something nearby that you can start by thanking him for.

† As a focus for your prayer today, pick one good thing in the world around you, and give thanks to God for it specifically as a gift God has given you.

For further thought

At some point in the day ahead, pause briefly and ask God to show you how God has been working with you recently.

June

Prayer in the New Testament letters

Christians bound together by mutual prayer

Read Ephesians 6:18–20

Pray in the Spirit at all times in every prayer and supplication … keep alert and always persevere in supplication for all the saints. Pray also for me, so that when I speak, a message may be given to me to make known with boldness the mystery of the gospel.

(verses 18–19)

I have friends who keep lists of people to pray for, and their particular needs. Somebody's relative is ill or has died. Someone is taking an important exam. Overcoming an addiction, setting out on a long journey, wanting good weather for the parish fête – a seemingly unending list of things that people hope God will provide, and about which they will seek the help of those who are known to be people of prayer.

Here Paul enlists the assistance of the people of Ephesus in the same way. He hopes that they will ask God to help him speak the gospel message boldly, recognising the difficulties that he faces. And he asks their prayers not only for himself, but for 'all the saints'.

Notice that there is no discussion here of how important these various needs are, or which ones should be given priority. Pray at all times for all people. God will decide how he will answer these prayers, in ways that are obvious answers to them, or in ways that are more hidden. The Ephesians are asked simply to pray, at all times and for all people. What comes after that is up to God.

Almost certainly, if others know of your Christian faith, you will have been asked to pray for them. They may or may not have told you what they are hoping for. You, too, are likely to have invited others to pray for you. There is a phrase, the 'communion of saints', that refers to this interdependence of believers. Our prayer today is one way of making that real.

† Lord, I hold before you today all those who have asked for my prayers, and all those who are praying for me. Keep us united in your love.

For further thought

You might like to write a list, at some time today, of those people you find yourself especially praying for at the moment.

Encountering God in your worries

Read Philippians 4:4–9

Rejoice in the Lord always ... Do not worry about anything, but in everything by prayer and supplication with thanksgiving let your requests be made known to God. And the peace of God, which surpasses all understanding, will guard your hearts and your minds in Christ Jesus.

(verses 4, 6–7)

A major aspect of my current job, helping to co-ordinate the mission of the Jesuit priests and brothers in Britain, is answering the enquiries that are sent in from all over the country and further afield. The members of the religious order itself have questions about their work and how it might best be developed. All sorts of other people want to know more about what we do, or why we do it, to offer their thanks or complaints.

It is said that a predecessor of mine, fifty years ago, could pick up the day's letters with these enquiries at 8:30 a.m. and have responded to them all by 10:00 a.m., leaving him the rest of the day to study, pray or relax. Then email was invented! Now the questions shower down night and day, and many of the correspondents seem to regard a two-hour delay in responding as tardy.

Of course, such pressure isn't really new. The people of Philippi in today's reading are encouraged not to worry about anything, but to let God be aware of their requests, so that they can then rest peacefully. In this way, the number of demands we face can become a blessing rather than a burden. In many of them, there will be something true, honourable, just, pure, excellent, commendable, even pleasing. Today's prayer invites you to look out for those aspects of whatever challenges you're facing just now. In this way they become places of encounter with God, rather than worries blocking his presence.

† 'Let nothing disturb you, nothing frighten you. All things are passing, God never changes. Patience obtains all things. Whoever has God lacks nothing; God alone suffices.' (Teresa of Avila)

For further thought

Where can you encounter God in today's letters, emails, texts or messages?

June

Prayer in the New Testament letters

The leader and the led

Read 1 Timothy 2:1–10

*I urge that supplications, prayers, intercessions, and thanksgivings should
be made for everyone, for kings and all who are in high positions, so
that we may lead a quiet and peaceable life in all godliness and dignity.
This is right and is acceptable in the sight of God our Saviour.*

(verses 1–3)

Eight months after Queen Elizabeth II died, her son Charles III
was crowned in Westminster Abbey in London. The coronation
ceremony, which had not been seen for seventy years, surprised
many by being deeply Christian. Much of it consisted of prayers
that Charles might receive from God all the gifts he would need
to be a good, dedicated and worthy king. Why? Not simply for his
own benefit, but so that, as today's reading says, 'we may lead a
quiet and peaceable life in all godliness and dignity'.

How much a constitutional monarch in a modern democratic
state can do to ensure this is perhaps debatable, but the principle
is a sound one. Any society has its leaders, and they can do much
to influence the lives of those they govern. Asking God to help
them do this well is an important aspect of any believer's prayer
life. And a 'quiet and peaceable life' can make it easier to recognise
the abiding presence of God in Christ Jesus.

Readers of *Fresh from The Word* may differ in their response
to what the letter to Timothy goes on to say about women. The
meaning of braided hair, gold and pearls, and expensive clothes
surely differs in different cultures and societies worldwide. But
we can all agree that a desire to be adorned with good works,
whether found in women or in men, is more important than these,
and also a reasonable gift to be sought in prayer.

† Lord God, bless all those in authority in my society, and grant them the gifts they
need to bring peace in our neighbourhoods, our countries, and in our world.

For further thought

What three gifts or qualities do you think are most needed in
anyone putting themselves forward for a leadership role?

14 June

The power of prayer in common

Read James 5:13–18

Are any among you suffering? They should pray. Are any cheerful?
They should sing songs of praise. Are any among you sick? They should
call for the elders of the church and have them pray over them … The
prayer of the righteous is powerful and effective.

(verses 13–14, 16b)

Lourdes in southern France is one of the great pilgrimage sites of the Christian faith. Every year hundreds of thousands of sick and suffering people visit the town. A few hope for a miraculous cure. Many more return repeatedly for the experience of praying alongside others, knowing the help and support that that brings. Cheerfully, they sing songs of praise. Humbly, they seek God's forgiveness for their sins. Together, they intercede for the sick and the suffering, praying for each other.

In looking this week at what the letters of the New Testament have to teach us about prayer, much of the focus has been on the individual believer. What happens when I set out to encounter God, and how might I deepen that meeting? But our week started with Pentecost, a gathering of the faithful in an upper room, together blessed with an outpouring of God's Spirit. So, it is good to be reminded, at the end of the week, of the power of communal prayer.

Part of that power comes from our ability to bolster each other's faith. I recognise in myself days when I am a fervent follower of Jesus, and other days when my doubts are to the fore. In fervour, I can support others; in doubt, I can draw on their strength. There was a reason that Christ founded the Church rather than merely summoning isolated individuals to companionship with him.

† In prayer today, I recall all those on whom I rely for their strength; and I thank God for those he enables me to strengthen in my turn.

For further thought

What have the New Testament letters told you this week about prayer – something new to you, or something you might be in danger of forgetting?

June

Prayer in the New Testament letters

Comfort and hope (from Isaiah 40–55) (1)

Notes by **Liz Carter**

Liz is an author, poet and editor living with long-term disabling illness. She writes about finding God's treasure in the midst of brokenness and how to explore peace when life doesn't go as planned. She likes Cadbury's chocolate and is proud to be a grammar pedant. She lives in Shropshire, UK, with her husband Tim, a church leader. She is the author of *Catching Contentment* (2018), *Treasure in Dark Places* (2020), *Valuable* (2023) and the *Newland Trilogy* (2023). Liz has used the NIVUK for these notes.

15 June
Words of hope

Read Isaiah 40:1–5

Comfort, comfort my people, says your God. Speak tenderly to Jerusalem, and proclaim to her that her hard service has been completed, that her sin has been paid for, that she has received from the Lᴏʀᴅ's hand double for all her sins.

(verses 1–2)

What does 'comfort' mean to you?

There's the physical comfort we need to feel safe in our world – the basics of nutrition and warmth. And then there is the comfort we all need in our deep places: in our emotions and our spirits, we need to know we are loved. It's this comfort we will be exploring over the next week.

The passages from Isaiah 40–55 are ones full of comfort and assurance. Isaiah is prophesying to his people who, two hundred years on from his time of writing, are broken by exile and asking many questions of God: Has he abandoned them? Why did he allow this to happen? These are questions that can be familiar to us, too, when we go through difficult times. As with the Israelites, God knows the words that will give us hope, and he whispers them to us today in tender echoes: 'Comfort, comfort my people.'

This week, then, think about what kind of comfort you need to receive. Do you need to hear how loved you are? Do you need to hear forgiveness? Do you need to sense the gentle touch of the Spirit on places that are weary and ragged?

† God of comfort, thank you that you are with me. As I go into this week, may I take hold of your whispers of hope. Amen.

16 June
Good news

Read Isaiah 40:6–11

'The grass withers and the flowers fall, but the word of our God endures for ever.' You who bring good news to Zion, go up on a high mountain. You who bring good news to Jerusalem, lift up your voice with a shout ... say to the towns of Judah, 'Here is your God!'

(verses 8–9)

I scroll through my news app, saddened by the chaos that seems to rule the world. There's rarely a good news story to be found, but when there is, it can lift me up and change my perspective.

The people of Israel had lived through a time when all the news was bad, when their homes had been smashed apart and they had been taken to a foreign country and scattered from their families. So, it's no wonder that the news of God gathering them back together and bringing them back from exile was news worth shouting about – God was coming in power to heal and to comfort and restore. The exiles desperately needed to hear this good news, to take hold of the truth that God was still holding them and had never let go.

Our lives in this world are short, like grass that withers away, but here we are reminded that our lives in God's plan are enduring, just like God's word, and that we can hold on to these truths in times when we are struggling. The good news of God's love for us resounds through eternity and breaks open the borders of transient time, and we are caught up with those echoes, living in the sure and certain hope of both eternal life and God's sovereign power with us right now, wherever we are.

So today may you be so filled with hope that you run over mountains in your soul and break down your borders to shout out the news: 'Here is your God!'

† Father God, thank you that your good news transcends all of time and breaks the power of all the bad news in my life. May I long to shout it out to all around me. Amen.

For further thought
Pray through your news feed or newspaper today and ask that God's good news will break through in healing and restoration.

June

Comfort and hope (from Isaiah 40–55) (1)

'Here is my servant'

Read Isaiah 42:1–7

I will take hold of your hand. I will keep you and will make you to be a covenant for the people and a light for the Gentiles, to open eyes that are blind, to free captives from prison and to release from the dungeon those who sit in darkness.

(verses 6–7)

In a dystopian novel I read recently, residents of the future city only get one chance to prove themselves worthy. If they do not, they are thrown outside the city walls and left to fend for themselves.

The Israelites must have felt that they'd failed God and proven themselves unworthy: Isaiah had given them multiple warnings to serve God and to turn away from evil, but they hadn't listened and so God allowed them to be taken into exile.

But God didn't end their story there. God didn't throw them out and ban them from his presence. Instead, God promised that he would send his servant to redeem and restore – because God is a God of multiple second chances, and not willing that any should perish. God did not abandon his people – even when they abandoned him. He had a plan in place because he knew they needed him to step in and save them; he knew they couldn't do it on their own.

This servant would be a bringer of justice, a gentle saviour who would serve, rather than be served. This passage has its ultimate fulfilment in Jesus, of course, and so these words are as much for you today. As you look around at the mess of the world, reflect on not only how God will always give you second chances to repent and be transformed, but also how you are called to bring God's light to the world and freedom to those in all kinds of captivity. You are invited to join in the work of Jesus – the light to all nations.

† Dear Father, thank you that you never abandon me, that you sent your Son to save me. Help me to take hold of your hand as you take hold of mine. Amen.

For further thought

Who do you know who is sitting in darkness? How can you pray for them and help them this week?

18 June

Sing a new song

Read Isaiah 42:10–16

Sing to the LORD a new song, his praise from the ends of the earth, you who go down to the sea, and all that is in it, you islands, and all who live in them. ...let them shout from the mountaintops. Let them give glory to the LORD ...

(verses 10–12)

The people have been silent for a long time.

Their poetry is forgotten. Their songs are unsung. Their music only resounds through their dreams. Now they sit by the river and weep as they remember how they once sang together, raising their voices in worship. How can they sing songs about their God now, in this strange, uncaring land?

But now they are released, and the very wilderness cannot restrain its praise. The ends of the earth resound with a new song of joy: God has overcome, and they have been made free.

Isaiah is reminding the exiles that God is for them and that at just the right time, he came in power to deliver them. Even though they had messed up, he would always fight for them. The song they heard in their dreams and wept for by rivers had never left them and was always weaving around them, even when their entire world seemed steeped in silence. And now they could at last join in with all their might: 'Sing to the LORD a new song!'

That song is still our song today, and every corner of our world is invited into its melody, because God sings it over all of us in his radical, inclusive story of salvation. We are not left alone in our desert places; we are lifted into eternal music where love strums the notes and joy shouts the lyrics. So today may you be assured of the hope and the future always being sung over you, and as you join in, may you be comforted.

† Lord, I sing a new song of praise to you today, joining in with the echoes across history of all your people worshipping your name. May I sing your song even when it hurts. Amen.

For further thought

Read Psalm 137:1–6 and reflect on how the Israelites felt. Where is your 'river of Babylon' today? How will you keep the song going?

June

Comfort and hope (from Isaiah 40—55) (1)

19 June
Called by name

> **Read Isaiah 43:1–7**
>
> *Do not fear, for I have redeemed you; I have summoned you by name;*
> *you are mine. When you pass through the waters, I will be with you;*
> *and when you pass through the rivers, they will not sweep over you.*
> *When you walk through the fire, you will not be burned.*
>
> (verses 1b–2)

It's a 'when', not an 'if'.

Isaiah doesn't pretend things are all going to be fine. He doesn't gloss over the reality of suffering or couch it in the language of 'maybe', but instead he calls it as it is: 'When you pass through the waters.'

When.

Sometimes as Christians we have been made to feel as though if we believe, everything will be good. We will be healed, we will have enough money, we will be free of all the things that bind us. And then, if these things don't happen, we feel that we are somehow failing God. As a disabled person, I have sometimes been told I don't have enough faith.

So, it is a relief to read words such as these, words that admit to the struggles we will all go through. It's a relief to see the stark honesty written across them: sometimes things are going to be overwhelming. But ...

But. The 'but' is even more important than the 'when' because it is where we find comfort. The waters may almost swallow us up, the fire may almost consume us, but God is there in the waves and there in the flames, walking with us and keeping us from being overcome.

We are called by name, and we belong to God. We are precious and honoured in his sight. God's heart has always been for restoration, and we can take hold of that here and now, even if it feels as though we are on the edge of drowning. So today, take hold of one truth: God walks with you.

† Lord, thank you that you call me by name, that you are with me in the fire, and I am not overcome. Help me to hold on to you and to praise you through my storms. Amen.

For further thought

Picture Jesus standing in front of you and calling you by name. His voice is tender and bursting with love. How do you respond?

20 June
A way in the wilderness

Read Isaiah 43:18–21

Forget the former things; do not dwell on the past. See, I am doing a new thing! Now it springs up; do you not perceive it? I am making a way in the wilderness and streams in the wasteland.

(verses 18–19)

You are almost consumed.

You've been dragging across barren wasteland so long you can't remember what flowers look like. Scrubby brown grasses wave listlessly in the unforgiving heat and harsh gravelly sand scrapes at your weary knees. You are raging with thirst and your soul is at the end of itself. Where is hope? Where is God?

Then you see it. You gaze at it warily: it must be a mirage, a pretence to taunt you once again. There's no water near here. But then there's a rumble under your feet like a thundering of mighty rivers, and your heart leaps. It's true. Water springs from the ground in myriad places, cascading over the baked ground and then over your upturned face as you marvel at its power. You drink it in and nothing has ever tasted so pure. It infuses you with energy and you dance among its fountains. There on its edges you see new flowers burst from the earth and they are more beautiful than you remember.

You are still in the wasteland. There's a long way to walk to get home. But now your walk is infused with something new – something that shimmers in the warm air before you and draws you onwards. All around you God is weaving the glory of hope. And a comforting whisper breathes through the air: Forget the former things. Forget the former things. I am doing a new thing.

Can you perceive it today? Can you dig into your imagination and join with God's work there? Can you taste holy water from the streams in your wasteland?

† Lord, thank you that you make a way through my wilderness and that your water of life refreshes and restores me. Thank you that you are doing a new thing in my life. Amen.

For further thought

Do you know someone who is in a wasteland – maybe even physically? How can you help them practically today?

June

Comfort and hope (from Isaiah 40–55) (1)

21 June
The Spirit poured out

> **Read Isaiah 44:1–8**
>
> *For I will pour water on the thirsty land, and streams on the dry ground; I will pour out my Spirit on your offspring, and my blessing on your descendants. They will spring up like grass in a meadow, like poplar trees by flowing streams.*
>
> (verses 3–4)

As I write this from my home in Shropshire in the UK, winter is approaching. In the winter I love to curl up by a roaring fire with a warm blanket and a good book: it is a place of comfort for me. We started last week in a place of comfort – not fleeting comfort, though, like a warm room or a good meal, but the lasting comfort of knowing we are saved and we are loved.

Isaiah loves to write about comfort and hope, and his book is infused with these things. He knows that his descendants will feel cut off and abandoned after their time of exile, and also knows that they will taste the freedom of restoration and the great blessing God will bring upon them and their future generations. He knows God will pour water on their thirsty land and also knows that one day the land will be fully redeemed within a new heaven and a new earth, where abundant life will belong to all who ask and joyous freedom will reign.

Isaiah is giving the people a new and astounding truth: the Spirit will be poured out. They have only known the Spirit upon individuals – prophets and kings – but now they are assured that the Spirit will be for all people. And we have the privilege of living in that reality, where the fresh water of the Spirit is poured on our thirsty ground, where we can know the Comforter beside us, lifting up our heads. As you go into the next week, may you live fully in the wonder of holy comfort and bask in hope that never fails.

† Holy Spirit, thank you that you are my Comforter, that you assure me with the hope of glory. Help me to take hold of this hope and offer it to all those around me. Amen.

For further thought

Read Ezekiel 47:1–12 and ask God to give you a picture of a river flowing where everything will live and where everything will be healed.

Comfort and hope (from Isaiah 40–55) (2)

Notes by **Catherine Sarjeant**

Catherine describes herself as living in a messy place in which she is being treated for complex PTSD. She lives in this messy place with Jesus and has a passion for helping others meet him in the reality of life. She co-leads a small house church learning together that God is with us in the midst, bringing order out of chaos. She is married with two teenage children. Catherine has used the NRSVUE for these notes.

22 June
There is no other

Read Isaiah 45:1–7

I call you by your name; I give you a title, though you do not know me. I am the LORD, and there is no other; besides me there is no god. I arm you, though you do not know me.

(verses 4b–5)

It's easy to assume that if someone is used of God to preach, to lead, to perform miracles, they must be godly. Yet here in our passage, God uses Cyrus as a prophetic voice to Israel even though, as he says, they do not know him. Despite this, God gives him a ministry (title) and empowers (arms) him.

This means that we need to be discerning – just because God has used someone, doesn't mean that they are godly. On the other hand, just because someone doesn't do things in the traditionally 'Christian' way, or have 'right' vocabulary, doesn't mean that God is not in their life.

When we put our trust in people based on the gifts or ministry that they exercise, we place both them and ourselves in danger – if their character is not as developed as their gifts, they will likely fall, with all too familiar consequences.

As a trauma survivor, I understand these dangers only too well, but there's a more positive side. If we don't always find Jesus where we should, we can often meet him in surprising places: with a Samaritan woman, tax collectors, the demonised, the sick. As we go through this week, look out for God in unexpected places!

† Lord Jesus, help me discern those who have not only been graced with your gifts, but have your heart.

God's patience

> **Read Isaiah 48:6–13**
>
> *You have never heard; you have never known; from of old your ear has not been opened. For I knew that you would act very treacherously and that from birth you were called a rebel.*
>
> (verse 8)

God's people, then and now, are called to represent who he is to a world that doesn't yet know him. But then, as now, we so often misrepresent him and ironically, the more God reveals of himself, the more of him there is to misrepresent! This passage expresses this dilemma – God longs to reveal more of himself and his purposes, but this rebellious people keep taking what they think they know and distorting it, turning everyone away from him.

In my early years as a believer, I absorbed views about God from preachers and other Christians, as well as the view prevalent in society. Many of the believers were godly and well intentioned and much of the teaching was sound. But alongside these were running themes – not just in what people said, but also the way they behaved, and these built a consistent picture that misrepresented who God is. Like many, I came to see God as distant and somewhat scary, and church as legalistic and transactional: if I did good and kept the rules then others/God would do good back to me; if I didn't he would shun me and instead of blessing me I would be cursed. Which meant when bad things happened, I had not only those things to deal with, but also the guilt of presuming I had been sinful and deserving of punishment from an irate Father.

Thankfully, I had an awakening where I saw that it is all about relationship with a loving and living God. Nothing outwardly changed, the pieces of the puzzle were identical; they just got rearranged and the proper picture became clear.

† Lord, thank you that what was hidden for so long has now been made clear in Jesus. Help us to live in the joy and love this brings.

For further thought

How can we better represent who God is, as individuals and as church?

You are not forgotten

Read Isaiah 49:7–18

Sing for joy, O heavens, and exult, O earth; break forth, O mountains, into singing! For the LORD has comforted his people and will have compassion on his suffering ones ... See, I have inscribed you on the palms of my hands.

(verses 13,16a)

Isaiah writes to a people still in slavery and deep distress and yet writes as if their release has already happened 'I have answered', 'I have helped'. They were in the place of darkness, but God's words, being in the present tense, provide a concrete hope: it is done, it is finished, it is assured – even though it is not yet.

It echoes Jesus' words on the cross, in that bleakest, most desperate of all places. As he is experiencing the full consequences of sin and brokenness, separation from the Father, darkness deeper than anything ever known – in that place, a cry of victory, a declaration of hope, 'It is finished!'

One thing I have learnt over the years is that God is faithful, but there is often a distance between the hope and the realisation of that hope – an in-between place of trust. Often, we step faithfully but see nothing noticeable changing, no massive breakthrough. It's a bit like a balloon filling up with air: the balloon gets larger, but nothing else changes. What we can't see is the air getting more pressured, feeling trapped by the balloon until finally, something changes – the balloon bursts, air rushes out ... freedom as the constraints and barriers are broken.

Maybe you're feeling the increasing pressure – circumstances pushing against hope, just like the balloon. Maybe the balloon has just burst – it's messy and uncomfortable. I spent seven years waiting for breakthrough from PTSD and when it came it wasn't my idea of the beginning of breakthrough (a collapse response in a public place)! Hear the words of Isaiah: freedom is coming.

† Thank you, Jesus, that even when you endured the worst, you spoke words of hope for us. Help me to hear those words when I feel far from you.

For further thought

Do you know someone who is feeling that pressure right now? How can you help them hear words of hope – and how can you co-work with God to be the fulfilment of that hope?

June

Comfort and hope (from Isaiah 40–55) (2)

25 June

Comfort even for the desert

Read Isaiah 51:1–6

For the Lord will comfort Zion; he will comfort all her waste places, and will make her wilderness like Eden, her desert like the garden of the Lord; joy and gladness will be found in her, thanksgiving and the voice of song.

(verse 3)

It's easy to assume that people are in a wilderness because of their own poor choices. Yet Israel journeyed through desert to get to the land God had promised. John the Baptist chose the desert as a place of ministry and the Holy Spirit led Jesus there after his baptism. Desert places, like any other, can be places of calling and growth. Maybe you are in a desert place, but that doesn't mean that you're not actively seeking God, nor that you are in the wrong place!

The key in the desert is to look where you have come from, what of God you have known in the past. Your identity is rooted in the fact that you were made in God's image – not in the current reality of the desert place.

Battling through the ongoing effects of trauma can seem like a desert place, but I have always known God with me, have always worked at seeking him. In the worst places where I can't see or hear him because the noise of trauma has become so loud, there's been great comfort in knowing his presence in the past, and knowing what he's done for others has kept alive the hope of better.

The truth is that beauty can be found in the desert. The rich colours and shifting hues, the majestic scenery, the starlit nights. And then, where you least expect it, fertile springs and a carpet of radiant flowers. A place of abundant life in and beyond the desert too. Salvation for ever, deliverance not only from the desert but from all the effects of the desert, joy and gladness are the destination with comfort in the journey.

† Lord, though I may be in a desert place, help me see you there with me. May we gaze together on the beauty, in the comfort of each other's presence.

For further thought

Meditate on some desert experiences that you have known. Without ignoring or minimising the challenges, what of God's presence and comfort did you encounter? What beauty did you see?

Comfort and hope (from Isaiah 40–55) (2)

Peace and salvation

Read Isaiah 52:7–10

The Lord has bared his holy arm before the eyes of all the nations, and all the ends of the earth shall see the salvation of our God.

(verse 10)

The ruins of our life are redeemed, and everyone will see the salvation that God has brought! It means that in the midst of the ruins, we still sing, because we have met God in that place and have confidence in a redeemed future. We have known his comfort in the middle of the mess, the arid waste of the desert, and *in that place* we rejoice – not because of the place, but because of his presence in that place.

For me, the day to day can be pretty bad, when trauma responses kick in and a bit of havoc ensues – yet even there, I know God with me, and his presence makes it walkable. It is genuinely horrid and yet, at the same time, filled with hope, because God reveals himself in the midst.

Sometimes that revelation comes directly – God co-working with me in my healing brings dignity and empowerment and, above all, a trusting relationship. This in itself is healing – the God of all authority not imposing instant healing, when in the past it was those in authority imposing who abused.

Sometimes though, it is through friends who have walked with me, not minimising my experience of the ruined places, but reminding me of the promise that I will see the full salvation of God. The passage begins by praising those who bring this good news of peace, salvation, redemption, and that ultimately our God reigns (verse 7). My experience echoes that – friends walking with me, me being that friend to others.

Waste places, see the salvation of your God. For one day soon, all will be redeemed.

† Lord Jesus, thank you that together we can sing for joy in the ruined places, knowing that all the earth will see the salvation you have won.

For further thought

Do you know someone who needs to have you walk with them, acknowledging the reality of the current situation, but encouraging them with this wonderful truth?

June

Comfort and hope (from Isaiah 40–55) (2)

God's everlasting love

Read Isaiah 54:1–8

Do not fear, for you will not be ashamed; do not be discouraged, for you will not suffer disgrace, for you will forget the shame of your youth, and the disgrace of your widowhood you will remember no more.

(verse 4)

The picture is of a lonely woman, sitting huddled in a small, confined tent. She is childless, her husband left her when she couldn't give him children. Shame and humiliation are her only companions. She feels hopeless, her world is small and constricted, she wants to give up. And into that place, God sees and speaks, saying in effect: 'Enlarge your tent, make space for the more that I will bring.'

Sometimes, our world can feel like that too. Even with lots of people around, we can feel alone, insignificant, small, ashamed. When I was a young person, having suffered abuse, I carried shame, in part, because I felt that I must be bad for such terrible things to have happened. The shame made me want to shrink and hide, just like the woman must have felt. In reality, the woman had done nothing wrong, and neither had I, but our worlds had shrunk, nonetheless.

God restores our agency – he encourages the woman to enlarge her tent. In full view of those who perhaps had got used to seeing her as small, or perhaps thought that she should be small, God says, 'Enlarge the site of your tent' (verse 2). Don't hold back, do not fear that enlarging will bring more shame, I will protect.

This is the good news! Shame is not the end of the story. God will remove judgement, condemnation, humiliation – and replace it with dignity, value, worth, significance.

Let's be people who speak out these words to those who see their world as small, who have been made to feel small and ashamed and worthless, and let's work with them to enlarge their tents.

† Lord, thank you for shielding me, for covering my shame, for working with me to enlarge the tent of my self-worth. Thank you for loving me and honouring me.

For further thought

Are there those you know who appear small or whose world has been made small? How can you help them 'enlarge their tents'?

28 June
God's offer

Read Isaiah 55:1–11

Now you shall call nations that you do not know, and nations that do not know you shall run to you, because of the LORD your God, the Holy One of Israel, for he has glorified you.

(verse 5)

These messages in Isaiah have been wonderfully encouraging to us as individuals: comfort in lonely places, abundance and beauty in deserts, joy knowing that ruins will be restored, shame replaced with dignity, smallness enlarged, life in all its fullness! But of course, the message is to a nation, not just individuals – indeed, it is a message of hope to all nations.

And this is one of the amazing things about God – he holds the needs of the individual and those of nations as equally important and is able to address both at the same time! And that's the message here – as individuals who are thirsty, we come to him. In the passage, God made a covenant with David as an individual. But the covenant extends out to the whole nation – as individuals respond as David did, the impact ripples ever outward and the nation is encouraged in faith and drawn together in unity.

And that's the fulfilment of God's plan for Israel – that as they are blessed individually and collectively by God's active presence amongst them, they become a blessing to all the nations around them, because even the 'ends of the earth shall see the salvation of our God' (Isaiah 52:10).

It isn't just comfort for us – wonderful and true though that is – it's much bigger than that! As we receive, as our tents are enlarged, as our understanding of God becomes bigger, people see the goodness and beauty, the glory of God. And they run to him. They discover as individuals 'who it was who asked you' and they ask him and he gives them living water (John 4:1–15) and food without cost (verse 1) – not because it is cheap, but because it is priceless.

† Father, thank you that we are part of such a great adventure – to see lives restored, waste places flourishing, joy breaking out. May we today carry that hope and that joy to the nations as we meet with people and share you with them.

For further thought

How big is your vision? Is it to see just your salvation or that of those you know and love? Or do you need to enlarge the tent so that your heart connects with God – not just for the few, but for the nations?

June

Comfort and hope (from Isaiah 40–55) (2)

179

Abundance and want

1 Plenty

Notes by **Dr Ruth Perrin**

Ruth is a writer, researcher and Bible teacher based in Durham, UK. She has a special passion for supporting the faith of young adults and has spent twenty-five years doing that in different ways. Her dream is to see generous, hospitable communities of God's people sharing life and faith with those who don't know Jesus yet. And to help tired, anxious Christians find times and places to rest with the God who really does love them. Ruth has used the NRSV for these notes.

29 June
The God who loves to bless

Read Deuteronomy 28:1–14

If you will only obey the LORD your God, by diligently observing all his commandments that I am commanding you today, the LORD your God will set you high above all the nations of the earth, all these blessings shall come upon you and overtake you.

(verses 1–2)

God promised Abraham his descendants would be blessed and become a blessing to many nations (Genesis 12:1–2). Long before Jesus was revealed as the ultimate blessing, God made a covenant with Israel which included 'terms and conditions' – the blessings and curses of Deuteronomy. Christian ideas on God's blessings have varied. Some consider them reserved for the new heaven and earth. Others take these verses as a personal promise not an ancient covenant. Neither view is the Bible's overall picture. However, these verses show three things: first, God's character – his desire for human flourishing and delight to bless; second, his concern for practical aspects of human life, not just eternity; and, third, this is a communal promise – God cares about individuals, but this vision is for a nation living in abundance. Starting this week's reflections, it's important to begin from these truths: God is good, his concern is holistic – but he longs for humanity to thrive, not just to bless individuals. Abundance means many things, not just personal wealth, health and happiness. Let's allow him to speak and perhaps shift our perspectives.

† Thank you for your desire to bless humanity, Father. Open our hearts this week to what you'd say about abundance in our lives and communities.

30 June
God's compassion and abundant possibility

Read Matthew 9:35–38

When [Jesus] saw the crowds, he had compassion for them, because they were harassed and helpless, like sheep without a shepherd. Then he said to his disciples, 'The harvest is plentiful, but the labourers are few.'

(verse 36)

Matthew situates this teaching from Jesus between miraculous healings of vulnerable people and the disciples' first mission. The Gerasene demoniac, a paralysed man, tax collectors, Jairus' daughter, a haemorrhaging woman and two blind men are all socially ostracised, living in pain and shame. Jesus restores them to abundance – life, health and community.

Matthew explains that these are not isolated incidents. Jesus travelled far and wide offering good news, dignity and hope. His motivation? Compassion. Jesus longs to bring comfort, peace and security to the confused, distressed and those who are suffering. A good shepherd leads sheep to abundant green pastures so they can thrive. Jesus wants the same for humanity.

He uses an agricultural metaphor to explain. Humanity is an abundant harvest: vast, ripe fields; vines weighed down with fruit; trees with bowing branches. Their need is so great, pain so overwhelming, confusion and lostness so vast. Jesus longs to harvest them to his Father's house, and explains the need is for those willing to carry his message of hope to them.

There are two challenges. First, do we feel compassion when we see people's need, or do we judge, or, overwhelmed, hide from it? Second, will we answer the call to be labourers, offering the gospel to those around us in distress? Not everyone who met Jesus became his disciple, and not everyone we bless will come to faith – but still, the world continues to be full of pain. There is a harvest ripe in our generation too and we are the ones God is calling to share the hope we have!

† Lord, soften our hearts where they are hardened to the world's suffering. Give us vision when we feel overwhelmed, courage to share our hope, and faith to see your Spirit transform lives.

For further thought

Who desperately needs God's love and to experience the power of his Spirit? Ask Jesus to show how he would have you bless them in his name.

June

Abundance and want – 1 Plenty

Abundant life in Christ – not what you might expect!

Read Matthew 7:1–7

Do not judge, so that you may not be judged. For with the judgment you make you will be judged.

(verse 1)

What does living an abundant life look like? Wealth? Comfort? Luxury? Not according to these words of Jesus. Instead, it looks like healthy relationships and wise living.

First, being gracious rather than judgemental and instead of criticising, being aware of our own failures. As we become mature, gracious people *then* we can bless others by helping them grow. Jesus is harsh with those who pass judgement without looking in the mirror, calling them hypocrites.

Secondly, wisdom with our treasures and who we share them with. Be they dreams, our hearts or the precious parts of ourselves. An abundant life does not look like chasing popularity, or giving ourselves to those who are not wise and kind. In the age of social media so many people 'overshare' for 'likes', or make foolish choices. Jesus calls his followers to reflection and wisdom, to be vulnerable with those who can really be trusted.

Thirdly, humility to bring our needs to God. Rather than independence and trying to fix everything ourselves, he teaches us to pray – asking God as a vulnerable child asks a parent for what they need. It's not a case of 'naming and claiming' or trying to manipulate God. It's having humility to know we don't have to be strong, because he is, and confidence that we are loved by a God who delights to give good gifts.

So, graciousness, wisdom and humility. A life of healthy relationship with others, ourselves and our Lord. That is what an abundant life looks like.

† Father, forgive our focus on material things. Help us grow in graciousness, wisdom and humility and to build abundant relationships with you and others.

For further thought

Which of these is the greatest challenge for you? Spend some time reflecting on why that is and bring it to the Lord to change in your heart.

Walking with humanity, God's abundant goodness

Read Leviticus 26:9–12

I will walk among you, and will be your God, and you shall be my people.

(verse 12)

These verses describe God's covenant with Israel, the promise of favour, fertility and food – on the condition that they obediently live as his people. They also show another promise – fellowship.

Part of the covenant blessing was God's presence, reminiscent of Genesis when he walked in Eden with humanity. Verses 11–12 promise more than material blessing – also relational blessing, God living and walking with Israel. This is God's great dream, to be reunited with humanity, to live with us in a tangible way. Ultimately, this longing was so powerful that he came in the person of Jesus to dwell and walk among us, as well as to make reconciliation possible through the cross.

Sometimes people have tangible encounters with God's presence. Often, they describe an inexpressible peace, a joy they can't articulate, a powerful sense of God's love that moves them to tears. These fleeting moments become foundational events in their faith, something they never forget. Whether in a prison cell, looking at a beautiful view, in an atmosphere of worship, or a movie theatre, God can and does sometimes make his presence felt.

However, even these are fleeting glimpses of his eternal promise that one day all those who call on the name of Jesus will powerfully and permanently experience his presence and love in a new heaven and earth. More than possessions and provision, the true blessing we will experience is God's wonderful presence. That is the deepest longing of both God and man, and one day we can be sure it will come to pass.

† Father God, you put eternity in the hearts of humanity. Make us those who long for relationship with you more than physical blessing and give us faith in your promise of eternal fellowship.

For further thought

Which is your priority – physical blessing or relationship with God? Consider the root of that and how you might set your eyes on the bigger prize!

Abundance and want – 1 Plenty

July

Blessed to be a blessing: abundant support

> **Read 2 Corinthians 9:1–15**
>
> *The one who sows sparingly will also reap sparingly, and the one who sows bountifully will also reap bountifully. Each of you must give as you have made up your mind, not reluctantly or under compulsion, for God loves a cheerful giver.*
>
> (verses 6–7)

In ancient Rome, charitable giving was rare. Although the emperor might occasionally give gifts, the poor were mostly expected to take care of themselves. However, as the church in Jerusalem faced persecution, famine and poverty, the apostle Paul began a collection for them from other congregations. This was a new idea, and the relatively wealthy Corinthian church appeared reluctant to keep its promise to contribute.

Paul exhorts them with various tactics: he shames them with the example of the impoverished but generous Macedonians and emphasises the importance of Christians keeping their word. But he focuses on two heart responses: gratitude and generosity. He reminds them that God has given them so much and is delighted when his people pass that blessing on in acts of generosity.

This is still a wonderful principle, recognising what we have been blessed with and then being generous with it. God's people have always been 'blessed to be a blessing' (Genesis 12:2). Here Paul is teaching gentile believers to embrace that way of living.

Human nature is to accumulate resources for status and security. Sometimes Christians similarly think that if we give, God will owe us interest. Paul flips this thinking around, encouraging gratitude first and generosity as a response. Generosity *is* a risk, but also a wonderful way of life. It *is* a blessing to bless others and be the answer to their prayers, and God *will* honour that. Even if all we can give is a tiny coin, or a moment of our time, we know God delights in the generous sacrifice of a grateful heart.

† Lord, everything we have comes from you. Make us grateful and show us how to live generous lives that bless others and delight you.

For further thought

Who might God be asking you to bless today? What might that generosity look like?

4 July
Embracing Christ's abundant victory

Read 1 Corinthians 15:51–57

'Death has been swallowed up in victory.' 'Where, O death, is your victory? Where, O death, is your sting?'

(verses 54b–55)

In a world where people fear death above all else, the apostle's words are striking. He has had a revelation: God has shown him a wonderful mystery. At the return of Christ, the sound of a victory trumpet will herald something astonishing. The dead will be raised, and God's people will be transformed into something imperishable and immortal. He doesn't have words to properly describe this, but it will herald a mighty triumph and the defeat of death.

Paul is exuberant, passionate, confident in what he has been shown. Death will not win. Jesus will.

What might it look like if we really grasped this? If we really were not afraid of death. If we really understood that we are freed from living in the shadow of sin. What would a fearless you look like? How would you think, choose, act differently? How might God use you? Wouldn't living in that faith, that confidence, that assurance of God's abundant victory be wonderful?

Paul had unique encounters with God and although we might not have those, embracing this sort of revelation still requires the Holy Spirit. These verses give us wonderful information, but to get it from our heads to our hearts takes a move of the Spirit. Living in abundant victory is an act of faith, and that is a gift from the Lord. So, what might you ask God for to enable this heart transformation? What do you need from him to embrace and live out the life of abundant victory? He delights to bless his children, remember!

† Thank you for your victory, Lord Jesus – for the freedom and hope it gives. Holy Spirit, please give us revelation to live that out in tangible ways until you return or call us home.

For further thought

What makes you afraid? What is stealing your peace? Ask Jesus to bring revelation of his abundant victory in those places. His perfect love drives out fear.

5 July

Abundance and lack – growing up into Christ

Read Philippians 4:10–13

I can do all things through him who strengthens me.

(verse 13)

So far, we've reflected on God's blessings and our responses, but here Paul explains how he reacts when life isn't materially abundant! The Philippian Christians have sent a gift to support him, and he is grateful. But his gratitude seems more for their love than the money itself.

He explains that he has learnt to be content whether he has more than he needs, or not enough. The secret is that his strength comes from the Lord. Paul is so certain of God's love that even when he has nothing he doesn't doubt, but presses in, experiencing supernatural strength. Likewise, when he has more than he needs he is grateful, but God's love hasn't changed.

Most of us find this a challenge. When things are financially difficult, we are tempted to wonder why God isn't blessing us. Are we being punished? Have we been abandoned? This is a sign of immature faith that is 'tossed to and fro'; God wants us to 'grow up in Christ' and when tested to stand strong, not doubt (Ephesians 4:14–15). Like a parent teaching a toddler to walk, sometimes God takes a small step back to draw us towards him, to stretch and strengthen our faith muscles. He has not abandoned us but is growing us into maturity, to a place where we draw our strength from him directly, not just the things he blesses us with.

I aspire to 'be content in all circumstances' (verse 12) but I'm a work in progress. How wonderful that God is abundant in grace and mercy for the little children toddling after him – like us!

† Loving Lord, help us remember the extent of your great love for us and to lean into you when we lack what we think we need. Give us your strength in our weakness, Jesus.

For further thought

Recording answered prayers or creating an 'Ebenezer' (memorial object) can remind us of God's faithfulness when we doubt. What might you do to memorialise God's goodness in your life?

Abundance and want – 1 Plenty

July

Abundance and want

2 Scarcity

Notes by **Christopher Took**

Chris is an Anglican from an open evangelical tradition. Currently living near the top of a tower block in inner London, he has lived in the English Midlands, Durham Castle and County Dublin. He runs a website for Irish election results, has had some success in the Sermon of the Year competition, chairs a residents' group on fire and building safety for his local council and is studying Biblical Hebrew with City Lit. Find more resources at his website https://biball.org. Chris has used the NIVUK for these notes.

6 July
The rich and the poor

Read Proverbs 22:1–16

The generous will themselves be blessed, for they share their food with the poor.

(verse 9)

Do you think of yourself as rich or poor? How do others judge your economic status? What would those from richer or poorer countries think? Material poverty and wealth are relative, and definitely depend on the eye of the beholder!

'Money can't buy happiness,' we're told. But not having enough for our needs is stressful and can lead to poor mental and physical health.

Scarcity is one of the central concepts of modern economic theory. Being a little cynical, it's all about allocating scarce resources to those who can afford them. But we are reminded blessings (not quite the same thing as happiness) come from allocating scarce resources to those who need them (verse 9).

Our passage starts by declaring that our character and reputation should be the most valuable assets we have (verse 1). Riches come from humility: fearing God leads to riches and honour and life (verse 4). It's not so much what others think of us, but what God thinks.

Developing our relationship with God can be costly, but there's no scarcity with God's grace.

Whatever our material circumstances, true riches can be ours.

† Help me understand what's truly valuable in this world and in my life, so I can share what I have with those who are poor.

7 July
Providing for the poor

Read Exodus 23:10–13

*Six days do your work, but on the seventh day do not work, so that
your ox and your donkey may rest, and so that the slave born in your
household and the foreigner living among you may be refreshed.*

(verse 12)

The Covenant Code (Exodus 20:22 – 23:19) can seem like a random
collection of rules. These regulations are presented as spoken
directly to Moses by God, in the context of the Israelites hearing
God's voice (20:22) and an emphasis on God as the only God
(20:23). Worship brings blessing (20:24).

Clearly, these requirements relate to the operation of a
sophisticated society, describing an extensive framework of
criminal, civil, moral, economic and liturgical laws. Penalties range
from fines to death. These are rules to be taken seriously!

Today's extract comes near the end of the Covenant Code – and
verse 13 is a final warning to observe the rules closely and not to
be distracted by other gods and idols.

In verses 10–12, we are given two patterns of 'six plus one' –
the first covering years and the second the more familiar weekly
Sabbath pattern.

Along with scarcity, productivity is another important economic
concept. The idea is to squeeze everything possible out of the
factors of production, whether that means buildings, capital,
machinery or people. The idea of leaving land unused for a whole
year might seem a complete waste. In the UK and elsewhere, it's
taken two or more centuries of struggle to gain legal protections
so people don't have to work sixteen-hour days, seven days a week.

The Bible insists we take care of the poor, the stranger, those who
work for us, and even animals – both domesticated (verse 12) and
wild (verse 11). That care for the poor and those on the margins
should be the central concern of society. It's putting Proverbs 22:9
into action, where blessings follow the generous.

† Lord, I pray that I might experience the healing of your Sabbath rest, and that I
would encourage and enable others to experience it too.

For further thought

Those on the margins of society need not only relief from poverty
but relief from stress. What can we do to provide rest and
refreshment?

8 July
The poor and justice

Read Leviticus 23:15–22

When you reap the harvest of your land, do not reap to the very edges of your field or gather the gleanings of your harvest. Leave them for the poor and for the foreigner residing among you. I am the Lord your God.

(verse 22)

The Festival of Weeks described in this passage is called the Festival of Harvest in Exodus 23:16 and 'the firstfruits of the wheat harvest' in Exodus 34:22. I happened to be writing this reflection on the Sunday my church held its Harvest Festival – a very different celebration in twenty-first-century London than in ancient, agricultural Israel. But the basic principles remain the same: giving thanks for what God has provided, donating the best of what we have for God's use, and sharing our blessings with others, especially those in greater need.

In the Christian calendar, the Festival of Weeks corresponds with Pentecost, when we think about receiving the Holy Spirit rather than giving our offerings. Of course, in many ways, there is nothing we can give in return for such a great gift as the Holy Spirit. As the carol 'In the Bleak Midwinter' asks: 'What can I give him, poor as I am?'[1] But this isn't a rhetorical question designed to imply we can't possibly be expected to give anything worthwhile. The answer is to 'Give my heart'. Or as Isaac Watts declares: 'Love so amazing, so divine: demands my soul, my life, my all.'[2]

We see an overwhelmingly generous God who gives us the gifts of his Son (according to 1 Corinthians 15:20, the firstfruits of the new creation) and his Holy Spirit. In our reading today, God chooses to declare who he is in the context of making provision for the poor – 'I am the Lord your God' (verse 22). A just God is always going to identify himself with those who suffer injustice.

† Show me, Lord, what of mine I can share – materially, spiritually and emotionally. Help me recognise both injustice and the opportunities you provide for me to share with others.

For further thought

Fortunately, we are spared the elaborate ritual around animal sacrifice, but does this mean we take our offerings to God less seriously than we should?

[1] Christina Rossetti, 1872.
[2] 'When I Survey the Wondrous Cross', Isaac Watts, 1707.

Abundance and want – 2 Scarcity

July

189

9 July
The Lord hears the poor

Read Psalm 34:1–7

Glorify the LORD with me: let us exalt his name together.

(verse 3)

This joyful psalm of confidence in God declares that the poor (verse 6) and afflicted (verse 2) will join with all God's people in rejoicing. The psalm is associated with a difficult time for David – he was living in self-imposed exile, fearing for his life, pretending to be insane, carrying the promise he was to be king but with his prospects not looking good (1 Samuel 21:10–15)!

We noted earlier the importance of character. David's faith in God is able to sustain him even when he has left behind all his friends, possessions and status. It's this strength of character that enables him to praise God in the midst of disaster and isolation, and to encourage others to join him in this worship.

There's an ongoing conversation in this psalm between God and his people. The context for this interaction is praise and worship, even though some of the people are afflicted, fearful, troubled or shamed. David invites them all to join him in exalting the name of the Lord.

The scarcity of material resources is no barrier to receiving blessing from God. Perhaps even more importantly, the psalm seems to emphasise that those in particular need will be heard by the Lord and he will respond to them. David's personal testimony (verse 6) is that God heard 'this poor man' and saved him.

The promise is not that those who cry out will find a place of physical safety. Rather the angel of the Lord (often taken as a prefiguring of Jesus himself) will come to them, surround them and save them. Let's glorify the Lord together!

† Thank you, Lord, that you are a God who hears and answers. Help me to encourage others to join me in worshipping you and may your praise always be on my lips.

For further thought

What's your experience of the sort of worship David describes? What can you do so that praise of the Lord is on your lips more often?

10 July
Not impressed by riches

Read Ruth 3:1–15

I will do for you all you ask. All the people of my town know that you are a woman of noble character.

(verse 11b)

Both Boaz and Ruth get mentioned later in the Bible as the direct ancestors of Jesus (Matthew 1:5), where it's clear they're also the great grandparents of King David. This is an obvious honour, even more so for Ruth as a foreign woman. Boaz notes Ruth's good reputation and 'noble character' (verse 11). As an impoverished outsider, Ruth may have had to resort to some creatively unorthodox but ultimately innocent actions in order to get noticed by Boaz.

If you are poor, life is often chaotic. Circumstances such as war, famine, economic recession and ill health are often beyond the control of individuals, especially if they are already the victims of injustice, discrimination or misunderstanding. Ruth – female, widowed, foreign – finds herself in a precarious situation. She is successful in attracting the attention of Boaz, even if her methods seem strange to us. 'Cover me,' Ruth asks, in effect proposing to Boaz and inviting him to extend his protection to her, lending her his honour (verse 9). A wonderful prefiguring of our cry to Jesus that his forgiveness might cover us, that he might honour us with his name.

The Bible is littered with examples of God using surprising people in surprising ways! The prophet Samuel was reminded, 'The LORD does not look at the things people look at. People look at the outward appearance, but the LORD looks at the heart' (1 Samuel 16:7).

It's too easy to discount and exclude those on the margins. We can make assumptions about abilities and attitudes without knowing the full story. Could we do better at seeing people the way God does?

† Lord, help me to see the world around me with your eyes. Everyone's story is different – help me to understand something of the value you see in those who might not get a second look.

For further thought

What impresses you about others? Are you influenced by factors that don't really matter? How can you spot more valuable qualities in people?

Good things for the hungry

Read Luke 1:46–55

...for the Mighty One has done great things for me – holy is his name. He has filled the hungry with good things but has sent the rich away empty.

(verses 49, 53)

Today's reading (often known as the Magnificat, from the first word of its Latin translation) is probably one of the most familiar passages of scripture. It combines wonder at the greatness of God with humility for his involvement with us as individuals.

The angel who visits Mary tells her (twice – Luke 1:28, 30) that she has found favour with God. It's Mary's character, not her status, which has led to God singling her out for the incredible honour and responsibility of bearing his Son.

As with David in Psalm 34 (see 9 July), Mary begins with praise and a call to worship. This is never a bad place to start and can be helpful on those days when we don't especially feel like praising God. Mary recalls the many ways God has demonstrated his faithfulness throughout history, and her confidence that he will continue to do so. God is objectively worthy of our praise – it doesn't matter what mood we are in!

But the truly powerful message from Mary's song is her description of the 'topsy-turvy' kingdom, where the world's view of power and success and importance is turned on its head. God distinguishes (verse 51) between those who appear humble and those who really are!

Instead of the allocation of scarce resources to those who can afford them (see 6 July), it's the hungry (those who can't afford food) who will be filled (verse 53). Those who hold positions of power and influence will be deposed, and those who think they have nothing to offer will be raised up (verse 52). O magnify the Lord!

† Ever-worthy Lord, may praise be on my lips! Like Mary, may I find favour with you and may I be willing to offer myself in your service.

For further thought

My favourite version of the Magnificat is from Roger Jones' musical, *While Shepherds Watched* (can be found on YouTube, e.g. at music.youtube.com/watch?v=bq8nytodPo4). Why not listen to Mary's song, spoken or sung?

12 July
An antidote to scarcity?

Read Genesis 47:13–25

There was no food, however, in the whole region because the famine was severe; both Egypt and Canaan wasted away because of the famine.

(verse 13)

This is another challenging passage, where a degree in ancient Egyptian economics might be useful! There are some problems with the text – in verse 21, did Joseph move people into cities (NIV alternative reading) or reduce them to servitude? The Egyptians ended up in bondage anyway (verse 25). Even servitude may not be a terrible experience with a wise ruler like Joseph, but (see Exodus 1:8) times change.

The biblical narrative is overwhelmingly positive about Joseph's character, even if at times we might sympathise with his brothers' irritation. He behaved with integrity regarding Potiphar's wife, was popular in prison and was trusted instantly by Pharaoh to lead Egypt through a monumental crisis, which he did with great success.

For Joseph, the preservation of life in Egypt was his priority when managing the scarcity of food (and then the scarcity of money) in the face of an enduring famine. His actions may seem like sharp practice to us, but he saved everyone from death, introduced a fair (for the times) taxation system and provided them with seed to restart food production when the famine ended.

Joseph acted in the best interests of those who were not God's chosen people. The worst consequences of the famine seemed to afflict Egypt (Canaan isn't mentioned after verse 15). Joseph could have been concerned just with his own survival and that of the Israelites back in Canaan. But he had a much wider perspective. He had an eventful life of ups and downs where God always looked after him.

It may seem counter-intuitive, but could the best response to scarcity be generosity?

† Help me, Father, to respond with prayerful generosity to those in need throughout the world. Help me be wise in how I spend my money, plan my time, use my vote and share my resources.

For further thought

Generosity isn't just about money. Is there something more you could do with your time, skills or other resources to help those in need?

Letter to the Hebrews (1)

Notes by the **Revd Dr Ash Barker**

Ash is a leadership developer, shalom activist, communicator and Pioneer Minister. He has lived and served on the front line of urban poverty for over thirty years, beginning in his native Melbourne, before twelve years in Bangkok's largest slum and, since 2014, Birmingham, UK. Ash has authored eight books and leads post-graduate courses with Nazarene Theological College. With wife Anji, Ash lives in community at Newbigin House in Winson Green, is Minister at Lodge Road URC and leads 'Seedbeds' for growing community leaders. Ash has used the NRSVUE for these notes.

13 July
Jesus' unique significance

Read Hebrews 1:1 – 2:4

Long ago God spoke to our ancestors in many and various ways by the prophets, but in these last days he has spoken to us by a Son, whom he appointed heir of all things, through whom he also created the worlds.

(1:1–2)

Today, we begin a two-week walk through the book of Hebrews. We are not sure of the author – Paul, Barnabas, Apollos, Priscilla are all suggested by some scholars – but what we can be certain of is that whoever they were, they knew Jesus. Their love for him inspires a passion to communicate that always leaves an abiding impact.

Through the whole book, encapsulated in the first verses, we are reminded of the unique significance of Jesus Christ. Uniquely through him, we have direct access to God; no longer do we need intermediaries of either people or rituals. Uniquely through him, we have a direct revelation of God; the Son is the radiance of God's glory. Not only this, but he is unique in his ministry – he and no other can purify sin and he alone sustains all things by his powerful word. And he is unique in position – even the angels acknowledge and serve him.

Jesus has become God's Message himself. In Jesus, the fullness of God's revelation has been made known. Through his teachings, his life and his sacrifice on the cross, we gain intimate knowledge of and access to the depth of God's love and grace.

† Creator Father, may our lives witness to Jesus' love, and may we never waver in our faithfulness to you, as you never waver in yours toward us. Amen.

The dignity of all humanity because of Jesus

Read Hebrews 2:5–18

What are humans that you are mindful of them or mortals that you care for them? You have made them for a little while lower than the angels; you have crowned them with glory and honor, subjecting all things under their feet.

(verses 6b–8)

The writer of Hebrews takes us on a journey into the depths of Jesus' humanity. In these verses, we are reminded that though Jesus is divine, he willingly took on human form. He became like us in every way, sharing in our experiences, our joys, our sorrows and our struggles, our brokenness.

Imagine the Creator of the universe, the one who spoke galaxies into existence, choosing to become a fragile, vulnerable human being. He subjected himself to the limitations of a human body, the trials of earthly life, and even betrayal, torture and death. Why? Because God loves and values people that much. All of us are of incalculable worth to God.

Yet, we live in a world where multitudes of people live and die without experiencing worth and dignity. War, poverty and torture are daily experiences for millions. Abuse and a deep sense of shame and worthlessness are a way of life for so many. How can we worship this Jesus and not be broken-hearted at the travesty of this contrast? God intends all people to be 'crowned with glory and honour' yet so often we have robbed them not only of their crowns, but of their humanity.

Let this insight inspire us today and throughout the week. May we find courage in the fact that our Saviour, who shared in our humanity, is with us every step of the way and wants all people we meet to flourish in dignity. In his name, may we all find justice, joy and shalom in the Holy Spirit.

† Creator Father, we thank you for the incredible gift of your Son. Help us to remember his humanity and see his image in others. Amen.

For further thought

As we face the week ahead and see suffering of all kinds, let us remember that Jesus, who was made like us, can be our source of strength and hope.

15 July
Jesus: the greatest liberator of all!

Read Hebrews 3:1–19

Jesus is worthy of more glory than Moses, just as the builder of a house has more honor than the house itself.

(verse 3)

Moses was undoubtedly a remarkable figure in Israel's history. He led the people out of slavery in Egypt, received the Ten Commandments on Mount Sinai, and served as a mediator between God and the Israelites. His faithfulness and obedience were unquestionable. Yet, in this letter to the Hebrews, we are reminded that Jesus is even greater than Moses. How could this be?

The passage opens by urging us to consider Jesus, the Apostle and High Priest of our confession. Jesus, unlike Moses, is not just a servant in God's house; he is the Son who built the house. Moses was a faithful servant within the house, but Jesus is the Creator and Sustainer of the house itself. He is the foundation upon which our faith rests.

While God used Moses to lead the Israelites out of oppression in Egypt, Jesus liberates us in even more profound ways today. God in Jesus empowers us directly to live out God's will, freeing us from the bondages of all sins and deaths. Moses provided the law and told us what God wants, but Jesus fulfilled God's will and showed us what is possible.

But if we are to be freed, we have a part to play: under Moses, the Israelites had left Egypt, but Egypt had not left them and had to be dried out of them in the desert. We can choose to cling on to the old ways, the ways that led to death and bondage; we can harden our hearts against the liberation Jesus brings.

Let's hold fast to our confidence in Christ and live free!

† Creator of all, help us fix our eyes on Jesus, and allow his grace, compassion and guidance to inspire us in our journey of faith and life.

For further thought

How can we trust in Jesus' leadership and follow him faithfully today? How can we lead others to a place of liberty when the road to it might seem frighteningly unfamiliar?

Letter to the Hebrews (1)

July

A Sabbath rest for the people of God

Read Hebrews 4:1 – 5:10

Sabbath rest still remains for the people of God, for those who enter God's rest also rest from their labors as God did from his.

(4:9–10)

In these verses, we are reminded of the promise of entering into God's rest. Just as God rested from creation on the seventh day, there remains a rest for his people. This rest is not merely a physical rest, but an ever more profound rest that comes through faith in Jesus Christ. It is so much more than just an absence from work.

The Hebrew word *shalom* can be helpful here. Shalom means harmony between God, people and place. This is the rest that comes when all creation is healed. The fight against evil and injustice is gone; all that is left is a profound contentedness won by Jesus. All striving ceases. And it is something we can have a foretaste of now as we allow Jesus to be the source of shalom in a restless and fractured world.

As we navigate the challenges and the busyness of our lives, let us remember that true rest and peace can be found in Christ. It is not about ceasing from physical labour for a day, but about finding rest for who and where we are in him. It's about trusting in his ultimate defeat of injustice and evil on the cross, where he provided forgiveness of sins and reconciliation for all things with God.

So, today, let us take a moment to soak in God's promised shalom. Let us lay down our worries and cast our concerns upon him and find courage in the promises of his word. Jesus offers us a rest that rejuvenates our spirits. May this rest in Christ renew and strengthen us for the journey ahead.

† Creator Father, we thank you for the promise of shalom found in Christ. Help us to enter into that rest and harmony through faith, trusting in his finished work and relying on his grace. Amen.

For further thought

Where, today, do you need to experience that perfect rest, that shalom that is promised in Christ? However busy you are, pause and meditate on the completed work of Jesus and allow him to whisper peace into your soul.

Letter to the Hebrews (1)

July

A warning against falling away

Read Hebrews 5:11 – 6:20

We have this hope, a sure and steadfast anchor of the soul, a hope that enters the inner shrine behind the curtain, where Jesus, a forerunner on our behalf, has entered, having become a high priest forever according to the order of Melchizedek.

(6:19–20)

We see in this passage a contrast between the steadfast, sure anchor that is God and the fickle, shifting allegiances of people!

The author of Hebrews begins here by expressing concern that the readers have become spiritually numb, struggling to connect with God's deepest concerns. It's so often the beginning of a falling away from fidelity in Jesus. It's something that most believers will encounter at some point in their journey – maybe it's where you are right now.

Sometimes circumstances in our lives make us question God's care of us or those we love, sometimes trauma numbs us to his presence, closing us off from his word. That which used to be an anchor, an immoveable certainty in our life, has come adrift, and remaining faithful to the former things becomes increasingly difficult.

For others, it may not be circumstances that have led to this place; it may simply be that we have drifted from dynamic personal relationship with God to a form of religious experience. The life and vitality that used to be there has become dulled with time and familiarity.

The writer compares these situations to soil that has received ample rain but produces only thorns and thistles – that which was fertile has become a fruitless wasteland. The good news is that we don't have to be wastelands! The writer encourages us to imitate those who through faithfulness and patience inherited God's promises. If your life feels like that at the moment, don't despair, don't allow guilt or shame to hold you in that barren place. God knows, God is with you, the anchor is still there.

† Creator Father, grant us the wisdom and strength to remain gritty in our faith. Keep us from falling away and enable us to inherit your promises of fruitfulness. Amen.

For further thought

How can we seek deeper understanding of God's concerns, so that we don't become numb to those around us?

18 July
Jesus like Melchizedek the priest of God

Read Hebrews 7:1–28

This 'Melchizedek, king of Salem, priest of the Most High God, met Abraham as he was returning from defeating the kings and blessed him,' and to him Abraham apportioned 'one-tenth of everything.'

(verses 1–2a)

The story of Melchizedek is extraordinary! Abram has just won a battle when he encounters this mysterious figure who seems to appear from nowhere and yet who Abram responds to as if it is God himself. Even the name is intriguing, meaning 'king of righteousness', and his title 'king of Salem' at a time well before Jerusalem existed. So, here we have one whose priesthood is without beginning or end, who is both king of righteousness and king of shalom and to whom Abram offers worship and a tenth of his spoils.

What are we to make of this and how does it impact us today?

Perhaps, like Abram, we need to be alert to the presence of God in unexpected places or people, to see Jesus in the smile of the stranger, to give time to the passer-by, to give of our resources to those outside our culture or our comfort zone. Perhaps this is the way in which we receive the peace of God and the righteousness of Christ.

It reminds us too that there is one to whom the rituals, the law, the sacrifices point who is greater than all of them. They are never an end in themselves, they are never to become idols, displacing the one to whom they point. Melchizedek and the one he represents came before the priesthood, the Temple, the Church – and his priesthood continues beyond all of those, because he is greater than they.

Jesus is our High Priest and King of Shalom. We can now experience a love that is capable of breaking down all barriers between God, people and places.

† Creator Father, help us to grasp the depth of Jesus' kingship and priesthood and the healing presence it provides. May we live each day in the confidence of his life and work with, by and for us. Amen.

For further thought

Consider the permanence of Jesus' priesthood and the temporary institutions which point to him. How can we avoid making these the focus rather than keeping our eyes on Jesus?

Letter to the Hebrews (1)

July

High Priest of a new covenant

Read Hebrews 8:1 – 9:10
And they shall not teach one another or say to each other, 'Know the Lord,' for they shall all know me, from the least of them to the greatest.

(verse 11)

The old covenant, established through the Mosaic law, had its limitations. It required constant sacrifices for the forgiveness of sins, and the earthly tabernacle was a mere shadow of God's reality. However, with Jesus' arrival, everything changed. He became the mediator of a new and better covenant, one that brings transformation at a much deeper level for all people and places.

Through the sacrifice of Jesus on the cross, God defeated the haunting power of death and sin over us. He didn't just enter an earthly tent but entered reality itself, appearing before the presence of God on our behalf. His priesthood is real, unchanging and effective.

The old covenant's rituals were symbolic, signs pointing to the ultimate reconciliation of all things to come. In contrast, the new covenant in Jesus is transformative, offering us forgiveness and power to change from within us and our communities. It writes God's laws on our hearts and minds, enabling us together to have an intimate and personal relationship with Jesus and empowerment by the Spirit to do God's will.

As we reflect on this passage today, let us be filled with gratitude for Jesus, our High Priest, and the new covenant he inaugurated by defeating death. We no longer need to rely on external rituals for change but can trust in his finished work on the cross.

May we embrace the transformation that comes through the new covenant, allowing God's word to be written on our hearts, minds and lives. Let us draw near to him with confidence, knowing that Jesus, our High Priest, intercedes for us and offers us forgiveness, grace and the promise of abundant life.

† Creator Father, we thank you for the new covenant made possible through Jesus Christ, our High Priest and King of Shalom. Help us embrace the transformation offered: your word written in our hearts and lives. Amen.

For further thought

What would you like Jesus to be praying for now as he stands at the right hand of the Father, interceding?

Letter to the Hebrews (2)

Notes by **Dortje Brandes**

Dortje, born in Germany, is the second of four children whose loving parents taught her about God from a young age. After finishing a degree in international business, her quest to travel the world and discover God's plan for her life led her to YWAM, an international missionary organisation that she worked with for six years. Today, she feels privileged to work for both a church and a business. Dortje loves nature, adventures, Jesus and being an aunt to her amazing nieces and nephews. Dortje has used the NIVUK for these readings.

20 July
The blood of Christ

Read Hebrews 9:11–28

How much more, then, will the blood of Christ, who through the eternal Spirit offered himself unblemished to God, cleanse our consciences from acts that lead to death, so that we may serve the living God!

(verse 14)

Do you enjoy mysteries? I love the thrill of escape rooms – sixty minutes to decipher clues, solve puzzles and unlock mechanisms for the ultimate 'escape'. On the other hand, with the same intensity that I love solving mysteries, it irritates me when I can't figure them out!

In a similar way, I'm humbled by the mystery of Jesus' sacrifice. It's a mystery beyond my human comprehension, a divine escape plan offering eternal freedom. While I may not fully grasp the entirety of this mystery, I marvel at the beauty of God becoming human and sacrificing his life out of love for us. I rest in the assurance that, despite my imperfections, I'm loved and saved by his blood.

In escape rooms, I search for clues that lead to 'freedom', much like the way Jesus' blood reveals the pathway to eternal redemption. It's a mystery not hidden in shadows but illuminated by divine love. Just as I relish 'Aha!' moments in solving mysteries, the writer of Hebrews celebrates the revelation of Christ's sacrifice.

† Jesus, thank you for your blood, thank you for giving your life. Help me understand the power of your blood even more, the redemption and freedom that it brings not only in eternity but also here and now.

21 July
A sacrifice once for all

Read Hebrews 10:1–18

For by one sacrifice he has made perfect forever those who are being made holy.

(verse 14)

Have you ever felt the need to earn God's forgiveness? If only you had humbled yourself more, tried harder, done better? On a cognitive level, I understand I'm forgiven, that Jesus has paid the price once for all. Yet, I'm surprised how often I try to earn God's mercy – thinking that reading my Bible more, praying more, shedding tears of remorse would make him more likely to answer my prayers. This reveals that, on a heart level, I haven't fully grasped the mind-blowing and life-changing truth of Jesus' sacrifice.

Hebrews 10:1–18 vividly portrays the limitations of the old covenant's sacrificial system which demanded repeated offerings to attempt to cover sins. Yet the true goal of the law was the realisation that out of our own strength, we will never be perfect, will never measure up. It's only through Jesus' sacrifice that we enter the presence of God. His sacrifice, offered once for all, becomes the eternal bridge between our imperfections and God's holiness. This profound truth dismantles the notion that I must continually prove my worthiness. It beckons me to lay down the heavy yoke of rule-keeping and endless striving to be good enough, inviting me to find rest in the finished work of Christ.

As I reflect on these words, I sense the freedom that flows from deeply understanding this truth. The burden of trying to earn forgiveness lifts, replaced by the grace that speaks a louder word than my shortcomings. Today, I reject the illusion of having to earn God's grace anew each day. Instead, I embrace the eternal truth that Christ's sacrifice covers me completely.

† Thank you, Jesus, for making me perfect before God through your sacrifice. I invite you into my striving, my attempts to be good enough, my efforts to measure up. Help me rest in the deep revelation that your sacrifice was once for all.

For further thought

Find something that enables you to reflect on the blood of Jesus – bread and wine or something that is evocative for you. Take a moment to reflect on Jesus' sacrifice and let the truth sink in even deeper that he has paid it once for all.

Letter to the Hebrews (2)

July

22 July
A call to persevere

Read Hebrews 10:19–39

...let us draw near to God with a sincere heart and with the full assurance that faith brings, having our hearts sprinkled to cleanse us from a guilty conscience and having our bodies washed with pure water.

(verse 22)

Have you ever feared God? When I was a kid my dad would have sudden anger outbursts, probably due to being very overworked. Once, one of my siblings accidentally dropped a glass, and my father started yelling and furiously stamping his foot. His anger felt utterly unpredictable, which made it even scarier. It took me years to realise how much these experiences affected my perception of God.

The passage begins by highlighting the privilege we have through the blood of Jesus to enter the most holy place to stand before God. When we draw near to him with genuine hearts and unwavering faith, we are embraced into his presence.

The writer proceeds to emphasise that persistent, wilful sin after understanding the truth results in severe judgement, akin to the punishment faced by those who rejected the law of Moses. The writer concludes with, 'It is a dreadful thing to fall into the hands of the living God' (verse 31). What a strange thing to write after the incredible encouragement of us having gained direct access to God. What is the writer's intention? To scare his readers?

The Bible instructs us to fear God, but not in the manner in which I feared my dad. A healthy fear of God is key to enduring the challenges and trials that confront us. 'In the fear of the Lord one has strong confidence' (Proverbs 14:26, ESV). I'm still on the journey of discovering what it means to fear God in a good way. Until I fully grasp this mystery I will cling to the hope that I can confidently approach my heavenly Father, all thanks to Jesus' sacrifice.

† Father, thank you for welcoming me to confidently stand in your presence. In a world full of fear, anxiety and terror, teach me what it means to fear you in a godly way.

For further thought

How have your experiences with your earthly father shaped your perception of your heavenly Father?

By faith

> **Read Hebrews 11:1–22**
>
> *And without faith it is impossible to please God, because anyone who comes to him must believe that he exists and that he rewards those who earnestly seek him.*
>
> (verse 6)

Have you ever wondered whether your faith is enough? This verse – 'without faith it is *impossible* to please God' (emphasis added) – used to frighten me. What if my faith isn't enough? Faith seemed to be this mysterious substance that some people have lots of, others a bit and some none. What is faith really?

'Faith is confidence in what we hope for and assurance about what we do not see' (verse 1). Why didn't God instruct the writer of Hebrews to explain faith in a simpler way?! Could anyone describe faith in a more cryptic manner?

The Greek word for 'faith' is πίστις (*pistis*) which can also be translated 'trust'. By trusting God, we comprehend that the universe was brought into existence by his command even if we don't grasp all the scientific mechanics. By trusting God, Noah built an ark to save his family, despite lacking a manual on 'Surviving on an ark with numerous animals'. By trusting God, Abraham offered Isaac as a sacrifice even though he didn't understand God's motives; he chose to rely on God's benevolence and believed that he could even resurrect the dead.

Faith means to trust. I may not comprehend the reasons, witness the grand scheme or see the outcomes in my lifetime. Nevertheless, I can actively choose to trust God. Choose to trust that he knows the bigger plan. Choose to trust that by nature he *is* good and thus his plans are as well. Choose to trust that he *is* love. And in moments when my trust in God falters, I invite the Holy Spirit to address whatever hinders my trust in our amazing, loving and good God.

† God, thank you for all those people who have gone before us, who wrote history with you not because of their greatness but because they chose to trust you. Help me deepen my trust in you.

For further thought

In what areas of your life is it easy for you to trust God? In what areas do you struggle with having faith in God? What helps you when you struggle to have faith?

24 July
What more shall I say?

Read Hebrews 11:23–40

These were all commended for their faith, yet none of them received what had been promised, since God had planned something better for us so that only together with us would they be made perfect.

(verses 39–40)

Occasionally, I find myself yearning to be like Moses, witnessing the Red Sea parting; like Gideon, triumphing over enemies with just three hundred men; like David, defeating the giant Goliath with just a sling. While Hebrews 11 might appear as a gallery of faith superheroes, a closer look unveils their flaws: Moses' anger, leading to murder; Gideon's fear, prompting him to hide; and David's moral lapses, such as adultery and orchestrating a murder. It wasn't their greatness, their amazing leadership skills, their super strength, but God working through them despite their imperfections and failures.

As tempting as a superhero life may seem, it entails sacrifices. Consider Marvel or DC movies – the hero pays a high price for saving the world. Moses was only a baby when he was separated from his family and raised by strangers. After spending forty years with the nagging Israelites in the desert, he was never to enter the promised land. Daniel was abducted as a juvenile, having to spend his life in a foreign land.

Hebrews 11:35–38 details living in caves, torture, flogging, imprisonment and death. Their commendation for faith contrasts with unfulfilled promises. These stories inspire yet challenge me – God working the miracles through imperfections but asking if I'm ready for the cost. How can I grow in character and deepen my relationship with God to endure trials and hardships? These reflections propel me not to just wish for miracles but to earnestly seek growth in character and trust in God – both in sickness and in health, for better and for worse.

† Jesus, I'm grateful that my imperfections and failures do not limit your ability to work miracles. Guide me in developing my character and faith so that I can navigate and endure the trials and challenges ahead.

For further thought

I invite you to grab a piece of paper and a pen. Write down every promise of God given to you personally. Reflect on which promises have already been fulfilled and which ones are yet to be realised.

Letter to the Hebrews (2)

July

25 July
A warning against refusing God

Read Hebrews 12:14–29

Therefore, since we are receiving a kingdom that cannot be shaken, let us be thankful, and so worship God acceptably with reverence and awe, for our 'God is a consuming fire.'

(verses 28–29)

Have you ever felt the desire for a delicious meal after a tiring workday, craving something satisfying but not wanting to invest much time in cooking? In those moments, options like frozen pizza or a frozen vegetable medley become enticing choices, often without a thorough consideration of the long-term consequences. So, I can sympathise with Esau who, confronted with hunger and the immediate availability of a delightful cooked meal, chose instant gratification over his rights as the firstborn.

In many parts of the world, we are increasingly captivated by instant gratification, with same-day deliveries and on-demand content. I find myself reminiscing about a time when patience and enduring wait times were intrinsic to daily life, when waiting a week for the next TV episode or days for a mail-ordered item from a catalogue used to be normal.

The author of Hebrews urges us to make every effort to live in peace with everyone and to be holy. Am I prepared to take the necessary steps to actively pursue holiness and peace? In which areas of my life is it more tempting to cling to anger or engage in gossip? And where do I succumb to sin merely because it seems easier than resisting?

Reflecting on my faith, I examine where I might be seeking shortcuts for instant gratification. Will I pursue God even if it requires time and sacrifice, such as reducing TV or phone usage? Will I patiently await God's guidance, or will I hastily seek answers elsewhere? Am I open to God speaking into my life? Will I adhere to his words, even if it comes at a cost?

† 'Search me, O God, and know my heart! Try me and know my thoughts! And see if there be any grievous way in me, and lead me in the way everlasting!' (Psalm 139:23–24, ESV).

For further thought

Where does the temptation of instant gratification hinder your relationship with Jesus? How can we cultivate patience and endurance, both for ourselves and to assist others, in a world that often encourages immediate satisfaction?

26 July
Keep on loving each other

Read Hebrews 13:1–25

So we say with confidence, 'The Lord is my helper; I will not be afraid. What can mere mortals do to me?' … Jesus Christ is the same yesterday and today and for ever.

(verses 6, 8)

I stare at the vault apparatus in our school gym. The fear of embarrassing myself starts to creep into every cell of my body. What if I don't manage to jump *over* it? What if I bump into the vault and everyone laughs? 'The Lord is my helper; I will not be afraid. What can mere mortals do to me?' As I say these words in my mind, courage begins to rise up. I start running and jump.

Psalm 118:6 has been a source of courage for me in numerous tough situations, extending way beyond the challenges of facing the vault in gym class. It's a verse that is incredibly precious to me. Therefore, I find it intriguing that the author of Hebrews quotes this exact verse.

As we approach the conclusion of the book, the author, before finishing with a blessing and greetings, imparts some final key instructions: keep loving one another, practise hospitality, remember those imprisoned and honour marriage. The author then urges staying free from the love of money and finding contentment in what we have. This guidance is anchored in God's promise, stating, 'Never will I leave you, never will I forsake you' (verse 5). So we say with confidence, 'The Lord is my helper; I will not be afraid. What can mere mortals do to me?' (verse 6).

Do I deeply believe that God will never abandon me? Is he not just beside me, but my helper? Jesus Christ is the same yesterday, today and forever.

† Thank you, Jesus, for being the same yesterday, today and forever. Thank you for your promise never to leave me. With you by my side, I don't need to fear what people might say or do to me.

For further thought

Reflect on your current life. How content do you truly feel? What do you perceive as lacking? In Philippians 4:11–13, Paul discusses the secret to contentment. What could this secret be, and how can you learn to be content in all circumstances?

Letter to the Hebrews (2)

July

207

Professions of faith

1 Recognising Jesus

Notes by **Stephen Willey**

Much of Stephen's ministry in the Methodist Church has been in areas of multiple deprivation. Currently based in Coventry, England, he encourages the use of the arts, especially among young and vulnerable people, to address mental health issues, develop community cohesion and explore spirituality. Stephen is interested in mission to the economic world, has worked to counter human trafficking, and is interested in exploring how the mission of the Church can be expressed in different economic contexts. Stephen has used the NRSVA for these notes.

27 July

Peter sees Christ: Son of the living God

Read Matthew 16:13–17

[Jesus] said to them, 'But who do you say that I am?' Simon Peter answered, 'You are the Messiah, the Son of the living God.' And Jesus answered him, 'Blessed are you, Simon son of Jonah! For flesh and blood has not revealed this to you but my Father in heaven.'

(verses 15–17)

Sometimes we see things clearly and are able to believe in them, but things are not always obvious. As a child, I remember my mum spotting a well-camouflaged bird in the countryside. Try as I might, I couldn't see what she was looking at. Peter responds to Jesus by saying, 'You are the Messiah, the Son of the living God,' and he is blessed. Perhaps the other disciples hadn't seen it, maybe they still didn't see it and were disappointed, indeed frustrated, when Jesus affirmed what Peter had spotted.

The year 2025 is the 1,700th anniversary of the Council of Nicaea, which produced the Nicene Creed. When we look at that creed, we might feel like Peter – very sure and very enthusiastic – or we may feel challenged, even doubtful, as we reflect on how we see God. Peter's confession doesn't come from the lips of any of the other disciples at Caesarea Philippi, although later on Martha also says those words (John 11:27). I trusted that my parents had seen a bird, but I might not have believed a person I didn't not know so well. As Peter declares his faith in Jesus can we trust him to be right?

† Living Christ, I too am your disciple. Help me to follow Peter's gaze and see that you are the Christ, my Saviour and Friend.

28 July
Belief and disbelief

Read Mark 9:14–27

...he fell on the ground and rolled about, foaming at the mouth. Jesus asked the father, 'How long has this been happening to him?' And he said, 'From childhood. It has often cast him into the fire and into the water, to destroy him; but if you are able to do anything, have pity on us and help us.' Jesus said to him, 'If you are able! All things can be done for the one who believes.' Immediately the father of the child cried out, 'I believe; help my unbelief!'

(verse 20b–24)

When I failed French for the second time, I was really disappointed and I decided I'd never take another language exam in my life. Fourteen years later, beginning to train for ministry, I was told that Greek was a compulsory part of my course. Another foreign language exam, and one I had to pass! Friends said, 'Of course you will pass your Greek' – but I wasn't so sure. I worked hard for that exam and, as the examination date approached, I felt reasonably sure I would get through, but I still doubted. Previous experience had led to considerable doubt and gloom in me. Imagine my surprise when I got my highest mark in Greek!

In Mark 9, the boy's father surely feels deep gloom and doubt. His boy's condition and prognosis seem so bleak. No one he'd approached could heal his boy. Jesus was making a huge impact on people at the time and perhaps they'd said to the father that this healer was authentic. Maybe they'd said, 'He can heal your boy.' But, while he was going to give Jesus a go, the father had serious doubts. It might be possible this time, but experience had taught him not to hope too much, not to give all his trust only to see his hopes dashed. 'If you can,' he pleads, but there is doubt. Jesus sees this and challenges him – you don't need to doubt me, he is saying – and then the man opens his heart: 'I believe, help my unbelief!' Jesus does not ask for more; that is enough! The child is made well.

† Christ, you healed the sick and bound up the broken-hearted. Open my heart to a greater belief in you, not just for myself, but for all those entrusted to my care.

For further thought

How important is it that I believe with my whole heart? What would Jesus say to me about my faith?

29 July
Thomas believes

Read John 20:26–29

[Jesus'] disciples were again in the house, and Thomas was with them. Although the doors were shut, Jesus came and stood among them and said, 'Peace be with you.' Then he said to Thomas, 'Put your finger here and see my hands. Reach out your hand and put it in my side. Do not doubt but believe.' Thomas answered him, 'My Lord and my God!' Jesus said to him, 'Have you believed because you have seen me? Blessed are those who have not seen and yet have come to believe.'

(verses 26b–29)

'Why are the sheep behaving in that way?' we asked ourselves in the half-light, as night approached. Running this way and that, the whole flock looked distressed and confused. 'Perhaps it's a fox,' Kathryn said, but I couldn't see one. 'Yes!' she said, pointing, 'over there behind the fence.' A fleeting shadow passed by on the other side of a fence. I could barely see it, but I could see enough – the shape of a fox running on the other side of the sheep, disturbing their peace. So, she had guessed correctly about the fox. But why was it so important for me that she pointed it out and, also, that I was able to see it?

Why is it so important to see for oneself? Thomas, unlike Peter at Caesarea Philippi or after the resurrection, appears to need time to think before being convinced. Thomas could see a change in the behaviour of the disciples, but maybe he was a bit of a pessimist. After a painful and disappointing two weeks he needed to see Jesus himself if the gloom was going to lift. Perhaps Thomas didn't entirely trust his friends. He said to them that he needed to see Jesus alive and wounded. He wanted to verify for himself that Jesus was behind this change. It seems to me from the passage that Thomas believed the moment he saw Jesus – before he placed his fingers in the marks of crucifixion and, in my mind's eye, Jesus gently takes Thomas's hand to trace his wounds.

† In your imagination, ask the risen Christ to take your hand. Perhaps he helps you to trace the wounds of crucifixion? Then ask Christ where he wishes to lead you.

For further thought

How trusting am I of others when they say their faith has changed their behaviour? How does my behaviour affect the faith of others?

In Jesus' name

Read Acts 3:11–16

...you killed the author of life, whom God raised from the dead. To this we are witnesses. And by faith in his name, his name itself has made this man strong, whom you see and know; and the faith that is through Jesus has given him this perfect health in the presence of all of you.

(verses 15–16)

In the town where I lived there were amusement arcades run by a few individuals who formed a network. When my mum was helping Andy, who was part of that network, he said, 'If there is anything I can do for you, just say.' A few months later I was looking for work, so my mum said to Andy, 'My son needs a summer job. I don't suppose ...' 'Sorted!' said Andy. 'He should go to Ian's Amusements and tell Ian that Andy sent him.' The next day I went to Ian's Amusements. 'Have you got any work?' I asked. 'Doubt it,' some employees said. 'Is Ian around?' I asked. A few moments later Ian appeared from a room at the back of the arcade. 'Hello,' he said cheerily, 'what can I be a-doing for you?' 'Er, my mum knows Andy and he said you might have a summer job?' 'Well, any friend of Andy's is a friend of mine,' he said. 'You can start tomorrow at ten!' It was not a fair way to get a job but sometimes knowing a name can open doors.

Peter says here in Acts that Jesus' name opened the door for a man who was born lame. Unlike Andy's name, which opened a door for me, returning a favour, the name of Jesus opened doors for a stranger in need. God's economy, which Peter is working for, does not require 'silver or gold' (verse 6) and evidently people whom others may have written off as unproductive, like this lame man, are welcome in Jesus' network!

† Jesus, grant us faith in your name as you open doors which offer hope and life for ourselves and those in the communities and churches where we are serving.

For further thought

Do I believe Jesus' name has the power to change things? Which doors would I like him to open in my life or my community?

31 July
Peter's witness that God exalted Jesus

Read Acts 5:27–32

But Peter and the apostles answered, 'We must obey God rather than any human authority. The God of our ancestors raised up Jesus, whom you had killed by hanging him on a tree. God exalted him at his right hand as Leader and Saviour, so that he might give repentance to Israel and forgiveness of sins. And we are witnesses to these things.'

(verses 29–32a)

Until the last shot in the tennis match between Stan Smith and Ilie Nastase, I held out for Nastase to win and refused to accept that any alternative outcome was possible. When the match ended, I was in tears and my older brother was jubilant, having successfully backed Smith. I was angry at my victorious brother! I loved the way Nastase played and expressed himself. I had identified with him and I struggled to admit that Stan Smith had actually won!

Identifying with a player, a team, or a particular viewpoint, true or false, can have a great power. When Peter witnesses to Christ, the religious authorities condemn him. Their attachment to a different worldview means a refusal to see as Peter sees. Peter risks suffering as a result of his desire to share Christ with those more powerful than he is.

Those who follow Christ often have a strong desire to share how they see God's involvement with the world. However, what some see may not be welcomed by others. In the fourth century, church leaders shared how they saw things with the creation of the Nicene Creed. Many years later, discussion about a short statement of belief, and whether it should be included in the creed, caused distress for the Church. Arguments about the 'filioque clause' led to a rift within the Church and became a barrier to unity. How hard it can be to see a brother or sister's point of view, when we have made up our minds about which side we are on.

† Generous God, we call you Saviour and Friend, and desire to follow your example. Help us to live our faith in ways that give you glory and release others from pain, guilt or grief.

For further thought

Would I ever be part of a gang or group that insists on its own rules and excludes others?

John the Baptist witnesses to Christ's nature and status

Read John 1:29–34

'I came baptizing with water for this reason, that [Jesus] might be revealed to Israel.' And John testified, 'I saw the Spirit descending from heaven like a dove, and it remained on him. I myself did not know him, but the one who sent me to baptize with water said to me, "He on whom you see the Spirit descend and remain is the one who baptizes with the Holy Spirit." And I myself have seen and have testified that this is the Son of God.'

(verses 31b–34)

If 'seeing is believing' we may discover we are not at all sure what we believe! I love to see the wonder on the faces of children watching a magic trick. What they have learnt (recently, in their case) cannot possibly happen, has just happened in front of their eyes! Adults, too, can be astounded when the card they chose magically rises to the top of the pack in the hands of the conjuror. More confusing, perhaps, are optical illusions where, in the same picture, sometimes you see one thing and sometimes another.

John the Baptist, though a prophet, did not know what was going to happen with Jesus until Jesus came for baptism. Then, with the eyes of a person of profound faith, as he saw the Spirit descend on Jesus, John was able to see who Jesus was. Here before him was the Lamb of God, the Son of God, the person with authority even to forgive sins.

Later on in his life, John, in prison, seems to have become doubtful about the one he had seen by the river all those days before. Had he been wrong? Was it an illusion? Despite his earlier experience, it seems that John wondered, while he was in his cell, if Jesus was the one who would set people free. John sent his disciples to ask, 'Are you the one?' Jesus replied, 'Go and tell John what you hear and see: the blind receive their sight … the dead are raised, and the poor have good news brought to them' (Matthew 11:3–5).

† Open my eyes, Jesus, so I might see more of your nature, who you really are; not just for me, but for the whole of creation.

For further thought

When have I seen other people's eyes open wide with wonder? Could anything make me doubt what I have seen?

Christ, in nature God, became humble

Read Philippians 2:5–11

Let the same mind be in you that was in Christ Jesus, who, though he was in the form of God, did not regard equality with God as something to be exploited, emptied himself, taking the form of a slave, being born in human likeness. And being found in human form, he humbled himself and became obedient to the point of death – even death on a cross. Therefore God also highly exalted him and gave him the name that is above every name.

(verses 5–9a)

When I meet a loved one at the airport I often feel overcome with emotion. It isn't as if I doubted that they would come through the arrivals gate, or that I have forgotten them – I know them very well! However, as they become visible in the crowd there is a point of recognition. It is almost like I see them properly for the first time. What joy! They have made it! We are reunited!

People in the early Church are fervently looking for Jesus. As they look, they discover more about God's nature, though they already know Jesus. This ancient hymn in Philippians reveals what they have discovered about Christ. The practice of looking for Christ in the Bible, in hymns and liturgy, or in a creed, is a bit like going back to the arrivals gate and meeting him once more.

Believers coming together to sing a hymn reminds me of a family, all together at the arrivals gate. Our common joy, when we see Christ, reminds us who he is for all of us, although each one knows him differently. We might say to each other, 'It is Jesus who became like a slave for us' or 'He suffered and emptied himself for us' or 'His name is above every name'. Recognising Christ removes the separation that could cause division, isolation or loneliness. Neither isolated nor alone, we see who Jesus is. We may embrace one another as we welcome our Saviour, encouraged by sharing our beliefs and singing this hymn which ends in praise.

† Risen Christ, you became empty, as a slave, that we might never be alone. May our prayers, and our expectation of your coming, keep us close to all who are persecuted or alone.

For further thought

Who do I wish to see at my 'arrivals gate' and who might stand there with me?

Order your *Fresh from The Word* for next year!

Thinking ahead, now is the right time to order *Fresh from The Word*.

Order now:

- direct from IBRA web shop (see below)
- from your local IBRA rep
- from the SPCK website: www.spck.org.uk
- in selected Christian bookshops
- from online retailers such as Amazon, Eden and others

To order your copy from IBRA

- Website: **ibraglobal.org**
- Email: **sales@christianeducation.org.uk**
- Call: **0121 458 3313 (from outside UK: +44 121 458 3313)**
- Post: **using the order form at the back of this book**

E-versions of *Fresh from The Word* are available through online retailers such as Kindle, Kobo and Eden.

How are you finding this year?

Let us know how you are finding this year's daily Bible reading notes. If you are on Facebook or X (formerly Twitter), we would love to hear your thoughts, as little or as often as you like!

www.facebook.com/freshfromtheword

www.twitter.com/IBRAbibleread

You can write in too: IBRA, 4 Regal Court, 6 Sovereign Road, Birmingham B30 3FJ

You're part of a global community!

Where are you?

You may read *Fresh from The Word* on your own, with a friend, or even a small group, but that's just the tip of the iceberg. You are part of a large, worldwide and wonderful community of readers, all reading the same Bible notes every day!

Fresh from The Word notes are translated, published and distributed by our amazing IBRA partners; of a 75,000 plus total copies each year, 51% are printed in English (in the UK and overseas) and 49% are printed in other languages.

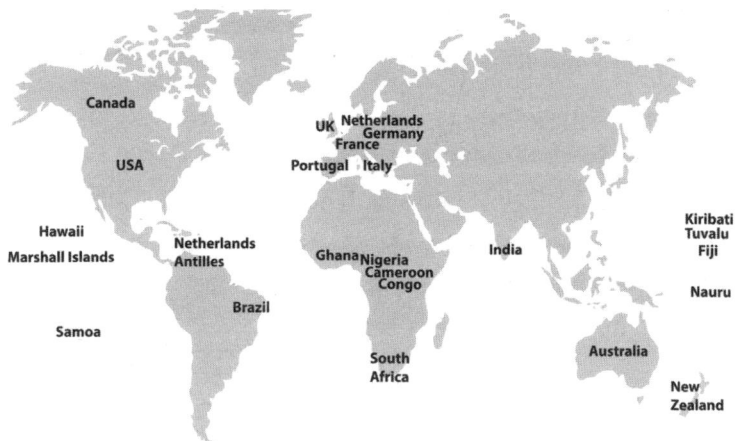

We have readers all over the world, in countries from A-Z: from Australia to the Bahamas, China to the Czech Republic, Hong Kong to Jamaica, the Netherlands and throughout Scandinavia, from St Kitts and Nevis, from the USA to Zambia and seemingly everywhere in between!

But where are you? We'd love to know!

Which part of the world is outside your window when you read your *Fresh from The Word*? Are you somwhere in the UK? Or reading this in India?

Please send us an email to: ibra@christianeducation.org.uk, or contact us via Facebook: www.facebook.com/freshfromtheword or X: www.twitter.com/IBRAbibleread

You are part of our IBRA family, and we'd love to get to know you!

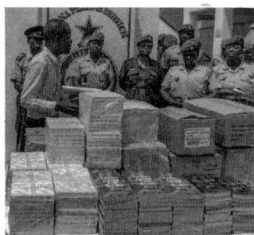

Two of our IBRA partners: AISSA in India and Asempa in Ghana

Professions of faith

2 Jesus is Lord

Notes by **Catrin Harland-Davies**

Catrin is a tutor at The Queen's Foundation for Ecumenical Theological Education, in Birmingham, UK, where she teaches New Testament studies and is Director of Continuing Ministerial Development. She is particularly interested in the development of ministry and church structures in the first century, and in how this might inform patterns of ministry and oversight today. Outside her teaching and research, she enjoys gardening, reading, walking and generally embracing middle age. Catrin has used the NRSV for these notes.

3 August
Jesus is Lord!

Read Romans 10:6–17

But what does it say? 'The word is near you, on your lips and in your heart' (that is, the word of faith that we proclaim); because if you confess with your lips that Jesus is Lord and believe in your heart that God raised him from the dead, you will be saved.

(verses 8–9)

'Lord' is a difficult title for many of us, with overtones of hereditary privilege or despotic rulers. Perhaps this is why I've always struggled with the declaration that 'Jesus is Lord'. I don't want to think of Jesus as despotic, and I don't like the highly gendered and authoritarian language that seems to align Jesus with the patriarchy. I'm more comfortable with the language of 'friend', 'brother', or perhaps 'teacher'.

But Paul's message shows another dimension to this title. He reminds us that the work of salvation is not ours to do. We are not asked to bring Jesus down from heaven, or to raise him from the dead. God has accomplished that, and all we need to do is to recognise it. We are witnesses to, not architects of, salvation.

In a world where an all-powerful Caesar was Lord, to proclaim Jesus as Lord was radical. And it remains radical today. It proclaims something greater than dictators, corporations or economic forces, and it lets go of the need to control our own destiny. Jesus is 'Lord' so that we don't have to be!

† Lord Jesus, when we feel powerless in the face of ruthless dictators or political and economic forces, help us to remember that you are Lord.

Mine be the glory ...?

Read 2 Corinthians 4:1–6

For we do not proclaim ourselves; we proclaim Jesus Christ as Lord and ourselves as your slaves for Jesus' sake. For it is the God who said, 'Let light shine out of darkness,' who has shone in our hearts to give the light of the knowledge of the glory of God in the face of Jesus Christ.

(verses 5–6)

I wonder what you understand by 'the god of this world'? Do you think of consumerism, or the cult of celebrity? Perhaps you have particular individuals or organisations in mind? These are all important readings, identifying idols which need to be removed.

I also wonder, though, whether there's an interpretation that comes much closer to home? Paul goes on to say that 'we do not proclaim ourselves'. And I find myself feeling deeply uncomfortable, because I suspect that I have too often proclaimed myself, instead of Jesus Christ as Lord. I don't mean that I have actively claimed to be divine, messianic or worthy of being worshipped – I think the danger is rather more subtle than that.

Sometimes, when I preach, I feel a sense of glowing self-satisfaction and pride. I've crafted a powerful and profound message, and I wait for the adulation that I deserve ... and all I get is polite 'thank yous'. At other times, I feel frustrated; my sermon was rambling and disorganised, and the message was unclear. But those are so often the occasions when someone will say, 'That really spoke to me.' I wonder whether that sounds familiar to you, as you preach, proclaim or seek to live God's love?

To be clear, I'm not suggesting that we should aim for mediocrity! We rightly do our best to give of our best. But are we sometimes driven by our own need to be admired or liked? Do we sometimes forget that it is only by God's grace that we can preach eloquently or minister God's love and care?

† Give me, loving God, the humility to put Christ at the centre of all I do and all I am, and to place my gifts at the service of the one who gives.

For further thought

This passage, read together with chapter 3, has often been used to justify antisemitism. Does the way we use scripture sometimes become 'the god of this world', allowing it to be used to justify the ungodly?

5 August
Making the good confession

Read 1 Timothy 6:11–16

Take hold of the eternal life, to which you were called and for which you made the good confession in the presence of many witnesses. In the presence of God, who gives life to all things, and of Christ Jesus, who in his testimony before Pontius Pilate made the good confession, I charge you to keep the commandment without spot or blame until the manifestation of our Lord Jesus Christ ... – he who is the blessed and only Sovereign, the King of kings and Lord of lords.

(verses 12b–15)

What strikes me about this passage is the huge climactic build in the status of Jesus. He starts off giving testimony before Pilate and facing death – vulnerable and human. Then, over three verses, he becomes 'our Lord', then 'the blessed and only Sovereign, the King of kings and Lord of lords', and eventually immortal, unapproachable, and worthy of 'honour and eternal dominion'. He climbs the ladder of royal seniority and ends up with eternal power or dominion.

And yet, he begins these few verses as a human figure in a human courtroom, giving testimony that includes 'the good confession' – the same 'good confession', presumably, that Timothy himself has given, as noted just one verse earlier. The word translated 'confession' (or, in some versions, 'profession') can also mean 'agreement'. Literally, it means 'the same word'. So this is not a unique, personal expression of faith, but rather an assent to something others believe too. Timothy has made that confession before witnesses, all of whom, presumably, had made it themselves at some point. And, before any of them, Jesus himself made it.

So, this is a statement of faith that brings Timothy into agreement – into fellowship, perhaps – with other men and women of faith and, crucially, into agreement – into fellowship – with Christ. We're never told what the specific wording of this confession is, but perhaps that doesn't matter. The point is that it's a statement of faith, and a statement of solidarity with the community of faith. When we state our faith, we stand with Christ, and shoulder to shoulder with all who have ever followed him.

† King of kings and Lord of lords, give me the faith to proclaim your glory, and the strength to stand firm among your followers from every time and place.

For further thought

What would be your 'good confession'? What summary of your faith could you proclaim with pride, in solidarity with centuries of Christians around the world?

219

So, that's who you are!

> **Read Matthew 14:32–36**
>
> *When they got into the boat, the wind ceased. And those in the boat worshipped him, saying, 'Truly you are the Son of God.'*
>
> (verses 32–33)

Have you ever had one of those moments where your knowledge of someone is deepened or completely transformed? Sometimes, they can be devastating moments of betrayal. But sometimes they can be positive and humbling: when the colleague we've always found difficult is the one to recognise that we need help and to offer it, or when we notice the person in real need, whose chief concern is to minister to the needs of another.

These are the kinds of moments which enable us to see more fully who that person is – to understand them more completely. And that seems to be what Jesus' disciples experienced in that boat. By this stage, they must have known that he was someone special. The very act of choosing to follow him would suggest that! But even so, they weren't prepared to encounter him in quite the way they just have. They have just witnessed him defying the laws of physics. And now he's controlled the very storm that was preventing them from reaching the shore! No wonder, then, that they cry out, 'Truly you are the Son of God!'

The Greek is ambiguous as to whether they see Jesus as *a* Son of God (a truly godly person) or *the* Son of God, but perhaps it's both. They see again, as so often before, God at work in him, but they also recognise something deeper – that they are somehow actually encountering God. Is the same true of us? Do we recognise God at work in others, and are we ready actually to meet with God through them?

† Loving God, help me to see you in the faces of my neighbours and to know you in the goodness I see. And grant that others may know you better through my life and actions.

For further thought

Where can you encounter God today? Could you end each day by giving thanks for three things that have helped you to know God better?

7 August
Being one

Read John 17:20–26

As you, Father, are in me and I am in you, may they also be in us, so that the world may believe that you have sent me. The glory that you have given me I have given them, so that they may be one, as we are one, I in them and you in me, that they may become completely one, so that the world may know that you have sent me and have loved them even as you have loved me.

(verses 21b–23)

This passage is surely one of the most beautiful expressions of the ideal of Christian unity, rooted in unity with Christ, that you will find anywhere. It may not have the analytical clarity of Paul's 'body of Christ' metaphor, or the scriptural weight of 1 Peter's 'spiritual house', but it is beautiful in its poetically paradoxical simplicity and complexity.

But it can be somewhat jarring to read it in context. The very next verse has Jesus go out to the garden where he will be arrested. Jesus prays for his followers to share in his glory – then immediately demonstrates a very unlikely route to that glory. I find myself wondering whether the disciples would really thank him for their participation in such glory (or, for that matter, for all the world knowing that they belong to him), once they realised what was involved!

Of course, that does seem to have been precisely their response, once things began to turn nasty, and who can blame them? But we know that the story doesn't end there. Unity with Christ turned out to be compelling enough to lead many of his followers, then and since, to choose precisely his path to glory – a journey possible only with such confidence in God's love. Even to those of us protected from persecution, the path of discipleship can be hard. But this isn't a path that we walk alone, or even alone with God. God's love is known and shown when we walk the path together, joined together as one through our collective oneness with the Father and with the Son.

† Righteous Father, make your name known to me and those who walk the path of faith with me, so that the love with which you love your Son may be in us, and sustain us.

For further thought

Give thanks for those who have walked with you in difficult times. How can you follow their example?

The cost of love

Read 2 Corinthians 4:10–14

[We carry] in the body the death of Jesus, so that the life of Jesus may also be made visible in our bodies. For while we live, we are always being given up to death for Jesus' sake, so that the life of Jesus may be made visible in our mortal flesh. So death is at work in us, but life in you.

(verses 10–12)

In my discipleship and ministry, I have never suffered the pain, indignities or hardships that Paul experienced as a result of his mission, nor anything close, thank God! I have, though, reached the point of exhaustion (physical and emotional). I have experienced heartache and even heartbreak. I have felt helpless, rejected and unfairly blamed. I'm not seeking sympathy; I'm not hard done by. Anyone who loves others risks all of this. Love means being present, even when it hurts. It means bearing the pain of others, when we have no answers or solutions to offer. It can mean becoming the focus of people's anger with God or the Church. It will often mean getting it wrong. To love is to be vulnerable.

I think this may be what Paul means when he speaks of carrying the death of Jesus in order to show the life of Jesus (only in his case there were also beatings, shipwrecks, arrest, the threat of death …). Loving the Church, loving God's creation, loving all people – this costs. It cost Christ, and it costs us. We can't show the kind of love that Christ lived to show without at times bearing the scars.

So what makes this kind of costly love possible? Surely it's that sharing in Christ's suffering also brings the promise of sharing in Christ's resurrection life. Loving others doesn't bring life only to them, but to those who do the loving. And that's because love isn't a series of actions or duties, but a way of life. In fact, it *is* life – life in all its rich, precarious, beautiful fullness.

† Loving God, help me to love others as you love me. Give me strength to bear their pain, patience to bear their anger, compassion to bear their suffering, grace to bear their rejection.

For further thought

What are the scars that you bear from loving others? What is the cost to you? And where do you find your support or respite?

9 August
Like mother, like daughter

Read 1 John 5:1–13

Everyone who believes that Jesus is the Christ has been born of God, and everyone who loves the parent loves the child. By this we know that we love the children of God, when we love God and obey his commandments. For the love of God is this, that we obey his commandments. And his commandments are not burdensome, for whatever is born of God conquers the world. And this is the victory that conquers the world, our faith.

(verses 1–4)

I've noticed that I'm turning into my mother. I see her in the mirror, and I hear her expressions when I speak. At the same time, as my children reach young adulthood, I look at them and see myself or my husband – or both!

This isn't just about genetics, but about values and learnt behaviour. Children imitate and learn from their parents – and not just their parents! My children were born into a wider community of family and friends, who shape who they are becoming, just as they continue to shape who I am. My children grow and learn in the same environment in which I am still growing and learning.

1 John suggests that we are children of God, nurtured and growing in the wider family of God, and that to love God is to love God's family. There is a slightly circular argument here. We know that we love God's children because we love God. And we show our love of God by obeying God's commands – foremost among which is to love the Lord our God with all our power, and to love others. So, we know we love others because we know we love God, and we know we love God because we love others.

But perhaps that circularity is the point. Loving God and loving God's children are the same thing. We can't say which comes first. Love is circular, not linear; like the wedding ring, love is without beginning or end. Love is eternal. And God is love. And we are God's children, growing ever more like God.

† Jesus our brother, help us to grow daily more like you, and to love God and one another with the same love that moved you in compassion, led you to the cross and overcame death.

For further thought

How have you grown a little more like God today, or what have you learnt about God that might shape who you are becoming?

Professions of faith – 2 Jesus is Lord

August

The Gospel of Luke (4)

1 Our priorities

Notes by **Kate Hughes**

Kate worked for the Church in Southern Africa for fourteen years. Since her return to the UK she has worked as a freelance book editor, mainly specialising in theology. She lives in a small council estate in Coventry and is involved in her local community, and she preaches regularly at her local Anglican church. Kate has used the NRSV for these readings.

10 August
Carrying our cross

Read Luke 14:25–35

Whoever comes to me and does not hate father and mother, wife and children, brothers and sisters, yes, and even life itself, cannot be my disciple.

(verse 26)

A recurring theme in the Old Testament is God reminding his chosen people that his covenant with them is a two-way thing. It isn't just a matter of God looking after Israel; in return, Israel has to obey God, put him first in their lives, their worship, their politics and their plans.

Following God's commandments involves much more than keeping rules about what you can eat or how you should spend the Sabbath. God has to come first, before everything else. Following God might involve leaving behind home and family, possessions, safety, facing the possibility of a terrible death – but the goal will make everything worth it. Jesus confronts people with the decision: are you for God or not? By coming as a human being, God in Jesus has made it as plain as possible that a decision needs to be made. The goal is the establishment of God's kingdom on earth. In this passage, Jesus challenges his hearers: 'Who is on the Lord's side? Who is prepared to give everything in order to work with me?' Israel is meant to be like salt, making all the difference to human life: don't end up in the bin when you could be citizens in God's kingdom.

† Lord, grant me the strength to truly follow you.

11 August
A lost sheep and coin

Read Luke 15:1–10

There will be more joy in heaven over one sinner who repents than over ninety-nine righteous persons who need no repentance.

(verse 7)

In yesterday's reading, Jesus stressed what is involved in following him. Nothing is more important. Today's reading shows what God does from his side, and how he helps people to be his followers.

The Pharisees make their routine response: 'He says he's a messenger from God, but he can't even keep the law!' But Jesus is keeping the law – God's law, the way God always behaves, with unshakeable love. He didn't just allow doubtful people to come close to listen to him, he positively welcomed them and ate with them. The tax collectors were generally hated: not only did they cheat their own people and work for the enemy, they also mixed with gentiles. The other 'sinners' might just have been poor people who couldn't keep the law properly because of poverty or the demands of their work. As Jesus' two stories tell us, the righteous considered these people 'lost'; they were never going to be welcomed by God. Yet exactly the opposite was true. God looks for the lost, he comes after them like a shepherd searching for a stray sheep and makes huge efforts to find them – like a woman who has lost one of her precious coins, possibly part of her marriage dowry, and turns the house upside-down to find it. And if one of these 'sinners' lets themselves be grasped by God, heaven itself has a party.

Jesus didn't just eat with those the Pharisees called sinners; he turned it into a party. But the Pharisees didn't think they needed to repent, so they missed out on God's party.

† Gracious God, without you I would be lost; thank you for finding me and rejoicing over me.

For further thought

Do you know how much you are loved by God? What can you do to help you remember this?

A son is lost

> **Read Luke 15:11–32**
>
> *But we had to celebrate and rejoice, because this brother of yours was dead and has come to life; he was lost and has been found.*
>
> (verse 32)

In those days, no one would have blamed this father if he had asked for his son to be killed – he had broken all the rules of how children were expected to behave towards their parents and the law was on the father's side. A lot of people listening to Jesus' story would have found the father's behaviour unbelievable. Even picking up his robe to run and meet his returning son was not how any self-respecting Jewish father should behave.

Too often we only ask God for help when we have tried everything else. We don't bother about him, or we don't believe that he can really love us. We blame him for bad things that happen to us or think that the bad things we have done are unforgivable. But this story tells us that this is an entirely wrong picture of God. The youngest son went as far away from his father as he could, yet was welcomed home with open arms.

Most of us are not spectacular sinners. Our failures can separate us from God, they can hurt other people and drive us to despair; but we do try to be good. Sometimes, however, we forget that the Church is a place for sinners, for helping people to change their lives by discovering the love of God. Like the older brother, we can feel taken for granted and can't share in God's rejoicing over sinners who repent. But God's love is huge enough for all his children. We can rejoice when someone changes the direction of their life, because it's great to share in God's joy.

† Dear Lord, I so often fail you, but always you welcome me when I come back home to you. Thank you.

For further thought

Do you know of anyone who has discovered God's love after a dark and difficult life? Share God's joy over their return home.

13 August
The shrewd manager

Read Luke 16:1–18

His master commended the dishonest manager because he had acted shrewdly; for the children of this age are more shrewd in dealing with their own generation than are the children of light.

(verse 8)

Tom Wright, in his book *Luke for Everyone* (SPCK, 2001), points out that nobody is honest in this story. As a Jew, the master couldn't charge money interest on his loans. Those in debt to him paid him in produce instead – oil and wheat. When the manager was sacked for fiddling the books, he wrote off some of the interest being paid on those loans. However, the rich man couldn't prosecute his ex-manager for stealing his interest because he himself was breaking the law by charging the interest in the first place.

We need to remember that Jesus is not giving (dodgy) financial advice here. He is telling a story, a parable. The story reminds his listeners that they, the Israelites, are supposed to be God's managers, keeping God's commandments, caring for God's world, spreading God's light. They are not doing a very good job and disaster is coming – in forty years' time, the Romans will crush a rebellion and destroy the Temple. The Pharisees' reaction to impending disaster is to tighten the rules, to make the nation more holy and exclusive so that God will have to rescue his people. Jesus, on the contrary, asks: 'What can you realistically do to deal with this disaster? How can you change your ways, not by ever-tighter rules that exclude people but by opening yourselves to others, using your possessions and your talents to make friends, to become the "light to the nations" that God wants you to be?' God's answer was the Church, which revolutionised society in the Roman empire by welcoming everyone into the household of God.

† Dear Lord, you offer me 'the glorious freedom of the children of God' (Romans 8:21, GNT); remind me every day that I don't have to earn it by keeping more and more rules.

For further thought

What is the difference between trying to get God on your side by a strict regime of rules and willingly doing what God wants in response to his love and forgiveness?

14 August
The rich man and Lazarus

Read Luke 16:19–31

...If they do not listen to Moses and the prophets, neither will they be convinced even if someone rises from the dead.

(verse 31)

Our city centre is full of homeless people and beggars. People tell me many of them are frauds, just trying to make money to buy alcohol or drugs. But it's not easy sitting all day hoping for a few coins, especially if you have slept badly in a shop doorway the night before.

Lazarus the rough sleeper is like the 'tax collectors and sinners' that Jesus makes his friends. They are all rejected by the rich people – the religiously secure Pharisees and the financially wealthy. Both groups think they will get preferential treatment from God in the afterlife. Their place is assured. So the rich man is shocked when he ends up in Hades and sees this beggar in heaven. He still thinks of Lazarus as a servant (or slave), there only to make his life more comfortable. When this is not possible, Lazarus must be sent on a different errand – to prevent the rich man's family ending up in Hades with him.

But the punchline of Jesus' story is that no Israelite should demand special treatment. It is all there, over and over again, in their scriptures: you must care for the poor, the widow, the orphan, the stranger, the refugee. They just need to start doing it, before it is too late. This is how God wants his world to be – this is the kingdom that Jesus comes to establish. Again, Jesus is asking 'Are you on God's side, like the tax collectors and sinners who see God's love and forgiveness in me? Or will you refuse to change?'

† Lord, help me to know you more clearly so that I may realise more and more that I cannot earn your love and forgiveness – it is your amazing gift to me.

For further thought

Is living by the kingdom values that Jesus showed in his life and death a way to earn your place in heaven, or is it a response to God's love shown to you?

15 August
Sin, faith and duty – kingdom values

Read Luke 17:1–19
Then one of them, when he saw that he was healed, turned back, praising God with a loud voice. He prostrated himself at Jesus' feet and thanked him.

(verses 15–16)

Repeatedly Jesus confronts the Pharisees when they criticise him for making friends with tax collectors and 'sinners', the little ones. Here he explains how, by contrast, his followers should behave. If the Pharisees insist on all these rules, most people just won't be able to keep them. Making people feel guilty and that God will reject them is simply unfair. It is throwing God's love back in his face. If someone acknowledges that they have done wrong, they must be forgiven again and again.

We can never pay back to God what he has given to us. By trying to follow the kingdom values that Jesus lived, we are not doing anything extraordinary – simply showing good sense! We are being truly human, living according to the maker's instructions.

It is the outsider, the rejected Samaritan, who shows the basic attitude to God we all need to have: gratitude. That we can overcome our sins, forgive the bad things done to us, love others, know God's love – none of this is due to our goodness or cleverness. It is God's love for us that enables these things to happen. The Jewish lepers who were healed rushed off to see the priest and get permission to go back to their homes and families; only another rejected outsider remembered to say thank you to Jesus as the representative of God's loving care. As Jesus said on another occasion to the chief priests and elders, 'the tax collectors and the prostitutes [and the Samaritans] are going into the kingdom of God ahead of you' (Matthew 21:31).

† I know no reason why you should love me, except that you are God and your nature is love. Help me to make gratitude the centre of my life.

For further thought

Think about your past life and your life today. Where have you seen God's love at work? How have you been forgiven and healed?

The Gospel of Luke (4) – 1 Our priorities

August

16 August
The coming of the kingdom

Read Luke 17:20–37

[Jesus] answered, 'The kingdom of God is not coming with things that can be observed; nor will they say, "Look, here it is!" ...For, in fact, the kingdom of God is among you.'

(verses 20–21)

These passages of 'apocalypse' in the Gospels and the book of Revelation have given rise to a lot of different interpretations. The word 'apocalypse' means 'revealing' (literally, in the original Greek, 'taking the lid off something'). Some people interpret this as the end of the world as we know it, the Second Coming of Jesus to finally bring in God's kingdom, God's rule on earth. But the people Jesus spoke to were facing a more imminent disaster, which would change the world as they knew it for ever. Following a Jewish revolt against the occupying Romans, begun in AD 66, and a declaration of independence, in AD 70, Jerusalem was besieged and sacked by the Roman army. Many Jews were killed, captured or fled their homes and, worst of all, the Temple was destroyed and its treasures taken to Rome.

For Jews, the Temple was the meeting place of heaven and earth, of God and his people. How could they worship God properly if there was no longer a Temple? But Jesus tells them that they need to be looking out for – and doing something about – what is already there: the real meeting place between God and his people is in Jesus. God has already started to establish his kingdom, but he needs people to join him, to commit themselves to believe, trust and follow Jesus. Again, Jesus is saying, 'Are you on God's side? Don't leave it too late: God is not only offering you his unshakeable love; he needs you to live it out and tell others about it, to be part of his kingdom.'

† O God, help me not only to be part of your kingdom, but to tell others about it by my words and actions.

For further thought

How can you be 'on the Lord's side' in your daily life, so that he can use you to bring in his kingdom?

The Gospel of Luke (4)

2 Seek out God's good gifts

Notes by **Ellie Hart**

Ellie Hart is a Bible teacher, writer, artist and the author of *Postcards of Hope* (BRF, 2018). She is passionate about reading the Bible in community, about understanding it well and allowing it to change our hearts and lives. She is especially enthusiastic about helping people to read and reflect on narrative in scripture. After ten years in overseas missions, she now lives in Derby, England, with her husband Andrew, three children and a disobedient but loveable brown dog. Ellie has used the NRSV and the NIV for these notes.

17 August
The persistent widow

Read Luke 18:1–17

In a certain town there was a judge who neither feared God nor cared what people thought. And there was a widow in that town who kept coming to him with the plea, 'Grant me justice against my adversary.'

(verses 2–3, NIV)

I heard once that when babies stop crying out for comfort, that's when you know there's a problem. It means they've lost hope that anyone will ever come.

In today's parable we meet a widow – too alone to send a man to represent her (as would have been usual), and, it seems, too poor to offer the bribe required by the immoral judge. She is powerless. We could understand if she were to give up. But this woman is both determined and audacious. She will not quietly accept that her destiny is to live with injustice. She speaks up, she continues to plead.

The purpose of the parable is not to reveal God as an uncaring judge but to encourage us to press into his true nature. A God who persistently seeks ways to bring justice would be touched by this woman's persistent cry. Her refusal to accept injustice and her passion for the poor and vulnerable echo God's own heart.

This can be our inspiration too – we persist because we know our cries align with who God is and that ultimately those cries will be joined by God's own cry, and justice will be done.

† Lord, help me when I run low on hope, when I want to give up, when I start to doubt your goodness. Help me to trust you, and to keep on crying out to you.

The Gospel of Luke (4) – 2 Seek out God's good gifts

August

18 August
One thing you lack

Read Luke 18:18–43

A certain ruler asked him, 'Good teacher, what must I do to inherit eternal life?'

(verse 18, NIV)

In the time that Jesus lived on earth, in the streets that he walked down, in the marketplaces he taught in and the homes he healed in, poverty was the normal way of life. Extreme taxation by the Roman empire had enabled a few people to become very rich indeed, while most became desperately poor. Those who went into debt lost their land and sometimes their freedom, while those few who were already rich grew even richer at their expense. No wonder Jesus caused such a stir when he came proclaiming a kingdom that was good news for the poor!

In the next two days we're going to meet two very rich men. Both have an encounter with Jesus, but they react in very different ways! The first is the rich ruler in today's reading. The thing that stands out to me is his question – 'what must I do to inherit eternal life?' It seems to come from his heart – but it's the wrong question! Gaining eternal life is not about what we do, but all about trusting God. Jesus, who knows the man's heart, challenges him. Can he walk away from his luxurious lifestyle and trust God instead? It seems he cannot.

You can't get a camel through a needle. It's not just very hard for those trusting in riches and comfort to follow Jesus. It's impossible. But what's impossible for humans is possible for God, and through his grace and mercy, hearts can be transformed, and the source of security shifted from possessions to God.

† Lord, help me when I want to cling on to material things, when I find my comfort and my sense of security in stuff. Help me learn to put my trust completely in you.

For further thought

Jesus is concerned to help people learn to live for eternity, and not for the short-term. 'Make sure your treasure is in heaven,' he said. This rich man couldn't shift his 'centre of faith'. How can you try to do that this week?

Zacchaeus the tax collector

The Gospel of Luke (4) – 2 Seek out God's good gifts

Read Luke 19:1–27

Zacchaeus stood there and said to the Lord, 'Look, half of my possessions, Lord, I will give to the poor, and if I have defrauded anyone of anything, I will pay back four times as much.' Then Jesus said to him, 'Today salvation has come to this house, because he too is a son of Abraham. For the Son of Man came to seek out and to save the lost.'

(verses 8–10, NRSV)

Today we come across another very rich man who meets Jesus. And this time we're going to see that, camels and needles notwithstanding, it is possible for a rich man to enter the kingdom of God!

Zacchaeus is introduced as a wealthy tax collector. The heavy and corrupt tax system of the Roman empire crushed ordinary people under the weight of its demands. When we hear that Zacchaeus was a chief tax collector the suspicion is all the more that his riches had come through the suffering of the weak and powerless. We've heard that the kingdom is good news for the poor, but can it possibly be good news for a man like Zacchaeus?

It's wonderful to realise that Jesus isn't put off by Zacchaeus' history! He sees beyond the sin to the lonely, isolated and perhaps misunderstood individual. And brings healing by asking for hospitality, by offering himself and his disciples as friends. And in that moment, the true Zacchaeus appears – a man after God's own heart – humble, generous, willing to give all he has for the sake of others. 'Today salvation has come to your house' (verse 9).

What a transformation the kingdom makes in Zacchaeus! As he accepts Jesus into his home, he is accepted into the kingdom of heaven.

I find this story – of the extraordinary transformation in Zacchaeus and of the impact that his transformation has on others – so challenging. It makes me ask myself, 'How am I being transformed?' and then, 'How is my life good news for the poor?'

† Lord, help me to live with my eyes fixed on what is to come, to be 'good news' for the poor who are within my ability to help, and to store up treasure in heaven.

For further thought

Being transformed by the kingdom is never a one-off! It's the ongoing work of a lifetime. How is God transforming your heart right now?

August

20 August
The triumphal entry

The Gospel of Luke (4) – 2 Seek out God's good gifts

August

Read Luke 19:28–48

As he rode along, people kept spreading their cloaks on the road. As he was now approaching the path down from the Mount of Olives, the whole multitude of the disciples began to praise God joyfully with a loud voice for all the deeds of power that they had seen, saying, 'Blessed is the king who comes in the name of the Lord! Peace in heaven, and glory in the highest heaven!'

(verses 36–38, NRSV)

'I was there! I'll never forget it!' My grandfather loved to tell the story of the coronation of Queen Elizabeth II. Crowds lined the streets of London, cheering and celebrating as the royal procession came by, everyone craning their necks (or climbing trees!) to catch a glimpse of the young queen in her golden coach. 'It was like watching history happen.'

In today's reading we have another royal procession. There's no golden coach and the crowds are significantly smaller. But this 'triumphal entry' really is a turning point, not just in Luke's narrative, but in history! Jesus rides into Jerusalem on a young donkey, just like Solomon on the way to his anointing as king. Other leaders might have ridden on a war horse, but to ride a donkey was to say, 'I come with peace'. This King who comes in the name of the Lord, comes to bring peace to the world …

It must have been amazing to be there. Perhaps a bit confused, and with no idea what was going to come next, the disciples were filled with joy and hope as they welcomed their King. As they shouted praise to God, no doubt they remembered the words of the prophet Zephaniah: 'Rejoice greatly, Daughter Zion! Shout, Daughter Jerusalem! See, your king comes to you, righteous and victorious, lowly and riding on a donkey, on a colt, the foal of a donkey' (Zechariah 9:9, NIV).

Jesus, our friend and our brother, is also the King who comes to reign in our lives and to bring peace.

† Lord, help me to serve you and celebrate you today as my King and the bringer of peace to my life. I pray that you will help me to be a peace-maker in the lives of others.

For further thought

How can we come in the same way – as children of the King of kings, in humility and service – despite the exhortation of others to 'big ourselves up'?

234

Parable of the tenants

Read Luke 20:1–26

Then the owner of the vineyard said, 'What shall I do? I will send my son, whom I love; perhaps they will respect him.' But when the tenants saw him, they talked the matter over. 'This is the heir,' they said. 'Let's kill him, and the inheritance will be ours.' So they threw him out of the vineyard and killed him. What then will the owner of the vineyard do to them? He will come and kill those tenants and give the vineyard to others.

(verses 13–16a, NIV)

I might have heard a hundred talks about the good shepherd (one for each of his sheep!) and another fifty on the prodigal son. But it's rare to hear someone speak on the parable of the tenants! But the Gospel writers had a limited wordcount! They carefully chose everything they included. So, we can be sure that there's treasure for us even in tricky places.

If we're going to make sense of this challenging parable, we need to understand who's who: the vineyard represents the people, the tenants those to whom God has entrusted them, the owner is of course God, and the son, Jesus. With that in mind, the message is clear – the people, instead of being nurtured as a good harvest for the owner, are being used and abused by the leaders for their own ends. The owner, seeing the distress of the people, decides to send his son, but the leaders don't even respect him, separating him from the people before killing him. The parable ends with God coming, bringing justice to those leaders and installing new, worthy ones in their place.

It's easy to see how upset the scribes and Pharisees would have been – so upset that they began to seek ways to fulfil the parable! But what does this say to us today? I suppose it is a deep challenge to all in leadership – are we leading people to God, building his kingdom, or like the leaders back then, are we leading them to our institutions, to pay our bills, to bolster our egos?

† Lord, help us to lead righteously in humility and awe, respecting the 'owner' and giving dignity to those we lead.

For further thought

How can the Church avoid becoming just another organisation based on power, seeking its own good rather than the good of those it is called to serve?

The Gospel of Luke (4) – 2 Seek out God's good gifts

August

22 August
Whose son is the Christ?

Read Luke 20:27 – 21:4

Then Jesus said to them, 'Why is it said that the Messiah is the son of David? David himself declares in the book of Psalms: "The Lord said to my Lord: 'Sit at my right hand until I make your enemies a footstool for your feet.'" David calls him "Lord." How then can he be his son?'

(verses 41–44, NIV)

People want so badly to pin other people down and define them. 'You're an arty type,' they say to me, or, 'You're a teacher.' And while it's true that I enjoy those things, I feel reluctant to accept one label that defines the limits of who I am or can be. I don't want to feel like a butterfly in a museum, pinned down and labelled!

Words, names, labels like these can of course be really helpful – they can act as shortcuts to predicting how people will behave, what they might say, how they might react. But when our knowledge of someone is limited by the label, if we never look beyond it, if we never take the trouble to get to know someone on their own terms, then we risk bigotry and prejudice.

All through the Gospels, people seek to label Jesus: good teacher, rabbi, carpenter, Lord, miracle worker, insurrectionist, blasphemer, Messiah, healer … Even the disciples, from John the Baptist's 'Are you the one?' to Peter's 'You are the Messiah, the Son of the living God' (Luke 7:19; Matthew 16:16).

Here, Jesus takes another label, 'son of David', and exposes the limitations of thinking about it in the traditional way. He persistently seeks to disturb the shackles that people want to place on him, on who he is. He longs for them to know God personally and not to be constrained by their narrow, religious understanding, their convenient, comfortable labels.

Perhaps we need to learn to interpret scripture through the lens of who Jesus is, rather than trying to define who Jesus is by our view of scripture.

† O Lord, thank you that you know me by name, by who I am in the deepest places. Help me to know you like that too.

For further thought

What are the labels people have placed on you? How can you live beyond the labels?

Signs of the end of the age

Read Luke 21:5–38

Truly I tell you, this generation will certainly not pass away until all these things have happened. Heaven and earth will pass away, but my words will never pass away.

(verses 32–33, NIV)

I imagine that at some point you will have listened to a sermon that takes the signs Jesus lists here and interprets them in the light of current geopolitical events. I always find them fascinating – whether it is the latest environmental disaster, the latest conflict or the latest economic or medical emergency, the cleverness with which scriptures are plucked from all over the Bible to explain how these events match up with end-times prophecies always amazes me!

Yet few of these sermons address the verses above. Jesus says that all these things will happen while the generation listening are still alive! Indeed, this seems to be the key – the motivation behind such passages is to encourage us, in all generations, to be ready to welcome Jesus in a way that people were utterly unprepared for when he came that first Christmas. Which means that every generation will be able to see signs of the end: there will always be wars and rumours of wars; in a fallen world, there will always be greed and poverty, always be religious persecution, always be natural disasters and man-made ones. These are the signs of a world and world system in free fall, with the enemy accelerating the plummet and our sinful choices fuelling the descent.

And we need to be ready to stand firm in such times, firm not so much on doctrine and labels, but firm in our faith in a God of love who will come and make things right, but who in this generation, right now, calls us to reveal that love to a world that so desperately needs it.

† Lord, help us to be light and love in a dark and, for many, frightening world, preparing everyone for your return.

For further thought

How can we help people understand the signs of the times whilst pointing them to a loving God?

Encouragement

Notes by **Immaculée Hedden**

Immaculée is from Rwanda. She served as National Intercession Co-ordinator for African Revival Ministries, and then with YWAM Rwanda before relocating to work with YWAM England in reconciliation ministries and counselling. While there, she met her husband, Richard, and together they wrote the story of how she survived the 1994 genocide in the book *Under His Mighty Hand* (2013). They are currently based in Rwanda serving in healing and counselling support ministry with YWAM. Immaculée has used the NIV for these notes.

24 August
Encourage the disheartened

Read 1 Thessalonians 5:12–18

Encourage the disheartened ... Rejoice always, pray continually, give thanks in all circumstances, for this is God's will for you in Christ Jesus.

(verses 14, 16–18)

On 2 April 1994, I felt led to start a time of prayer and fasting for my country Rwanda. The Lord spoke many things during that time and I heard him say, 'He puts his word on my mouth,' which I later realised was an encouragement to me to write down what he had said so that others would also be encouraged.

On 6 April 1994, the plane carrying the Rwandan president was shot down and crashed into the garden of his house near the airport. The pre-planned genocide against the Tutsi was set in motion and we could no longer move with freedom. Many times, people's hearts were failing, and they were overcome with fear and worry. But the Lord frequently gave me scriptures and words which I wrote down on pieces of paper which my cousin and her children read. For them and others, they were key promises from God and up till now they remember it. Some of them have made the choice to follow Jesus. Sometimes my cousin still reminds me how those words were meaningful to her and her children.

Encouraging the disheartened is a precious ministry that we can all be involved in.

† Lord, open my eyes to see the disheartened around me. How can I encourage them in word and deed?

25 August
Comfort my people

Read Psalm 24:1–3

The earth is the Lord's, and everything in it, the world, and all who live in it; for he founded it on the seas and established it on the waters. Who may ascend the mountain of the Lord? Who may stand in his holy place?

(verses 1–3)

Everything comes from God. The earth, everything we see, even those things we cannot see. The earth is his masterpiece. We too are his masterpiece, the apple of his eye. As we contemplate this truth, how does that impact the perspective of our life, our possessions, our relationships, our resources? May verses 1 and 2 reframe how we view what we 'own' and how we use it.

At the beginning of Genesis we read that God established the earth upon its foundations during Creation week, and then later, the post-Flood promise of Noah's time, that all life will never again be destroyed by flood and that he has set a boundary for the waters never again to cover the earth (see Psalm 104:9). Is God still in control of his creation or will our rebellion change all that?

As fallen creatures in a fallen world, just how do we enter into the presence of a holy God? We do it by welcoming Jesus into our lives. He is the only one who can cleanse us, through his blood, because he has paid the price through his crucifixion, when all our sin was laid on him.

In my native Rwanda many people shed blood during the genocide. It is amazing that Jesus can bring them back to having a pure heart and clean hands because of his atonement. We are all free in Jesus when we truly repent and believe. This is comfort to all of God's people, whom God calls 'my people'.

† Heavenly Father, give us the revelation of Jesus, the only one who enables us to stand in the holy place.

For further thought

Who in your circle of influence needs to know the one who will enable them to stand in the holy place?

Encouragement

August

Imitating Christ's humility

Read Philippians 2:1–4

Do nothing out of selfish ambition or vain conceit. Rather, in humility value others above yourselves, not looking to your own interests but each of you to the interests of the others.

(verses 3–4)

Writing from prison and knowing his execution was close at hand, the apostle Paul appealed to the believers in Philippi to make his joy complete. He not only wanted to know that the church had received encouragement from Christ, but that they also manifested the life of Christ in their midst. Much of that life is demonstrated by being other-focused: looking to the interests of others, valuing others above ourselves. The encouragement in today's passage is to godly ambition. This is ambition that is focused on God and fulfilling his will. When we do this, the outcome will be a life of loving and serving others in a way that reveals God. The way of the world and the flesh is often serving self and pleasing self. Jesus empowers us to change that. We die to our old nature and live to the new nature he has given us.

The Bible says those who are guided by the Spirit are children of God. When I'm in difficult situations, especially when challenged by people's need, I like to ask the question 'What would Jesus do if he were here?' If I'm sensitive to the Holy Spirit, I ask for help and guidance to act like Jesus would if he was here physically. Living in this broken world, sometimes the actual needs are hidden, and sometimes people are confused or even dishonest about what they need. That's why I enquire of the Lord to understand his will. I seek his perspective and guidance for effective responses to needs around me. I want the Lord to protect my heart of compassion and servanthood.

† Lord, bring to mind those things we need to let go of in order that we can live a life of loving and serving others in a way that glorifies God.

For further thought

What areas of your life consist of self-serving? Will you ask Jesus to change you to reflect his humility and servanthood?

Do not be discouraged

Read Deuteronomy 31:1–8

The LORD your God himself will cross over ahead of you …The LORD himself goes before you and will be with you; he will never leave you nor forsake you. Do not be afraid; do not be discouraged.

(verses 3, 8)

Today we read of an amazing encouragement and assurance to the Israelites before they crossed to the promised land. The Lord said he was going ahead of them as well as with them. That's a big encouragement. He said to both Joshua and the Israelites, 'Do not be afraid; do not be discouraged.'

When I read about Moses in this scripture, I feel sad. He was a great leader of God's people but when God told him that he would not go with them, it made me sad. The people of Israel were probably also sad to lose him, their leader who had been with them all of the time. It makes me wonder if they were grieving because of losing Moses. When we as believers lose people who are special to us, this scripture can speak to us that when such things come, we shouldn't be discouraged or afraid because the Lord will never forsake us. We experience grief whenever those things happen to us, but we aren't alone. We should be reminded of this. As much as God gave this promise to the Israelites, that promise also belongs to us.

This reminded me about the time I lost someone very special to me. In my devotions that day the Lord spoke to me that whatever has happened to me, he is going to be with me. That was a great comfort to me at that time.

He will keep in perfect peace those whose minds are steadfast because they trust in God (Isaiah 26:3). Focus on the Lord because he is always with you.

† Lord, we pray for your people, that they will have your steadfast love and know that they are not alone.

For further thought

What causes you to believe that you are alone? What will be helpful for you to realise that God's presence is with you?

Encouragement

August

The God who rescues

Read Psalm 18:1–19

*I called to the L*ORD*, who is worthy of praise, and I have been saved from my enemies.*

(verse 3)

The Lord is the Lord who rescues us. In verses 1 and 2, David starts by expressing his love for the Lord. He then goes on to proclaim that the Lord is his rock. Indeed, Jesus says he is the rock – the bedrock, in Greek, the *petros*. He says God is my fortress. If the Lord is the fortress, what does that mean? You have somewhere protected from the enemy, somewhere where you can rest, heal and regain strength. So David, as a warrior, says that the Lord is his fortress and his deliverer.

How do we access that place of refuge? For David and us, the key is our relationship, our friendship, with God. There's no greater friend than having the Lord as our best friend. David had built a relationship with God that wasn't shaken by anything. When David was in front of the giant Goliath, he wasn't afraid. He told Goliath he would kill him just like any lion he used to kill. Are you like David who said he would kill Goliath like a lion or bear? Or are you frightened in front of one of the giants (1 Samuel 17:36–37).

The Lord is the one who rescues us from our enemies. The story of David encouraged me to find my strength and trust in the Lord, to make him my refuge. During the genocide against the Tutsi in Rwanda, one man tried to kill me. He put away his gun after I rebuked the enemy at work in him.

† Lord, help us to put our trust in you, and know that with you we have overcome all the power of the enemy, and we have the one who rescues us from all the power of the enemy.

For further thought

So who is your giant? How do you react when the giant comes your way?

29 August
Now to him who is able

Read Ephesians 3:7–21

I pray that out of his glorious riches he may strengthen you with power through his Spirit in your inner being, so that Christ may dwell in your hearts through faith. And I pray that you, being rooted and established in love ...

(verses 16–17)

In today's passage, Paul is reminding us that the gifts we have we were given by God's grace through Christ. This is nothing to boast for ourselves. Whether we have a big public, visible ministry or one that is largely unseen, if it is to be effective in the kingdom, we need to serve with humility and thanksgiving, recognising that we're enabled by the one who has given all these things to us, and enables us to do it. Trusting in his ability means that in a time of discouragement, we look to the one who is able to accomplish what he has put in us and entrusted us to do.

When God called me to go to the nations, I couldn't see the way. Even sometimes my friends said that I was in confusion, because they couldn't see how that would happen. With human perspective there was nothing tangible to prove that what I said would be true – I am from Rwanda, I had no resources, I could not make this happen. So, sometimes they said, 'Is it really God who told her?' But I knew that I had been told by the one who is able and what he said I have been seeing fulfilled with my own eyes. Up till now I have travelled to more than twenty nations around the world serving him and speaking about his goodness and testifying to his love.

Don't look to yourself as insignificant or someone who is a nobody but look to him who is able to do it for you and through you.

† May we be rooted in love and established in Christ, to see the height, breadth and depth of your love. May we see everyone as part of your family.

For further thought

Who is enabling you to do what you do and where do you get your strength?

Encouragement

August

243

Encouraged through the word of God

Read Acts 15:30–35

But Paul and Barnabas remained in Antioch, where they and many others taught and preached the word of the Lord.

(verse 35)

We all need to be encouraged by the word of God. In this world where we have many distractions, it's important that we remember to set apart time to read the word of God and listen to what the Holy Spirit tells us through his word. Growing up as a young Christian, I've seen this work in my life. When I faithfully follow this devotion, the Lord frequently uses it when I face adversity and different needs.

Sometimes this can be in dramatic, life-changing ways. At others, the impact may be less obvious, but the kingdom is built each time we respond to his word. During the genocide, the need for God to speak was obvious and I would always ask the Lord's advice any time I needed to make a decision. At one point, it had become unsafe to stay at my cousin's house and I planned to move to some friends in the neighbourhood to take refuge. But in the night, as I sought God's word, the Lord showed me not to go there so I went to the nearby Gisimba orphanage instead. When I arrived there, I was told that the friends I had planned to stay with had already fled from their house. If it wasn't for God's guidance and mercy, I would have died a terrible death, because they were no longer there.

Jesus said, 'Man shall not live on bread alone, but on every word that comes from the mouth of God' (Matthew 4:4). I am alive to testify to that.

† Help us to read and hear your word as our daily bread.

For further thought

What is your daily bread? Is it social media or news, or do you go to the Bible?

Without a name (unnamed people)

Notes by **Jane Gonzalez**

Jane is a Roman Catholic laywoman. Retirement has offered her opportunities to spend more time in Spain, where she and her husband have a home, but also to indulge her creative side. She is currently writing haikus (seventeen-syllable poems), illustrating them with her own photos. Other projects include weaving and collage. In between all this, she finds time to play golf (badly) and remains an active member of her local parish, particularly in the Justice and Peace group. Jane has used the NRSVCE for these notes.

31 August
Unsung heroines and heroes

Read 2 Kings 4:8–17

He said to his servant Gehazi, 'Call the Shunammite woman.' When he had called her, she stood before him. He said to him, 'Say to her, Since you have taken all this trouble for us, what may be done for you?'

(verses 12–13a)

Names are important. One of our first questions on the birth of a new baby is, 'What have you called him/her?' Our name gives us an identity, roots us in history. It is something that we share with every human being. It is no surprise that the Nazis gave numbers to the inmates of their camps – stripping them of their names and their dignity. In effect, dehumanising them. To be unnamed is to be without a voice, or a history – to be unremembered.

But here we are, this week, reflecting on just such people – unnamed figures from scripture, whose identity we can only guess at or speculate on. Belatedly, perhaps, we are giving them the attention they deserve and honouring them in the remembrance. Their names may be lost or hidden but their words and actions speak volumes. Their humanity shines through. If we want to lead lives of Christian discipleship, then theirs is the example to follow.

The Shunammite woman, for instance … here is a woman of integrity, compassion and generosity who gives without the expectation of reward. But, as Mark says of another unnamed woman, 'what she has done will be told in remembrance of her' (14:9).

† Father, give me the grace to open my heart and my hands to whoever is in need. May your will be my guide in all I do or say.

A story seldom told

Read 2 Kings 5:1–5

Now the Arameans on one of their raids had taken a young girl captive from the land of Israel, and she served Naaman's wife. She said to her mistress, 'If only my lord were with the prophet who is in Samaria! He would cure him of his leprosy.'

(verses 2–3)

History was always one of my favourite subjects at school. And the past continues to fascinate me. If we go to a quiz evening at our local pub or school, I will always be the person eager to choose the history round to get us bonus points!

The way history is taught has changed radically over the years. There is more attention paid to social and domestic history – to the stories of 'ordinary' women and men. Their contribution to the shaping of nations is considered as valuable or worthy as that of the powerful or influential. Feminists coined the term 'herstory' in the 1960s, to challenge the idea that history was about 'his' story – the overwhelming concentration of study on the feats and achievements of men. Of course, the word 'history' has nothing to do with personal pronouns – but it is right to reconsider how the recording of world events, for many centuries, favoured one particular group or continent.

Salvation history is no different. So many critical moments and decisions hinge upon the action or words of people like the two unnamed women here. Although of very different status, culture and creed, they unite to help Naaman find healing. A servant, captive and an alien, has the courage and the compassion to suggest he goes to a Jewish prophet; his wife, a wealthy pagan, has the wisdom and discernment to listen and accept what her servant says.

How much more healing and grace might there be in our own communities if we put aside our differences and listened to each other?

† Father, help me to listen out for the still, small voices that speak your words to me. Give me ears to listen and eyes to see and hands to do your work.

For further thought

'Everyone is God speaking. Why not be polite and listen to him?' (Hafiz, fourteenth-century Persian poet). Who will speak God's words to you today?

Extra, extra, read all about it!

> **Read Mark 1:29–31**
>
> *Now Simon's mother-in-law was in bed with a fever, and they told him about her at once. He came and took her by the hand and lifted her up. Then the fever left her, and she began to serve them.*
>
> (verses 30–31)

I am a great fan of the cinema. All aspects of film and film-making fascinate me. I am the person who remains in the cinema watching the credits roll long after everybody else has left. The sheer number of people responsible for bringing a film to the screen is astounding. Unlike the early days of cinema, when only the 'big names' got a credit, nowadays anyone who plays the smallest part in the production has their name included. It is a far cry from those early days when the 'cast of thousands', the extras populating crowd scenes or busy in the background, got no mention as individuals. They were actors with so-called 'bit' parts – unimportant and anonymous. Recently, the word 'extra' has been replaced with the term 'supporting actor'. It better reflects the true nature of their role. Small though their contribution might seem, without it the film would be poorer and less realistic.

Our readings this week are full of 'bit players' or the supporting cast. In many respects, it is as if we have frozen the frame in a recording and can take just a little time to look around the edges at the people who often warrant little or no attention. Here is an older woman, sick with fever and then healed. In typical Markan fashion, there is no hiatus between sickness, cure and service. But freezing the frame allows us to concentrate on her for a moment, to reflect on a life of quiet service and steadfastness, to take her hand as Jesus does and look at her with love.

† Father, give me eyes to look at my sisters and brothers with love. Help me to remove the plank from my own eye before criticising or disparaging others.

For further thought

Take time today to freeze the frame. Are there unnoticed or ignored areas of your life where you need to pay attention and take action?

Without a name (unnamed people)

September

For all the saints

Read Mark 12:41–44

A poor widow came and put in two small copper coins, which are worth a penny. Then he called his disciples and said to them, 'Truly I tell you, this poor widow has put in more than all those who are contributing to the treasury.'

(verses 42–43)

As I write this, summer in Spain is ending and there is a distinctly autumnal feel in the air. The poet Keats called autumn the 'season of mists and mellow fruitfulness'. I find I often misquote this as 'melancholy' fruitfulness. For me autumn has a poignancy and is tinged with sadness. I celebrate the anniversaries of the death of my parents and uncle as summer dwindles and that of a much-missed friend as winter approaches. In the midst of my own personal remembrances, my faith tradition celebrates the feasts of All Souls (31 October, Halloween) and All Saints (1 November).

Anniversaries and days of remembrance give us the opportunity to recall our beloved dead and the chance to reflect upon their lives. On All Saints' Day, we reverence not only those women and men who are officially recognised as Christian heroines and heroes. We honour the memory of the unsung millions whose contribution to the growth and flourishing of the Church throughout the ages has too often been discounted or forgotten. How often have we heard it said that 'so-and-so is a real saint'? Or listened at a funeral to the account of a local saint – the man or woman who will never be officially canonised but who lived a life of charity and love and who made a real difference to those around them?

Here in our reading is such a saint. Jesus calls his disciples to recognise her, to witness discipleship in action. Here is a role model for us all. A woman of the utmost devotion, faith, hope and trust …

† Father, the widow gives everything she has and journeys with complete faith. Give me the courage to risk all in your service.

For further thought

If we are comfortably off, giving money may not be much of a sacrifice. Can you sacrifice your time or attention? Who needs these more than money?

The best laid plans

> **Read Mark 14:1–9**
>
> *Truly I tell you, wherever the good news is proclaimed in the whole world, what she has done will be told in remembrance of her.*
>
> (verse 9)

Recently, I was telling the story of how I came to learn Spanish. Aged fourteen, I had to choose subjects for the exams that would come along two years later. I already had a plan for the future. I would study history and English and have a career as a teacher. My final subject choice was between Spanish, needlework and chemistry. For me, this was a no-brainer! It had to be the language as I hadn't the skills necessary for the other two. In the event, I fell in love with Spanish from the first lesson. I did my degree in it and I never became a teacher.

Human beings love to make plans, however. We dream of what we might do with our lives. We have ambitions and hopes. We want to make our mark in some way. To achieve our fifteen minutes of fame, as the artist Andy Warhol predicted will come our way ... But what do we want to be famous for? How will we be remembered?

The unnamed woman is remembered for one act of startling generosity. She blesses the final days of Jesus' ministry. Amidst all the gathered worthies and hangers-on, she performs an act of grace and reverence and then vanishes.

It would be beautiful to be remembered for something as spectacular. Just as beautiful, though, is to be recognised for a life lived through unhistoric acts – a life of quiet fidelity to the gospel. We believe that God has a plan for each of us. Our achievement is to have cooperated with him to see it fulfilled.

† Father, you know my hopes and dreams. I ask you to fulfil them but only if they accord with your will. Help me to accept and perform whatever you ask me to do.

For further thought

Imagine you are at your own wake. How do people remember you? How would you wish to be remembered?

Without a name (unnamed people)

September

Hidden depths

Read Mark 14:12–16

Go into the city, and a man carrying a jar of water will meet you; follow him, and wherever he enters, say to the owner of the house, 'The Teacher asks, Where is my guest room where I may eat the Passover with my disciples?'

(verses 13–14)

I'm not quite sure who first posed the following question, but it is one that I sometimes use in faith formation sessions: 'If you were on trial for being a Christian, would there be enough evidence to convict you?' It's designed as a challenge to get people thinking. What would a prosecutor say to the jury to convince them that I was indeed a Christian? In the society in which I live, am I prepared to stand up and be counted? Am I prepared for martyrdom, metaphorically if not literally?

Many of our sisters and brothers in faith face actual persecution, imprisonment or death for being a Christian. Throughout the ages the martyrs have paid the ultimate price for bearing witness to the gospel. They are, rightly, cited as examples of faith and courage.

But we know that martyrdom is not for all of us, for the majority. Jesus knew it too and understood. He had secret followers – Nicodemus who 'came by night' and Joseph of Arimathea (John 19:38–39) were two. These facilitated the burial of Jesus but must surely be in a long line of those who tacitly helped his mission. Those who for some reason could not openly declare themselves for Jesus. Somebody offered a room for the Passover and arranged for another to show the way. Someone made sure that Jesus could have a final meal in safety. Others, whose deeds are forgotten, played their part. It is tempting to criticise a lack of courage or commitment in others – but would we, from our place of security and comfort, have acted any differently?

† Father, thank you for the gift of faith. Thank you that when faith falters and I fall, you raise me up, strengthen and console me.

For further thought

What can you or your faith community do in solidarity with Christians who suffer persecution? Consider supporting organisations like Open Doors (www.opendoorsuk.org) or Aid to the Church in Need (www.acnuk.org).

6 September
What's in a name?

Read John 20:1–10

So she ran and went to Simon Peter and the other disciple, the one whom Jesus loved, and said to them, 'They have taken the Lord out of the tomb, and we do not know where they have laid him.'

(verse 2)

One of the best features of our digital society is the ease with which we can access information and find out facts and figures. Gone are the days when, if you hadn't a shelf full of reference books, you were obliged to wait for the library to open! The internet has its pitfalls, of course, but its value to those studying and researching is invaluable. At the touch of a computer keyboard you can have all the learned and erudite works you need at your fingertips.

The erudite and learned among our theologians have long speculated on the identity of the unnamed disciple here. He calls himself 'the disciple Jesus loved'. Many translations call him the 'beloved disciple'. So, was he John the evangelist, or Lazarus, whom we know Jesus loved? Is he a symbol of the perfect follower or is he someone known to the community he addresses, who self-deprecatingly refers to himself thus? Rather like saying, 'Yours truly …'? Is he lost forever?

Does it matter? We will never know his identity, in this life. And, with all due respect to our scholars, for most of us, struggling to follow Jesus day by day, it's a moot point. An interesting diversion. What is important here, for me, is the concept of being loved or being the beloved, the object of total, unconditional love and attention. God doesn't have favourites. We are all his works of art, as Paul tells us (Ephesians 2:10), and each of us, named or unnamed, famous or living in obscurity, is beloved and precious and unique in his eyes.

† Father, you created me in love and your love holds me and supports me. Help me to be true to myself in all I do so that I might draw others to know you.

For further thought
'You are precious in my sight.' Take some time to reflect on Isaiah 43:4–5. How can you respond to God's loving care?

Readings from 1 Samuel (1)

Notes by **Deseta Davis**

Deseta is Assistant Pastor of a Pentecostal church in Birmingham, UK. Her main vocation is as a prison chaplain helping to bring hope to those who are incarcerated. Having obtained an MA in Theological Studies, she previously worked as a tutor in Black Theology bringing the study of theology to a range of people who had not considered such study. Deseta is married to Charles, and they have two grown-up children and a granddaughter. Deseta has used the NIVUK for these notes.

7 September
Hannah's vow

Read 1 Samuel 1:1–18

Lord Almighty, if you will only look on your servant's misery and remember me, and not forget your servant but give her a son, then I will give him to the Lord for all the days of his life, and no razor will ever be used on his head.

(verse 11)

As we start the book of Samuel this week, I am reminded of the text in Deuteronomy 7:12–14 which states that if Israel was obedient to God and obeyed his commands, no person, animal or even the land would be barren or lose their offspring.

Yet, it was the women themselves (rather than the nation) who were blamed and shunned for not being able to have children, especially sons. Infertility brought severe disgrace to a woman, being seen as a curse or punishment. This was particularly difficult for Hannah, being severely mocked by her husband's second wife who had already borne him sons.

For years Hannah wept bitterly and prayed in deep anguish of soul, making an astounding promise to God that she would give the very child she so desperately wanted back to God, forever!

How many of us cry out to God in prayer! We want the 'thing' so badly that we make promises that we cannot keep. False promises – 'God if you save me from this, I will ...' – then as soon as we are 'saved' from the situation we forget what we promised to God.

But when God remembered Hannah, she also remembered her vow to him.

† Lord, if I have made promises that I haven't kept, help me meditate on those and allow your Spirit to teach me.

8 September
A vow fulfilled

Read 1 Samuel 1:19–28

...they brought the boy to Eli, and [Hannah] said to him ... 'I prayed for this child, and the LORD has granted me what I asked of him. So now I give him to the LORD. For his whole life he will be given over to the LORD.'

(verses 25, 27–28)

Hannah eventually becomes pregnant and bears a son, whom she calls Samuel which means 'asked of God' or 'heard by God'.

As soon as Samuel is born, Hannah sets about fulfilling her promise to God in preparing for Samuel to be given away for life.

Hannah did not know whether she would ever have another child; all she knew was that her shame and disgrace had been taken away. Whether this would be her one and only son or not, she would fulfil her vow to God. She would give her son to the priest for life.

Today, Hannah may have been judged as a very bad mother. Social workers and lawyers may have been involved. How can she give her child away to three men after being weaned (between the ages of two and five traditionally)? Eli who was seen as a bad father and his wicked sons. What life would Samuel have?

There are many people in the care system today. Labelled as 'care leavers', several of them end up in the criminal justice system. Living the never-ending cycle of being released and returning to prison within months, if not weeks.

It is sometimes deemed that the next step from care is prison. However, even though Eli was not a good father and his sons were not good examples, Samuel, far from entering prison, became a prominent prophet and priest to Israel. He became one of the most respected leaders, in a time when there was no open revelation. Life may be difficult in care but as Samuel demonstrates, it does not have to end negatively.

† Loving, caring God, so many young people are in homes or with families that do not care well for them. Please help them to buck the statistics and become prominent people in society.

For further thought
Where is your nearest children's home? What part could you play in helping to care for and mentor the children?

Readings from 1 Samuel (1)

September

The call of Samuel

Read 1 Samuel 3:1–21

The Lord was with Samuel as he grew up, and he let none of Samuel's words fall to the ground. And all Israel from Dan to Beersheba recognised that Samuel was attested as a prophet of the Lord.

(verse 19–20)

Samuel was a young child but had learned to minister to the Lord in the tabernacle as a menial worshipper. He did not know he was in training to become the next prophet and priest. In those days, the word of the Lord was rare so Samuel did not know the Lord's voice when he called. Yet he heard the voice and thinking it could only be from Eli, the person he knew, he responded to Eli. Eventually God speaks to him directly.

This was one of the few cases of an audible voice from God in the Bible and spoken to a young child. God calls him by name and gives him a prophecy about Eli and his sons that they will die as a punishment, which Eli accepts. Although the prophecy was nothing to do with Samuel, this could be seen as the call into his own ministry, as young as he was. By the time Eli and his sons die, Samuel is ready to take up the position of prophet and priest. However, even though all Israel knew that Samuel was confirmed as a prophet of the Lord, he did not assert his authority over Eli whilst he was alive. He continues to serve Eli until he is recognised as a prophet in his own right and succeeds Eli after death.

We sometimes need to sit under a leader who may seem 'wayward', whilst God continues to build our character and make the way for us to follow his calling. We do not have to force our way in. What God has planned, he will do!

† Faithful God, with all the hustle and bustle of life, it is sometimes difficult to hear your voice. Help us to be good listeners, obedient to your word and good followers.

For further thought

Reflect on what God has called you to do in your life. How will you fulfil it?

10 September
As if by magic

Read 1 Samuel 4:12–22

The man who brought the news replied, 'Israel fled before the Philistines, and the army has suffered heavy losses. Also your two sons, Hophni and Phinehas, are dead, and the ark of God has been captured.' When he mentioned the ark of God, Eli fell backward ... and he died

(verses 17–18)

After a very severe defeat from the Philistines, Israel deemed it as God's disapproval upon them. However, rather than repenting and asking God for guidance, the sons of Eli: Hophni and Phinehas decide to take the Ark of the Covenant to the war effort, hoping it would protect them. The Ark was deemed as the very presence of God and rather than seeking God, they try to manipulate God into helping them. However, the Ark was captured by the enemy and the prophecies of Samuel came true, Hophni and Phinehas were killed.

This spiralled into a cycle of events: Eli, hearing the Ark had been captured, fell off his seat and died. It did not seem that he mourned for his sons as much as for the Ark of the Covenant. Then the wife of Phinehas, on hearing of the death of her husband and father-in-law, goes into labour and bears a son whom she calls Ichabod – stating that the glory of Israel had left. She also promptly dies.

At times, like the priests, we treat the things of God as if they are magic. We go back to the same old 'formula', that seemed to work once. 'Abracadabra, it worked before' we cry! We expect God to 'fulfil' his role. We try to manipulate rather than seek God for new guidance. Whilst in a given situation, we may need to sit and reflect and find out what God would have us to do rather than taking it into our own hands and expecting God to help 'as if by magic'.

† Righteous God, please forgive us for using you as if you are a magic formula. May we seek you for guidance rather than just expect you to turn up when we require or demand.

For further thought

Has God always 'shown up' when you expected him to? What did you do when he didn't?

11 September
The people turn back to God

Read 1 Samuel 7:1–12

*So Samuel said to all the Israelites, 'If you are returning to the Lord
with all your hearts, then rid yourselves of the foreign gods and the
Ashtoreths and commit yourselves to the Lord and serve him only, and
he will deliver you out of the hand of the Philistines.'*

(verse 3)

The Ark after it was captured spends seven months in Philistine
territory and causes no end of problems to the people who are
desperate to get rid of it. Once it is returned to the Israelites, it
spends twenty years in Kiriath Jearim in the house of Abinadab
where it is treated with respect and honour.

Although the Ark is back, the people were no more right with
God than before. The cities were in ruins, armies defeated and they
continue to be under Philistine domination. During this time, all
Israel mourned because it seemed the Lord had abandoned them.

We get no word of Samuel during the time of the problems
with the Ark, but then he calls for repentance, a change of heart
and the putting away of the foreign gods. He encourages them to
return to the Lord.

We look at today's world and we sometimes despair because
we wonder where God is in all this! It may seem that God has
abandoned us. But there is generally something that we ourselves
may have to do. The children of Israel had a change of heart, they
started to seek the Lord and eventually turned back to God.

We have an obligation to reflect on where we are individually,
even in this very difficult time. Have we left our first love? Have we
turned away from God to the things that are not of him? If so, we
need to turn back to God and as we seek him with all our heart he
promises, 'I will be found by you' (Jeremiah 29:13–14).

† God of the universe, we turn our hearts to you. May we seek you, find you and
be the light that is needed in this difficult time in the world.

For further thought

Reflect on Jeremiah's admonition to seek God with all our hearts.
How do we find him?

Readings from 1 Samuel (1)   **September**

12 September
Heed the warnings

> **Read 1 Samuel 8:1–22**
>
> *But the people refused to listen to Samuel. 'No!' they said. 'We want a king over us. Then we will be like all the other nations, with a king to lead us and to go out before us and fight our battles.'*
>
> (verses 19–20)

After the death of his mother Queen Elizabeth in 2023, Prince Charles was crowned and became King Charles III. It was a very stately affair. Many people came from home and abroad to see this historic occasion. Even people who were not monarchists took time out to watch the whole affair. No doubt, there were some countries that wished they had a monarchy to celebrate. It brought a lot of good publicity to the UK, even though there were a few people protesting.

Israel saw the other nations with a king and stated to Samuel that they wanted an earthly king like the other nations. However, their nation was never a monarchist nation, they were a theocratic nation, where God ruled. So as much as Samuel felt rejected, God confirmed they were rejecting him rather than Samuel. No matter how Samuel warned them of what the king would do, they would not heed the warning and demanded a king.

The people had turned back to God – yet they rejected him at the first chance. There are many ways that God tries to warn us today. It may be through a child or a well-learned, respected leader, but many times we have made up our mind and will not listen to anyone. We ignore the consequences because we want it so badly. The grass may look greener on the other side, the other nations may seem happy, but it's not always what it seems. The pomp and ceremony may be lovely at the time, but there are always penalties to not heeding the warnings!

† Pray for your leaders, ask God to direct them to be examples to other nations. Pray that they will be willing to stand out from the crowd and do what is right.

For further thought

What was the last warning you did not heed? What were the consequences?

Readings from 1 Samuel (1)

September

13 September

Be the one!

Read 1 Samuel 9:15 – 10:2

Saul answered, 'But am I not a Benjamite, from the smallest tribe of Israel, and is not my clan the least of all the clans of the tribe of Benjamin? Why do you say such a thing to me?'

(verse 21)

During a recent course we were taught that research had found that only 'one in three' leaders finish well. The Leading with Integrity module of the course showed some pictures of people who had fallen along the way and had not finished well. We were a class of approximately sixty people, and it struck me that two-thirds of the leaders in that room would not finish well. This was a very sobering thought.

Saul in today's text started off very well, very humble – he stated, 'I'm only from the tribe of Benjamin, the smallest tribe in Israel, and my family is the least important of all the families of that tribe!' He was humble indeed and did not tell anyone that he had been anointed king by Samuel. However, as time goes on, Samuel's warnings that we spoke of yesterday begin to materialise. King Saul becomes egotistical and treats the people with disdain eventually trying to kill the future King David, his greatest ally.

Sometimes a person's greatest gift can become their downfall. Like Saul, God may give us a role or position that is meant to help others. However, rather than staying close to God we can become self-centred and conceited believing that we are deserving of the gift and no one can take it away. We then start to treat people with disrespect, forgetting that all good gifts come from God. We start to lack integrity and live for ourselves. If we are not careful, we may end up like Saul, as one of the two-thirds, rather than being the one!

† Lord, help me live a life of integrity, that I might be one of those who finishes well.

For further thought

What is integrity and how do we live it out in everyday life?

Readings from 1 Samuel (2)

Notes by **John Birch**

You can read John's biography on 25 May. John has used the NIVUK for these readings.

14 September
Saul rebels

Read 1 Samuel 13:5–15

Saul remained at Gilgal, and all the troops with him were quaking with fear. He waited seven days, the time set by Samuel; but Samuel did not come to Gilgal, and Saul's men began to scatter. So he said, 'Bring me the burnt offering and the fellowship offerings.' And Saul offered up the burnt offering. Just as he finished making the offering, Samuel arrived and Saul went out to greet him.

(verses 7b–10)

It's easy to read this passage and think we'd do just the same as Saul. There's an ongoing war against the Philistines, and Saul, Israel's first king, has assembled an army he considers sufficiently large. But situations on the ground change quickly. Now they face an enemy 'as numerous as the sand on the seashore' (verse 5) and equipped with thousands of two-man chariots. Things are not looking good and panic sets in. There's a mass desertion of the Israelites, hiding anywhere they can or fleeing across the Jordan.

With his army seriously depleted, Saul desperately needs God's help and advice. His decision to go ahead with a sacrificial offering ignores Samuel's instruction to wait for him. When the prophet appears, he is angry, telling Saul he's been very foolish in not keeping God's command. His reign as king will be short, and there would no longer be a future dynasty with his name.

There are consequences following many of the decisions we take in life. However, when we feel out of our depth or in danger, it is good to know that God is with us, and a prophet's presence is no longer essential for an answer to our prayers!

† Loving God, we thank you for your continuing presence through the peaks and troughs of our individual journeys of faith.

David and Goliath

Read 1 Samuel 17:8–58

Then Saul dressed David in his own tunic. He put a coat of armour on him and a bronze helmet on his head. David fastened on his sword over the tunic and tried walking around, because he was not used to them. 'I cannot go in these,' he said to Saul, 'because I am not used to them.' So he took them off. Then he took his staff in his hand, chose five smooth stones from the stream, put them in the pouch of his shepherd's bag and, with his sling in his hand, approached the Philistine.

(verses 38–40)

Picture the scene, a confrontation between Israelite and Philistine armies facing one another over a valley. Victory is possible if someone can defeat the giant called Goliath, who is daily taunting the terrified Israelites. Enter our hero David, on an errand for his father and hearing Goliath's words echo across the valley. What David hears is someone mocking 'the armies of the living God' (verse 26). His anger is enough to bring him in front of Saul and offering to kill Goliath with his own hands.

A terrified Saul gladly accepts the offer, handing David his tunic and armour, possibly to take some credit for, or share in, David's victory. Refusing the offer, David chooses instead to fight simply with five stones and a sling. To David, this is not a fight between two nations, with its focus on a giant and a shepherd. This is God's battle and victory is inevitable, which it proves to be, and the enemy scatter in panic.

Life presents us with many battles, though rarely with giants! More frequently, we have mountains to climb and obstacles to overcome, often seeming insurmountable. David found the courage and strength he needed through his faith in God, and in facing the threat of Goliath, he chose the armour of God rather than that of Saul. David was not seeking glory but standing up to the Philistines' insults against God's name. A reminder for us to have courage in standing up for what we believe when others mock our faith or God's name.

† God of justice, we pray for all those who face persecution for the faith they live and proclaim.

For further thought

Throughout the world Christians face far more than the taunting of Goliath for their faith. Check out the websites of organisations such as Open Doors, which highlight this issue.

16 September
David and Jonathan

Read 1 Samuel 19:1–7

Jonathan spoke well of David to Saul his father and said to him, 'Let not the king do wrong to his servant David; he has not wronged you, and what he has done has benefited you greatly. He took his life in his hands when he killed the Philistine. The LORD won a great victory for all Israel, and you saw it and were glad. Why then would you do wrong to an innocent man like David by killing him for no reason?'

(verses 4–5)

Relationships can become difficult over time, as we find with Saul and David, now an essential member of Saul's team and a close friend of Jonathan, his son. David has quickly risen to the highest rank in Saul's army. People celebrate his bravery every time the army marches through a town, much to the detriment of Saul's own standing. Saul fears David as a potential rival and decides there is only one solution: David must die. But he underestimates the strength of Jonathan and David's friendship, strong enough for Jonathan to do all he can to stop Saul from killing his friend. Eventually, Saul's mood changes (temporarily) and he says that David will not be harmed.

Sometimes we forget this is a story about people such as us, prone to mood swings, wanting to be in control, and becoming unstable and jealous when things do not go as we would like. We have seen this perhaps among people we know, and certainly in the politics of many countries, where jealousy can so easily lead to oppression and death.

Jonathan takes a risk in warning David, and another in standing up to Saul and persuading him that killing David was the wrong way to go. His goal, apart from saving his friend's life, was reconciliation for the good of Saul and the nation, as David had proved himself such a capable army commander. Relationships are often precious, as with David and Jonathan, and we should celebrate those that mean so much to us.

† Bless those who we call our friends, and be there when relationships are strained, your love and grace overcoming our weakness.

For further thought

Think about your own relationships, at work, home and social, and how your words and actions might sometimes cause friction.

Readings from 1 Samuel (2)

September

David and Saul

Readings from 1 Samuel (2)

September

Read 1 Samuel 24:1–12

See, my father, look at this piece of your robe in my hand! I cut off the corner of your robe but did not kill you. See that there is nothing in my hand to indicate that I am guilty of wrongdoing or rebellion. I have not wronged you, but you are hunting me down to take my life. May the LORD judge between you and me. And may the LORD avenge the wrongs you have done to me, but my hand will not touch you.

(verses 11–12)

Saul had a 'complicated' relationship with David. He recognised David's skill and usefulness to him as an army commander but resented his popularity, seeing it as a threat to his status. David, meanwhile, meant no harm to Saul and indeed respected his divine anointing as king. He was also married to Saul's daughter Michal, and best friends with his eldest son, Jonathan, almost part of the family. But that did not stop Saul's personal vendetta, and so David, the future king, feels forced to go into hiding as a fugitive on the run.

In our reading, Saul has with him three thousand skilled soldiers, outnumbering David's troops who are hiding in a large cave near the Dead Sea, by five to one. And in that cave, David has a unique opportunity to kill the man who has been relentlessly pursuing him. However, his conscience holds him back. God had rejected Saul, but for David he was still the anointed king, and deserved due reverence.

I don't live in a country where its leader considers themselves divinely appointed but am aware that many millions do live under the control of autocratic leaders, demanding full allegiance from their citizens, with imprisonment or death a threat for those who challenge their power.

I am reminded that God wants us to respect those in authority, but also that Jesus was not averse to criticising those who abused their positions of power, which seems to have been, in part at least, David's approach in his response to Saul.

† God of justice, be with all those in positions of authority, that they might use their influence for the common good and not for personal gain.

For further thought

We live in an increasingly unstable world, with global conflicts and a growing distrust of those in control. How might the worldwide Church speak more clearly into these issues?

18 September
The Witch of Endor

Read 1 Samuel 28:3–20

Samuel said, 'Why do you consult me, now that the Lord has departed from you and become your enemy? The Lord has done what he predicted through me. The Lord has torn the kingdom out of your hands and given it to one of your neighbours – to David. Because you did not obey the Lord or carry out his fierce wrath against the Amalekites, the Lord has done this to you today. The Lord will deliver both Israel and you into the hands of the Philistines, and tomorrow you and your sons will be with me. The Lord will also give the army of Israel into the hands of the Philistines.'

(verses 16–19)

In Israel, anything that could be described as occult practice was strongly condemned by the priestly laws, as it could involve false gods and demonic powers. Saul had recently expelled all mediums and spiritists, in full accord with Mosaic law. But now, with Samuel's death and faced with a huge Philistine army and no advice from God, a desperate Saul seeks advice from one of the mediums thrown out of the country. It was dangerous both spiritually and physically, as Endor was close to the Philistine encampment. The medium he meets knows her life might be in danger, but Saul swears an oath on the Lord's name that she will not be punished and asks that she summon Samuel.

It was never going to end well! Even the medium is shocked to see Samuel, and the news that comes is grim. Rejected by God because of his sins, Israel will now fall into the hands of the Philistines, Saul and his sons will die, and the kingdom will pass to David.

I have noticed a growing number of practitioners offering spiritual experiences, including mediums, locally. Someone told me there's a God-shaped hole in all of us, yet so many try filling it with the wrong things. Some may be looking for the spiritual experience without the 'baggage' of church, and maybe we need to consider that in the way we do outreach, to enable those who are searching to fill that precious hole in their lives with the One who fits it perfectly.

† Loving God, may all those embarking on a spiritual journey see your hand reaching out to them and, with your grace, fill that God-shaped hole in their lives.

For further thought
Should the Church be reaching out more effectively to those on some kind of spiritual search or journey, who do not see their needs being met within what we currently offer?

Winning back that which was lost

Read 1 Samuel 30:3–20

When David and his men reached Ziklag, they found it destroyed by fire and their wives and sons and daughters taken captive. So David and his men wept aloud until they had no strength left to weep. David's two wives had been captured – Ahinoam of Jezreel and Abigail, the widow of Nabal of Carmel. David was greatly distressed because the men were talking of stoning him; each one was bitter in spirit because of his sons and daughters. But David found strength in the LORD his God.

(verses 3–6)

David is now established in Philistine territory, in Ziklag – a small city gifted to him during his flight from Saul and from where he organises undercover and brutal raiding parties while carefully avoiding conflict with his benefactor. Saul had continued to pursue him, but David again showed that he meant the king no harm. Now David returns home to discover that Ziklag has been destroyed in a raid, his two wives captured (his other wife Michal had been taken back by Saul) and the men remaining in the city are distraught at their own losses, and angry with him.

Unlike Saul, David did not panic, but found strength and direction from God. There is encouragement in knowing that he can find the enemy, which he does with the assistance of an abandoned Egyptian slave. All those captured, along with items stolen, are recovered and even more taken back as plunder. In a gesture resembling one of Jesus' parables, David insists all plunder will be shared equally between his soldiers, those who stopped halfway through exhaustion, and those who completed the task. All will receive the same, because ultimately the plunder is not his but the Lord's. This would become a legal statute. He also shares plunder with elders of Judah in Ziklag, an expression of gratitude for their help when fleeing from Saul, and to others further afield in Judah. It would not be long before David assumed his new role as king, and here we see him preparing the way!

† Faithful God, you accept us, imperfect as we are, and use us in the building up of your kingdom. For such grace and mercy, we thank you.

For further thought

David was by no means perfect as a human being yet chosen by God to be king. Have you felt called by God to do something, and dismissed the idea as improbable? Keep listening, and next time, be positive and step out in faith!

20 September
Death of Saul

Read 1 Samuel 31:1–13

When the people of Jabesh Gilead heard what the Philistines had done to Saul, all their valiant men marched through the night to Beth Shan. They took down the bodies of Saul and his sons from the wall of Beth Shan and went to Jabesh, where they burned them. Then they took their bones and buried them under a tamarisk tree at Jabesh, and they fasted seven days.

(verses 11–13)

Saul has been on a downward spiral in this week's readings, through fear, jealousy and losing the trust of God. Much time had been lost in his relentless pursuit of David, who truly meant him no harm. We have a king whose power is on the wane, feeling isolated, whose imminent death has just been prophesied.

A perfect time for the Philistines to strike! Which they do with such power that the Israelites scatter before them. Soon Saul lies badly wounded and his three sons lie dead. Saul avoids total humiliation by falling on a sword, but what follows is not an easy read, with their bodies abused and put on display as trophies. But amidst the blood of battle, we find an act of bravery and compassion, as the men of Jabesh Gilead remember Saul's kindness to them in the past, and retrieve the bodies so they might be reverently buried beneath a tamarisk tree, a symbol of hope and blessing in the Bible.

How do we best remember those who have died? I have heard several eulogies read out in funeral services that revealed things I never knew about someone I knew. It makes me realise how little we really know about the lives of those around us, our friends, distant relatives, the local church fellowship. Sometimes we only see what we want to see. Many would be glad that Saul was dead, but for some, here was someone who was remembered not for his failures, but for his kindness.

† Thank you, Lord, for those who through their lives have revealed your love quietly in word and deed, an example for us to follow.

For further thought

Who are the people who have influenced your own journey of faith through their lives, or in their written or spoken words, and what have they taught you?

Balance

Notes by **Liz Clutterbuck**

Liz is a Church of England priest who combines parish ministry with a ministry-training role for the Stepney Area of the Diocese of London. Additionally, she has a research interest in exploring how church impact can be better measured, so that we can learn how missional initiatives work best and where. Liz is passionate about social media, film, baking and travel – and loves it when she manages to combine as many of her passions as possible! Liz has used the NRSV for these notes.

21 September
Everything in balance

Read Ecclesiastes 3:1–8

For everything there is a season, and a time for every matter under heaven ... a time to weep, and a time to laugh; a time to mourn, and a time to dance.

(verses 1, 4)

Tomorrow, 22 September, is the autumn equinox in the northern hemisphere. It is one of two days in the year (alongside the spring equinox) when the sun is exactly above the equator and day and night are equal length. This week's readings are therefore all on the theme of balance, encouraging us to consider what scripture teaches about this and how it impacts our spiritual lives.

These famous words from Ecclesiastes are often heard at funerals, where the grief of loss is balanced with the joy that our loved one has entered the kingdom of heaven. In mourning, we remember that just as all are born, so all die; that life includes weeping as well as laughing; planting as well as harvesting – we cannot have one without the other. This is the balance of God's creation.

For those living in countries far from the equator, the passing of the year is marked by nights shortening and lengthening. The moments of balance are rare and can easily be missed. In contrast, for those nearer the equator, the balance of night and day can seem unremarkable or monotonous. Let us take the equinox this week as an opportunity to celebrate it!

† Take time to consider the contrasts you are currently experiencing in your life. Lift these situations to the Lord in prayer.

22 September
Seedtime and harvest

Read Genesis 8:20–22

As long as the earth endures, seedtime and harvest, cold and heat, summer and winter, day and night, shall not cease.

(verse 22)

A few years ago, a friend invited me to join her in marking the autumn equinox by walking a labyrinth built into a local cemetery park. The act of engaging with the labyrinth was, in itself, an act of balance: walking into its centre, we were invited to prayerfully lay down what we were carrying at God's feet; as we walked back out, we were to consider what God was calling us to take back up. When walking a labyrinth, the inward and outward paths are the same length and the aim is to do both at the same speed – although there is often the temptation to rush out once the centre has been achieved!

The equinox provides us with the opportunity to reflect upon the passing of time. We are nearly three-quarters of the way through the year; in the northern hemisphere, our season of heat is almost over and cold weather is approaching. It is a reminder that, whatever else may be going on in our lives, God's creation continues unabated.

God's words to Noah mark a fresh beginning following the Flood. God's people are promised that never again will God curse the ground in this way. For much of the world, September is also a time of fresh starts marked by the new academic year. Even for those who are not in education, it can feel like an opportunity to start over, to make a fresh commitment to work, loved ones or to faith.

† Creator God, we give thanks for your promise to us and the gift of your creation. May we never forget that you are at work in the turning of the seasons.

For further thought
What are your hopes for the rest of the year? Spend some time in contemplation and bring them before God.

Balance

September

23 September
Fields need to rest, too

Read Leviticus 25:1–7

For six years you shall sow your field, and for six years you shall prune your vineyard, and gather in their yield; but in the seventh year there shall be a sabbath of complete rest for the land, a sabbath for the Lord.

(verses 3–4a)

In many denominations, sabbaticals are offered to church ministers every few years. In the Church of England, clergy are entitled to this three-month break from parish ministry every decade, beginning ten years after ordination. It is an amazing gift to ministers and is directly inspired from these verses in Leviticus.

We may not all be entitled to this kind of sabbatical, but every week is an opportunity to put God's words to Moses into practice, working six days and then observing a Sabbath for the Lord.

In our busy world, there are lots of things that can get in the way of our practising of Sabbath. Even if we work a five-day week and have a two-day weekend, we can still fill that time 'off' with activities that aren't necessarily bringing us rest or closer to God.

A friend of mine has a discipline of a weekly 'tech Sabbath'. Every Friday evening, he turns off his phone and puts away his computer – his final action is posting to social media the phrase: 'the work isn't done, but it is time to stop'. For twenty-four hours he does not touch technology, reading books and magazines instead, and spending time with loved ones. By literally turning off, he is able to rest. Every week when I see his post, I am in awe of his commitment to this practice.

Our lives may not be compatible with such an approach, but it is crucial for us to balance work with rest. We cannot thrive by working 24/7 and we do not honour God if we try to.

† God of all times and seasons, show us how to praise you in our resting as well as in our working. Help us to keep your Sabbath holy in our lives.

For further thought

What does Sabbath look like in your life? What could you put in place to ensure that you keep a Sabbath in your life?

Balance

September

24 September
Day and night, light and dark

Read Genesis 1:14–19

And God said, 'Let there be lights in the dome of the sky to separate the day from the night; and let them be for signs and for seasons and for days and years.'

(verse 14)

I love a good sunset! I will often time a walk through my local park for the hour before sunset and sit on a bench to watch the sky change colour. It feels rather magical to leave home in daylight and an hour later return in the dark. In England, we might refer to a really beautiful sunset as 'the sky putting on a good show' – delighting in such a gorgeous natural phenomenon.

There is a balance in night turning to day, and day turning to night. Both are marked with the beauty of the sun's appearance or disappearance. But of course, day to night does not mean light to dark – even at night, God's creation lights the sky.

The moon and stars have provided humanity with a natural calendar for centuries. As it wanes and waxes, the moon shows the passing of months – while particular constellations of stars become visible in certain seasons.

Living in London, I miss out on the beauty of the night sky because of light pollution, but it's always a joy to experience it when I'm in the countryside and can look up and marvel at it. We may not need the night sky in the same way our ancestors once did, but we should not forget the glorious detail of God's creation.

God never leaves us without light. God never leaves us.

† God of the stars of night, thank you that you never leave us without your light. There is always light, never darkness.

For further thought
Look up which constellations are visible where you are and see if you can find them in the night sky.

God and Caesar

Read Matthew 22:15–22

Then he said to them, 'Give therefore to the emperor the things that are the emperor's, and to God the things that are God's.' When they heard this, they were amazed; and they left him and went away.

(verses 21b–22)

The Pharisees' amazement at Jesus' answer to their question about taxes shows that they had not expected him to support the payment of tax to the Roman empire. Instead, Jesus is showing them that it is impossible to live solely focused on living the most spiritual life possible; we are 'in the world' even though we are no longer 'of the world'.

There is much that can be said about this interaction, but continuing with our theme of balance, it shows that we cannot simply cut ourselves off from society and ignore what is around us. We need to balance our beliefs and values with the affairs of the world.

Jesus directed his listeners to give to the emperor what belonged to him, and to give to God what was God's. We are therefore encouraged to balance our giving of resources to what is required of us and what we are able to offer freely. We pay our taxes while also giving to our church or to charities.

The twentieth-century theologian Karl Barth suggested that Christians should read both the Bible and newspapers but interpret the newspaper with their Bible. In other words, we should make staying in touch with current affairs part of our prayer life, balancing God and the world together.

Today, we consume news in a whole range of formats – it may be phone notifications and social media posts rather than a daily newspaper – so it is much easier to become overwhelmed by the events of the world. By bringing our Bible and our prayers to the world there is hope of balance.

† God, we lift our world to you, where its noise can drown out our prayers. Help us to balance our lives on earth with our lives in your kingdom.

For further thought

Look at how you balance your time and money given to God and that given to the world. Does it feel balanced?

26 September
If we live or if we die

Read Romans 14:5–9

We do not live to ourselves, and we do not die to ourselves. If we live, we live to the Lord, and if we die, we die to the Lord; so then, whether we live or whether we die, we are the Lord's.

(verses 7–8)

We exist in the balance of life and death. We are aware of both the fragility of life and the good news that in Christ we have received the gift of eternal life.

This should not mean that we live fatalistically. It's not a case of 'eat, drink and be merry for tomorrow we may die'! Instead, we are called to live lives that glorify Jesus and provide those around us with a taste of his love for us.

I draw great inspiration from the stories of those Christians who have gone before us. Many churches use a calendar of saints in their daily prayers – Christians whose works, prayers and writing have continued to shape the Church long after their death. But I also seek out the stories of ordinary saints. People whose names do not appear in the history of the Church, but whose legacies live on in their local church or neighbourhood.

Since moving to my current parish, I've learnt much about the ordinary saints of this church – those who died years before I arrived and those whose funerals I have taken since I arrived. Tower blocks in the parish bear the names of my predecessors in ministry, unbeknown to most of the residents – a legacy to lives lived in the Lord.

We cannot seek this legacy ourselves. To do so would be at odds with living in the Lord. All we can do is seek to live the life God has given us, so that in both life and death we are for God.

† Thankful to you, Lord, for this new day, we lift our lives to you and ask that you show us what it means to live in you today.

For further thought

Who are the ordinary saints that inspire you? Find time to share their stories with someone else.

Balance

September

271

27 September
Balanced body

Read 1 Corinthians 12:14–26

But God has so arranged the body, giving the greater honour to the inferior member, that there may be no dissension within the body, but the members may have the same care for one another.

(verses 24b–25)

How is your body feeling today? It can be easy to forget the role of our physical bodies in our spiritual lives, but something that my spiritual director encourages me to do at the start of our sessions is to check in on my body. If I'm physically uncomfortable, then it will be a distraction during our time together.

We know that emotions can manifest themselves in physical symptoms. If we are emotionally out of balance, then our bodies are likely to be too. We all have different bodies, but each of us will know what it means for us to feel balanced – whether that's an absence of pain, eating well, sleeping enough or being healed of illness.

Paul's famous illustration of the Church as a body is all about balance. The Church is made up of all sorts of people – those who might feel as insignificant as a little toe, all the way through to those who believe they are the brains of the operation – but in fact, all are equally indispensable.

It is a reminder that not only do we all have a part to play in the Church, it is impossible to be a lone Christian. We are the body of Christ and it is a body made up of many parts. It cannot function well unless the body is balanced, but that is not easy to achieve.

† God, we are the body of your Son Jesus Christ. Bind us together as a Church so that we may be united in our work for your kingdom.

For further thought

Spend some time thinking about your body. Where is there imbalance? What do you need to become balanced?

New settings, new challenges

1 A travelling, wandering race

Notes by **Erice Fairbrother**

Erice is an Anglican priest in the diocese of Waiapu in Napier Aotearoa New Zealand. For the last two and a half years she has been privileged to serve as Chaplain at Hukarere Māori Girls' College in the Hawke's Bay region – the last remaining Māori girls' college in New Zealand. In her spare time, she enjoys writing, publishing and performing poetry. Erice has used the NRSV and ESV for these notes.

28 September
Faith – journeys into the unknown

Read Genesis 12:1–3, 10–20

Go from your country and your kindred and your father's house to the land that I will show you … and in you all the families of the earth shall be blessed.

(verses 1, 3, NRSV)

We begin this week with a directive from God. Go! Leave everything you know. It will work out for you and others. What a command! And what trust in God's voice follows!

For go they did, beginning a journey into unknown places until famine led them on into Egypt. We can only guess at how their faith in that original call was tested. Was it a loss of trust in God's promise that led Abram to give Sarai to Pharaoh in order to save his own life? As the week progresses, we will explore how that original call to 'go' was experienced and tested. How God's people responded to their leaders, the challenges they faced and God's own faithfulness when the faith of his people dimmed.

Such human stories! Stories of testing that open us up to the reality of falling down in the face of testing, coming to know true humility, only to find the blessing of God's constancy remaining with us still.

† Thank you, Lord, for your faithfulness throughout my life so far. Help me to keep listening for your call on my life in the days ahead.

Who, me? Yes, you!

In the 1980s, I was elected by the National Teachers' Union to be part of a team leading teacher pay talks, including making our case to the government. Feeling terribly inadequate, I questioned my ability to do it. Who, me? Years later, when I was invited to be Chaplain at Hukarere Māori Girls' College, I again questioned my suitability. I was very conscious that culturally I am a descendant of a colonial settler family, with only minimal exposure to the Māori language. Who, me?

Moses, being unsure of his ability, was not afraid to question his suitability with God. To which God replied, 'I will be with you' (verse 12). Really? Moses is still not convinced. Another question. Another reply. Finally, Moses accepts the call to lead, trusting the promise that God would be with him. He stepped up and led. And the people were delivered because of him.

A call on our life is not always about being the best, the most spiritual, the most able, the most educated or perfect. God saw in Moses, qualities that he could not yet see in himself. In the 1980s, I never saw myself as an advocate in education, or later, as a chaplain able to work in a different cultural context. No matter what our abilities, God sees us as he has made us; he knows what we are capable of in his world. This trust in us deepens our trust in him. Who, me? Yes, you! And the promise he gave to Moses remains 'I will be with you.'

† Here I am, Lord. Show me where you want me to serve, and grant the assurance to know that I will not be alone.

For further thought

Is there someone in your journey who has been God's voice saying, 'I will be with you'? Let them know how much their presence means to you.

No turning back

Read Exodus 14:26–31

But the people of Israel walked on dry ground through the sea, the waters being a wall to them on their right hand and on their left. Thus the Lord saved Israel that day from the hand of the Egyptians.

(verses 29–31a, ESV)

This story reminds me of one of the most life-changing decisions I ever made. Fifteen years old and convinced that God had 'called' me, I literally crossed the road to the Anglican church in our town and asked to be baptised an Anglican. At the time I could not foresee it would mean no going back to familiar worship practices and relationships. Nor was it possible to imagine the journey; its challenges, disappointments, testing and the deep growth that lay before me.

We make decisions all the time. Big or small, they are moments of conversion, when we reset our vision or when the direction of our lives is irrevocably changed. I crossed a road, the Israelites crossed a dry seabed, but in both cases, they were moments of definitive change. No matter how it is for any of us, what enables us to sustain a change in direction is a good question.

What enabled the Israelites to survive ultimate change? After all, there was for them, and for many in our own time who are escaping trauma or oppression, no turning back. Those ancient refugees had left everything, except their faith. Faith may not have been a conscious priority as they fled. But later reflection revealed the faithfulness of God's saving presence (verses 30–31a) – rekindling that faith, evoking worship (verse 31). It's not always easy to see God's presence during the difficult challenges we encounter on our journeys. Often that awareness comes later when on reflection we discover the presence which has held us before, continues to hold us still. Embracing us, drawing us on.

† Give thanks for the times God's presence has held you in the hard times and brought you to safety.

For further thought

How has your faith been challenged, revisited and renewed on your spiritual journey thus far? What do you continue to hold on to? What have you left behind?

New settings, new challenges – 1 A travelling, wandering race

September

1 October
Beware of what you wish for

Today's passage overlaps with one read recently, on 12 September. We'd encourage you to reflect, not only on Erice's words here, but also the way in which the Holy Spirit can speak to us through different writers, in different situations, from the same passage.

Read 1 Samuel 8:10–22

But the people refused to listen to the voice of Samuel; they said, 'No! But we are determined to have a king over us, so that we also may be like other nations and that our king may govern us and go out before us and fight our battles.'

(verses 19–20, NRSV)

We read this while debates about government and leadership across the world continue. In New Zealand, dealing with the consequences of colonialism is challenging. How we will be as a nation in the future rests on remembering our past and addressing it. For many facing those memories is one of the hardest challenges.

Samuel too is faced with a challenge from his people – a request to appoint a king over them. God calls their attention to the ultimate social abuse and injustices that come with investing power in one person. It's not what they want to hear, and their request becomes a demand. What they want, the decision they have made, is set. Even God's past faithfulness to them disappears in the face of it.

In our Anglican communion service, we hear the words of Jesus as we break bread together: 'Do this to remember me.' Remember where God has been for us in the good times, where he has been in the toughest times of our lives. They are memories that keep God's constant faithfulness a living reference point for us in the choices we have to make on a daily basis. To remember keeps us from letting our own wants and desires overwhelm God's will for us.

'Beware of what you wish for' is a common saying. It could sum up Samuel's warning to the Israelites. It is a good reminder for us. To remember when our own wants and desires threaten to dim our 'memory of him'.

† Let me never forget your goodness to me, O God, and keep me faithful, even when I want things to go my own way.

For further thought

What memories of God's faithfulness can you draw on in times of trouble? Perhaps write them down or be creative in creating a source of such memories.

Keeping it simple

Read Micah 6:1–8

What does the LORD require of you but to do justice, and to love kindness, and to walk humbly with your God?

(verse 8b, NRSV)

God is clearly frustrated. Ignoring his warnings, his people have chosen to go their own way, with disastrous results. Yet despite his frustration God responds not so much with judgement, but with a lament – and at the heart of lament is grief. Micah reveals a God who grieves, a God emotionally impacted by human actions: 'O my people, what have I done to you?' (verse 3). In that agonising cry God's ancient lament foreshadows Jesus' lament over Jerusalem on his way to the cross. Grief for the loss of the divine/human relationship God ordained at creation. A relationship that makes us fully human, partners with God in building his community on earth.

Yet we too, like the Israelites, can choose to follow our own way, imagining we know best, making choices that impact God's work in our communities. After some discussion, a decision was made to rename our Christmas Market the Summer Market. Why? The word 'Christmas' was felt to be a bit exclusive. On a global scale, our choices now threaten life itself. God's gift of a life-sustaining earth is abused and ravaged, his life-giving oceans thoughtlessly polluted, the vulnerable and poor ignored. God's lament continues. In the voices of the suffering, the grief-stricken and the silenced, his cry continues: 'O my people, what have I done to you?'

What will it take for us to restore our relationship with God? God himself makes it simple: prioritise justice, be unconditionally kind and in all humility walk with him. So simple! Yet – can we trust God that it is enough?

† Pray for grace to live simply with God and for the humility to trust that God will use us to alleviate things for those who lament in our own time.

For further thought

We can be overwhelmed by the laments of the poor, the oppressed and those suffering around us. Set aside time to pray for those who minister to them in God's name.

New settings, new challenges – 1 A travelling, wandering race

October

3 October

Being present

Read Jeremiah 29:1–14

Seek the welfare of the city where I have sent you into exile, and pray to the Lord on its behalf, for in its welfare you will find your welfare.

(verse 7, NRSV)

We began this week with God directing Abram to go. For the exiled in Babylon, we can only imagine the longing, the yearning to go, to go back home. This time, however, God sends a different message. Remain. Settle where you find yourselves. He warns against listening to those who are telling them what they want to hear, planting false hopes for a return. His message is clear. Ignore those voices and instead settle down where you find yourselves. Furthermore, pray for your neighbours as well as for yourselves, for that will bring the peace and well-being you long for.

Calls to remain, to stay, to be still, recur throughout scripture. In our reading today, it is God's response to his people at a particular time in their exile. Later the psalmist exhorts his readers to be still; Jesus, in the agony of Gethsemane, calls his disciples to remain with him (Psalm 46:10; Matthew 26:36–41). Stillness in the Psalms is a call to listen, to learn and know God. In the garden, the disciples are to 'remain' actively; to watch, to pray. The elders in exile are to build communities, build positive relationships with those among whom they find themselves and to do it with prayer.

To pray is to connect with God. To be still is to find wisdom. To watch is to see what is real and engage with what is. The message to the elders seems counter-intuitive, yet it became a pathway to peace and wellness. In a world of great unrest, perhaps it is a message for us too. To be present, to be still, to pray.

† Help me, Lord, to learn to stay in the present with you, to discern your will for me anew each day.

For further thought

How do you stay present with people and with God? What new disciplines can you use to help with this?

4 October
Priorities

Read Haggai 1:1–11

*Now therefore, thus says the L*ORD *of hosts: Consider how you have fared. You have sown much, and harvested little; you eat, but you never have enough; you drink, but you never have your fill; you clothe yourselves, but no one is warm; and you that earn wages earn wages to put them into a bag with holes …Why? says the L*ORD *of hosts. Because my house lies in ruins, while all of you hurry off to your own houses.*

(verses 5–6, 9b, NRSV)

The people of Judah, having returned from exile, immediately rebuild their homes and lifestyle. Meanwhile the Temple lies in ruins. Haggai is quick to draw the comparison. He makes the connection between their good life failing to satisfy, and their failure to make God's house the priority. Worship, the source of all that satisfies, flowing into every part of life.

We could do well to heed Haggai and his call to reset priorities. We live in a world where the pursuit of wealth, of celebrity status and the accumulation of possessions, is a never-ending obsession. A pursuit that increases the divide between the few who have and the many who have not. What would Haggai make of us? What would he call us to pay attention to?

This week we have encountered God speaking directly into the reality his people find themselves in. When it is time to leave, he leaves with them; when it is time to stay, he stays with them; when it is time to look at ourselves, he lets us see honestly, yet always with the hope of restoration. At the heart of all our readings is a God who never loses sight of us. For Haggai, to lose sight of God is a judgement on Judah's priorities.

We end this week with a challenge to take stock of our own priorities as God's people at this time. To reset, letting God be present and seen in us; so that the world doesn't lose sight of the source of the peace and hope it so desperately longs for.

† My soul sings with thankfulness that even when I have let you fade from sight, you have never lost sight of me.

For further thought

Take time to do a faith 'stocktake'. What needs a reset? What needs to be celebrated?

New settings, new challenges – 1 A travelling, wandering race

October

New settings, new challenges

2 A changing Church?

Notes by **Mark Mitchell**

Mark, a humanitarian aid worker, has journeyed across the globe, from the Pacific to Ukraine, responding to disasters and conflicts. His passion lies in practically demonstrating God's love to those affected by adversity. Through his work, Mark has witnessed first-hand the importance of unity, acceptance and inclusion in diverse and often challenging contexts. Based in New Zealand with his wife and two daughters, Mark enjoys time with his family and exploring the Wellington hills with his dog while listening to a good podcast. Mark has used the NIV for these readings.

5 October
Don't rush to judgement

Read Acts 5:33–39

When they heard this, they were furious and wanted to put them to death. But a Pharisee named Gamaliel, a teacher of the law, who was honored by all the people, stood up in the Sanhedrin and ordered that the men be put outside for a little while.

(verses 33–34)

In today's reading we find three groups of people facing judgement: 1) The jailers who had lost the prisoners they were guarding. The fear of severe punishment loomed over them. 2) The high priest and Sadducees faced the judgement of these Jesus-followers who were accusing them of killing Jesus. 3) Peter and the disciples who were accused of false teaching and judged by the authorities as dangerous.

In the midst of this complex situation, Gamaliel emerges as a beacon of wisdom. He reminds us of a fundamental truth: ultimately, there are just outcomes to our choices. If man-made, they fade away, but if from God, they are eternal.

Sometimes we allow the fear of how others might judge us, to rob us of the dreams and calling God has for us. Take inspiration from Peter and the disciples. Keep doing what you believe God is calling you to do, even in the face of adversity.

Today, let us reflect on our own lives. Are we quick to judge ourselves, doubting our own callings and dreams? Are we allowing external judgements to stifle our true potential?

† Lord, grant us the strength to trust in your timing and persevere in our callings despite what others may say.

Making poverty history

> **Read Acts 4:32–37**
>
> *All the believers were one in heart and mind.*
>
> (verse 32)

Does this sound like your church, or the Church of today? Are we truly of one heart and mind? Increasingly, it seems that the world is divided along partisan lines and in too many cases this is true of the Church as well. Yet, we know that a Church divided against itself will not stand (Matthew 12:25). Perhaps we are in danger of losing sight of the main thing? When Jesus was asked, 'What is the greatest command?', he summarised the law as loving God and loving your neighbour (Matthew 22:34–40) – two points but indivisible.

And love looks outwards, looking to bless. When we strip all away and focus on this it becomes easier to remember that our blessings are not for us alone and it makes sense of the phrase 'no needy person among them'. It doesn't imply absolute wealth equality but underscores that no one should suffer or be in need within a caring community. Social support systems, even where they exist and work, are never enough; needs are so often more than just financial or physical. Spiritual and emotional poverty also cries out for relief.

As we strive to reduce the impacts of poverty, let us remember that the unity of heart and mind in the early Church was not a mere coincidence but a result of their dedication to loving God and their neighbours. In our divided world, this unity remains the key to addressing all forms of poverty and building a more compassionate and just society.

† Lord, help us unite as one in heart and mind, focused on loving you and our neighbours, so that we can see an end to poverty, both material and spiritual.

For further thought

In a divided world, how can we in the Church model true unity? How can we meet the needs of those around us, transcending mere financial assistance to encompass the holistic well-being of all?

New settings, new challenges – 2 A changing Church?

October

Change takes courage

Read Galatians 2:1–14

When I saw that they were not acting in line with the truth of the gospel, I said to Cephas in front of them all, 'You are a Jew, yet you live like a Gentile and not like a Jew. How is it, then, that you force Gentiles to follow Jewish customs?'

(verse 14)

Change isn't simple; it requires courage and accountability. In the passage, we see the importance of confronting those who resist change, and this process can be both challenging and delicate.

First, let's acknowledge that change, whether in our personal lives or within a community, is difficult. Meaningful change demands courage; it often means stepping into the unknown, leaving behind familiar routines, and facing uncertainty. However, this courage alone may not suffice. For the disciples, change meant putting aside religious doctrine, the very essence of what had been instilled in them from a young age. They may have been used to seeing Jesus reinterpret scripture, but this was new territory again. And to be called out on it by Paul can't have been comfortable, but this leads us to the second point – accountability.

Accountability plays a crucial role in facilitating change. When individuals or groups are hesitant to embrace change, it often takes others who care to hold them to account, to urge on and encourage, particularly when the unknown starts to become uncomfortable. The role of 'accountability partner' also requires courage. Telling someone (in love) when they are heading in the wrong direction is challenging and requires boldness and conviction.

So, as we navigate the complexities of change, let us remember that it's not merely about having the courage to change but also the compassion to support and hold accountable those who may be hesitant. In this way, we can collectively move towards positive transformations in our lives and communities.

† Heavenly Father, grant us the courage to embrace change in our lives and communities, recognising that it often leads to growth and improvement. Help us approach those who resist change with empathy and understanding. Amen.

For further thought

How can we become agents of positive transformation? Remember, even in the face of reluctance, the power of empathy and courage can lead us to new possibilities.

What about the gentiles?

Read Acts 15:22–29

It seemed good to the Holy Spirit and to us not to burden you with anything beyond the following requirements: You are to abstain from food sacrificed to idols, from blood, from the meat of strangled animals and from sexual immorality. You will do well to avoid these things.

(verses 28–29)

Yesterday, we read about the change that was required in reaching out to the gentiles. In today's reading (it's worth reading the whole chapter), we see the early Christian Church questioning how to relate to the gentiles who clearly had different customs and practices. The decision reached during this meeting holds significant lessons for us today.

As we read this passage, it prompts us to reflect on our tendency to judge others based on our own standards. We often measure people and cultures against our familiar norms, which can lead to misunderstandings and division. However, God created the richness of diversity, each culture reflecting his goodness in its unique way. It's essential to recognise that differences aren't necessarily about being better or worse; they are simply different. I am fortunate in my work to be able to travel often and experience many very different cultures. I often reflect on the fact that we are all created in God's image, yet many people I engage with look and act very differently from me. By seeing these differences, I believe I get a fuller picture of who God is and his character.

This understanding can help break down barriers and embrace the beauty of diversity. But in our pursuit of harmony, we must also acknowledge that there are some absolutes, principles and values that transcend cultural differences.

The message from this passage is clear: we should not create unnecessary barriers or emphasise trivial differences. Instead, we must focus on the core values that bind us together.

† Lord, help us embrace the beautiful diversity in your creation, understanding that differences do not make us better or worse but uniquely reflect your goodness. Guide us to find common ground and unity in the celebration of our differences.

For further thought

In our interactions with people from diverse backgrounds, let us seek to understand, appreciate and celebrate the unique perspectives and qualities they bring, while holding firm to the timeless values that unite us as God's children.

New settings, new challenges – 2 A changing Church?

October

283

What about food?

Read Romans 14:18–23

Do not destroy the work of God for the sake of food. All food is clean, but it is wrong for a person to eat anything that causes someone else to stumble. It is better not to eat meat or drink wine or to do anything else that will cause your brother or sister to fall.

(verses 20–21)

In today's reading, the apostle Paul addresses the delicate issue of navigating differences within the Christian community. While the context of this passage revolves around dietary rules, its message holds true for various aspects of our lives where we encounter diversity.

We are all unique, with distinct backgrounds, preferences and beliefs. Just as we hope for acceptance and understanding from others, we must extend the same courtesy to our fellow believers. However, it's crucial to remember that accepting others' differences doesn't guarantee they will reciprocate.

As Christians, we bear a particular responsibility in these situations. Paul emphasises the need for us not to cause our brothers and sisters to stumble or fall into sin. Our actions and choices should reflect a commitment to unity and peace, especially in the face of differences. This is a repeated theme from Romans 12:18, which says, 'If it is possible, as far as it depends on you, live at peace with everyone.'

Paul urges us to be mindful of one another's consciences. While we may have the freedom to engage in certain practices or enjoy specific freedoms, we must consider the impact on others. It's not about compromising our beliefs but rather exercising sensitivity and love towards our fellow Christians.

In a world where diversity abounds, it is challenging to navigate differences and ensure that our actions do not lead others astray. We must approach these situations with prayerful consideration and a genuine desire to preserve harmony within the body of believers.

† Heavenly Father, grant us the wisdom and discernment to navigate differences in a way that upholds unity, peace and love within the Christian community. Amen.

For further thought

In a world characterised by diversity, our faith calls us to a higher standard of love and respect.

New settings, new challenges – 2 A changing Church?

October

10 October
What about slaves?

Read Philemon

Perhaps the reason he was separated from you for a little while was that you might have him back forever – no longer as a slave, but better than a slave, as a dear brother.

(verses 15–16a)

In the book of Philemon, Paul addresses a sensitive issue – the return of Onesimus, a former slave who had likely wronged his master, Philemon. The focus here is on Philemon's response. Will he choose to forgive and embrace Onesimus as a brother, or will he claim what he might perceive as being his right and re-enslave Onesimus?

Before we think of Philemon, imagine the turmoil in Onesimus' heart as he returns to his old master, uncertain of his reception. The memories of past mistreatment and fear must have weighed heavily. Yet, he goes back willingly. His only hope was that he believed that Philemon, influenced by Paul's letter and his belief in Christ, would receive him with forgiveness and compassion, rather than anger or punishment.

This raises an important question for us. How do we receive those who were once enslaved, at least metaphorically? Do we label them by their past, as slaves to sin, or do we see them as equals, friends and individuals with inherent dignity, forgiven and set free? In principle, our response may be, 'Of course!' But what if they had wronged us previously? Would we still welcome them as family?

There is another reminder of how to welcome those who wronged others. Remember the story of the prodigal son, where the father rushes to welcome his son from afar, celebrating with a feast (Luke 15:11–32). It's a reminder of the warmth and wholehearted acceptance that comes with receiving someone who was lost.

Unfortunately, we don't know how Philemon treated Onesimus on his return, but we can know how we will receive others.

† Let us open our hearts, O Lord, to receive those who seek refuge and freedom. May we welcome them with love, as you welcome us.

For further thought

As we reflect on Philemon's story, let us consider how forgiveness and acceptance can break the chains of division and prejudice in our own lives. Are there people we need to welcome back into our lives?

New settings, new challenges – 2 A changing Church?

October

285

All are welcome

Read Galatians 3:23–28

So in Christ Jesus you are all children of God through faith.

(verse 26)

In the rich tapestry of our Christian faith, we find a resounding message of inclusion and unity. Galatians 3:23–26 beautifully encapsulates this message, reminding us that in Christ, all are welcome.

The passages we've explored this week reflect the complexities of judgement, change, unity and the celebration of diversity. Each of these themes contributes to the overarching narrative of God's inclusive love for all.

Galatians 3:28 tells us, 'There is neither Jew nor Gentile, neither slave nor free, nor is there male and female, for you are all one in Christ Jesus.' This profound statement breaks down the barriers that often divide humanity. It emphasises that in Christ, all distinctions disappear and we become one family.

The message is clear: every individual, regardless of their background, social status or gender, is equally embraced by the boundless love of Christ. It's a reminder that the doors of God's grace are wide open to all who seek him.

The challenge, as we've seen throughout the week, is how we apply these key themes to our situation. This isn't simply a historical footnote about how the early Church dealt with them; it's a call to us to engage in a similar way – with those outside our community as well as those within the community of faith with whom we perhaps disagree. The extent to which we do this is the extent to which we build the kingdom of God as opposed to simply building our own narrow interests.

† Lord, help us to fully embrace the message of unity and inclusion found in your word. May we live it out in our daily lives, welcoming all who seek you with open arms and loving hearts.

For further thought

The message of inclusion challenges us to create a welcoming and accepting community that transcends all boundaries and divisions. Let us reflect on how we can better embody this message in our lives, inviting others to experience the love and unity found in Christ.

Samaria and the Samaritans

Notes by **Dr Delroy Hall**

Delroy is a trained psychodynamic psychotherapist with over thirty years' experience as a pastor and bishop. He is CEO of Delwes Consultancy which specialises in loss, depression, anxiety, clergy stress, Black male suicide and cultural competence. Primarily, he is committed to dealing with human pain while developing trust, so people can recover and thrive. As a former 400-metre hurdler, he is training to compete in various aqua bike events. He is married with twin daughters. Delroy has used the NKJV for these notes.

12 October
A mix of people and gods

Read 2 Kings 17:24–34

They feared the LORD, yet served their own gods.

(verse 33a)

We begin this week by reflecting on this interesting line in the biblical text as we see the development of a nation. Will the new people gathered in Israel come to know and serve the new God? Or, as a marginalised group, will they stay with their old way of life, giving them their identity?

It reminds me of something my mother used to say of some people who were aware of the gospel but continued to do their own thing. From the Caribbean folklore they were called 'worldly wise'. They were generally men, and a few women, who were well versed in scripture and who could recite huge portions of the Bible. Though thorough in biblical knowledge, their lifestyles had not changed. They allegedly knew all about God, but they did not have a transforming relationship with him.

In today's reading, how would it work out for those who had been transported to this foreign land? Would they take this opportunity to discover the real God? The final verse tells us that they never did.

How many times have we wished our friends and families would take opportunities to get to know Jesus, but instead, they persist in their old ways? How can we live in such a way as to encourage real relationship?

† Lord, help me to surrender my whole life to you and not be half in and half out. Amen.

A faithful few

> **Read 2 Chronicles 30:1–12**
>
> *For the king and his leaders and all the assembly in Jerusalem had agreed to keep the Passover in the second month. For they could not keep it at the regular time, because a sufficient number of priests had not consecrated themselves, nor had the people gathered together at Jerusalem.*
>
> (verses 2–3)

Reflecting on this biblical text I am reminded of the words often attributed to the anthropologist Margaret Mead: 'Never doubt that a small group of thoughtful committed citizens can change the world. In fact, it's the only thing that ever has.'

We are living in a time where how many 'likes' we get on our social media posts can determine whether we feel useful or not. But popularity is not a useful benchmark. Here we see a group of people humbling themselves to follow the Lord despite experiencing the opposite of popularity – being scorned and mocked. We can read those words with ease, but we often do not take into consideration the levels of courage needed to make such a step.

I am reminded of my own Christian ministry where, on many occasions, no one turned up for Bible study – but I persisted, and people started to attend, after quite some time. I recall a ministerial peer who held a Bible study with one person for over a year until others, who were church members, started to appear.

Maybe you are in such a situation right now. The odds are stacked against you in your job or within church ministry. Your vision is seen as folly and people are laughing at you. My encouragement to you is simply this: start, see what happens, learn from what you do and continue.

† Father and Friend, let us learn from you. You are not asking us to wait on big numbers to start a new ministry or project. You want us to start and see your hand at work.

For further thought

As you read the scriptures, within your heart who do you identify with? The mockers or the small group? It is easy to be a mocker, but a follower requires courage and strength.

An offer to help refused

Read Ezra 4:1–3

*But Zerubbabel and Jeshua and the rest of the heads of the fathers'
houses of Israel said to them, 'You may do nothing with us to build a
house for our God; but we alone will build to the LORD God of Israel, as
King Cyrus the king of Persia has commanded us.'*

(verse 3)

Adversaries wanting to help build a project of honour. Really!

Historically, the Samaritans held a mix of Israelite beliefs and
their own traditions – as we saw a couple of days ago, this lack of
clarity can distract from real relationship with God. Yet they were
offering much-needed help – how tempting that must have been.
But Zerubbabel and Jeshua and the rest of the leaders understood
that exile and the destruction of the Temple had arisen precisely
because of this lack of holiness, and they were right to refuse the
help even though the Samaritans were saying the right things.

We can be in a similar situation where offers of help abound,
but we can sense the 'spirit' of the giver is not right. One of the
things I quickly learnt in church leadership is that you can have a
need for certain gifts in order to start or progress a ministry and
be tempted to make use of someone because they have the skills,
gifts and talents. But if they do not have the character that comes
from a life transformed by relationship with Jesus, disaster follows.

This is not just a dilemma for church ministry but for workplaces
too. Such lessons are learned the hard way. In one of my
pastorates, I was accused of holding a certain person back in their
ministry. When I left the church and another incumbent came, this
person was given centre stage in the life of the church and it soon
became clear to the congregation why I did not allow the person
anywhere near the pulpit.

† Lord, help us to see beyond what we can see. Amen.

For further thought

You may be in a difficult situation and in need of serious help.
Before you decide whose help to accept, take a step back, wait,
think, pray and then act.

Samaria and the Samaritans

October

15 October

Not ready yet

Read Matthew 10:1–6

Do not go into the way of the Gentiles, and do not enter a city of the Samaritans.

(verse 5)

'Nothing happens before its time.' I used to hear that so often from my African Caribbean elders. I am not sure if I believed it then and I am still unsure … The Old Testament is full of stories of God's plans being delayed by grief, fear or just plain disobedience. But it is true that we can sometimes press for things to happen when the time has not yet arrived, and we must wait.

Such a time is highlighted in our scripture today – Jesus himself would one day go out of his way to visit Samaria, but the time was not yet. The big question is, how do we know when to wait and when to make progress in our own motivation?

One of the things I realised as a pastor is that we can spend time and energy in ministry where folk are not yet ready to respond to the good news of Christ, the ground is not yet prepared for the good seed. But if we spend that same amount of time and energy in other places, we reap a bountiful harvest of new people for Christ. The key is discernment and listening to the prompting of God.

The gentiles were not ready, but the Israelites were and, discerning this, Jesus gave his direction. Of course, that didn't mean that all would be ready to respond. There were still words of warning to prepare the disciples for some of the hostility they would face – and the same is true for us today – though a people may be ready it will not always be plain sailing.

† Loving Saviour, help us to discern where we should spend our time as we spread your good news to a lost world.

For further thought

We are called to evangelise the world, but is it possible our endeavours could be more effective if we discerned who we should talk with, and when?

Samaria and the Samaritans

October

16 October
Overcoming barriers

Read John 4:1–10

He would have given you living water.

(verse 10b)

The story of the woman at the well has been told on many occasions. She is from an ethnic group shunned by the Jews; she is a woman with no standing in their culture. And she is judged because of her multiple marriages and current sinful state. She is ostracised by her own people; in her wildest dreams she could not have expected the Messiah to come to her.

Yet come he does – and reveals who he is to this marginalised woman in a way that he declines to do for anyone else in scripture.

In doing so, Jesus does not sidestep the issues but deals with them all while respecting her humanity as being created in the image of God. Jesus enters a bold conversation of love with this woman; he listens to her without judging and hears a yearning that perhaps others have missed. And in loving compassion, he gives her what her soul has been longing for – acceptance, significance and peace. As a man, I have no idea how this woman may have felt in that culture, but I have worked as a counsellor for over three decades and continue to be amazed at what can happen with the power of giving people space to talk about the things that are bothering them the most.

Perhaps men had rejected her because she couldn't bear them children. Perhaps her sense of disgrace and loneliness had shaped her decision-making.

We are so often caught up trying to solve the presenting issue, so quick to judge, that we fail to hear the heart cry, fail to see the deepest need.

† Divine Lord, hear us in our dark times and remind us to offer kindness when we hear the pain of others. Amen.

For further thought

Some may criticise the plight of this woman, but all of us, when we hit hard times, want to be treated with kindness, mercy and compassion. Don't you?

Samaria and the Samaritans

October

17 October
Open to believe

Read John 4:19–42

Sir, I perceive that You are a prophet.

(verse 19b)

To perceive is to 'find out by seeing', 'to discern', 'to look at', 'to behold'. The many definitions of 'to perceive' capture what has taken place in the life of the Samaritan woman. There are many stories of Jesus having conversations with different people – from fishermen to the religious elite. Some responded to his words, others didn't understand them. Still others, understanding, rejected them. What makes the difference? This woman had everything stacked against her – she didn't share Jesus' cultural or religious background, she was hurting and broken, marginalised and lonely. She had every reason to be blind to God, but instead, perceives what others miss. Psychologist Carol Dweck might describe her as a nameless Samaritan woman, with a growth mindset, warm towards God, open to believe.

And perceiving this, Jesus has journeyed to this unexpected place to meet this unnoticed woman. And creatively, non-judgementally, he teases open that warm heart so that it can receive his love. He sets aside religious differences about where they should worship, cultural distinctions about whose ancestor is more important. And he defuses the stigma by revealing that he knows about the sixth 'husband' without being critical. And then he uses her current circumstance to reveal her real need. Day after day, painfully she came to collect water, only to be thirsty again. An echo of her inner thirst for love and companionship – man after man, but still she yearned for one who would truly love her. And in Jesus, she found him.

May we be equally creative and attentive to God's Spirit as we seek to share his love with those we would perhaps shy away from.

† Divine Listener and Friend, during those sacred moments of sharing the gospel, teach us how to listen to the depth of a living soul.

For further thought
We never know what is in people's lives until we start to listen to them. Let us endeavour to have a growth mindset so that we can listen to people well and minister effectively.

A mission field

Read Acts 8:14–17

Then they laid hands on them, and they received the Holy Spirit.

(verse 17)

There is almost an unexpected shock/surprise that Samaria was open to God's word. In this reading there is a flurry of missionary activity which results in the new believers being empowered by the Holy Spirit to be witnesses in a place that had previously been seen as difficult and hard to reach.

This new mission field – or church plant – happened almost by accident. A woman, who could not keep long-term relationships, no doubt emotionally and psychologically broken by her unsuccessful marriages, was used by God as a catalyst to spark a revival in a so-called difficult and hard-to-reach part of the society.

I recall years ago a Church of England vicar emphasising that in our ministry we need a Lazarus – someone who had been given up on by the community, but who Jesus can use in his kingdom. I would concur and say every ministry needs a nameless Samaritan woman to become the catalyst in a congregation. Of course, it may be uncomfortable for some to have someone like this in the congregation, but loving others isn't always comfortable, for us or for those we are trying to love!

Is there a Samaritan woman in your neighbourhood who the church can be intentionally praying for? Is there someone in your congregation who can begin talking with such an individual and see how the Lord directs? I suspect in all our communities there are many Lazaruses and Samaritan women. See if you can find them.

† Father, give us a heart to pray, find, befriend and love the Lazaruses and Samaritan women in our communities. Amen.

For further thought

Loving the Lazaruses and Samaritans in our communities can be challenging, but as we lean into such challenges there we will grow, love and understand God and his way more deeply.

Samaria and the Samaritans

October

Persistence

Notes by **Shirlyn Toppin**

Shirlyn is a presbyter in the Methodist Church. She believes passionately in the preaching of the word of God, without compromise, and exercising a pastoral ministry of grace. She enjoys various forms of leisure, reading and shopping. Shirlyn has used the NRSVA for these notes.

19 October
Abraham bargains with God

Read Genesis 18:16–33

Suppose there are fifty righteous within the city; will you then sweep away the place and not forgive it for the fifty righteous who are in it?

(verse 24)

What might be the possible outcome if you bargain with God? In today's reading the bargaining over the salvation of Sodom points our attention to God's justice. Abraham successively presented his pleas while bravely decreasing the number from fifty to ten. Surely he was 'pushing his luck' with such intense persistence. In fact, God actually encouraged Abraham's intercessory prayers. God initiated the process by revealing his purpose to Abraham, which moved him to bargain persistently because of his understanding of God's purpose and mercy.

The temptation to bargain with God is always present, which most of us have done at one point or another. Even those who claim to not believe in God bargain with him. 'If you help me win the lottery, I'll help the poor'; 'help me to pass this exam and I will go to church.' Does bargaining work with God? Unlikely, given the account of Jephthah's negotiation with God (Judges 11:30–31) and the conclusion of Abraham's bargaining for Sodom. While God will encourage our persistence in prayer, he doesn't answer through bargaining, but in accordance with his will.

As we explore this week's theme of persistence, may we perceive how liberating and enriching it is to persevere despite challenges.

† Loving Father, let your will be done in all things. Amen.

Isaac's persistence in his actions brings reward

Read Genesis 26:12–33

He moved from there and dug a well, and they did not quarrel over it; so, he called it Rehoboth saying, 'Now the LORD has made room for us, and we shall be fruitful in the land.'

(verse 22)

Expulsion, envy and contention – if they were not character-building lessons for Isaac, they certainly positioned him to exemplify the saying 'patience is a virtue'. Cutting off his water supply made him unable to provide for his flocks. He kept moving for the sake of keeping the peace, and his persistence in action in the end was rewarded. He had the water rights in Rehoboth. What would have caused most people to give in despair had the opposite effect on Isaac. Persistent action was victorious.

It's hard to understand why God allows complicated and unnecessary issues in our lives. What is the point? What is God preparing us for? What lessons can be learnt? More often than not we eventually come to an understanding of that particular difficult period. God is at work even when we cannot see it; he is 'making room', creating opportunities beyond our wildest imaginations.

Those seeking refuge or asylum in many countries may find identifiable experiences like that of Isaac. Like him, they desire acceptance not criticism; self-determination not suppression; compassion not cruelty. Like him, they might wonder when God might intervene so that they too could say 'the Lord has made room.' But God's intervention comes in different ways, sometimes directly, sometimes indirectly. Perhaps God is asking you to 'make room' for the powerless and hopeless, to persistently cry out on their behalf even if it appears ineffectual. Isaac's tenacity reminds us that it could be rewarding.

† God, thank you for the spirit of perseverance when confronted with hurdles. Help us to trust you in every situation. Amen.

For further thought

There are times when we have to accept God's slowness to intervene, but it doesn't mean he is unaware of our needs.

Persistence

October

21 October
Request granted

Read Matthew 15:21–28

'I was sent only to the lost sheep of the house of Israel.' But she came and knelt before him, saying, 'Lord, help me.' ... Then Jesus answered her, 'Woman, great is your faith!'

(verses 24–25, 28a)

Exclusion generates feelings of unworthiness. Peer pressure and unwarranted opinions have reduced many to compromise and conform to public expectations. Standing out of the norm is not socially acceptable and can be seen as a deliberate act of rebellion, causing further isolation.

Today's reading reveals a confrontation with someone whose faith enabled her to refuse the accepted parameters and who, doing so, exemplifies persistence in the face of discouragement and insults. This Canaanite woman was the outsider in that society – a gentile, a woman, an uninvited guest. Nonetheless she was a woman of faith who recognised in Jesus the one who could fulfil her urgent request.

She could have walked away after hearing the statement, 'I was sent only to the lost sheep of the house of Israel.' She could have tucked in her request, listened to her pride and slunk off. Instead, rather than allowing the chilling words of rejection to direct her path, she chose to follow her knowledge of Jesus to be even bolder. Tenacity won because the Canaanite woman refused to give up. She believed and hoped that mercy would prevail in her situation, and it did – her request was granted.

The woman's action has much to teach us about persistent faith when we feel as if God is ignoring our prayers. Persistent faith is unyielding and does not give up easily. It breaks down barriers so that even the outsider can experience blessings. It's a revelation of the grace of God, which resulted in answered prayers.

† Loving Lord, 'hear my prayers and let my cries come unto you' (Psalm 102:1). Amen

For further thought

Persistence was key in the text for answered prayer. Have you ever experienced a similar response in your prayer life?

Persistence

October

22 October
Persistence in mercy

Read Matthew 18:15–17, 21–22

If another member of the church sins against you, go and point out their fault when the two of you are alone … if you are not listened to, take one or two others … If the member refuses to listen to them, tell it to the church.

(verses 15–17)

Confrontation, ownership and forgiveness for the restoration of relationships is reflected in today's theme 'persistence in mercy'. Jesus pointing out the manner for dealing with conflict within the Church and with each other makes us uncomfortable. But it is a much-needed process to prevent us from minimising the harm done by mistaking it for mercy. Persistence in mercy starts with confronting the offender. Failure to do so may indicate that the offence doesn't matter and the offender's behaviour is justifiable. Persisting in mercy should hopefully result in the person taking ownership, therefore paving the way for genuine forgiveness to ensue.

Persistence in mercy highlights that ignoring a conflict is futile and naive. Relationships have been broken either because of refusal to accept that there is a dispute or because of a lack of insight as to how to address it. We could probably recall uproars in meetings over trivial matters that triggered issues left simmering for months, perhaps years. Conflict does not disappear – sooner or later it erupts causing irreparable damage.

Persistence in mercy reminds us that we cannot lose sight of the kingdom's perspectives. Hostility, dysfunctionality and pride distort our ability to keep our eyes on the goal and the ultimate prize, which will be unpacked in tomorrow's notes. Persistence in mercy advocates connectedness. Jesus often spoke about his 'oneness with God', reaffirming how we should be with one another. Jesus' command is clear. Can we afford to dismiss it at the risk of our relationship with God and others?

† Lord, help us to be merciful and to follow your directives for healing and reconciling. Amen.

For further thought
Persistence in mercy is needed for the sustaining of relationships. Is there anyone you might need to pursue?

Through it all

Read 2 Corinthians 11:24–33 and Philippians 3:13a–14

...forgetting what lies behind and straining forward to what lies ahead, I press on towards the goal for the prize of the heavenly call of God in Christ Jesus.

(Philippians 3:13b–14)

Why is it important for us to be persistently hopeful? Let us take a look at Paul's reasoned declaration in today's reading. Pressing on, looking ahead or moving forward was Paul's intent to complete God's call to discipleship and service, and to the ultimate destination of heaven. Commitment to God's call compelled Paul to give a defensive account of his labours and sufferings to the Corinthian church, as 'the signs of a true apostle' (2 Corinthians 12:12). Past failures, successes, shattered promises and unrealised dreams were exactly that: the past. What was ahead was unknown to Paul, but he trusted in the all-knowing God with an unwavering confidence.

Since we are assured that persistence, remaining hopeful, is rooted in trusting God, what happens when that confidence is shaken? No one is immunised against criticism, disappointment and sorrow – it's a passage of life. Our response, on the other hand, is the defining factor to whether we retreat, or press through it all like Paul. He had a glimpse of the prize – not one of tangible temporariness but timeless/eternal.

I was told by an unbeliever when I expressed hope in Christ's return that it was meaningless daydreaming to believe in heaven and eternity. For that person, only the here and now mattered. For them, there was nothing beyond this present reality – unlike Paul's resolute trust in God who has made great provisions for those who believe in him. What awaits us in heaven is worth far more than any struggles we face here on earth. Hope requires perseverance.

† Heavenly Father, let no barrier hinder my confidence and hope in you. Give me courage to faithfully endure. Amen.

For further thought

How do you persevere when confidence wanes and hope seemingly diminishes?

The demands of persistence

Read Hebrews 12:1–13

Therefore, since we are surrounded by so great a cloud of witnesses, let us also lay aside every weight and the sin that clings so closely and let us run with perseverance the race that is set before us.

(verse 1)

For a runner in a long race or marathon, knowing the course helps to keep up momentum and motivation with each step. Knowing your ultimate goal will help you to remain focused and pace yourself. Becoming discouraged or distracted is not a viable option, even if the race seems unending. Every race demands the runner to be persistent, irrespective of impediments seen and unseen.

We know that God has good plans for us. We know that God will never abandon us. We also know that faith helps us to persevere when things go awry. In spite of all the 'knowing', life-changing encounters filled with difficulties and suffering can make us question God's intentions leaving us feeling 'weighed down'. Yet, the demands of discipleship necessitate that we run continuously the Christian race, even though we are discouraged by life events or disappointed with people.

Both good and bad things could be deterrents as we press forward in faith. Persistence is demanding. But you and I are not the first to run the Christian race, evident in the reading: 'since we are surrounded by so great a cloud of witnesses …'. Yes, many people have run this race of faith before us, faithfully enduring to the finish line.

Successful running of the race demands single-minded determination. Jesus could have become unfocused and taken his eyes off his purpose and destiny. He was determined. He was committed. He persisted.

† Lord God, help your children to trust in you when the race of faith seems too demanding. Amen.

For further thought

Consider what may distract you from reaching the finish line.

Persistence

October

25 October
Be encouraged – God will be with you

> **Read Isaiah 41:10–14**
>
> ...do not fear, for I am with you, do not be afraid, for I am your God; I
> will strengthen you, I will help you. I will uphold you with my victorious
> right hand.
>
> (verse 10)

Fear is universal! Fear interrupts our lives and spiritual growth. God
is aware of our tendency to fear, but he does not want us to be
consumed by fear. Isaiah reminds us of five promises God made to
the Israelites, which were applicable then and now. Promises made
to give them confidence that they did not need to fear. Promises
to encourage them to trust in him. Promises to inspire faith in God
and be equipped for any battle or storm.

'I am with you' – God is with us at all times and in every
situation, whether good or bad. Nothing we face is bigger than
God. Assurance of his presence with us in all circumstances should
instil trust and not fear.

'I am your God' – God is faithful. He is always there when we
face difficulties. We need to keep our eyes fixed on him. Whatever
we might be fearful of, we need to surrender it to the one who
sits on the throne.

'I will strengthen you' – God gives us courage to face all our
battles. He is the solution to all of our fears.

'I will help you' – We can do nothing without God. We need his
divine help as we persevere in our discipleship.

'I will uphold' – God reassures us that he will keep us from
falling.

Fear is daunting, but God is unswerving in his promises, which
are 'Yes' and 'Amen'. Persist in his promises and be encouraged
that he will be with you.

† Gracious Father, I pray that you will fill me with your love that I might overcome
my fear. Amen.

For further thought

Meditate on 2 Timothy 1:7. How does this encourage you in the
context of today's reflection?

Persistence

October

Letters to Titus and Jude

Notes by **Paul Cavill and Tom Hartman**

Paul and Tom are friends who meet for fellowship and lunch as often as their timetables permit, which is quite infrequently, despite Paul being retired. Paul is an author and specialist on English place names and the faith of ancient peoples. Tom is a zoologist who has specialised in evolutionary genetics and firmly believes that dinosaurs are the key to teaching children about anything. They form an unlikely group, but it seems to work. They have used the NIVUK for these notes.

26 October
An example to all

> **Read Titus 1:1–16**
>
> *[An elder] must be hospitable, one who loves what is good, who is self-controlled, upright, holy and disciplined. He must hold firmly to the trustworthy message as it has been taught, so that he can encourage others by sound doctrine and refute those who oppose it.*
>
> (verses 8–9)

When you read through Paul's letter to Titus, a friend and co-worker residing on the island of Crete, you might be shocked at him quoting the defamatory remarks deriding Cretans for being 'always liars, evil brutes, lazy gluttons' (verse 12). His point, of course, is that we do not have to live according to the stereotypes with which we are sometimes labelled – we can be different.

Paul had selected Crete as a strategic crossroads for shipping routes where there would be manifold opportunities to spread the gospel. A beacon in the Mediterranean. He left Titus on Crete to finish off what he had started, but it was not an easy task. How do you change a culture? Paul is quite clear: it is by example. So, he lists the qualities essential in a church leader in both actions and belief.

Paul and Titus were working with people who were quite different from them. But, by striking up conversation, being led into holy living by the Spirit and holding to the example of Christ, they were preparing the Christians on Crete – sometimes slowly and cautiously, but at other times with confidence and specific rebukes, to challenge the culture and transform it.

† Lord, help us to transform the world and to hold fast to the example that you have set before us in your Son, our Lord.

A message to slaves

Read Titus 2:1–15

Teach slaves to be subject to their masters in everything, to try to please them, not to talk back to them, and not to steal from them, but to show that they can be fully trusted, so that in every way they will make the teaching about God our Saviour attractive.

(verses 9–10)

Surely if Paul believed that there is 'neither slave nor free', as he stated boldly to the church in Galatia (Galatians 3:28), then he should be championing freedom and equality? So what is he doing here when he tells slaves to be dutiful and try to please their masters?

For context, in the New Testament era, the term 'slave' was often used to describe a variety of conditions that included indentured servitude, economic servitude and chattel slavery (the form that we think of when we hear 'slave'). Slavery could result from a variety of circumstances, such as being captured in war, paying off a debt or voluntarily entering service as a form of employment due to economic hardship. Such 'slaves' included those with special skills such as doctors or being literate or musical. In Roman times, there were structured ways for slaves to gain their freedom – a practice known as manumission.

Even with that understanding, what Paul requires (Galatians 3:28) is a breathtakingly bold and radical approach. When slaves, whatever their background, became Christians they were to be welcomed as equals – yes, their legal or contractual circumstances hadn't changed, but the essence of the relationship was transformed. No longer were they to be treated as beneath, but as peers. And this radical change would ultimately lead to a wider transformation by holding true to the values of Jesus through whom all change for good will come about.

† Lord, help me to confront the values of the society in which I live that are not upheld by your truth and good news; and renew me, by your Spirit, to be more like your Son.

For further thought

How can we all confront the slavery that is still prevalent throughout the world?

A timeless message from a different culture

Read Titus 3:1–15

He saved us through the washing of rebirth and renewal by the Holy Spirit, whom he poured out on us generously through Jesus Christ our Saviour, so that, having been justified by his grace, we might become heirs having the hope of eternal life.

(verses 5b–7)

Paul's letter to Titus is centred on working through a cultural stereotype to help a fledgling Christian fellowship to integrate into Cretan society and yet be distinct from it. Paul is not fazed by this at all. He can, in one moment, talk about the virtues of a good Christian life, and in another, be planning Titus' trip to Nicopolis to be with him during the winter.

Paul was very much a man of his time, but he also articulated truths that are timeless and for everyone. He intersperses heavenly theology (as in our extract above) with earthly practicality regarding pointless debates. His overriding concern is that the good news of Jesus Christ is there to make the whole of society better. His practical advice is to ensure that the Church does not become an enclave separated from society, nor become so similar to it that there is no distinction in behaviour or values. The Church is to be a transformative fellowship, a worshipping community that faces God and, by the power of the Holy Spirit, is an example of a holy people.

How to represent Christ in a culture that is different or antagonistic is a common theme within the scriptures. We ask (as in Psalm 137), 'How shall we sing the Lord's song in a strange land?' Only by prayer, careful study and in humility are we able to dialogue with the culture into which the Lord has placed us, to transform it and not be conformed to it.

† Lord, keep us in step with your will as we negotiate the maze of our lives. Help us to be honest and realistic disciples presenting the risen Lord wherever we find ourselves.

For further thought

Consider how much of our lives and those of our fellowships are conformed to the world and how much they are able to transform the world.

Letters to Titus and Jude

October

Contend for the faith

Read Jude 1:1–4

I felt compelled to write and urge you to contend for the faith that was once for all entrusted to God's holy people.

(verse 3)

We live in an often-confusing world. It can be hard to know what or who to believe. Leaders of various sorts often say one thing and do another. More and more sophisticated technology can be used to con and deceive us. People talk of our time and outlook as being 'post-truth'.

Something similar was the case in the church Jude was writing to. Plausible teachers were undermining the truth of the gospel and deceiving the people. Their message affected mind, body and spirit. It was based on an argument that God's grace permitted people to indulge freely in sin. It encouraged immorality – as many of the surrounding pagan religions did – and it denied the lordship of Christ.

Jude was so troubled by this situation that he changed his whole approach to writing, from gentle encouragement in his planned letter, to stern warning in the letter we have, that he felt compelled to write. He urges the Christians to fight for the faith that God has revealed to them, and his condemnation of the false teachers suggests practical ways to do this: Christians should stand firm on the sovereignty of Jesus; they should maintain purity in mind and body; and they should consciously keep themselves in the truth and grace of God.

Jude's encouragement is to distrust the message of teachers who do not live out the faith. Faith involves mind, body and spirit. And truth matters.

† Father, in the many distractions and temptations of the world, help us to be people of integrity and truth.

For further thought

How can we best 'contend for the faith'? What part do you individually have to play?

Persevere in the faith

Read Jude 1:5–11

...on the strength of their dreams these ungodly people pollute their own bodies, reject authority and heap abuse on celestial beings ... these people slander whatever they do not understand.

(verses 8, 10)

I happened to be walking past a stadium when the game inside finished and thousands of people poured into the street – going in the opposite direction from me. It was almost impossible to make any headway against that human tide; just standing still was difficult enough. Some of them shouted at me for trying to get past them. Going against the flow physically, mentally or spiritually can be really hard.

W B Yeats, the twentieth-century Irish poet, pictured an apocalypse very different from the one in the Bible. In his poem 'The Second Coming', he writes of people's attitudes before the dread event: 'The best lack all conviction, while the worst/ Are full of passionate intensity.'[1] Jude writes about the false teachers with their visions and passion, their free abuse of things they don't understand. It is not hard to see parallels with the passionate rhetoric used in various media today, but particularly in social media. Measured defence of faith and virtue (how old-fashioned that is!), and reverence and respect for God are mocked, and followers are often carried along by the enthusiasm and emotion of the slanderers.

Jude twice (verses 5 and 11) reminds his fellow Christians that God is not to be mocked, using examples of God's judgement from scripture and tradition. We don't have to join in and follow the passion and pressure of the crowd. We can stand firm, however loudly we are shouted at, and leave the judgement to God.

† Pray for yourself, and for people you know who are facing persecution, mockery and abuse for their faith.

For further thought

How do you stand or go against the flow in your work or personal relationships? What encourages you to persevere? What do you find particularly difficult? How can you encourage others facing the same issues?

[1] W B Yeats, 'The Second Coming' (published 1920).

Letters to Titus and Jude

October

31 October
Beware false teachers and loose talkers

Read Jude 1:12–19

These people are grumblers and fault-finders; they follow their own evil desires; they boast about themselves and flatter others for their own advantage.

(verse 16)

A poster put up in public places in Britain during the Second World War read 'Careless talk costs lives'. Idle chatter in wartime could possibly give away important information to the enemy that could endanger people. Jude is very critical of the obvious ungodliness of the false teachers in his letter: he mentions in today's reading how they pervert the central communion rite of their church by selfishness and faction, when it should express their unity as they share the body and blood of Christ. But he also shows how ungodliness appears in the little things as well as the big things. Grumbling, fault-finding, boasting, flattery and scoffing are the thin end of the wedge and often lead on to more serious sin. These things are careless talk, holding precious things cheaply, leading people astray: they quench the Spirit and foment division. In the end, Jude affirms, careless talk like this costs lives.

The Bible has a lot to say about talking. Jude's brother, James, warns in his letter against loose talk, saying that the tongue 'corrupts the whole body' (James 3:6). Jude agrees and reminds the church of the apostles' warning about loose talkers in the last times. Holding our tongues can be a long and difficult discipline to learn and practise: it is vital, not only for ourselves, but also for the Church.

† Pray with Paul (Colossians 4:6) – let my conversation be always full of grace, seasoned with salt, so that I may know how to answer everyone.

For further thought

How can we disagree with other Christians without disrespect, and agree with each other without self-satisfaction?

1 November
Blessing

Read Jude 1:20–25

But you, dear friends, by building yourselves up in your most holy faith and praying in the Holy Spirit, keep yourselves in God's love as you wait for the mercy of our Lord Jesus Christ to bring you to eternal life.

(verses 20–21)

'The quality of mercy is not strain'd …/ It is an attribute to God himself.' So says Portia in William Shakespeare's play *The Merchant of Venice*, in a plea for justice tempered by mercy. Jude has been very severe in this letter about the false teachers and their ungodliness. Here, though, in his closing encouragements, he switches focus from them to the faithful Christians in the church. And his theme is mercy. In the opening greeting, he prays for God's mercy to be abundantly present in the church; at the end, he tells the church to wait for God's mercy to be revealed; and he urges the church to practise mercy towards others in the face of the disruption of the false teachers.

Sometimes we can be tempted to give up on the weak or waverers; we are sometimes tempted to give up on ourselves when we are weak or wavering. But God's mercy is not strained, or limited, or effortful: Jesus has all the power and the mercy to bring us into his presence 'without fault' (verse 24), perfect in his sight. Neither should our practice of mercy be strained, or limited, or effortful because mercy is, indeed, an 'attribute of God' that he shares with us. By exercising mercy, we build up our faith and keep ourselves in God's love. Jesus said in the Sermon on the Mount, 'Blessed are the merciful, for they will be shown mercy' (Matthew 5:7). We are 'twice blessed', as Portia says, in giving and receiving mercy.

† Glorious Lord, thank you for your mercy on us. Help us when we find it hard to be merciful to others.

For further thought
We don't talk a lot about mercy these days. What does mercy look like in practice?

Letters to Titus and Jude

November

Searching for shalom (1)

Notes by **Ian Fosten**

Ian Fosten has ministered within the United Reformed Church in Norfolk, Suffolk and on Holy Island (Lindisfarne). He is director of a community theatre in Lowestoft where he lives with his wife and two younger children. He runs open-mic poetry readings, edits book reviews and has a particular interest in landscape and spirituality. Ian has used the NRSV for these notes.

2 November
Desperately seeking peace

Read Exodus 2:23–25

The Israelites groaned under their slavery and cried out … God heard their groaning, and God remembered his covenant with Abraham, Isaac, and Jacob. God looked upon the Israelites, and God took notice of them.

(verses 23b–25)

Peace-seeking is a universal human ambition. Quite apart from specialist individuals working to make peace between warring factions and armies, yearning for peace is part of everyday experience – whether it is relief from the neighbour's barking dog, our own squabbling children, from worry about money, past trauma or unrequited love, we often equate peace with the cessation of something undesirable and intrusive. By contrast, the Hebrew word *shalom*, which is usually translated as 'peace', has a much richer meaning. As well as having this familiar sense of release from conflict, it carries with it a sense of completeness, of things being in the right place, of at-home-ness. It is this last attribute which particularly speaks to me as I read in the book of Exodus about the oppressed and enslaved people of Israel – they yearned for freedom to be themselves, make their own choices, live without fear and in a place where they could truly be at home.

As this week unfolds, we shall journey through parts of the Bible on our own quest to understand and, I hope, come to know more deeply God's gift of peace – shalom!

† In seeking peace, dear God, take me beyond avoiding difficulty or duty. Rather, let me be open-minded and open-hearted enough to receive your gift. Amen.

3 November
Seeking peace in wealth

Read 1 Timothy 6:6–10

*Of course, there is great gain in godliness combined with contentment
… For the love of money is a root of all kinds of evil, and in their
eagerness to be rich some have wandered away from the faith and
pierced themselves with many pains.*

(verses 6, 10)

A teenager I know can be powerfully optimistic. When he has set his heart on acquiring a branded hoodie or the latest version of a video game, he thinks, 'If I can only get this, then I shall want for nothing else'. I don't doubt the sincerity of his optimistic belief, but equally, I don't doubt that after wearing the hoodie a couple of times or playing the game for a month or two, he will see something else which will unquestionably make his life complete … until the next thing! I cannot be too judgemental of this young person, for I too can display his optimistic outlook, and isn't unsatisfiable consumption the main driver behind many economies in the world?

That being so, our reading from 1 Timothy is both countercultural and challenging. In a society driven by 'more is better', how do we bear honest witness to the truth that 'enough is best'? I once attended a church discussion where a man was proudly describing his family's chosen minimal lifestyle – no car or TV, a frugal diet and so on. When he'd finished speaking, my friend, who I knew was struggling with the material demands of his own family, burst out, 'Yes, but how can I witness in that way without seeming as self-righteous as you have appeared to me!'

Maybe our best witness is built upon desiring, prioritising and growing the quality of contentment – itself an expression of shalom – in which we neither make a flamboyant display of deprivation, nor let ourselves be uncritically enthralled by consumerist hype.

† Teach me, Lord Jesus, to recognise when I have enough. Save me from wanting what I do not need. Free me to be generous with all that I have. Amen.

For further thought

When we pray, 'Lead us not into temptation', does over-active avarice feature on our list of possibilities?

Searching for shalom (1)

November

4 November
Seeking peace in personal suffering

Read Mark 5:24b–34

Now there was a woman who had been suffering from haemorrhages for twelve years … she said, 'If I but touch his clothes, I will be made well.' …He said to her, 'Daughter, your faith has made you well; go in peace, and be healed of your disease.'

(verses 25, 28, 34)

When we speak of faith we may well reach for words like 'strong', 'powerful' or 'heroic'. Faith is something to aspire to, to aim for, in order that, with enough application on our part, we might gradually accumulate more of it. On first reading, the story of the woman who had been ill for so long supports this understanding. Doesn't Jesus spell it out when he says, 'Your faith has made you well'? But reading the story again I am struck by the woman's faith, and even more so by her desperation – she has tried all other potential cures, presumably putting her faith in those practitioners too, but without success. Her secretive, despairing lunge at Jesus' cloak was perhaps not so much a sign of complete confidence as the action of someone with nothing left to give, or lose. If this was so, then it leads me to see faith less as a personal quality to develop and more as a gift given when we come to God in Jesus empty-handed and unable to mend whatever is wrong with us.

The story concludes in a way that is inspiring, instructive and, of course, delightful. The Gospel writer sets out the result – the woman's physical disease is cured, and whilst that is great in itself, there is more. By listening to her story and removing the social stigma that went with her illness, Jesus sees that her life is made well physically, mentally and socially. She is no longer incomplete but living in peace – shalom!

† Today, dear God, I have nothing to trade and nothing to give. Instead, accept my emptiness – and with open hands I am ready to receive whatever you know that I need. Amen.

For further thought

Faith has little to do with how strong we are – but plenty to do with how well we acknowledge our weakness.

5 November
Peace in wisdom and understanding

Read Proverbs 3:13–24

Happy are those who find wisdom, and those who get understanding ...
She is more precious than jewels, and nothing you desire can compare
with her ... Her ways are ways of pleasantness, and all her paths are
peace. She is a tree of life to those who lay hold of her.

(verses 13, 15, 17–18a)

When my son was learning to read, we would try to make time each day to sit together with the book he had from school. He made progress but it seemed quite slow and laboured and our reading times felt a bit more of a duty than a shared pleasure. I often felt that in tackling the printed words he was somehow having to go through an additional process because he couldn't 'see' what was 'obvious' to me. Only when he went to a different school several years later was his dyslexia identified and appropriate help given.

Whilst words may never come completely easily to my son, I have noticed over the years that he is stronger in qualities such as empathy and an ability to appreciate context and the bigger picture. He has clear emotional sense and understanding – he is, undoubtedly, becoming wise.

Wisdom is rarely considered, much less given pride of place, by parents wanting their children to 'do well'. Exam results and sporting wins are much easier to quantify and display – and boast about! Society tends to reward high-flyers and big achievers more readily than quieter folk who make their way with thoughtfulness, understanding and generosity. In today's reading, the compiler of Proverbs helps to redress that imbalance. Proverbs shows that wisdom is indeed a prized commodity, for it is close to the Father's heart and underpins the purpose and integrity of all creation. Where wisdom and understanding are truly valued, there we will encounter peace – shalom!

† Lord, you know the goals I set and how I would like others to see me. Help me set being wise as more important than being popular, and understanding more important than being 'right'. Amen.

For further thought

Speaking wisely and with empathy, admitting uncertainty, is more important than sticking to a 'party line'.

Searching for shalom (1)

November

311

He restores my soul

Read Psalm 23:1–6

The LORD is my shepherd, I shall not want. He makes me lie down in green pastures; he leads me beside still waters; he restores my soul.

(verses 1–3a)

Do you sleep well? I hope so, but if, like me, you don't always, then this piece is particularly for you.

What is it about the small hours of the night that creates a fertile ground for dark thoughts, worries and past regrets? Why do harrowing images from the evening news or tiresome memories choose to surface at just the time when you most need to rest and draw refreshment for the coming day? I'm sure there are plenty of explanations out there, but if the problem persists what can be done? Here is something that helps me.

Instead of tossing and turning I deliberately bring to the front of my mind a treasured memory of a scene that is from half a century ago – a riverside meadow in Kent, England. With teenage friends I was on a cycle ride, and we stopped to rest. The weather was sunny and warm, trees were in full leaf and the river flowed slowly enough for one boy to rescue his shoe which had fallen in. Nothing otherwise of note happened, and after a while we cycled on our way – but there was something about that pause by the river meadow which was given and complete, and which embedded itself indelibly in my mind, my heart and my soul. It was an experience and a definition of peace – shalom.

Fifty years ago, I discovered and still draw upon what the writer of Psalm 23 had also learned was at the core of God's friendship with us – shalom, the peace of God that quietens and restores my soul.

† Lord, I do not ask that you spare me from troubled thoughts – only that in even the darkest times you will give me the means to know your gift of peace. Amen.

For further thought

Allowing God to 'restore our soul' is essential. We neglect this task at our peril, and we must never be too busy to let it happen.

Searching for shalom (1)

November

Peace comes through Jesus Christ

Read Zechariah 9:9–10

Lo, your king comes to you; triumphant and victorious is he, humble and riding on a donkey, on a colt, the foal of a donkey ... and he shall command peace to the nations.

(verses 9–10)

I read this text from Zechariah and write this reflection as another violent conflict erupts in the world. By the time you are reading it I hope and pray that hostilities will have ceased, though sadly but realistically, the likelihood is that the same deadly cycle of violence and loss will have reared its ugly head elsewhere. What hope and lasting peace can be found in such a self-destructive, broken world?

In answer to that question Zechariah, speaking around 500 BCE, offers what sound like contradictions: God's agent/king 'shall command peace to the nations' and he'll do that triumphantly and achieve victory, yet at the same time he will display humility and arrive, not on a warhorse, but on a joke animal – a young donkey. Unless Zechariah was deluded, this unconventional bringer of peace overturns how the world's business has been conducted. Historically, militarily powerful empires (religious or secular – it seems to make little difference) have washed like the tide across the nations, leaving the seeds of inevitable future conflict in their wake. When Zechariah's words find expression in Jesus, they are neither a wishful hope nor an abstract paradox, but are grounded in the lives of real people.

For Jesus, peace-making is personal and particular.

In my youth, when others sang vaguely about giving peace a chance, the US folk singer Tom Paxton unwittingly caused a prayer pathway to form from Zechariah, via Jesus and into the rest of my life, as he and a concert audience in Croydon, England, sang 'Peace will come'[1] and that the longed-for peace might start with us.

† I despair, I rage, I turn off the news, but you are 'Prince of Peace' and you call me to the work of your kingdom – so, Lord, let it start with me. Amen.

For further thought

Christianity does not say, 'Jesus will sort it': it requires us to say, 'What can we do to help build the kingdom?'

[1] Tom Paxton, 'Peace will come', 1972.

Searching for shalom (1)

November

Peace through the Spirit's presence

Read Romans 8:5–11

*For those who live according to the flesh set their minds on the things
of the flesh, but those who live according to the Spirit set their minds on
the things of the Spirit ... to set the mind on the Spirit is life and peace.*

(verses 5–6)

As a young minister in the 1980s, I helped out at a youth camp
near Oxford, England. The style of the event was charismatic
Christian with lively music, talks and prayer and healing ministry.
The climax of the weekend was an evening meeting during which
the standing congregation was urged to invite the Holy Spirit into
their lives. One by one people fell (gently and safely) to the floor,
leaving just me and one other standing. After a while the meeting
concluded with a praise time and a happy crowd spilled out into
the night. As I walked out into the dark, glad to be alone, I asked
God, 'So what happened – why didn't I fall over in the Spirit too?'
I am sure that God answered, immediately, 'But we talk anyway!'

Four decades later, and despite my natural inclination to find a
quiet corner away from other people's demands, I still find that I
am closer to God and more alive to the Spirit when I make myself
be open to others and take on (with varying degrees of reluctance)
kingdom tasks that I'd prefer to avoid but which need to be done.
Does this mean I am at peace? Not in a conventional sense, for
I am more often unsettled and restless until I get on with what
needs to be done. And in doing what I believe God asks of me, I
invariably know that, as in a dark field once near Oxford, I am held
within God's purpose and God's peace – shalom!

† Dear God, by your Spirit gather up my fearfulness and other failings, yet still help
me play a useful part in building your kingdom. Amen.

For further thought

Don't be too earnest about seeking God's peace – shalom. It might
already be close by, just waiting for you to notice!

Searching for shalom (2)

Notes by **Jan Sutch Pickard**

Jan is a poet, storyteller and liturgist living on the Isle of Mull, having served for six years on the staff of the Iona Community and then as an Ecumenical Accompanier (peace monitor) in Palestine and Israel. Living in West Bank villages, she learned the daily greeting *Salaam* – heart-achingly close to the Hebrew *Shalom*, both words meaning 'Peace'. As a member of the Iona Community, Jan shares this belief: the gospel commands us to seek peace founded on justice. Jan has used the NIVUK for these notes.

9 November
Do not worry

Read Matthew 6:25–34

See how the flowers of the field grow … If that is how God clothes the grass of the field … will he not more clothe you? …seek first his kingdom and his righteousness … do not worry about tomorrow, for tomorrow will worry about itself.

(verses 28b, 30, 33–34)

Moving house can be one of life's most stressful experiences, as I know from personal experience – I moved house this year. It was hard work (although I was blessed with help from family, friends, neighbours). I was worried too, about what might go wrong, whether I'd have the stamina. But now (thank God) I'm sitting writing this in my new home.

It sits in a grass plot on an open hillside. Folk told me that I'd need to find someone to cut my 'lawn'. But I left it uncut, wanting to see what would grow. As I settled in and started to unpack, I watched a meadow springing up, many varieties of wildflowers with grasses that bloomed, seeded and blew in the wind. After the loss of leaving my old home and the anxieties of beginning again, watching the grass grow was balm to my spirit.

Then and there, I was mindful of many folk in this world who are on the move for reasons they have not chosen: refugees from war or persecution, families displaced by the climate crisis.

† With conscience and compassion, may we put prayer into practical action, be helped to see our own anxieties in proportion and calmed by God's healing Spirit, like the wind over the grasses.

10 November
Out of the wilderness

Read Isaiah 32:14–20

The Lord's justice will dwell in the desert, his righteousness live in the fertile field. The fruit of that righteousness will be peace … My people will live in peaceful dwelling places, in secure homes.

(verses 16–18a)

A green field, a grove of trees, glowing in autumnal gold or dancing with spring leaves … a blasted landscape of mud and shell holes, trees mere charred stumps. That was the same place, before and after the Battle of the Somme (in the 1914–18 war). And now, more than a hundred years later, someone searching for where a grandfather died in the mud may find a serene green field again, or a forest.

The book of Isaiah reflects the changes that happen across the face of this world from the way that we humans live in it: wastelands created by human conflicts and 'natural' disasters caused by our use of fossil fuels resulting in wildfires and floods that we handle badly. Yet the same texts celebrate the way that, in spite of our worst efforts, the natural world has the power to heal itself: through the work of the Holy Spirit; and, paradoxically, human beings may be part of this healing. In the words of Martin Luther King Jr – 'The arc of the moral universe is long, but it bends toward justice.'[1] Peace is possible: as long as it goes hand in hand with justice.

I think of this as I gaze out on what was recently a wild-flower meadow around my new home on the Isle of Mull, Scotland. It has just been strimmed, so that the land can rest through the winter. I am wondering how I can share this new-found space, this peace I am experiencing, with those who have so little. Maybe putting it into words is one way?

† Spirit of God, may we respect and care for your creation, and let its peace, in turn, heal us.

For further thought

What do these words mean to you: 'The fruit of righteousness will be peace; its effect will be quietness and confidence for ever'?

[1] Martin Luther King Jr, 'Remaining Awake Through a Great Revolution', speech given at the National Cathedral, 31 March 1968.

11 November
A faith that sings

Read Acts 16:22–34

About midnight Paul and Silas were praying and singing hymns to God, and the other prisoners were listening to them. Suddenly there was such a violent earthquake that the foundations of the prison were shaken.

(verses 25–26)

In the chaos caused by the earthquake in Philippi, a terrified jailer called for lights, to see what was happening. Before that, there was darkness, the pain of shackled people who'd been brutally treated, anger, uncertainty, fear of those imprisoned together or alone. And there in the dark, there had also been singing.

When I was arrested for demonstrating against the nuclear submarines at Faslane in Scotland, I spent several hours in a police cell. I didn't suffer brutality, simply the due process of the law (as I and others were, technically, 'breaching the peace'!). In our separate cells, we were not left in the dark: the lights were on constantly, glaring down on hard surfaces. Time had been arrested because my watch was confiscated. But I was connected to other people because – in other cells – seasoned campaigners, who were also ministers of the church, could not be prevented from singing: South African freedom songs, Scottish folk songs and hymns. (Was the quality of the singing – or lack of it – a reason for our early release?)

Seriously, the singing raised my spirits and those of all the other detainees. It encouraged me with the faith and commitment that we had in common. As did the joyful, prayerful time together when released in the middle of the night, and the meal that friends prepared for us to share.

† Thank you, God, for song that lifts our hearts and expresses our faith, for shared meals that celebrate community.

For further thought

Read – if possible sing – Charles Wesley's (1738) hymn 'And Can It Be?' about conversion, where faith leads to action: 'I woke, the dungeon flamed with light/ My chains fell off, my heart was free/ I rose, went forth and followed thee.'

Searching for shalom (2)

November

Encouragement in the search

> **Read 1 Thessalonians 4:13–18**
> *Therefore encourage one another with these words.*
>
> (verse 18)

To be honest, I find these words challenging, rather than comforting. It's a powerful picture of the return of Christ, the last judgement, the resurrection of all who have 'fallen asleep' in Christ. This word-picture resembles the frescoes by Michelangelo in the Sistine Chapel, the crowded canvases of Jan Van Eyck. But these masterpieces alienate rather than awaken my faith. I meet God in other ways.

Would I use this particular scripture passage, or point to those pictures, to encourage someone grieving the loss of someone they love? I don't think so.

Then what? Compassion and our common humanity mean that we can't just cross the road, ignore grief that's too raw, feelings for which we can't find the words.

Today I heard from a friend for the first time since his wife died. Told of her sudden illness, I had tried ringing, left messages, sent emails, cards: no response. Rumours of loss and distress, but no clear communication: grief can put up barriers like that. Suddenly a message has come, that he'll be on the island next week. Face-to-face talking may be more helpful than all my feeble efforts.

What I can also offer is a project, begun with these two friends in mind. After my wildflower meadow was cut, sawdust (which should outlast months of rain) was used to outline a labyrinth on the turf. I've been walking its gentle pilgrimage in silence, turning to face hills, sky, sea, homes, distant horizons, holding in my heart friends, living and dead, in God's presence.

Encouragement without needing words.

† Loving God, you bless those who mourn, through the empathy and down-to-earth care of others. Encourage us all to believe that death does not have the last word.

For further thought

Find (online perhaps) pictures of the last judgement (or: judgment) by the artists mentioned above. How do they speak to you?

13 November

Perseverance

Read Romans 5:1–5

...we also glory in our sufferings, because we know that suffering produces perseverance, perseverance, character; and character, hope.

(verses 3–4)

I'm remembering a time when I trespassed in an olive grove. Imagine two middle-aged women coming to the edge of a road cut through farmland, crouching until the coast is clear, then scuttling across. Afaf, a Palestinian, was taking me to see her farm, on land cultivated by her family for centuries, before being claimed by an Israeli settlement.

When I met her, she and her brother were the last Christians in a small West Bank town, where she had been Principal of the girls' school. She did not preach to the girls, but her faith clearly shaped her consistent and caring leadership. Other Christian families had emigrated to Europe or the USA. Afaf chose not to leave her home and the fruitful courtyard garden she'd tended over many years, or her Muslim neighbours, with whom she shared meals, mutual respect and moral support. For her, as for other Palestinians, persevering by staying put was a prophetic act, a reminder that justice is needed for all.

As an Ecumenical Accompanier, I enjoyed her company and learned a lot from her, in her home and school. And she took me trespassing!

In the olive grove, Afaf made mint tea and we shared flat-bread and hummus. She told me that these long-lived, life-giving trees are seen as symbols of *sumud*, an Arabic word rich in meaning: steadfastness, patience, persistence, perseverance. I am still encouraged by her faith, her *sumud*.

† Thank you, God, for those – near or far – who 'remain in Christ', whose steadfastness encourages us. (Name at least one in your heart.)

For further thought

What is happening in the 'Land' we call 'Holy' right now? Search the news, pray about what you learn, donate to an organisation working for peace.

Searching for shalom (2)

November

A path that leads home

Read John 14:15–21
The Spirit of truth [promised by Jesus] … lives with you and will be in you.

(verses 17–18)

A neighbour asked: 'This pattern laid out in your garden – what's all that about? What is a labyrinth anyway?'

I'm sorry if readers using these notes earlier in the week were confused by that word. Yet confusion comes with this ancient tradition of making patterns with a meaning. They're easier to experience with feet on the ground rather than by long explanations. In a maze, anyone can get lost, but labyrinths have a single winding path which in the end will lead home, to the heart of the pattern. Following one slowly can be a kind of spiritual journey, a pilgrimage. It's said that the labyrinth set into the floor of Chartres Cathedral in the Middle Ages was there for folk prevented by infirmity or warfare from going on pilgrimage to the Holy Land. In our conflicted and distracting modern world, this reflective practice can still have value.

Drawing a labyrinth creates something like the intertwining patterns of Celtic art, found in the Book of Kells. Illustrating such great Gospel books was, for medieval monks, an act of devotion to God's beautiful and complex nature. It communicates the presence of God's Spirit. It also reminds me of the complicated statements – words turning and turning to find meaning – found in passages from John's Gospel. I don't find such text easy to follow. I need patience, persistence!

There are many different ways of sensing the presence of God's Spirit: reading a book, singing in a cell, picnicking in an olive grove, walking a labyrinth, watching a wild-flower meadow grow. Thank God for all of these.

† Thank God for all of the above, and any other ways you are aware of God's Spirit at work.

For further thought

Learn more about labyrinths; if possible find and walk one!

Preparing a place

Read John 14:1–3

Do not let your hearts be troubled … My Father's house has many rooms … And if I go and prepare a place for you, I will come back and take you to be with me that you also may be where I am.

(verses 1–3)

I began with moving house: a stressful time, but hopeful, too, giving the opportunity to be somewhere with more space, living, at last, on one level. I can't be smug because I live in a country with a shortage of affordable housing. I know I'm fortunate, seeing elsewhere those who wage war choosing civilian targets, destroying homes of ordinary people. I'm aware that right now the whole of humanity is living through – seeking to survive – a climate crisis threatening our common home, the earth.

After my move, I looked back at the place where I'd lived for a quarter of my lifetime: it wasn't a perfect place, but it had been there when I needed it; as familiar as my own body. I felt a sense of bereavement.

Beginning the work of making the new house my own, I thought hard about how I wanted to use it: shelves for books still to be read (a place of lifelong learning), space for stillness and reflection, light for plants to flourish, a kitchen table ready to feed guests, with room for all comers. It would still not be an 'ideal home', but a place with integrity, of welcome for friends and strangers in all their diversity.

I imagine God's house (with its many metaphorical rooms!) must be like this. I believe that, wherever we are, in this life or whatever is to come, God's Spirit of hope will go before us, God's Spirit of faith will find us when we feel lost, God's Spirit of love will still be there beside us.

† Compassionate God, we pray for those displaced by war or natural disaster [name somewhere in the news] and those in our own country whose lives are insecure, who long for a place to call 'home'.

For further thought

List organisations that help the homeless or campaign for better housing. How can you support them? Is such practical action a long way from John's search for future hope?

Searching for shalom (2)

November

Gold

1 The value of gold

Notes by **Raj Bharat Patta**

Raj is proud to celebrate his identity in multiple belongings: Dalit, Christian, Asian, (Im)migrant, India, UK, church, academic, postcolonial, public sphere, husband, father and friend. He currently serves as a minister of the Methodist Church and completed his PhD from the University of Manchester. He is a member of the Interfaith theological advisory group of the Churches Together in Britain and Ireland and sits on the Cliff College committee and on the steering group of the Centre for Theology and Justice in the UK. Raj has used the NRSV for these notes.

16 November
And God created gold!

Read Genesis 2:10–14
And the gold of the land is good.

(verse 12)

Gold from the times of antiquity has always been considered to be valuable – as a metal it doesn't lose its character or value with the passing of time. Gold is also considered as a symbol of safety, risk diversification and is seen as a smart investment. In the Indian context, 'Akshaya Tritiya' ('eternal third day') is part of the Hindu calendar, when people buy gold as it is thought to be auspicious.

Why did the writers of the biblical creation story mention gold in this way? The reason I think is that Adamah, animals (Genesis 2:7, 19) and the minerals like gold (verse 12) all are made out of the soil. In this way, the first created human, the animals and the minerals share the commonality of the soil in their nature – and it is all good.

From the perspective of human beings, gold might be considered very precious in comparison to the rest of the creation, but from the perspective of the Creator God, all are good and have the same source. Perhaps our meditation on the 'gold of the land' today is an invitation to seek the spark of the divine, the preciousness in all of God's creation, for all have their origin in the soil of the earth.

† Creator God, help us to see like you the goodness in all of the creation, for everything and everyone is equally precious in your sight. Amen.

A golden proposal

Read Genesis 24:15–27

When the camels had finished drinking, the man took a gold nose-ring weighing a half shekel, and two bracelets for her arms weighing ten gold shekels.

(verse 22)

This is a beautiful story of God's faithfulness to Isaac and his servant and it is often read at Indian Christian betrothal ceremonies. A problem arises though if texts are appropriated to uphold patriarchal traditions – the story is not intended to endorse a dowry system or marriages arranged by men!

Why does Abraham send his senior servant to look for a wife for Isaac not from the daughters of Canaanites, but from his own country and from his own relatives? Again, we must be careful – it was not to ensure the purity of a class or caste; it was to ensure the clarity of witness. If those who had a relationship with God diluted that by embracing other worldviews, the knowledge of God would be lost – and all nations would miss out on the blessing of knowing him.

What does the gold represent here then? The servant gives it, not as a payment or an inducement, but as a thank offering that God has been faithful. He gives it in response to the worth, the character, that Rebekah has shown in generously serving this foreigner. And in so doing she has reflected the very character of God, precisely fulfilling the reason for the mission the servant had been sent on.

A critical reading of the texts helps us to dig out the gold that liberates people from oppressive traditions and systems.

† Thank you that as we seek your ways, you free us and fulfil us beyond our imagination.

For further thought
Are there texts that we use or have heard used in ways that endorse our traditions rather than build the kingdom?

Gold – 1 The value of gold

November

Don't store up gold

Read Deuteronomy 17:14–17

...also silver and gold he must not acquire in great quantity for himself.

(verse 17b)

Along with many nations, Indian politicians, when declaring their assets – including gold – are shown to be amongst the richest segments of the nation. At the same time, India is the nation with the highest population of those defined as poor.

Today's reading warns against leaders who might be tempted to use their position for personal gain. The instructions about choosing a king make it clear that possessing wealth and assets does not qualify someone for leadership, but rather those who are called to leadership should be serving people with equity, justice and peace, ensuring liberation for all.

And when we consider the greatest King, Jesus, we see exactly this. He who had all things dispossessed himself of riches in order to identify with the poor. If riches, gold, silver and wealth were signs of divine blessings or a qualification for leadership, then Jesus should have been the richest person who ever lived on our planet! But Jesus' way is to pitch his tent among the weak and the vulnerable, taking his birth in poverty and living his childhood as a refugee.

Being a disciple of Jesus is not about acquiring gold and silver; rather it is about a cross and suffering.

How do we free ourselves from this alluring lie – that wealth and status equals God's approval and blessing? Wouldn't it be wonderful to be led by those who served rather than having to serve those who lead?

† God in Jesus, we thank you for choosing to identify with the weak and the poor. We thank you for calling us to serve. Amen.

For further thought

In what ways can we in our church identify with the weak and the poor in our communities today?

The arrival of the Queen of Sheba

Read 1 Kings 10:1–13

...then she gave the king one hundred and twenty talents of gold ...

(verse 10)

Two things strike me from this passage:

First, I recognise a mutual respect between the Queen of Sheba (probably modern-day Yemen, but possibly Ethiopia) and King Solomon of Israel. They celebrated each other's gifts and shared the resources of their lands with one another, including in this case gold and silver. In our twenty-first-century world when antisemitism and Islamophobia are increasing, with hate crime and conflict accelerating, this text challenges us to strive to build bridges of peace and justice, rooted in mutual respect and celebrating each other's gifts and resources.

Secondly, in coming, the Queen of Sheba reminds Solomon of the divine plan for Israel to draw all nations to God through their demonstration of his nature and character. She came, intrigued by what she had heard, and if indeed she was from Ethiopia, went back and sowed the seeds of faith in her nation that would be brought to life in Acts 8, as the official of a future queen (Candace) is baptised by Philip. Her visit underscores that Solomon became king to execute justice and righteousness (verse 9) to reflect God's ways. That's how Jesus leads his kingdom and how he invites his followers to live for the cause of love, peace and justice in our world today.

Perhaps whenever we are too engrossed with the preciousness and price of gifts or the value of gold, instead of being impressed by its value, we can use it, as Solomon did, as a reminder of what is of true worth: mutual dignity and respect tokens that are reminders to execute justice and righteousness.

† Lord, thank you for the gifts we receive from you and others. May we be more impressed by the love that underpins them than the value of the gifts themselves.

For further thought

Next time you give a gift to your friends and families, think of the message that your gifts will convey to them. Perhaps your gifts should be symbols for love, peace and justice.

Gold – 1 The value of gold

November

20 November
Offerings of gold

Read 1 Chronicles 29:1–9

Then the people rejoiced because these had given willingly, for with single mind they had offered freely to the Lord.

(verse 9)

We have seen how easy it is to confuse material wealth – gold – with blessing. Yet Psalm 133 tells us what blessing really is: 'life forevermore' – abundant life, life in all its fullness. More, the psalm tells us how this blessing is won – when there is unity. How appropriate then is today's reading, people coming together with 'single mind' to generously and wholeheartedly give of the very substance that is so often mistaken for blessing. In freely letting go of what the world counts as valuable, the people received that which was of inestimable value.

And it is inspired by David, encouraging the people to give to the building of the house of God. His passionate speech includes that as a king he has provided all that is required for its building. In addition to that, because of his devotion to the house of God, David makes a personal offering that he has as a treasure of his own to the house of God. On hearing David's speech and witnessing his own first freewill offering to the house of God, the leaders made their own freewill offering to the treasury of the house of God. At this sight everyone rejoiced for they had all given willingly, with one heart and mind to the Lord.

Drawing a relevance of this text for our context today, as leaders, we inspire others, not by making them feel guilty, not just by selling the vision with passion, but by our example. The people knew how to worship, because David had danced before them in worship, he had played an instrument, had written songs for them to sing. They knew how to give, because he had given – as a king and as an individual.

† God, the giver of life, help us as a Church to lead by example in giving our offerings. Amen.

For further thought

In what way is your local church or group leading by example in giving offerings for the flourishing of life in the creation of God?

Gold – 1 The value of gold

November

21 November
A house of gold

Read 2 Chronicles 3:1–8

He overlaid it on the inside with pure gold ... He overlaid the upper chambers with gold.

(verses 4b, 9b)

The Golden Temple of India, an iconic Sikh Gurudwara, which is situated in the city of Amritsar in the state of Punjab, is not only an architectural marvel to see, but also a sacred place of worship, symbolising peace, unity and selfless service. People who have visited this place testify to how serene it is, offering solace to the soul, for this place is open to people of all faiths and none.

In today's text, we read about Solomon's fine, meticulous architectural details in the building of the Temple of the Lord. He takes great care with the building, overlaying gold both inside the building and outside. Not only is what is immediately visible beautiful, but that which would be hidden from many is given equal attention. It reminds us of Jesus' words about the need to be clean inside and out, our private, unseen thoughts and lives need to have as much attention as the more visible aspects. Our bodies, which are temples of the Holy Spirit, can be transformed by him to metaphorically be inlaid with what is of true beauty, true worth – the gold of the fruit of the Spirit.

It perhaps also points to Psalm 139 where Solomon's father describes the care with which God knows us, the detailed understanding of what makes us who we are – a knowledge which leads to his love for us and his pride in us. To God, we are as beautiful and resplendent as that physical Temple, and he is pleased to dwell in us.

† Lord, thank you for the care you bestow on me and for the beauty that you create in all of us.

For further thought
How do you view yourself? Spend some time reflecting on how God sees you in the light of this passage.

Gold – 1 The value of gold

November

What gold can't buy

Read Job 28:12–19

But where shall wisdom be found? And where is the place of understanding?

(verse 12)

Can money buy everything in this world? Can gold and silver gain everything this life requires? The Beatles famously wrote of money that it 'Can't Buy Me Love'.[1] But Job in his conversations to his friends explains that wisdom can't be bought with gold either. Indeed, nothing that is normally seen as valuable (including the topaz from Ethiopia, perhaps linking us to the wisdom that the Queen of Sheba witnessed) can be used to purchase it. Wisdom, it seems, is priceless.

Where then can wisdom be found? Well, wisdom is far more than simple knowledge. Knowing the facts might make us informed, it doesn't make us wise! Wisdom requires experience, understanding and perspective as well as knowledge. The hymn 'Immortal, Invisible' speaks of 'God Only Wise' – only he has the perspective, the knowledge and the experience to fully grasp the true situation; we, as Paul suggests, 'see in a mirror, dimly' (1 Corinthians 13:12). And yet, how often we make judgements, how often we make decisions based on our own narrow perspective and limited knowledge. How rarely we rely on God's direction, his insight, his wisdom.

We value wealth, we value celebrity, we value long life, yet through this week we have seen that while gold (and all the other things we value) has its place, it is only when it points to that which is truly valuable that it really glistens.

† God of wisdom and understanding, help us to acknowledge the limitations of gold, help us to see the brighter, more wonderful truths to which it points. Amen.

For further thought

It is said that, 'Knowledge is knowing that a tomato is a fruit, but wisdom is knowing not to put it in a fruit salad.' What do you need wisdom for today?

[1] John Lennon and Paul McCartney, 'Can't Buy Me Love', 1964.

Gold – 1 The value of gold

November

Gold

2 Better than gold

Notes by **Christopher Took**

You can read Christopher's biography on 6 July. Christopher has used the NIVUK for these notes.

23 November
Wisdom: a better choice – better than gold

Read Proverbs 8:1–21

Choose my instruction instead of silver, knowledge rather than choice gold.

(verse 10)

For those people with access to good nutrition and modern health care, increasing lifespans mean the celebration of golden (and even diamond and platinum) wedding anniversaries has become more common. Doing anything for fifty years is an incredible achievement, but it's still a linear advance over twenty-five, thirty or forty years.

This week we are going to look at the claims the Bible makes about certain things being better than gold. These claims aren't for something being a slight improvement over the alternatives on offer, rather they encourage us to imagine and embrace an exponentially superior experience. We aren't talking about an upgrade from steerage to first class, rather the difference between crawling on the earth and interstellar travel!

In Proverbs, Wisdom is often personified: in our passage, as someone calling out to people as they pass (verses 2–3). Frequently, this depiction of Wisdom is associated with the Holy Spirit. Perhaps here we have those entering the city being exhorted by God himself to embrace wisdom, knowledge and instruction because these are more valuable than precious metals or exquisite gems. Galatians 5:22–23 describes the fruit of the Spirit, and Proverbs 8:19 reminds us this fruit exceeds everything of earthly value.

† Holy Spirit, at the start of a new week, fill me afresh with your wisdom, love and understanding. Help me to hear and understand your word so I can walk with you in righteousness and justice.

For further thought

How big a part does your imagination play in your spiritual life? Is there potential to develop your imagination in your relationship with God?

Commandments sweeter than honey and more precious than gold

Read Psalm 19:7–14

*The decrees of the L*ORD *… are more precious than gold, than much pure gold.*

(verses 9b–10a)

Our world is awash with sugar and even sweeter artificial alternatives. Some of the world's biggest brands with near-universal recognition seem to be little more than sugar and water. But in biblical times, honey was one of the few sweeteners available and a rare treat. That's why the psalmist parallels honey with gold (verse 10). However tasty sugar and even honey are, they provide an instant but short-lived reward. The aim of following the Lord's commands is to build something of eternal worth (verse 9) and greater reward (verse 11).

The psalmist lists the benefits of adhering to God's word: refreshment for the soul, wisdom, joy and understanding (verses 7–8). But he also identifies a problem for would-be servants: our own failings and distorted worldviews are serious blocks to developing the sort of character and lifestyle God demands (verse 12).

The Hebrew Bible does a thorough job of examining the human condition and identifying the problems preventing fallen people having a full relationship with a perfect God. The idea of this relationship enduring beyond death and despite our failings is hinted at in the Old Testament, but the concept of resurrection and re-creation to enable us to live with God for ever was developed in the centuries before Jesus was born. That process of resurrection and new creation was demonstrated and begun with Jesus, but sometimes we lose sight of what this means for us.

Even without our understanding of how Jesus' death and resurrection bridges the gap between sinful people and loving God, the psalmist has total faith he 'will be blameless, innocent of great transgression'. A sweet promise for us!

† Lord God, help me to value your word and meditate on it in my heart, so I can follow your ways and be innocent of great transgression.

For further thought

Is there enough honey in your understanding of God's commands? Can they be a burden rather than a source of refreshment?

Delight in God's law that's more valuable than gold

Read Psalm 119:127–136

Because I love your commands more than gold, more than pure gold, and because I consider all your precepts right, I hate every wrong path.

(verses 127–128)

Today's reading reflects much of what yesterday's had to say. Psalm 119 is an elaborate (and lengthy) meditation on the importance of the law of the Lord. On one level, nearly every verse is a variation on 'Your statutes are wonderful; therefore I obey them' (verse 129). But this must be a vitally important truth if it's repeated so many times. And we don't just have repetition from the psalmist – we have delight! (This delight is mentioned explicitly nine times in Psalm 119 and implied many more.)

The psalmist has no doubt about the value of God's commands: he loves them 'more than gold, more than pure gold' (verse 127). He is distressed by those who don't follow the Lord's teaching (verse 136) yet he is also aware of his own failings when he prays: 'turn to me and have mercy on me' (verse 132).

In the Gospels we have warnings about the unhelpful directions that an apparent love of the law can lead people into. The Pharisees were renowned for their study and 'love' of the law, and yet Jesus warns our righteousness must 'surpass that of the Pharisees and the teachers of the law' if we are to enter (experience, establish) God's kingdom (Matthew 5:20). The law is not an end in itself; if it's loved like that, the love will become selfish, harsh and ultimately worse than useless.

The psalmist is not writing about legislation and regulation but describing love and relationship. He sees life and light in God's words – something we're privileged to see clearly in Jesus, God's living Word (John 1:14) and the Light of the world (John 8:12).

† Heavenly Father, may I delight in your word as I read it with understanding, and may my love for your word increase my love for you and for others.

For further thought

Are you in danger of falling into the same trap as the Pharisees?! How can you guard against legalism and grow in love?

Gold – 2 Better than gold

November

Tested to be like gold

Read Job 23:1–10
But he knows the way that I take; when he has tested me, I shall come forth as gold.

(verse 10)

The delight of yesterday's reading turns to the depression of today's. We are thrilled by the psalmist's relationship with God and his confident walking in the Lord's way. But we know life isn't always like that. One of the reasons we should meditate on God's word (Psalm 19:14) is to prepare us for more challenging times.

Job goes from success to disaster. It seems God has deserted him. His friends try to comfort him and make sense of his situation. In our passage, Job responds to Eliphaz's suggestion that Job's misfortune was caused by his sin, and that if Job repents, all will be restored.

Job is wiser than that and has greater integrity. Even if he doesn't know why disaster has befallen him, he knows it is not a punishment for his sin. At a time when Job feels abandoned by God (verses 3, 8–9), he knows that God has established and will uphold his innocence for ever (verse 7).

It's far easier to trust God when things are going well, when we know where the next meal is coming from, and we can see the way ahead. At those times it might feel we have a strong faith, but true confidence that our faith will sustain comes not in the easy times, but in the more challenging periods of our life.

In such times, instead of fear, worry or bitterness taking all our energy, faith provides the space in our hearts and minds for change to happen, and our character becomes refined like gold – and Christ is seen.

† Help me, dear Lord, to know the truths of your word, so that when I feel lost, I will know you are still with me.

For further thought

Has your faith helped you get through testing times? How can you prepare for any challenges ahead?

27 November
Refined like gold

Read Malachi 3:1–12

He will sit as a refiner and purifier of silver; he will purify the Levites and refine them like gold and silver.

(verse 3a)

The people were supposed to bring tithes and offerings to the priests (the Levites) as tokens of the love they had for God and the neighbours whose needs their gifts would supply. They were an expression of God's compassion and justice. But the Levites had become corrupt, and the people were withholding offerings, using this as an excuse. In our reading, God declares that he will refine the priests and challenges the people to do what is right.

If refining is to happen, it cannot be by accident. Refining gold involves heating it to over 1,000°C – way beyond the capability of domestic ovens, but that is seriously hot – if our circumstances are going to reach those temperatures, it will feel seriously uncomfortable! Without understanding what God is doing and why, it is easy to mistake the events that God uses to refine us as a punishment, and these negative connotations are reinforced when we see the word 'testing', with the association to unpleasant exams. But the testing described here is not to see whether we have passed or failed some divine exam; it's to reveal things that need to be removed so that they don't tarnish or distort the image of God in us.

In that context, Malachi 3:10 is a remarkable verse: 'Test me in this.' He isn't asking the people to undergo anything that he is not willing himself to endure. Is there anything in him that is less than pure gold – is he trustworthy, is he really love? Will he provide for me if I have left myself without enough as I generously give to those in need, as I bring in the 'full tithe into the storehouse'?

† Lord God, when I face challenges and trials, help me to hold fast to your promise of abundant blessings for all who trust in you.

For further thought

Is it easier to remember and meditate on verses with a positive message? Should more time be spent on uncomfortable verses?

Faith more precious than gold

Read 1 Peter 1:3–9

...the proven genuineness of your faith – of greater worth than gold, which perishes even though refined by fire.

(verse 7)

Peter tells us that in Christ, we have been born into a hope for this life and into an inheritance for the life to come that will never tarnish. We recall from the last couple of days that refining is the process of removing that which distorts the image of God in us. Peter says that having completed this process, that dazzling image will never again be spoiled (verse 4). What a wonderful assurance for the future – but more than that, what a great encouragement for the present. As we suffer 'grief and all kinds of trials', as God uses these to refine us, the result is that Jesus is revealed (verse 7b) – something of far more value than even refined gold – which unlike Jesus, will pass away.

It has echoes of Paul's words in 1 Corinthians 13 – that those things built on faith, hope and love continue into eternity. What a marvellous legacy for us to be able to shower people with that blessing now and inherit from us after we are gone – no wonder our response is one of glorious joy and praise!

But how is this achieved? How can we reveal Jesus when we have never seen him, Peter asks. The answer is simple: we love him and believe in him and that brings a joy in the present that sustains us even as we are being refined.

† Lord Jesus, help me to be aware of those around me in need, so I can serve them and you from love and compassion rather than the thought of any reward.

For further thought

What is the balance of suffering and rejoicing in your life (verse 6)? What could you do to increase the rejoicing?

A city of gold!

Read Revelation 21:15–21
The wall was made of jasper, and the city of pure gold, as pure as glass.

(verse 18)

The picture of the new Jerusalem is big – really, really big! Its volume is over ten billion kilometres cubed, an image demonstrating that there is enough space for everyone. And that's just the city, one part of the new heaven and earth. The language of Revelation struggles to describe the incredible beauty and splendour of the new Jerusalem because it will surpass anything we can imagine.

The city will be of purest gold, with every impurity removed. And unlike the city in Proverbs 8, where Wisdom needed to call out to people as they entered, the people entering this city will already be full of wisdom, knowledge and love. Just as the gold used to construct the city will be pure, so will all the people who inhabit it. All the struggles in this life to build our faith and character, and to develop our relationship with God, will find their full reward and realisation when we reach the new heaven and earth, and enter the new Jerusalem.

And God has already begun his creation of the new heaven and earth by giving Jesus his resurrection body. And we are promised a new body for the new city. 'So will it be with the resurrection of the dead. The body that is sown is perishable, it is raised imperishable' (1 Corinthians 15:42). Faith greater than gold leads to a body greater than gold, living with God for ever in a city of gold!

It turns out that the full revelation of Jesus isn't the end at all, but rather the real beginning.

† Creator God, thank you for beginning the renewal of your creation through Jesus' resurrection; strengthen my faith so I can live that resurrection life now as fully as possible.

For further thought

The Great Divorce by C S Lewis is one answer to the question 'what will heaven be like?' Definitely worth a read! C S Lewis, *The Great Divorce* (Geoffrey Bles, 1945).

Gold – 2 Better than gold

November

335

The character of God: the God who comes

1 The hope of Israel

Notes by **Kate Hughes**

You can read Kate's biography on 10 August. Kate has used the NRSVA for these notes.

30 November
Decision time for Mary

Read Luke 1:26–38

Then Mary said, 'Here am I, the servant of the Lord; let it be with me according to your word.' Then the angel departed from her.

(verse 38)

The Mary who was called by God to give birth to his Son was a teenager from a small town in the Middle East: probably dark-haired and tanned, used to helping her mother in the house, fetching water from the well, looking forward to having a new life when she was married to Joseph. Why does it matter that Mary seemed such an ordinary Jewish girl?

Because how God came to earth when he decided once and for all to deal with the mess that human beings had got themselves into is important. He wasn't born in a royal palace, with a princess for his mother. He came to where people were: to an ordinary girl, in an ordinary village – and amazingly Mary said yes to God's request. This is what makes her so special: not her place in society or her good looks, but her faith that if she said yes to God, God could deal with everything else.

Stories about great men and women, people who changed history because of their obvious bravery or intelligence, can be inspiring – but also daunting. Most of us are not like them, our lives are ordinary. In the next week we are going to look at 'The God who comes' in Advent as the one who was foreseen and looked forward to by God's chosen people, culminating in the faith of that teenager in Nazareth. May we be inspired!

† O God, help us, like Mary, to say yes to you when you ask us to work with you.

For further thought

Who are your heroes and heroines of the faith? What is it about them that inspires you?

One of the little clans of Judah

Read Micah 5:2–4

But you, O Bethlehem of Ephrathah, who are one of the little clans of Judah, from you shall come forth for me one who is to rule in Israel.

(verse 2a)

Ruth, King David's great-grandmother, settled in Bethlehem with her second husband Boaz (see the book of Ruth) and three generations later David was born there. He moved away once he was called by the prophet Samuel to become ruler of Israel, but Bethlehem was still regarded as the place from which God's ultimate ruler, the Messiah, would come. So it was not exactly an unknown town.

But it was still a very ordinary town. There was no king's palace there, no beautiful buildings. Just houses, fields, probably a synagogue and an inn. When Jesus – the Messiah – was born there, it was overcrowded, noisy, full of people returning to the town of their ancestors to register for the census. The little party of a man and his very pregnant wife, exhausted by their journey from Nazareth, trying in vain to find a room for the night, would not have stood out from the crowd. Eventually someone let them sleep in the ground floor of their house, where the animals spent the night.

Our God is a God who can use the unimportant, the inadequate, one of 'the little clans' – an ordinary town, a tired, worried man, an exhausted woman, a noisy night, a stable – to bring about great events and a world-changing action. He can use us, too, to establish his kingdom in the world, to show his love as Jesus did.

† God, who works through the ordinary and the inadequate, work in me today.

For further thought

At the end of today, look back at the ways in which God has used you and helped you this day.

The character of God: the God who comes – 1 The hope of Israel

2 December
God the shepherd

Read John 10:11–18

I am the good shepherd. I know my own and my own know me.

(verse 14)

Being a shepherd was a full-time job. In fact, shepherds were regarded in Jesus' time as second-class Jews – there was no way they could keep the law, eat the right food, get to synagogue. They had to stay with their sheep, and a close bond developed between sheep and shepherd. The shepherd led the sheep, walking in front of them, and the sheep trusted him to take them to good pasture, protect them from wolves and keep them safe. And if one of them was silly enough to get lost, separated from the rest of the flock, the shepherd would search until the lost sheep was found.

This is the God who comes to us in Jesus. Jesus shows us in all he says and does what God is like. Above all, he shows us that God loves us; he cares for us just as much – more – than that shepherd on the hillside. God is with us always, he leads us, he protects us, he knows us and enables us to know him, he doesn't abandon us when we are stupid or sinful. We are his own flock, his own people.

'I am the good shepherd,' says Jesus. And 'Whoever has seen me has seen the Father' (John 14:9), who is also the good shepherd for all his creation.

† Thank you, Father, that like a good shepherd you always take care of me.

For further thought

What difference would sharing God's shepherding skills make to your own relationships?

3 December
The Son who is sent

> **Read Isaiah 9:6–7**
>
> *A child has been born for us, a son given to us.*
>
> (verse 6a)

The title of these Advent notes is 'The God who comes'. The God who comes is Jesus. Jesus, who shows us as a human being what God is like. Shows us God translated into terms that we can understand, because we too are human beings. Jesus is the Son – the spitting image of his Father, united to him, working with him on the same project of repairing the relationship between God and human beings, obeying God, trusting God. Jesus, as a true son, shows what God's love for us is like in everything he says and does. And this is the child, the Son, that is given to us by God. The ruler who will establish and uphold the kingdom of David (verse 7).

Only that's not quite the kingdom that God comes to establish. Jesus rarely, if ever, got called 'Wonderful Counsellor, Mighty God, Everlasting Father, Prince of Peace' (verse 6). God in Jesus came to confront and defeat evil, to show human beings a different way of living, to free them from slavery to sin, to show them the peace that comes from knowing that they belong to God, they are part of his family, and his love is unshakeable – even if in his Son he was rejected, betrayed and crucified.

† Thank you, Jesus, for showing us the unshakeable love of God, who treats us as his beloved sons and daughters.

For further thought

Hold in your mind today that nothing can separate you from the love of God shown in Christ Jesus (compare with Romans 8:39).

4 December

God the ruler

Read Genesis 49:10–12

The sceptre shall not depart from Judah, nor the ruler's staff from between his feet, until tribute comes to him; and the obedience of the peoples is his.

(verse 10)

I didn't choose the readings for this week, and I must admit, when I came to write these notes, I did wonder what on earth this reading had to do with 'The God who comes'! On reflection, I think it has to do with the God the Jewish people expected to come and the God who actually came.

The people of Israel had a difficult history: slavery in Egypt, wandering in the desert, battling with the resident tribes of the Promised Land, kings who were sometimes great and sometimes terrible, occupation by Assyrians, Greeks and Romans, exile in Babylon. It's not surprising that they looked forward to a time when God would intervene to set things right by sending his chosen one, the Messiah, to defeat all Israel's enemies and establish his kingdom, in which all peoples would obey him.

And that time did come – but not as the Jews had foreseen. So different was God's coming, in fact, that many of them failed to recognise his Messiah, who dealt with human sinfulness not enemy armies, who died the physical death of a criminal, defeated death not the occupying Romans, and established a kingdom of peace that was open to all 'the peoples' as equal citizens, not as subdued enemies.

The resurrection of Jesus showed that we are now living in the first days of God's kingdom, even if it has not yet fully come.

† God, who raised Jesus from death, help me to live this day as a citizen of your kingdom.

For further thought

What does it mean to live now as a citizen of God's kingdom?

The character of God: the God who comes – 1 The hope of Israel

The bread of life

> **Read John 6:25–40**
>
> *For the bread of God is that which comes down from heaven and gives life to the world.*
>
> (verse 33)

Bread plays an important part in the life of Jesus. He feeds people by multiplying a few small loaves; he teaches his disciples a prayer that asks God to 'give us today our daily bread'; he compares faith to yeast that enables bread dough to rise. Bread means life: for many people in the world, bread is part of their staple diet; without it they will die of starvation. Those who can supply bread enable people to live.

At the beginning of chapter 6 of John's Gospel, Jesus feeds five thousand people, multiplying a boy's picnic rolls to feed all those who are tired and hungry. Not only does everyone have enough, but there are also a lot of leftovers. God's loving provision for everyone he has created is that they should have the means to live. As bread gives life, so does God's care for his people enable them to live the true life he has created them to have.

There is plenty of God's bread to go round: 'Whoever comes to me will never be hungry' (verse 35). We can always trust and call upon God's life-giving, unshakeable generosity. At the end of his earthly ministry, at his final meal, Jesus uses bread as a symbol of the life that God will continue to give in abundance to all who eat it. In nearly two thousand years, God's bread supply has never run out, even if our distribution of it makes it appear as if it has.

† Thank you, Lord, that you continually supply me with bread, the life-giving strength of your love.

For further thought

When we pray 'Give us today our daily bread', what does this mean for the millions in the world who are starving for lack of bread?

The character of God: the God who comes – 1 The hope of Israel

The light will shine

Read Numbers 24:15–19

I see him, but not now; I behold him, but not near – a star shall come out of Jacob, and a sceptre shall rise out of Israel.

(verse 17a)

The Israelites are trekking through the wilderness, passing through the lands of various tribes. Sometimes they get permission to pass through, sometimes they have to fight their way through. When they get to the territory of Moab, they camp on the bank of the River Jordan, opposite the city of Jericho. Balak, the king of Moab, decides that, rather than fight the Israelites, he will try to get rid of them by getting Balaam, a man in contact with God who could foretell the future, to curse them – anything to make them go away.

Balaam dithers about whether to obey Balak or God (Numbers 22–23), but eventually he goes to look at the Israelites. Instead of cursing them, however, as Balak wants, he blesses them, as God tells him. In today's reading, Balaam foresees a future Israelite who will be like a star, a new ruler for the world. It will be many centuries before that horde of ex-slaves marching across the desert becomes a settled nation and a kingdom, before a star rises, but God is faithful to his people and the star will be God himself, who will say 'As long as I am in the world, I am the light of the world' (John 9:5); God himself who will be the light that 'shines in the darkness, and the darkness did not overcome it' (John 1:5).

† Lord Jesus, may your light shine upon us like a bright star, driving away all our darkness.

For further thought

The world often seems a very dark place. Where and how can you see God's star shining in it?

The character of God: the God who comes

2 A great light

Notes by the **Revd Canon Helen Van Koevering**

After living in Mozambique in a post-conflict context for twenty-eight years, Helen, raised in England, moved to the USA with her family in 2015. Helen had served as a parish priest and Director of Ministry within the Anglican Diocese of Niassa, northern Mozambique, between 2004 and 2014. She is now Rector of St Raphael Episcopal Church in Lexington KY where her husband serves as Bishop. Her children are now all grown and married, and Helen now delights in being a grandmother! Helen has used the NKJV, NIV and RSV for these readings.

7 December
I am the light of the world

Read John 8:12–30

I am the light of the world. He who follows Me shall not walk in darkness, but have the light of life … It is also written in your law that the testimony of two men is true. I am One who bears witness of Myself, and the Father who sent Me bears witness of Me.

(verses 12, 17–18, NKJV)

'I am the light of the world.' These words are a reflection on the evening ceremony in the Temple courts, when two giant Menorahs, the many-branched candlesticks, were lit and illuminated the whole the Temple court. Jesus means to fulfil his words in the world through the life of his followers, because the world is in darkness. Just as the world is in darkness before the day's sunrise. The sun's rays slowly break through the night, make the birds sing, bring colour to the fields and cities, and wake the sleeping. The sunrise does not make the world, but strengthens a life not seen in the darkness, life which belongs to the very nature of the created world. The sunrise fills the life of the world.

With the life of God coming into the world, through Jesus, with the Spirit's power, so we may see the world that the Light reveals, be energised and fulfilled in walking with the Light, and find our path together through life. Take time today to relax in that gentle, beautiful vision of sunrise, and breathe in Jesus' statement: 'I am the light of the world.'

† Jesus, you are the light of the world, the light of life for us all. This is good news for the world. Be our light today. Amen.

343

People have seen a great light

Read Isaiah 9:2–5

The people walking in darkness have seen a great light; on those living in the land of deep darkness a light has dawned. You have enlarged the nation and increased their joy … you have shattered the yoke that burdens them.

(verses 2–4a, NIV)

Every year in Advent, we light a candle for joy. We anticipate joy in our Christmas celebrations, in the fun of gift-giving and receiving, in gathering with family and friends. Some churches remember that some may not be joyful at this time of the year – they may be lonely, mourning, away from family and friends – and a special candle-lighting service or 'Blue Christmas' may be supportive for them.

Yet we look towards Christmas as a celebration of promise and possibilities because the Christ child came, Emmanuel, God with us. Joy and rejoicing in this day brings about a people's celebration, and joy shared generously overflows, is multiplied through increased 're-joy-cing' with others' joy. The exultation and joy of the people is spoken of metaphorically in our reading, as the answer to oppression and war. Through that metaphor we come to see that further war, plunder and bloodshed is not the answer to war, plundering and bloodshed. The answer to all of this is joy, expressed in the face of it, because of the promise. Only peace can avenge violence. Only mercy can disarm wrath. Only love can answer hate. Only life can defeat death. In Isaiah as a whole, we see God's coming as leading to a reversal of fortunes, in unexpected and joy-inspiring ways. As many a poor community in our world will show you in exuberant worship, joy is the response, the answer, to the God who came amongst us.

† Lord, may we rejoice to remember your coming amongst us this year. Open our eyes to see opportunities to increase joy around us today. Amen.

For further thought

Whoever you meet today, find a way to let joy overflow. It could be as easy as offering a smile!

9 December
A fortress

Read Psalm 94:17–23

*When I said, 'My foot is slipping,' your unfailing love, L*ORD*, supported me. When anxiety was great within me, your consolation brought me joy. But the L*ORD *has become my fortress, and my God the rock in whom I take refuge.*

(verses 18–19, 22, NIV)

My father was a wise man of few words. I remember him once encouraging me through a tough time with a simple proverb, 'It is always darkest before the dawn.' We hear that in Psalm 94, which paints a picture of just how dark it has become for the faithful who sit and wait for God to act and expose wickedness, and the pride that says, as in Psalm 10, 'There is no God'.

When the Old Testament comes to a close, a 400-year time of God's silence begins before John the Baptist comes to those waiting for God's light to arrive in Jesus' birth. Psalm 94 is a psalm for Advent because Advent is a time to look back to the dawning of this light. This psalm calls for justice, protection, comfort and peace, just as our world does still. Advent speaks of the coming of Christ as an expectation and promise to bring the dawn of the light of God to our world undone by sin. Advent will remind us of the final appearance of Christ as the promise of true justice coming as light to be seen by all. And Advent encourages us to trust in the strength of the love of the God who holds us in the palm of his hand, as strong as any fortress of old.

† Light of God, remind us this Advent of your promise of the strength of your love and justice. Your presence and promise is like a fortress for our lives. Hold us to you, we pray. Amen.

For further thought

Who can you care for and support today? Who needs to hear of the strength of God's love and care for them? Pray for them.

The character of God: the God who comes – 2 A great light

10 December
I am the gate

Read John 10:1–10

So Jesus again said to them, 'Truly, truly, I say to you, I am the door of the sheep ... I am the door; if any one enters by me, he will be saved, and will go in and out and find pasture.'

(verses 7, 9, RSV)

Today's reading comes from the passage in John 10 where Jesus is compared to the shepherd of the sheep. But in verse 9, the focus is on Jesus as the door or gate of the sheepfold. It's perhaps easier to compare Jesus to a shepherd than a gate. Perhaps those listening didn't understand the figure of speech either, because Jesus 'doubles down' on this figure of speech, repeating that he is the gate for the sheep, and his purpose is that the sheep 'may have life, and have it abundantly' (verse 10).

In Mozambique, I learned that the 'gate' for the sheep (and goats) was indeed a shepherd. At night, the animals were herded into a raised enclosure, and the shepherd would then sleep the night in the entrance. No person nor animal could enter nor leave without stepping over or awakening the shepherd. The gate and the shepherd were the same, there for the well-being and thriving of the sheep, which was abundant life for them!

Jesus heals the man blind from birth in John 9. The Pharisees are supposed to be the shepherds of Israel, caring for, protecting and nourishing the people. They expelled the healed blind man from their community, more concerned about guarding their power and authority than being shepherds. The blind man receives his physical and spiritual sight, believes in who Jesus is, joins his community of followers and knows the gift of new life, here and now, with the One whom God sent, Jesus Christ.

† Loving God, you care for us as the shepherds care for their sheep. Thank you. Open our eyes to the meaning of the abundant life you provide for us. Amen.

For further thought

Try writing a psalm of thanksgiving for God's care, provision and protection of you and your community.

The character of God: the God who comes – 2 A great light

December

346

11 December
Raise up a righteous branch

Read Jeremiah 23:3–8

I myself will gather the remnant of my flock out of all the countries where I have driven them and will bring them back to their pasture, where they will be fruitful and increase in number.

(verse 3, NIV)

Our choices have consequences and over generations, the people of Israel, under the leadership of kings, had made choices that ultimately led them to be scattered amongst other nations. Now, Jeremiah points to a time when God himself will replace those earthly leaders, and as a shepherd, lovingly guide them back to a place of fruitfulness.

Of course, most of us don't live under kings, and many of us no longer live in agrarian societies – perhaps we need new metaphors for leadership before we start imagining God as the good CEO or President!

Nevertheless, we understand the picture – just as sheep need a shepherd to guide and protect them, the people of Israel needed responsible leaders (shepherds) to provide for them. Wise leadership matters, whether in nations, businesses or the Church. Of course, we are all responsible for our choices, but when those in authority make decisions, they have a profound effect on those they lead – and they are held doubly responsible if they mis-lead people or abuse them.

This passage speaks of God's promise to raise up a branch who will reign wisely to save Judah and Israel. And this new leadership will focus on justice and righteousness in the land. God will begin again with a 'righteous branch' of the house of David, a wise shepherd will be enthroned, and the people will find shelter and life underneath and connected to that branch.

† Holy God, by your initiative, we follow your Son as your righteous branch. Connected to and known by him, we can know your loving, abundant care for us all. Amen.

For further thought

What does this metaphor of Jesus as the 'righteous branch' of God mean to you and your community?

The character of God: the God who comes – 2 A great light

December

12 December
I am the true vine

Read John 15:1–7

I am the true vine, and my Father is the vinedresser ... Abide in me, and I in you. As the branch cannot bear fruit by itself, unless it abides in the vine, neither can you, unless you abide in me.

(verses 1, 4, RSV)

What would it mean for the Church, for each of us, to live abiding in the vine: part of those branches connected to Jesus as described in the passage? If Jesus is the vine and we are the branches, how does this relationship set us apart from the society in which we find ourselves? The imagery of the vine and branches speaks of interdependence and interrelationship, emphasising the necessity of our connection to Christ for spiritual nourishment and growth.

This metaphor points to the love of neighbour as expressed to all outside of our immediate and normal circles, just as the sheep follow and are cared for by the good shepherd. The image of the sturdy vine – Jesus – sustaining and thriving through all challenges, offers a powerful symbol for the Church today, illustrating how our strength and vitality come from our unbreakable bond with him.

We are to cling to Jesus in order to reveal God's boundless love for all. It isn't just a question of being a vine comprised of difference and diversity, but being part of the vine that becomes a beloved community of followers of Jesus. Bearing fruit is about recognising and investing in the love of God in Christ Jesus, not as self-made people, but for and with others. Pruning and bearing fruit isn't about judgement but about growth that makes the vine stronger and healthier.

In all our beautiful diversity this is our real purpose: to abide in Christ.

† God, may our worship and life as a Church draw us towards abiding in you and your word. May we be fruitful as the body of Christ in our day. Amen.

For further thought

What are your thoughts and reactions to the purpose of the Church today as abiding in Jesus Christ? Does that change in the worship, ministry and mission of and with your church?

Humility exalted

Read 1 Peter 5:1–6

Shepherd the flock of God which is among you … all of you be submissive to one another, and be clothed with humility, for 'God resists the proud, but gives grace to the humble.' Therefore humble yourselves under the mighty hand of God, that He may exalt you in due time.

(verses 2, 5–6, NKJV)

Yesterday, I saw the tattoo of a young man that declared, 'You are God'. As we close this second week of looking at 'the God who comes' such a self-exalting comment is in stark contrast to the one who was God but who came humbly. In our passage, we read about the humility of God amongst us, and the humility that is needed to feed others, lift others, and serve others in an awareness of the grace of God. Humility is all about responding to God's love and grace in the way we relate to one another, hearing the invitation to be part of the change that our neighbours, communities and world need. It's about being God's hands and feet in the world today.

Our reading today has a specific message for the diversity within Christian communities. The letter of 1 Peter describes these relationships in a distinctly reciprocal way. Some have responsibilities to the overall community, but this letter clarifies the obligations of all. There is no hierarchy of concern and work except as in mutual relationships. In fact, the letter flattens hierarchy 'under the mighty hand of God'. Abiding and connected in the branches of God's vine, we recognise our part in being, not God, but God's light in our world.

† Hold me always in the branches of your love and care. Teach me to draw life from your presence, strength and hope from your beloved community, and to be lifted up by the awareness of your grace and love always. Amen.

For further thought

How might I serve God in others today?

The character of God: the God who comes – 2 A great light

December

The character of God: the God who comes

Notes by **David Painting**

You can read David's biography on 18 May. David has used the NRSVUE version for these notes.

14 December
Conspiracy!

Do not call conspiracy all that this people calls conspiracy, and do not fear what it fears or be in dread.

(verse 12)

Conspiracies: whether it's a supposed NASA conspiracy to fool people into thinking we landed on the moon, a government conspiracy to force us to be vaccinated or a liberal conspiracy to rig an election – we do seem to enjoy a conspiracy theory!

Perhaps it's the comfort that comes from feeling as if we are on the inside, the sense of importance that comes from 'knowing' things that others don't, or the camaraderie of huddling together in a select group against a hostile, unbelieving world.

Sometimes though, I think the conspiracy theory is designed to deflect our responsibility in a situation. We construct a theory that blames our circumstances on the actions of some other group, thereby excusing ourselves. We know that being honest about things is the only way to improve them, but that's easier said than done!

Well, it turns out this isn't a new phenomenon – the people of Israel had begun to look everywhere else but themselves to explain why things were going so badly wrong. Anything to avoid looking at their own choices: their persistent rebellion.

Instead, they, and we, are called to focus on the one who comes to reveal the truth. He alone can be our sanctuary, the only source of real security.

† Lord, thank you that you are the way, the truth and the life. Help me not to be distracted by the lies that the enemy sows.

For further thought
Invite God to gently reveal any areas where you have been blaming others when actually, you need to take responsibility.

The character of God: the God who comes – 3 The way

A prophet

> ### Read Deuteronomy 18:14–22
>
> *Although these nations that you are about to dispossess do give heed to soothsayers and diviners, as for you, the LORD your God does not permit you to do so. The LORD your God will raise up for you a prophet like me from among your own people; you shall heed such a prophet.*
>
> (verses 14–15)

Yesterday we thought about conspiracies – false words that bring false comfort, that distract from the truth. And today picks up that theme – people claiming to speak authoritatively on God's behalf but who do not. What they say might be factually correct or even come to pass, but that doesn't make them a prophet – as our passage says, true prophets will be like God.

Paul encountered this: 'These men are slaves of the Most High God, who proclaim to you the way of salvation' (Acts 16:16–18). What the girl said was factually accurate, but she spoke because her owners demanded it as a means of earning money, not out of a compassionate heart for the unsaved – and that turned the facts into something the enemy could use as a lie to misrepresent the heart of God.

Prophecy is about representing God – not just his words, but who he is – and to do that we must 'speak the truth in love' (Ephesians 4:15). What is spoken must emanate from the heart and character of God, otherwise, even though what is being said may be factually correct, it cannot be a message from God who *is* love.

And that is the heart of this passage – God will raise up prophets and you will be able to tell them apart from the others because they will not only speak that which is factually accurate, but they will speak it in the way God would speak it – out of his heart, his character. If what is said and the way it is said does not sound like Jesus – the one who came – then it isn't God.

† Lord, thank you that you speak the truth. Thank you that you do so motivated by love and that your words are filled with that love.

For further thought

Test prophecy – does it line up with what you know about God, does it sound like Jesus, does it invite, is it filled with compassion and understanding? Or is it judgemental, condemning, insistent, commanding and lacking empathy? Is it rooted in love or founded in fear?

The character of God: the God who comes – 3 The way

December

16 December
I am the way

Read John 14:6–10

Jesus said to him, 'I am the way and the truth and the life. No one comes to the Father except through me. If you know me, you will know my Father also. From now on you do know him and have seen him.'

(verses 6–7)

I am infamous for having a poor sense of direction. When our children were in the car, if I suggested a short-cut, they would beg me not to take it, knowing how long the 'short-cut' might take … When we lived in Romania, locals would often stop me and ask directions. I dread to think how many of them are still wandering around on the basis of my well-meaning but likely inaccurate directions.

Many systems, religious and secular, commend themselves as 'the way' to holiness, success, salvation, prosperity, love or all five … But Jesus doesn't point us to a book of rules, doesn't require a system. Instead, he points to himself, to his character, to his person, to his example – and says, 'I am the way'.

And he explains why – he and the Father dwell in each other – they share the same character, the same values, the same everything. They are, in practice, one. If the destination is the Father, then the way is the character and nature of Jesus. You can't come, be in relationship with the Father, if you don't share the family likeness.

Let's be clear: Christianity isn't the way, the truth and the life. Nor is knowing the Bible back to front or belonging to a particular denomination, or even the Church in general. Indeed, if we make any of these things our way, our truth, our life, they become idols displacing the one – the only one – who claims that he embodies all of these.

Jesus comes, God comes and lives amongst us to show us the way, to be the way.

† Lord, thank you that you didn't come to leave instructions, but to walk with us. Thank you for leading me in paths of righteousness.

For further thought

How do we keep to the way, the truth and the life rather than the ways of the world or the ways of our religious traditions?

17 December
He will see his offspring

Read Isaiah 53:9–12

Yet it was the will of the Lord to crush him with affliction. When you make his life an offering for sin, he shall see his offspring and shall prolong his days.

(verse 10)

'Who could have imagined his future?' (verse 8). This is the prophet's response to what he sees in the snapshot of the moment – and it is unspeakably dreadful. There is no hope here, no possibility of a last-minute reprieve, just the relentless march towards injustice, to a tortured, humiliating death and a borrowed grave. Elsewhere, seeing the same, Isaiah asks, 'Who can speak of his generations?' – there is nothing beyond this, it ends here.

And there are times in our lives where this resonates. We look at a snapshot of our circumstances, see where we have come from, look at where the road inexorably leads, and we can see nothing beyond. The demise of our career, of a long-term relationship, of reputation, of life itself, perhaps.

And the enemy and those he influences flock around us, their voices adding to the insistent thoughts of our own mind – it is hopeless, the ending of the story, already written in cruel, cold immutable writing.

Yet and yet … We trust in a God who writes a better ending, who tears up the version that the enemy would write, the ending that we would predict – and by his blood writes an impossible, wonderful, miraculous, resurrection-infused ending!

And Isaiah glimpses it – despite the evidence, despite the circumstances – trusting in God's character, he declares: 'He will see his offspring.'

Death will not have the last word.

And we have the same hope. The same power that was at work raising Christ from death is now at work in us. However bleak the picture, however certain the predictions, the God who comes can write a better ending!

† Lord, thank you that you write a better ending than we could possibly imagine!

For further thought

In what areas of your life, or the lives of those you love, are you trusting for a better ending? How can you encourage and support those for whom life currently seems hopeless?

The character of God: the God who comes – 3 The way

December

353

An everlasting covenant

I will make a covenant of peace with them; it shall be an everlasting covenant with them, and I will bless them and multiply them and will set my sanctuary among them forevermore.

(verse 26)

As a child I had problems with arithmetic. Why should one plus one equal two? When I joined one piece of my railway track to another, one plus one remained one – I still had one railway track even if it was now longer. Earlier in this chapter, Ezekiel gives the people a similar puzzle. He has two sticks and joins them together – two become one. In a similar way, Paul describes marriage – the two become one.

This is the business of God – he who is three and yet one, constantly working towards creating unity from diversity – in our passage, one kingdom out of the divided nations of Israel and Judah pointing towards a greater unity than even that. More, Ezekiel says that this is no temporary solution; the work of God is to bring a permanent wholeness, a permanent shalom in an eternal covenant that knows no end.

This is good news for us – in a world where nations are divided, where people within a nation are polarised against each other, where individuals are fractured, where humanity wars against nature and where mankind is separated from God – the news that God can bring healing and unity is good news indeed!

We reflect of course on how that unity has been won each time we share communion. Ultimately, it is by the broken bread, the poured out wine, symbols of the broken body and shed blood by which wholeness comes. A wholeness that embraces the presence of God, for ever.

† Lord, we give you thanks for your broken body and shed blood, that through your brokenness we can be made whole.

For further thought

Are there people with whom you need to restore unity? Are there parts of yourself that are fragmented that need help reuniting?

19 December
Behold, I stand at the door

Read Revelation 3:14–22

Listen! I am standing at the door, knocking; if you hear my voice and open the door, I will come in and eat with you, and you with me.

(verse 20)

The passage begins with serious words of challenge and rebuke – the Laodiceans' blindness to their true condition and their tepid response to the gospel is making God sick – it is a stark rebuke!

Yet, as with all the Father's discipline, it comes with hope and an action plan – open your eyes to the truth, repent when you have understood it, recognise that God does all of this motivated by a loving desire to be in relationship with you.

We see that encapsulated in verse 20. First, Jesus knocks – he initiates the possibility of relationship. Secondly, it isn't the knocking that inspires us to open the door, it's his voice. Thirdly, the first meal shared is the one we provide ('I will come in and eat with you') and lastly, Jesus prepares the meal for us ('and you with me').

He waits – God humbles himself, Omnipotent God, who could tear down the door in a moment, stands and waits on our response. Nor is it the constant banging on the door, it isn't the relentless logic of the gospel that stirs us, it is the voice of Jesus. It is the revealed character of a servant-God, it is the loving tone as he speaks our name that gives us the courage to open ourselves to him – trusting that he will deal kindly with us.

And when we open he comes in, not to take control, but to enjoy what we have provided. He begins where we are, not where we should be, not where we one day will be, but joyfully sits at our table and eats with us – honouring who we are.

† Lord, we trust you with our true self, we open ourselves to you. Come in, we pray. You are welcome.

For further thought

Sometimes we are anxious about opening the door to God because we are ashamed or because we fear his displeasure at what he might find. But he already knows – he doesn't want to come in to berate, but to eat with us. Knowing this, what difference does it make? Will you open the door?

The character of God: the God who comes – 3 The way

20 December

I am the resurrection and the life

Read John 11:21–27

Jesus said to her, 'I am the resurrection and the life. Those who believe in me, even though they die, will live'.

(verse 25)

'I am the resurrection and the life' – life is the very essence of who God is – it flows from him, can only be found in who he is, and without it, physical life is death; with it, physical death cannot contain the resurrection life that still exists! This is surely one of the most profound revelations that Jesus brings.

Martha is distressed, disappointed, that Jesus didn't come sooner and heal Lazarus – and we can understand, empathise with her distress – as indeed Jesus does. We pray earnestly for something, knowing that God is capable of answering, and yet that which we have prayed for doesn't happen. The message is simple and challenging – keep believing, there is a bigger miracle on offer than that which we longed for.

More than a wonderful healing, they will soon see a dramatic resurrection! Not the resurrection that Martha alludes to, when all will be raised on the 'last day', but a more immediate miracle than even that.

But there is a bigger miracle that we can all experience. Not everyone who is sick will be healed, and even when they are, they will still face death. And even if they should be resurrected like Lazarus, they will still one day die. And yes, all will then be raised on the last day, but here is the greatest miracle. The God who comes, comes today through the fruit sown in our life. Everything we do that is founded on faith, hope and love are eternal representations of who God is and they radiate out from us in a never-ending wake whose impact never dies.

† Lord, we are so grateful that our lives live on beyond us. Thank you that we will one day rejoice with you in all that we have accomplished.

For further thought

How does the knowledge that the effectiveness of your life continues beyond you affect how you live?

The character of God: the God who comes – 3 The way

December

356

Emmanuel: God with us (1)

Notes by **Stella Wiseman**

Stella is a priest in the Church of England where one of her passions is the intersection of faith and creativity. She spent many years in journalism and writes fiction for children and young adults, and also runs an annual poetry competition and a regular craft market, seeking to build a community of creative people linked with the Church. She has three adult children, a husband and ten cats. Stella has used the NRSVA for these readings.

21 December
Arise! Shine! The night is nearly over

Read Isaiah 60:1–6

For darkness shall cover the earth, and thick darkness the peoples; but the LORD *will arise upon you, and his glory will appear over you. Nations shall come to your light, and kings to the brightness of your dawn.*

(verses 2–3)

If you live in a country with a cold, dark winter, it can be a tough season. There are more illnesses and deaths in winter, more accidents, more depression, and, of course, the land seems dead too. And even if where you live this is a bright, sunny season, there will be times when life feels dark and difficult. Whether this darkness is linked with our own personal circumstances or those of the wider world, with its wars and disease and the inexorable heating of the planet, or a combination of personal and global factors, it can feel hard to see a way out.

This is something we can see in today's passage – there is a sense of impenetrable darkness which covers everything. And yet …

When faced with darkness there is no point in trying to chase it away. We need light to dispel it and that is just what is promised here. The greatest light of all is coming, the brightest dawn – that of the Lord, God with us, not some far distant deity but a God with us in the darkness, difficulty, pain, joy, happiness and celebration of human life. That is a light to welcome this Christmas.

† Loving God, thank you for your light which the darkness will never overcome.

Emmanuel: God with us (1)

22 December
Who's who?

Read Matthew 1:1–17

An account of the genealogy of Jesus the Messiah, the son of David, the son of Abraham.

(verse 1)

There is a British TV series called *Who Do You Think You Are?* in which celebrity guests trace their family histories back as far as they can and uncover all sorts of surprises. There is often hardship and conflict along with unexpected twists and compelling storylines. Rather like Jesus' family history, in fact!

Matthew starts the exciting story of the life, death and resurrection of Jesus by making it clear where he fits in with the story of God's people, right there in the line which stretches from Abraham, a man who followed God's call, through David, the great king of Israel. The Jewish people were expecting a new king who would be descended from David and here he is at last.

One of the beauties of Jesus' family tree is that it isn't straightforward and it doesn't pretend that everyone in the past led blame-free lives, nor that they were from just one nation. Jesus came from a line which includes exiles, refugees, men who exploited women, at least one sex worker, the sort of people whom a lot of us shun or at the very least, refuse to see as equals. 'Well, that person was the black sheep of the family,' we might say, glad that we are 'at least better than that'. Maybe it is time to pause and think just how inclusive God is and how God loves and dwells in everyone, including those we might ignore or look down on.

After all, they are all part of Jesus' family.

† Loving God, thank you that you welcome us and can work through us all, whatever our backgrounds or behaviour. Help us to remember how inclusively gracious you are.

For further thought

Often it is only in retrospect that we can see where God has been working. Remembering this can encourage us when times are difficult.

Emmanuel: God with us (1)

December

23 December

The obedience and kindness of Joseph

Read Matthew 1:18–25

...an angel of the Lord appeared to him in a dream and said, 'Joseph, son of David, do not be afraid to take Mary as your wife, for the child conceived in her is from the Holy Spirit. She will bear a son, and you are to name him Jesus, for he will save his people from their sins.'

(verses 20–21)

The scandal! Utter, terrifying scandal! Mary, a young woman, was to marry Joseph, and now she was pregnant and not by him. By rights she should have been shunned or worse. Joseph was, Matthew says, someone who obeyed the law, and the law he followed stated that both the man who had made Mary pregnant and Mary herself must die. It is hard to begin to understand what Mary must have felt, or what her parents or Joseph must have felt.

Joseph is represented here as a kind man as well as a law-abiding one, and he decided to try to limit the shame and punishment by calling off the marriage quietly. She might then have lived with her parents until they died but what would have happened then? Her life would have been ruined.

Joseph was, however, not just lawful, not just kind, but obedient too, and that obedience saved the day. He had a dream in which an angel told him that he should still marry Mary because the baby growing in her came from the Holy Spirit and would save people from their sins. Joseph must have wondered what was happening! First his wife-to-be was pregnant, then an angel told him still to marry her and that somehow the child would be the people's Saviour. But, however puzzled he was, he obeyed and the story could continue to unfold in yet more wonderful ways.

† Loving God, we praise you for your love, poured out for all in Jesus, and give thanks for the obedience of Mary and Joseph. May we obey you, even when we don't see the whole picture.

For further thought

Joseph would have been within his rights to insist on punishment for Mary, but his actions show that there is always room for grace-filled kindness.

Emmanuel: God with us (1)

December

359

24 December
The star in the East

Read Matthew 2:1–6

In the time of King Herod, after Jesus was born in Bethlehem of Judea, wise men from the East came to Jerusalem asking, 'Where is the child who has been born king of the Jews? For we observed his star at its rising, and have come to pay him homage.'

(verses 1–2)

The wise men, the kings, the magi, maybe three, maybe more, following the star in search of Jesus and then presenting him with gifts of gold, frankincense and myrrh. No Christmas story would be complete without them, would it? Yet only Matthew recounts it while Luke concentrates on lowlier folk – shepherds in the field. Why, though, were they so significant to Matthew and why does he write about King Herod and all Jerusalem being frightened?

The wise men were probably astrologers, looking to the stars for information about what was happening in the world. They were almost certainly gentiles rather than Jews and perhaps Matthew was emphasising Jesus was a king that not just Jews would recognise but all other nations too. In fact, he might well have been recalling the passage we read a few days ago in Isaiah: 'A multitude of camels shall cover you, the young camels of Midian and Ephah; all those from Sheba shall come. They shall bring gold and frankincense, and shall proclaim the praise of the LORD' (Isaiah 60:6).

No wonder King Herod was worried. These wise men had arrived looking for a rival king, someone who might threaten his rule. Of course, what he didn't appreciate, but what Matthew knew, was that this was a king with a difference. Not some short-term temporal ruler whose kingdom was of this world and who ruled by fear – like Herod did – but a king who is for everyone and who rules with love.

† Loving God, we thank you that your love is for everyone, whoever we are, whatever our background or status.

For further thought

The wise men perhaps used divination which the Hebrew law forbade. Yet they are celebrated as some of the first people to recognise Jesus. Jesus welcomes all.

Emmanuel: God with us (1)

December

25 December
Make a joyful noise this Christmas

Read Psalm 98

Make a joyful noise to the LORD, all the earth; break forth into joyous song and sing praises.

(verse 4)

A very joyful, blessed Christmas to you! It truly is a day to celebrate and the psalmists knew how to celebrate! Today's reading is a psalm of joy in praise of the wonderful things that God has done. It was a psalm written for an occasion long before Jesus was born but it absolutely resonates throughout the ages, reminding us that God's steadfast love and faithfulness are for ever.

The psalmist was celebrating God's relationship with Israel, but with the coming of Jesus, the Christ, God born as a human, we see that this love stretches far beyond the Israel of the original psalm. Absolutely everyone is part of God's people, and not just every person but the whole of creation. Even the fields are clapping their hands and the hills are singing together with joy, which is a wonderful, poetic and celebratory image.

This is a psalm of praise in the past; a psalm of praise for today, especially as we celebrate the birth of Jesus, the Christ; and also for the future as the psalmist reminds us that God will judge all nations with righteousness. It reminds us that God is holding everything, past, present and future, and holding us, safe in the arms of everlasting love.

So today let's sing a new song and make the most joyful noise possible to tell the world that God is here. Happy Christmas!

† Loving God, we are awed by and give thanks for your love and your glory, seen in nature and seen in Jesus, born a tiny human baby. God around us and God with us.

For further thought
Psalm 98 is echoed in Mary's song of praise in Luke 1:46–55, the Magnificat. Mary knew she was praising the God whose love is for ever.

Emmanuel: God with us (1)

December

361

26 December

Offering treasures

Read Matthew 2:7–12

When they saw that the star had stopped, they were overwhelmed with joy. On entering the house, they saw the child with Mary his mother; and they knelt down and paid him homage. Then, opening their treasure-chests, they offered him gifts of gold, frankincense, and myrrh.

(verses 10–11)

Their long, hard journey was over at last and, filled with joy, the wise men entered the house and knelt down before the baby Jesus, there with his mother. What was everyone thinking and feeling at that moment? The wise men were probably expecting something grander than a simple house with a simple, young peasant girl, which is what Mary almost certainly was. And Mary must have been astonished when a group of foreign dignitaries arrived and knelt down in front of her new baby, then produced gifts of great value. Perhaps baby Jesus slept through it all!

It may be that events had been so strange for Mary already that she simply took it all in her stride and accepted that these sorts of things happened when God was involved, but it is tempting to wonder what she thought of the gifts. They were strange ones indeed and very valuable, the sort that people at the time would bring to someone who was their superior, whom they wanted to impress. There was gold for a king; frankincense, which comes from a tree resin and is often seen to represent divinity; and myrrh, another tree resin which was used in embalming.

We don't know exactly why the wise men brought these gifts but it is tempting to think that they represent Jesus as a king and God, but a king and God who would die and rise again. The whole purpose of Jesus represented here on earth in gifts given by strangers from another land. Again, this is God for everyone.

† Loving God, may we too worship you and give you the gift of ourselves this Christmas.

For further thought

The wise men continued to recognise Jesus as more important than earthly kings by listening to their dream and not returning to Herod, risking his wrath.

27 December
Refugees in a strange land

Read Matthew 2:13–15
Now after they had left, an angel of the Lord appeared to Joseph in a dream and said, 'Get up, take the child and his mother, and flee to Egypt, and remain there until I tell you; for Herod is about to search for the child, to destroy him.'

(verse 13)

The early months with a new baby can be exhausting and a mother may not want to travel far, if at all. Imagine then being forced to flee your home, taking your baby and a few belongings with you, and walking for miles, always fearing that those who wish you harm will catch up with you, not knowing where you will end up.

That is what happened to Mary and Joseph and their young baby here in Matthew's Gospel. That is what happens to countless refugees, forced to flee for their lives because of war or violence, or because of extreme conditions which mean they must seek food and shelter elsewhere. How terrifying it must be. How could this have happened to God's Son? How can this happen to anyone?

Jesus and his family were refugees and once again here is God, intimately involved in the suffering of the marginalised and in the messiness of humanity. God needed sanctuary in a foreign land, among strangers, dependent on their kindness and welcome. It is the same today. Later in the book of Matthew (chapter 25), Jesus says that when we feed the hungry, care for the sick and suffering and welcome the stranger, we are doing the same for him. Jesus is there with those on the edges.

† Loving God, teach us to see you in all whom we meet, especially in those we may be tempted to reject or despise.

For further thought
Instructions to care for refugees appear many times in the Bible – for example, 'you shall love the alien as yourself, for you were aliens in the land of Egypt' (Leviticus 19:34).

Emmanuel: God with us (1)

December

Emmanuel: God with us (2)

Notes by **Erice Fairbrother and Hukarere Māori Girls' College**

Hukarere Māori Girls' College in Hawke's Bay was founded over a century ago in the Anglican faith in Aotearoa New Zealand. The story of their incredible evacuation without loss of life in the terrible cyclone of February 2023 has been widely told. Erice Fairbrother (see her biography on 28 September) is Chaplain at the college and has written these reflections with some of the girls: Zsana Dimitro, Karani Wilkie, Alizae Adsett, Quayeshia Rahiri and Cherish Whaiapu. Erice and the team used the NRSVA (Bilingual Edition Aotearoa).

28 December
Flight to safety

Read Matthew 2:16–18

A voice was heard in Ramah, wailing and loud lamentation, Rachel weeping for her children; she refused to be consoled, because they are no more.

(verse 18)

Cyclone Gabrielle hit New Zealand in February 2023. That night the senior girls at Hukarere Girls' College hostel remember police visiting to make sure they were safe as the storm grew. Hostel Manager, Amelia, like Joseph in the passage, came from a line of indigenous forebears and that evening, understanding where the real danger lay, Amelia repeatedly visited the nearby river. Finally, its warning, like that of the angel, was clear.

Take the girls and flee.

The readings this week catch fragments of memories of that experience, when the students too had to 'get up', help the younger ones gather what they could and put them in the vans. And then, only when the younger ones were on their way to safety, they recall being driven through the storm, the darkness thick around them.

For Jesus and his family, this was their lived experience as they fled the oncoming torrent of Herod's murderous jealousy.

Jesus understands what life can throw at us, the fear, living with uncertainty, the courage that is needed. And knowing that, he walks alongside us and does not leave us.

Emmanuel. God with us.

† Thank you that you kept us safe, Lord. May others know your peace in their lives when life takes unexpected turns, and they are afraid.

29 December
A different return

Read Matthew 2:19–25

And after being warned in a dream, he went away to the district of Galilee. There he made his home in a town called Nazareth.

(verses 22b–23a)

So much is unsaid here! Fleeing to an unfamiliar land, waiting with a longing to return. What sustained them?

When Hukarere Hostel was evacuated, it was, in the words of the students, 'the routine' that was sustaining, so that they were able to feel 'happy to have somewhere'. The daily practice of *karakia* (of Morning and Evening Prayer) was an important part of that routine. Yet even as they were escaping in the increasingly heavy rain, one of the senior students called out from the back of the van – '*Whaea*! We forgot the Prayer Book!' Amelia the manager, however, had one, and when they arrived at the Marae that night, as they went to settle to sleep, one of the students led them in Evening Prayer.

In the time that followed, through various relocations, it was this routine led by these students that gave structure, a way of being held together, of knowing God was with them.

Their time in 'Egypt' lasted for two and a half school terms before they could return. And like Jesus, the return was to something completely different. Finding the school buried under debris and silt, their hostel and all that was in it completely lost, they too made their home in a different 'district' altogether. Here in a new place and new hostel, the daily practice of *karakia* was re-established at their homecoming.

Did the holy family have a routine? Was it centred on their faith and relationship with God? Joseph continued to dream; the hostel continued to pray. Here is a faith that sustains even when it too seems lost.

† May I never forget that you are with me always, even when I am not always ready to be with you.

For further thought

Have you experienced sudden overwhelming loss? Take a moment to reflect on what sustained you then and what sustains you now.

Emmanuel: God with us (2)

30 December
God with us – how do we know?

Read Isaiah 63:7–9

...in all their distress. It was no messenger or angel but his presence that saved them, in his love and pity, he redeemed them.

(verse 9a)

Several years ago, a student asked me, 'How do we know it's God?' It was a good question! In a world where communications and messages are not always trustworthy it is a very real contemporary question. Our reflections this week have described God speaking in dreams, even in the flow of a river. For Isaiah, God is recognisable as the one who hears human distress – a distress so often experienced when we're hit by the unexpected, by unprecedented upheaval, times of unimaginable loss and grief. His love 'is steadfast' (verse 7).

The reality that God was with us in such times often comes later. The time to look back and reflect is different for everyone. As we reflected in the light of our reading for today, the hostel seniors could recognise the work of God in their manager and a Catholic boarding school who took them in that night. The God who loves and saves was shown in the presence of the Old Girls of Hukarere, who came and cared for them, embracing them in a love that was steadfast, reassuring them that they were safe.

God with us. Ultimately, we can understand and acknowledge the reality of his presence as located in our real-life experiences. In the first instance, as the students put it – 'it is the love and support, and friends' that means everything. This week following the celebration of the birth of Christ – the God who became one of us – is a good time to consider and remember those who have been the presence of God for us.

† Give us grace to see you, wherever and however you have been at work in our hardest of times. We thank you as we remember those who have shown us your steadfast love.

For further thought

Processing previous distress can bring peace to past experiences. As the new year begins, find a safe friend to help process any that you still hold alone.

Emmanuel: God with us (2)

December

31 December
Thankfulness, the heart's reply

Read Psalm 148

Young men and women alike, young and old together! Let them praise the name of the Lord.

(verses 12–13a)

What an amazing outpouring of thankfulness in this psalm!

The loss of our school and the incredible saving of over fifty lives at the hostel on the night of the cyclone evoked an outpouring of love and thankfulness from all over New Zealand. The boarders were overcome with the gifts that were delivered, funding from so many organisations that poured in, the unconditional hospitality of strangers. Churches opened their doors so we could have rooms to teach in, offering kindness without reservation. We moved from place to place often, the students rising to the challenge even while still grieving and uncertain. And then the news! A place was found for the school and was being prepared for us.

It was not during that time, but later in the process that feelings of thankfulness began to emerge. It wasn't a lack of gratitude that held us back – sometimes trauma and dealing with the aftermath just take up all our emotional energy.

Then, in our reflections one day, one of the students mentioned feeling thankful – and there was a moment of naming it; thankfulness for the gifts, for letters and cards from other school students, for the churches that opened their buildings to us. Remembering their generosity of spirit was the beginning of our spirits being lifted, and though we used different words, we with the psalmist and the rest of the country were praising the Lord.

Perhaps expressing thankfulness needs to come when the heart is ready. Ready to open to God in response to his steadfast love and presence. Recognising that not only is God with us, but we can be with God too. Praise the Lord!

† Give thanks for the gifts that you have received from God over the past year.

For further thought

Recall a situation where you have been a blessing to someone, when you could be their Emmanuel at that time, and give thanks.

Emmanuel: God with us (2)

December

IBRA scheme of readings in the next edition

Finding Jesus
1 Finding the young Jesus
2 Encounters

The Gospel of Matthew (1)
1 Christ's ministry begins
2 Instructions and reassurance

Names: people and place

Readings in Ruth

Maintaining unity
1 Unity in the body of the Church
2 Living in unity

Readings in Romans (1)
Righteousness in God alone

Exile and home
1 Driven away
2 The way home

The Gospel of Matthew (2)
1 Voices of Holy Week: from cheering crowd to lone prayer
2 From death to resurrection

Grace (1)
The restorative grace of God

Pride and prejudice

The Gospel of Matthew (3)
1 Help and healing
2 Signs and lessons

Doubts and fears

Grace (2)
1 God's gracious gifts
2 Receiving and giving

Readings from Isaiah 1–39 (1)
1 Rescued from judgment
2 The trumpet sounds

Character of the prophets

Parables: in the Old and New Testaments

Readings in Romans (2)
1 Dead to sin, alive through Christ
2 Fruits of God's Spirit

Mental health and faith

The Gospel of Matthew (4)
1 Questioning and establishing the authority of Jesus
2 Understanding what is important

Seasons of life
1 Nurture
2 Maturity

Wisdom

Readings in Isaiah 1–39 (2)
1 Provision from God
2 Delivery through God alone

Authority and governance

Stolen from God: on the subject of slavery

The Gospel of Matthew (5)
1 Insights
2 Warnings

Setbacks and comebacks
1 Reason for hope
2 Confounding expectations

Readings in Romans (3)
1 Love and harmony
2 Respect one another

Treasure

Verses from Thessalonians (epistles 1 and 2)

Symbols of Advent
1 Foreshadowed from ancient times
2 Words of the prophet

Symbols pointing to Christ: seven great 'O's

A Saviour comes: Gospel stories
The Christmas story in different gospels

Leftovers

IBRA International Fund

IBRA brings together readers from across the globe, and it is your donations and support that make it possible for our international partners to translate, print, publish and distribute the notes to over a hundred thousand people. Thank you.

Are you able to make a donation today?

How your donations make a difference:

Your donations make a tremendous difference to our IBRA International Partners, enabling them to support people in their local communities to grow in a deeper knowledge of God.

£15 can print 15 copies of *Fresh from The Word* in India
£25 provides 500 IBRA reading lists for a country that does not currently receive IBRA materials
£50 provides 40 copies of *Fresh from The Word* in Nigeria

Our partners are based in ten countries, but the benefit flows over borders to at least thirty-two countries all over the world. Partners work tirelessly to organise the translation, printing and distribution of IBRA Bible study notes and lists in many different languages, from Ewe, Yoruba and Twi to Portuguese, Samoan and Telugu!

Thousands of copies of *Fresh from The Word* are printed here in the UK, and our overseas partners produce tens of thousands more in English and then translate the book you are reading to print many more in various local languages. With the reading list also being translated into French and Spanish, then distributed, IBRA currently reaches over 700,000 Christians globally.

Faithfully following the same principles developed in 1882, we continue to guarantee that your donations to the International Fund will support our international brothers and sisters in Christ.

If you would like to make a donation, please use the envelope inserted in this book to send a cheque to International Bible Reading Association, 4 Regal Court, 6 Sovereign Road, Birmingham, B30 3FJ or go online to ibraglobal.org and click the 'Donate' button at the top of the page.

Would you leave a legacy to help continue our mission?

IBRA's work over the past 143 years and *Fresh from The Word* are only possible through you, the readers, and your donations.

A gift in your will to IBRA's International Fund will help continue our Bible reading legacy. We guarantee that 100% of your legacy will pay for the continuation of our work.

'And the good news must first be proclaimed to all nations.'
Mark 13:10 (NRSVA)

It was the vision of Charles Waters to empower people in Britain and overseas to benefit from the Word of God through the experiences and insights of biblical scholars from around the world.

In his diary entry on 1 January 1862 he wrote,

'Let me live to Thee, O Lord; and oh, if it be Thy will, let me be a shepherd of Thy sheep, and a means of saving many souls!'

If this humble man only knew of what his work has achieved! For the last 143 years, every day people have had the ability to read God's word through IBRA, and been able to gain personal wisdom, insight and guidance.

We know that is over 52,000 days' worth of readings. Our community has been in over 43 countries, we've had thousands of writers and millions and millions of readers.

Please leave a legacy today to keep Charles' vision alive, and our mission being fulfilled.

The Fellowship of Professional Workers in India shares *Fresh from The Word* Bible reading notes with Christians in the secular workforce.

To find out more please contact our CEO, Zoë Keens
Call: 0121 458 3313
Email: zoe.keens@christianeducation.org.uk
Write to: IBRA, 4 Regal Court, 6 Sovereign Road, Birmingham B30 3FJ.
We'd love to hear from you.

International Bible Reading Association partners and distributors

A worldwide service of Christian education at work in five continents

HEADQUARTERS
IBRA
4 Regal Court
6 Sovereign Road
Birmingham
B30 3FJ
United Kingdom
www.ibraglobal.org
ibra@christianeducation.org.uk

SAMOA
Congregational Christian Church in Samoa
CCCS
PO Box 468
Tamaligi
Apia
Samoa
asst.gsec@cccs.org.ws / lina@cccs.org.ws

Congregational Christian Church in Tokelau
c/o EFKT
Atafu
Tokelau Island
hepuutua@gmail.com

Congregational Christian Church in American Samoa
PO Box 1537
Pago Pago, AS 96799
American Samoa
gensec@efkasonline.org /
nfalealii@efkasonline.org

FIJI
Methodist Bookstore
11 Stewart street
PO Box 354
Suva
Fiji
mbookstorefiji@yahoo.com

Ekalesia Kelisiano Tuvalu Church
Congregations in Suva, Kioa, Lautoka and Labasa
31 Ratu Sukuna Road
Nasese
Suva
Fiji

GHANA
Asempa Publishers
Christian Council of Ghana
PO Box GP 919
Accra
Ghana
gm@asempapublishers.com /
info@asempapublishers.com

NIGERIA
IBRA Nigeria
David Hinderer House
Cathedral Church of St David
Kudeti
PMB 5298 Dugbe
Ibadan
Oyo State
Nigeria
ibndiocese@yahoo.com

SOUTH AFRICA
Faith for Daily Living Foundation
PO Box 3737
Durban 4000
South Africa
ffdl@saol.com

IBRA South Africa
The Rectory
Christ Church
Cnr Constantia Main and Parish Roads
Constantia
Cape Town 7945
South Africa
Terry@cchconst.org.za

DEMOCRATIC REPUBLIC OF THE CONGO
Baptist Community of the Congo River
8 Avenue Kalemie
Kinshasa Gombe
B.P. 205 & 397
Kinshasa 1
DR Congo
ecc_cbfc@yahoo.fr

CAMEROON
Redemptive Baptist Church
PO Box 65
Limbe
Fako Division
South West Region
Cameroon
evande777@yahoo.com

INDIA
All India Sunday School Association
House No. 9-131/1, Street No.5
HMT Nagar, Nacharam
Hyderabad
500076
Telangana
India
sundayschoolindia@yahoo.co.in

Fellowship of Professional Workers
Samanvay
Deepthi Chambers, Opp. Nin.
Tarnaka, Vijayapuri
Hyderabad 500 017
Telengana State
India
fellowship2w@gmail.com

Fresh from The Word
Order and donation form

IBRA

Use this form to order next year's edition at this year's price!	Quantity	Price	Total
AA240208 *Fresh from The Word*		£13.99	
10% discount if ordering 3 or more copies			
UK P&P			
Up to 2 copies		£4.75	
3–8 copies		£8.35	
9–11 copies		£10.75	
If ordering 12 or more copies please contact us for revised postage			
Western Europe P&P			
1 copy		£9.95	
If ordering more than 1 copy please contact us for revised postage			
Rest of the world P&P			
1 copy		£15.95	
If ordering more than 1 copy please contact us for revised postage			
Donation Yes, I would like to make a donation to IBRA's International Fund to help support our global community of readers.			
£5.00 ☐ | £10.00 ☐ | £25.00 ☐ | £50.00 ☐ | Other ☐			
TOTAL FOR BOOKS, P&P AND DONATION			

Title: _____ First name: _____ Last name: _____

Address: _____

_____

Postcode: _____ Tel.: _____

Email: _____

Your order will be dispatched when all books are available. Payments in pounds sterling, please. We do not accept American Express or Maestro International. HOW WE USE INFORMATION ABOUT YOU AND RECIPIENTS OF YOUR INFORMATION: We will use your information in performance of your contract with us and the provision of our services to you including our legitimate interests. For further details please view our full privacy policy and your rights at www.ibraglobal.org/privacy

CARDHOLDER NAME: _____

CARD NUMBER: ☐☐☐☐ ☐☐☐☐ ☐☐☐☐ ☐☐☐☐

START DATE: ☐☐ ☐☐ **EXPIRY DATE:** ☐☐ ☐☐

SECURITY NUMBER (LAST THREE DIGITS ON BACK): ☐☐☐

SIGNATURE: _____

Card details will be destroyed after payment has been taken.

Please fill in your details on the reverse

Gift Aid declaration *giftaid it*

If you wish to Gift Aid your donation please tick the box.

☐ I am a UK taxpayer and would like IBRA to reclaim the Gift Aid on my donation, increasing my donation by 25p for every £1. I understand that if I pay less income tax and/or capital gains tax than the amount of Gift Aid claimed on all my donations in that tax year, it is my responsibility to pay the difference.

Signature: _____   Date: _____

Thank you so much for your generous donation; it will make a real difference and change lives around the world.

Please fill in your address and payment details on the reverse of this page and send back to IBRA.

☐ **I enclose a cheque (made payable to IBRA)**

☐ **Please charge my MASTERCARD/VISA**

Please return this form to:

IBRA
4 Regal Court
6 Sovereign Road
Birmingham
B30 3FJ

You can also order through your local IBRA rep or from:
• Website: ibraglobal.org
• Email: sales@christianeducation.org.uk
• Call: 0121 458 3313
• Ebook and Kindle versions are available from Amazon, Kobo and other online retailers.

IBRA
Registered Charity number: 1086990